Clara C...

May 1972

Nelson
and the Hamiltons

BY

JACK RUSSELL

SIMON AND SCHUSTER
NEW YORK

SBN 671–20324–X
Library of Congress Catalog Card Number: 70–79638
Designed by Edith Fowler
Manufactured in the United States of America
by H. Wolff Book Mfg. Co., Inc., New York

Contents

A SECTION OF ILLUSTRATIONS
WILL BE FOUND
FOLLOWING PAGE 128.

Nelson
and the Hamiltons

CHAPTER ONE

The First Meeting

THERE IS no doubt that they approved of each other from the beginning.

Apart from the opinions generally expressed by their contemporaries that they were all three unusual and attractive people, both Captain Nelson and Sir William Hamilton wrote pleasantly about each other after their five days together, and kept up a friendly correspondence for the next five years. As for Lady Hamilton, she dictated her impression of the meeting to Nelson's biographer, James Harrison, a few weeks after the hero's death at Trafalgar.

> On Sir William Hamilton's returning home, after having first beheld Captain Nelson, he told his lady that he was about to introduce a little man to her acquaintance, who could not boast of being very handsome: "but," added Sir William, "this man, who is an English naval officer, Captain Nelson, will become the greatest man that ever England produced. I know it, from the few words of conversation I have already had with him. I pronounce, that he will one day astonish the world. I have never entertained any officer at my house, but I am determined to bring him here. Let him be put in the room prepared for Prince Augustus."
>
> Captain Nelson was, accordingly, introduced to her ladyship; and resided with Sir William Hamilton during his short stay at Naples: and thus commenced that fervid friendship between the parties, which continued to glow, with apparently increasing ardour, to the last moment of their respective existences whom it has been Lady Hamilton's severe lot to survive.

Of course, nobody believed a word of it! If they were generous, they said that her ladyship's memory was playing tricks again; and, if they were cruel, that she intended to possess Nelson dead, as she had Nelson living.

What?—if Sir William had never put up a naval officer before, he must have neglected his duty as British Ambassador! But Great Britain had been at peace for the last ten years, before her ladyship ever began to do the honors of the Palazzo Sessa; not a warship would have gone to Naples, certainly not on a mission as important as Captain Nelson's. Well then, this little man—unknown, unmarked by battle, unhonored at the time, remember—what could he have said in a few words of conversation with Sir William, who, whatever else he was, was no fool, to make him believe that he would *one day astonish the world?* Why, exactly that. Harrison gives the precise words a few lines later.

"Sir William," said he, in consequence of the dispatch made use of in obtaining the Neapolitan troops, "you are a man after my own heart: you do business in my own way! I am, now, only a captain; but I will, if I live, be at the top of the tree."

Lady Hamilton's reminiscence is borne out by the fact that the little captain made a point of telling his friends what a good man he was and what a great one he was going to be. Sir William, in believing him, was in good company with Lord Hood, Sir John Jervis, and all Nelson's commanders in chief, who put their confidence in him and gave him the opportunities to prove himself.

They met on Wednesday, September 11, 1793. They met in turbulent times.

In time, as in space, only the largest objects are visible at a distance. A man standing five miles from a mountain can see nothing but the mountain, whereas a man standing in a wood at the foot of the mountain cannot see the mountain at all. A step further—viewed from a vantage point over London, the dome of St. Paul's dominates the city, but the laborer who dug the foundations, the artisan who laid the pavement, the mason who built the pillars that support the dome, may not have lived to see it finished. People may be conscious of great events happening around them, they may participate in, even cause, great events; but only a prophet can adopt the position of posterity, and as many see through their posteriors as through their eyes.

The French Revolution rises from the pages of history books like a paper castle from a child's book of fairy stories when it is opened. On many pages there is nothing but the French Revolution, with Fox prophesying glory and Burke prophesying doom; as if work and play, what Sir William Hamilton called "The whole art of going thro' life tollerably," had stopped and people stood still to witness some monstrous birth. Nothing stopped in England. There was as much interest in the recent return of King George

III to his senses—he had addressed an oak tree as the King of Prussia in Windsor Park and chased Fanny Burney through Kew Gardens—as in the capture by the Paris mob of the Paris prison. Society was as pleased that Mr. Pitt, the Prime Minister, had resisted making the profligate Prince of Wales Regent, as it was that the French were apparently trying to give themselves a British constitution.

There was then, more than now, a leaven of complacency in the upper crust. It had the intellectual respectability of a philosophy and the sanction of an established religion. The philosophy may be summed up in Pope's "Whatever is, is right." As for religion, it was no accident that, to Nelson, God and Providence were the same conception, or that his father, the clergyman, once wrote to him, "Your lot is cast, but the whole disposing thereof is of the Lord: the very hairs of your head are numbered—a most comfortable doctrine." Providence would provide. On the whole it did.

For three years, from 1789 to 1792, Englishmen looked askance at what was going on across the Channel, without losing the main view that it was better to be at peace than at war. At that time, of course, war had none of the hideous connotations that have accrued to it in this century. No one protested against war because it was immoral, only because it was unreasonable. But there were, occasionally, circumstances that made war appear eminently reasonable.

At the beginning of February 1793 England went to war because the French threatened her most treasured possession—her security. The war in which Nelson and the Hamiltons met, loved, and died—Lady Hamilton died six months before Waterloo—was fought for national security, commercial security, and constitutional security. Security—and a touch of intolerance. "I hate a Frenchman," said Nelson. "They are equally objects of my detestation, whether Royalists or Republicans—in some points, I believe the latter are the best."

When it began, Louis XVI had been dead nearly a fortnight, Paris was governed by a body of hopeful and bloodthirsty idealists in the Convention, France was split by civil war and ringed by an alliance of outraged monarchs. There was a French army in Holland that had nettled John Bull, and, as if furious at Mr. Pitt for not seizing his opportunity to destroy them while they were divided and facing a formidable coalition, the Convention declared war on England.

Nelson was pleased. "My Dear Fanny," he wrote to his wife from London, "*Post Nubila Phoebus*—your son will explain the motto—after clouds come sunshine." The clouds were five years ashore on half-pay, living with her in his father's parsonage in Norfolk. The sunshine was the sea, a ship, and the chance of fame and fortune, with fortune coming a bad second.

In this February 1793 Nelson was in his thirty-fifth year and had both his arms and eyes. Apart from the previous five years, he had been at sea almost continuously since he was twelve. He had risen quickly in rank and favor under the patronage of his uncle Maurice Suckling, who had been Comptroller of the Navy, and Admirals Sir Peter Parker and Lord Hood, and he was a post captain of fourteen years' standing. He was known as a dedicated and uncommonly active officer with serious and slightly eccentric manners—he was old-fashioned in his dress and the length of his queue and never got drunk. He had not been in any battles but had distinguished himself in an ill-fated expedition against the Spaniards in Nicaragua in 1780, and again in the years 1784 to 1787 in putting down an illegal trade by American ships with the Leeward Islands.

It was on the island of Nevis that Captain Nelson married the widow Nisbet on March 11, 1787. Frances Herbert Nelson was at least five months older than her second husband (assuming that the inscription on her memorial in Littleham church is correct); her first had died after a brief marriage leaving her with a son, Josiah, born in 1780. Fanny was the niece of Mr. Herbert, the President of Nevis, who was descended from an Earl of Pembroke; she was proud of her Herbert connections and seldom left the name or the initial H off her signature.

It was a love match. "Not," said Nelson, "what is/vulgarly/no I wont make use of that word commonly called love . . . my love is founded on esteem the only foundation that can make love last." Well, it was not any other sort of match, because Nelson had no fortune and neither did Fanny until Mr. Herbert died in 1793, and then she brought him £4,000.

Fanny was retiring, dark-haired, genteel, with a faded prettiness like a rose that never bloomed, and a martyr to colds. When they returned to England, they went, for the sake of economy, to live at Burnham Thorpe with the Captain's father, the Reverend Edmund Nelson. Fanny sniffed away five Norfolk winters before her husband's departure released her to the milder climate of Bath. Nelson took Josiah to sea with him. Fanny failed to give him a child, but in that respect, as in another, perhaps he failed her.

Nelson's ship was the *Agamemnon,* a two-decker of sixty-four guns and a fine example of eighteenth-century warships, the most practical and tasteful fighting ships ever built. He sailed with a division of Lord Hood's fleet for the Mediterranean, where he had never been before. There he had his first experience of waiting off Toulon for the enemy to come out.

The enemy had no intention of coming out. Toulon was a Royalist city, less antagonistic to the British fleet than to the French government. In August 1793, when the army of the Convention marched into the south of France, the city fathers promptly surrendered to Lord Hood and invited him to defend them.

To the free world, and that is how the courts of Europe saw themselves, here was a great opportunity to destroy the revolutionary forces in France. The best part of the French navy and its first harbor were in their hands. They had now to be held against the Convention army, which was at Marseilles slaughtering *les enfants de la patrie* for their Royalist tendencies.

Lord Hood chose Captain Nelson for the important service of carrying dispatches to the courts of Sardinia and Naples, requisitioning the troops they were to provide in return for British subsidies. And so, on September 11, 1793, the little man came to Naples.

That place was in a flurry of excitement and anticipation. Whoever had come to Naples under the British flag would have been received with joy and feted as Nelson was. "Our daily prayers," wrote Sir William, who never said them, "are for the sight of a British Fleet in the Bay of Naples."

Many men have lived worthier lives than Sir William Hamilton, but it is difficult to think of any who lived a more agreeable one. He complained, of course, of its slight imperfections and considered himself a philosopher for bearing with them.

He was born in 1730, the grandson of a Duke of Hamilton on his father's side and an Earl of Abercorn on his mother's. As that lady was governess to Frederick Prince of Wales's children, and, so scandal said, something else again to Frederick Prince of Wales, he grew up with the future King George III as his playmate. He was a younger son of a younger son and had no fortune. When he was twenty-five and serving as an officer in the Footguards, he made up for this deficiency by marrying an heiress. Catherine Hamilton brought him a Welsh estate worth £5,000 a year and a love that lasted the twenty-seven years of their marriage. He used her money to buy pictures and her love as a retreat from several less enduring loves.

In 1764 William Hamilton entered the diplomatic service, for which, by breeding and manners, he was eminently suited. His friendship with the King made him an ambassador, or envoy extraordinary and minister plenipotentiary, as they used to say. Catherine's health and his own tastes made his place of residence Naples. He came to a country famous as the warm and luxurious playground of the ancients; to a city famous for its palaces, for the theatrical splendor of its setting; to a court famous for the boisterous simplicity of its young King.

Ferdinand, born in 1751, was the third son of King Charles III of Spain. Charles had appropriated the Kingdom of the Two Sicilies (Naples and Sicily) from the loose hegemony of the Austrian Empire. His eldest son was mad and had to be restrained from assaulting any woman in sight. His second son became mad—he was that pitiable creature Charles IV, the dupe first of Godoy then of Napoleon. So when Charles succeeded to the Spanish throne, he left the Two Sicilies to Ferdinand, who was eight years old and not mad—but he was kept simple on the theory that any study might damage his brain. This boy king was brought up to indulge his passions for hunting and horseplay in the company of servants, and to mix with the lowest sort of people at whom he shrieked the colorful vulgarisms of the Neapolitan language. He was consequently natural, single-minded in his pursuit of pleasure, and very popular with the least intelligent, and therefore greatest number, of his subjects.

When Hamilton arrived at Naples, the King was thirteen and the country was under the influence of Spain. Four years later Ferdinand married Maria Carolina, the sixteen-year-old daughter of the Austrian Empress, Maria Theresa. Another daughter, Marie Antoinette, was to marry Louis XVI.

Maria Carolina had the manners and appearance of a queen—Ferdinand had the manners and appearance of a farmhand. She had the will to rule, and on the few occasions her husband resisted it she nagged and screamed at him until he fled from the room. Her influence and policies were Austrian and, compared to those of Spain, liberal. On the birth of her first son in 1775, she claimed her right to sit in the Council of State and within a year she was the ruler of the kingdom. She had a fault, and Hamilton wrote, "It is well to own, and indeed the Emperor Joseph told me so himself when at Naples, that all the daughters of Maria Theresa had very tender hearts susceptible to sudden and violent impressions." Scandal said she took lovers, but as she bore her husband seventeen children it was probably only scandal.

The third important person at Naples, whose name was linked with the Queen's in this last respect, was John Acton. He came from a family of English baronets, though he was born in France in 1736. He served in the French and Tuscan navies with distinction. In 1778 he was sent to Naples to reorganize the Neapolitan navy. He was ambitious, and a bachelor, and became the Queen's favorite and Minister of Marine. An honest and industrious minister, in a court full of dishonest and idle ones, he was soon indispensable to the carrying on of government and virtual prime minister. Hamilton found him a friend and an ally and awarded him the ultimate accolade when he said, "I can perceive him to be still an Englishman at heart."

It was a time, the only time since the Roman Empire, when the leisured class of Europe devoted itself to the scientific enjoyment of life, and the unleisured classes devoted themselves to the leisured class. The pursuit of culture and the deliberate cultivation of taste were the full-time occupations of hundreds of civilized ladies and gentlemen who perambulated Europe. Naples was the southern capital of this civilized society. They came for the sunshine and the music, for the flowers and the arts, for Pompeii and Vesuvius—and for the British there was the added attraction of the British Ambassador.

Lady Craven remembered: "Sir William and Lady Hamilton" (this is Catherine who, Dr. Burney said, was the finest piano player in Italy) "constituted for a time the great pleasure of the Court. . . . His superior understanding and philosophic turn of mind made him a most interesting man. In every branch of science and polite literature he excelled, whilst the versatility of his character constituted the most extraordinary composition." He was tall, athletic, aristocratic, had easy manners and a fund of anecdotes which increased every time a noble traveler succumbed to the local Hebes or Ganymedes. William Beckford called him "The first of connoisseurs—not only in the fine arts, but in the science of human felicity."

Sir William, who was made a Knight of the Bath in 1772 for staying where he was, had a collection of several hundred paintings and sketches. It was a cabinet collection, representative of the taste of the day for rather gloomy romanticism, but the works of Leonardo da Vinci, Rubens, Rembrandt, Hals and Vandyke also graced the walls of his residence, the Palazzo Sessa. He made the two greatest collections of Greek vases ever to leave Italy, one of which may still be seen in the British Museum. He owned for a time the masterpiece that came to be known, from the name of its purchaser, as the Portland Vase.

He made experiments with electricity, kept a tame monkey, and planted an English garden in the grounds of the royal palace at Caserta. He had a house at Caserta and a pretty villa on the coast at Posilipo. He played the cello and kept his own band of musicians. Vesuvius was his particular study and his observations on volcanoes in papers to the Royal Society, whose president Sir Joseph Banks was his friend, were published under the title *Campi Phlegraei*. He hunted regularly in the winter season with the

King, in the grand battues which were Ferdinand's delight. Thousands of beaters were employed and the slaughter of wild boars, deer, hares, even hedgehogs when nothing else appeared, was immense.

One of Ferdinand's less attractive habits was to cut up the dead animals and to invite the ladies of the party to watch him as he worked, up to his elbows in blood, and dangled the parts suggestively in front of their eyes. Another one was described by Sir William to his correspondent Sir Nathaniel Wraxall.

"When the King has made a hearty meal, and feels an inclination to retire, he commonly communicates that intention to the noblemen around him in waiting, and selects the favoured individuals, whom, as a mark of predilection, he chooses shall attend him. 'Sono ben pranzato,' says he, laying his hand on his belly, 'Adesso bisogne una buona panciata.' [I have dined well, and now I need a good easing of the belly.] The persons thus preferred then accompany His Majesty, stand respectfully around him, and amuse him by their conversation during the performance." Even at a time when the commode was a useful piece of furniture—Nelson's was in the bottom right-hand drawer of a completely innocent-looking chest—this was thought rather old-fashioned.

Ferdinand's other arrangements were more modern, positively liberal. In the grounds of Caserta, at San Leucio, he established a silk factory and a colony largely composed of peasant girls. He made the laws and laid down Christian precepts, and provided a hospital, a school and a church. It was a proper little welfare state, though, of course, the cynics knew better. "Scandal says," said Lady Holland, "their establishment answers the double purpose of seraglio and nursery."

Cynicism, complacency turned sour, was fashionable. Kotzebue, the forgotten German playwright whose *Pizarro* Sheridan made the hit in London, remarked, "From the terrible Italian jealousy the stranger has nothing to dread; it is no longer to be found except in novels. The husband does not lay the slightest obstacle in the way, and even that doubtful animal the *cicisbeo* exist no more. Conjugal Fidelity might be here depicted as flying or concealing itself from ridicule." Sir William had been living in Italy for thirty-four years when Nelson came for the second time to the Palazzo Sessa.

In 1782 Catherine declined and died. The first Lady Hamilton was a shadowy figure (there was an even more shadowy daughter who died in 1775). She was a pious lady who longed to convert her husband so that they might meet more often in a better world than they had in this. Her last wish was that he should be buried beside her in the Welsh church where she knew she was going.

Sir William was a philosopher. "My study of antiquities," he wrote once, "has kept me in constant thought of the perpetual fluctuation of everything. The whole art is, really, to live all the *days* of our life; and not, with anxious care, disturb the sweetest hour that life affords—which is the present! Admire the Creator and all his works, to us incomprehensible; and do all the good you can upon earth; and take the chance of eternity without dismay." This too was a very comfortable doctrine.

The summer of 1784 found the Chevalier, as he was known in polite Neapolitan circles, on leave in London. There, in the house of his nephew Charles Greville, he met the girl who was to succeed and eclipse Catherine as the second Lady Hamilton.

She was the daughter of poor parents, Henry and Mary Lyon, of the hamlet of Nesse in the Wirral, Cheshire; born on April 26, 1765, and christened Amy sixteen days later. On her father's death, she was taken to live with her maternal grandmother, Mrs. Kidd, in Hawarden, across the River Dee. As soon as she was big enough, she was put into domestic service.

Somehow or other she came to London—perhaps her mother took her there to exploit her budding charms. She was a beauty and beauty has always been a negotiable commodity; but Amy was too wild, too uncalculating, to wait for the main chance. After another short spell in service, she threw caution, and clothes, to the wind, and posed as the "Goddess of Health" in a pseudo-medical exhibition at the Adelphi. While Dr. Graham lectured on the virtues of mud baths and exercises, his unwashed and idle audience gawped at Amy on her pedestal. Among the crowd of Bond Street loungers and loose fish were some brighter sparks of society, and she soon found a new occupation.

A fashionable sea captain, John Willet Payne, the friend and companion of the Prince of Wales, was credited with her seduction. From him she graduated to Sir Harry Featherstonhaugh of Up Park. In the sedate surroundings of this aptly named spot, the fiercely beautiful young girl was indulged in every frolic her wild temper sought—until Sir Harry dropped her for breaking the only rule of propriety recognized by the Up Park set. She became pregnant by him.

She fled home to Hawarden and turned in panic to the one person she had met whose appraisal of her suggested that his interest might survive the tragedy—the cool-eyed Greville. After the birth of "little Emma," she returned to London with a new name, Emly Hart, and a new protector.

19

Greville gained a seventeen-year-old mistress on the cheap, and her mother as housekeeper into the bargain.

He kept her for four years in a small house in Edgware Row, near the unfashionable retreat of Paddington Green. In the spring of 1782 when Emly came to live with him, Charles Greville was thirty-three and a bachelor. He was a younger son of the Earl of Warwick and his mother had been the favorite sister of Sir William Hamilton. He had £500 a year from the family estate, and, as a Member of Parliament, an excuse for an occupation. He paid Mrs. Kidd a small allowance to keep "little Emma" at Hawarden, and gave Emly £20 a year spending money. In return she counted the pennies and kept house for him, helped by her mother, who, having mysteriously become Mrs. Doggin, marked her rise in station by calling herself Mrs. Cadogan.

Greville taught Emly how to spell and she became Emily. He engaged a music teacher for her. She became Emma, and they lived in secluded and respectable sin. It was not sin as far as she was concerned. No, he had saved her from sin. It was—well, it was goodness. They were in love. At least she was. Greville once wrote to Sir William, "It does not become a FRS to give way to his passion."

This FRS collected geological specimens. There was a mania for collecting—pictures, statues, coins, books, all sorts of ancient art, and rubbish, lumped together and called virtu. Clothes were worn until they stank, lice popped out of powdered heads, Mr. Bramah's water closets were the exception rather than the rule, but everyone had a collection. (Even Nelson collected Nelsoniana for his Nelson Room.) Europe was ransacked for treasures, first by wealthy Englishmen, who paid for them, and then by triumphant Frenchmen, who stole them. One of the most assiduous ransackers was Sir William Hamilton, and his agent for accepting commissions in London was his nephew.

Greville collected stones. Emma stayed home being grateful and good, except when her temper broke the bounds of Paddington Green. A mistress had her situation somewhere between a servant and a wife, with more duties than the first and fewer privileges than the second. There were few places where she could appear in company with Greville; few people he could meet that she could meet, and they were usually artists, who could not be offended by her company and would not presume to try to seduce her. When he introduced her to George Romney, Greville insured that, had she spent the rest of her life as Mrs. Hart of Edgware Row, she could never be forgotten.

Romney, who was besotted with the girl, painted her in at least two dozen different attitudes. She was his inspiration, his favorite model, his only model in a way, because once he had seen her, all his portraits of women had a bit of Emma in them. He recorded her as one of the most beautiful creatures of that, or any other, age.

Sir William thought so too and spent many afternoons gazing at the girl. Though there were nearly twenty years between uncle and nephew, they were very much alike. They were both younger sons, with the need to acquire a fortune and without the inclination to work for it. Their tastes were similar—how similar! Emma was soon calling them Pliny the Elder and Pliny the Younger, after the two whose lives, as Sir William delighted in telling her, so closely resembled those of their modern counterparts.

When the Plinys went off to inspect the Elder's Welsh estate, which the Younger managed and was anxious to inherit, Emma traveled to Hawarden to collect "little Emma." With the little girl, she revealed a side of her character which her situation demanded must be repressed. She told Greville, "When she comes and looks in my face and calls me mother, endead I then truly am a mother; for all the mother's feelings rise at once and tells I am and ought to be a mother." Poor Emma. Poor "little Emma." Before long she was sent away to be brought up in a respectable household. The relationship was never acknowledged, though they were to meet again.

"Little Emma" was sacrificed to propriety, *bienséance* they called it then. Emma was to do something very similar later.

At the close of the year 1784 Sir William was preparing to return to Naples. He flirted with Emma under his nephew's calculating eye, and invited them both to visit him to enjoy the pleasures, the *agrémens*, of the southern city. How Emma came to Naples and Greville did not is a story worthy of Ben Jonson. Everyone appears at his worst, behaves abominably, and is better off at the end than he was at the beginning.

It began with a joke. Shortly after his arrival at Naples, Sir William made a proposition to Lady Clarges which she mistook for a proposal of marriage and politely declined. "The Devil fetch me if I meant to propose," he wrote to his nephew, "though I ever after have thought she would suit me well."

It was no joke to Greville. The next lady might accept and an offspring would put him out of his inheritance. He was not even certain he had an inheritance. "They say here that you are in love," he wrote back. "I know you love variety, and are a general flirt, and of the 60 English, what with widows and young married ladies, an amateur may be caught. . . . If you did not chuse a wife, I wish the tea-maker of Edgware Row was yours, if I could without banishing myself from a visit to Naples." This was very nephewly!

Sir William's answer is missing, but he could not have closed the subject, as Greville pursued it on May 5, 1785. (Letters took about a month to reach Naples.) He said that he was now considering marriage himself. Lord Middleton had two daughters with £20,000 apiece and the second was available. Could he present himself as a gentleman with expectations and without encumbrances? Sir William had only to do him one favor and himself another. Emma was but twenty, "and at your age a clean and comfortable woman is not superfluous."

Sir William replied that he had already made his will leaving everything to his nephew. But with regard to E., while she loved Dear Charles, she could only esteem and suffer him. There were risks. "It would be fine fun for the young English travellers to endeavour to cuckold the old gentleman, Signr. Ambassador, and whether they succeeded or not would surely give me uneasiness." If Greville married, he would allow Emma £50 a year; if he did not, he would rather see them both at Naples than Emma alone, "for I am sensible I am not a match for so much youth and beauty."

Greville immediately sent Lord Middleton notice of his prospects. (It was in vain and he died a bachelor.) Of the unsuspecting Emma, he told Sir William, "You know that, added to her looks, so cleanly and sweet a creature does not exist, and she is handsomer than when you saw her here."

Old Pliny hesitated. He was concerned about his virility. And what would the world say in this bizarre game of consequences?

"You will be able to have an experiment without any risque," came the reply. "You need not fear domestic duty, women always require what men give them reason to expect . . . and as I consider you as my heir-apparent I must add that she is the only woman I ever slept with without having ever had any of my senses offended, and a cleanlier sweeter bedfellow does not exist." As for the world, "You know we are not accountable to the world further than not to offend against *bienséance*."

And so it was agreed.

That such a transaction could have been made by two civilized and urbane gentlemen, who might have been bargaining for a horse not a woman, is only a measure of the morality of the day. It was considered odd, slightly ridiculous, that a mistress should pass from nephew to uncle, but there was no fuss, no censure, and it was well known once Emma was established in Naples. Greville later became a member of the Royal Household, and

Queen Charlotte had a very strong sense of propriety. Sir William kept his post for another fifteen years.

It will appear that the transfer of Emma from Paddington Green to the Palazzo Sessa was a very reasonable way of solving a difficult problem. The alternatives for her were a dull life in the country on a tiny allowance, or a return to the downward ways of Up Park.

In March 1786 Emma and her mother set out for Naples. She went reluctantly and only on the understanding that Greville would join her in the autumn. And here was a new problem. Having got her out of the Younger Pliny's bed, how were they going to get her into the Elder's?

She arrived on her twenty-first birthday, a tall, fair-complexioned girl with blue eyes, long auburn hair to her heels, and a tempestuous will of her own. Sir William was kindness itself. She had her own apartment overlooking the sea, a carriage and servants, a dress of Lady Hamilton's, a shawl, and more dresses were being made for her in muslin for the hot weather. Sir William was more than kindness, and she told Greville sharply in a letter, "Nobody shall be your heir-apearant."

In the following three months she wrote every week to Greville, telling of the pleasant life, of boating and bathing at Posilipo, of everyone's admiration and the amorous advances of the King himself, of painters painting her and of language, singing and music masters instructing her; telling of Sir William's polite but persistent importunities and her resistance to them; telling of her love, her love for her Greville, until she cried out, "Oh, my heart is intirely broke."

He answered the last letter, but in such a way that she exploded, "How, with that cool indifference, to advise me to go to bed to him. Sir Wm! Oh, that worst of all! But I will not, no I will not rage. If I was with you, I would murder you and myself booth . . . nothing shall ever do for me but going home to you. If that is not to be, I will except of nothing, I will go to London, their go into every excess of vice tell I dye, a miserable broken-hearted wretch, and leave my fate as a warning to young whomen never to be two good; for now you have made me love you, you made me good, you have abbandoned me; and some violent end shall finish our connexion, if it is to finish." She ended, "It is not to your interest to disoblige me, for you don't know the power I have hear. Onely I never will be his mistress. If you affront me, I will make him marry me—God bless you for ever."

This, written on August 1, was goodbye. Sir William had to wait for his inheritance until the very end of the year, but Emma was not going back. She was playing the part of a discarded lover, and the speech in the

23

letter would have done very well in a play. She would have made a first-rate actress—"Damn Mrs. Siddons!" as Nelson said—and Greville, who was a scientific observer, knew it.

"Emma's passion is admiration," he wrote to Sir William, "and it is not troublesome, because she is satisfied with a limited sphere, but is capable of aspiring to any line which would be celebrated, and it would be indifferent, when on that key, whether she was Lucretia or Sappho, or Scævola or Regulus; anything grand, masculine or feminine, she could take up, and if she took up the part of Scævola, she would be as much offended if she was told she was a woman as she would be, if she assumed Lucretia, she was told she was masculine."

This is remarkably acute. What he says is that Emma can play any part, and play it with such conviction that she becomes the part she is playing. It explains many of the changes in her character which otherwise appear arbitrary and even contradictory, and lead her accusers to charge her with insincerity and pretentiousness.

Both Greville and Sir William expected her to leave Naples that winter. She fooled them both, or gratified them both. She certainly gratified Sir William. She summed up the situation on December 26, 1786, "I am a pretty whoman and one can't be everything at once; but now I have my wisdom teeth I will try to be ansome and reasonable."

In the year that Nelson and his wife went to live in the Norfolk parsonage, Emma settled permanently in the Palazzo Sessa. Sir William, who found as much delight in her accomplishments as in her beauty, became more and more enraptured with her. The girl in her gauzy dress, who looked, and some said sang, like an angel, was the jewel of his collection, to be polished and cherished. Emma repaid him with gratitude and the love she associated with it, and with her good behavior. She was accepted by the English, petted by the Neapolitans, and praised by the Court as a model of virtue. But she could not go to Court. She was inside the moral pale, but outside the social one. The Queen could only be civil at a distance. Some traveling ladies scorned her company, while their husbands sought it. She began to feel the indignity of her situation, and by the winter of 1789, when she had lived with Sir William for three years, she felt secure enough in his affections to overcome it.

She set about getting him to marry her in a very characteristic way, by spreading the rumor that they were already married. "It is very natural for her to wish it," wrote the Chevalier to Sir Joseph Banks, who had heard the story, "and to try to make people believe the business done, which I suppose has caused the report in England." He had no objection to marrying

Emma. On the contrary, it would secure her company for the remaining years of his life. There was an obstacle if the Queen of Naples refused to acknowledge her even after the marriage, but this disappeared when the Queen, who was already disposed in Emma's favor, intimated that she would certainly receive her as Lady Hamilton.

All this took time. In the eighteenth century everything that required a person to go from one place to another took a lot of time. It makes the history of the age tolerable because seldom more than one event took place in a day—there was not time for another. Dinner took up the best part of the day. People seemed to move slowly and to tire quickly. If Sir William had to write a dispatch, he complained of being fagged to death. Activity was highly prized. Nelson's activity, which would not be considered as remarkable today, was praised to the skies. There is a sneaking feeling that Nelson, Napoleon and Wellington were as great as they were because they got up earlier than anyone else and neither ate nor drank as much.

It was not until the summer of 1791 that Sir William and Emma were once again in England. Horace Walpole met them at the Duke of Queensberry's villa at Richmond. "There were Sir William Hamilton and Mrs. Harte; who, on the 3rd of next month, previous to their departure, is to be made Madame l'Envoyée à Naples, the Neapolitan Queen having promised to receive her in that quality. Here she cannot be presented where only such over-virtuous wives as the Duchess of Kingston and Mrs. Hastings —who could go with a husband in each hand—are admitted." In fact they were married in Marylebone Church on September 6, 1791.

Sir William was sixty-one, and his bride twenty-six. If Charles Greville harbored any resentment against his former lover, or any anxiety about his future inheritance, they were soon dissolved. Sir William was the same amiable uncle, and Lady Hamilton treated him like an aunt. Of course, the wedding did not escape notice. Peter Pindar, the rhyming gossip, had his fun.

> O Knight of Naples, is it come to pass,
> That thou hast left the gods of stone and brass,
> To wed a deity of flesh and blood? *
> O lock the temple with thy strongest key,
> For fear thy deity, a comely She,
> Should one day ramble, in a frolic mood.

. . . .

* It is really true—the Knight is *married* to a beautiful *virgin*, whom he styles his *Grecian*. Her attitudes are the most *desirable* models for *young* artists.

25

Yet should *thy Grecian goddess fly the fane,*
*I think that we may catch her in Hedge-Lane.**

Even the peripatetic Casanova gibed at the marriage. "He was a clever man, but ended by marrying a young woman who was clever enough to bewitch him. Such a fate often overtakes a man of intelligence when he grows old. It is always a mistake to marry, but when a man's physical and mental forces are declining, it is a calamity."

They were in England a few months only, but it was long enough to revitalize the gloomy Romney into a new burst of portraits, and to astonish society with Emma's unique attitudes and bravura singing.

The attitudes probably developed from Emma's poses as the "Goddess of Health." She mentioned them first in 1787 when she asked Greville to send her a shawl: "Now as I have such a use of shawls, and mine is worn out. Sir William is miserable. For I stand in atitudes in them." Sir William produced and stage-managed each performance, as Goethe recorded on his visit to Naples.

> The old Knight has had a Greek costume made for her, which becomes her extremely. Dressed in this, and letting her hair loose, and taking a couple of shawls, she exhibits every possible variety of posture, expression, and look, so that at the last the spectator almost fancies it is a dream. One beholds there in perfection, in movement, in ravishing variety, all that the greatest of artists have rejoiced to be able to produce. Standing, kneeling, sitting, lying down, grave or sad, playful, exulting, repentant, wanton, menacing, anxious—all mental states follow rapidly one after another. With wonderful taste she suits the folding of her veil to each expression, and with the same handkerchief makes every kind of head-dress. The old Knight holds the light for her, and enters into the exhibition with his whole soul.

Horace Walpole heard Emma sing. "Oh! but she sings admirably; has a very fine, strong voice; is an excellent buffa, and an astonishing tragedian. She sung Nina in the highest perfection; and there her attitudes were a whole theatre of grace and various expressions." Nina was her speciality. "Her Nina," wrote Romney, "surpasses everything I ever saw, and I believe, as a piece of acting, nothing ever surpassed it. The whole company were in an agony of sorrow." After one concert, Gallini, who managed the opera house in Hanover Square, offered to engage her, and Sir William replied pleasantly that he had engaged her for life.

The Hamiltons returned to Naples in the winter of 1791. They

* The resort of the Cyprian corps, an avenue that opens into Cockspur Street.

stopped in Paris on the way, and Emma was presented to Marie Antoinette, and carried a letter from her to her sister Maria Carolina. The ex-model and ex-mistress was now truly Madame l'Envoyée, the ambassadress twixt Queens.

Sir William had taken a risk. A man who marries his mistress risks offending every woman into whose society he introduces her. A man of sixty-one who marries an infamous beauty of twenty-six risks offending every man who cannot credit himself with the courage to do the same. He wrote hopefully to Walpole, "It has often been remarked that a reformed rake makes a good husband. *Why not vice versa?*" And more confidently to Sir Joseph Banks, "Lady Hamilton has nothing to do with my public Character but Their Sicilian Majesties are so good as to receive and treat her as any other Travelling Lady of distinction. She has gained the hearts of all, even of the Ladies, by her humility and proper behaviour, and we shall I dare say go on well. I will allow with you that 99 times in a hundred, such a step as I took would be very imprudent, but I know my way here and here I mean to pass the most of the days that I can have a chance of living. Without a Woman you can have no Society at home, and I am sure you will hear from every quarter of the comfort of my house."

Emma's favorable reception at Court and the marked attentions shown her by the Queen were the real reasons for her success. Visiting ladies who wished to be presented to the daughter of Maria Theresa were obliged to seek an audience through the daughter of Mrs. Cadogan. And the reason why Maria Carolina smiled affectionately at Emma Hamilton was a political one.

When the shock of the first crisis in France had passed, Naples was calm. Some *émigrés* arrived, cursing French politics, but their influence was balanced by that of patriotic clubs, formed by French merchants and some idealistic sprigs of the Neapolitan nobility, who fancied a change. Liberal opinions, and the mystic cant of Freemasonry, were tolerated by the Queen, who felt secure in the shelter of the vast Austrian Empire. In February 1790 her brother Leopold became Emperor, and she strengthened the link between Naples and Vienna by marrying her eldest daughter to his son Francis. Another daughter was married at the same time to the Grand Duke Ferdinand of Tuscany. The whole royal family went to Vienna for the weddings, the round trip took eight months, and returned with a comfortable feeling of security.

Suddenly in March 1792 Leopold died. Maria Carolina was grief-stricken. She had more than one reason to cry, because the new Emperor Francis II was too young and inexperienced to deal coolly with the succession of crises emanating from France. A month later the Convention declared war on Austria.

On land the Austrian army appeared invincible. Naples, however, was vulnerable from the sea, and the first sea power in the world was Great Britain. That is why Maria Carolina patronized Lady Hamilton and, through her, the elderly Chevalier, the British Ambassador. As the threat from France increased, so did the Queen's friendship for Emma.

In December 1792 a French squadron under La Touche Tréville sailed into the Bay of Naples, bringing an emissary from the Convention who, in the uniform of a common grenadier, marched into the Court and demanded recognition for the new Republic. Sir William was ill at the time; he had a bilious fever that nearly took him off. Emma received daily letters from "her devoted friend, Charlotte," as the Queen signed herself.

Any chance of an accommodation with France was cut off with the head of Louis XVI. In the aftermath of fear and repression in Naples, the Republican sympathizers, who had openly welcomed Latouche, were driven underground. A treaty was entered into with England, providing for Neapolitan troops to be made available in return for a subsidy and the presence of a British fleet in the Mediterranean.

Early in September a Spanish ship brought the news of the capture of Toulon, by the Spaniards of course. This caused the flurry of excitement and anticipation into which Captain Nelson sailed on September 11, 1793.

As the *Agamemnon* dropped anchor, a boat came alongside with an invitation to the Captain to visit the Neapolitan flagship, where, by chance, he was presented to King Ferdinand. He assured the King that Lord Hood, and not the Spaniards, had received the surrender of Toulon. "The Spaniard," said the King, "had *Trompe Trompe.*"

Nelson went ashore, taking Josiah with him, as he made a point of introducing his midshipmen to polite society whenever possible. He met Sir William and had his famous few words of conversation. In the evening, there was a conference with Acton, who had succeeded to his baronetcy and was now Sir John. It was decided that 6,000 soldiers should be sent to Toulon, 2,000 of them before the end of the week. His business done, Nelson went to bed in the room prepared for Prince Augustus. The Prince, George III's sixth son, had curtailed his Italian holiday and was on his way home.

For the next three days Nelson was royally entertained. He visited the vast palace at Portici, near Vesuvius, which had a highway running through the middle of it, but with all that was the Queen's favorite palace. He was not presented to Maria Carolina, because she was expecting her sixteenth child. He dined with Acton in glittering company, and was given a letter in the King's hand for Lord Hood. He had asked for such a letter and it was a great favor to get it, because it took so long for Ferdinand to write it. All the time, Sir William was with him, interpreting for him, and Emma was fussing about him, and, when he was out, she fussed about Josiah.

"Lady Hamilton," Nelson wrote to Fanny, "has been wonderfully kind and good to Josiah. She is a young woman of amiable manners and who does honor to the station to which she is raised." So he certainly knew something of Emma's history.

September 15 was a Sunday, and the day chosen for a royal visit to the *Agamemnon*. There was a heavy swell in the bay, too heavy for a King, and the visit was postponed to one o'clock the next day. Nelson dined at the royal palace in the city and had the seat of honor at Ferdinand's right hand.

They were all up early the next morning to see the troops march down to the harbor to embark. Then the Captain of the *Agamemnon* gave a breakfast party on board his ship for the British at Naples. There were Sir William and Lady Hamilton, the Bishop of Winchester, Lord and Lady Plymouth, Lord Grandison and his daughter, and a whole lot more, eating and drinking—and the seamen looking at them enviously because they had little enough to eat and drink, and in all the preparation for the party and the King's visit no water or provisions had been taken on board.

It was noon, and Nelson was preparing to send his guests ashore to make room for the King, when a message arrived from Acton that a French warship with three vessels in convoy had been sighted off the south of Sardinia. The scene was changed in a second. The Bishop, the lords and ladies were hurried over the side, there were hasty farewells as the boats bobbed away and the *Agamemnon*'s sails were unbent and shaken out in the breeze. She sailed, with empty champagne bottles rolling across the decks, leaving King Ferdinand open-mouthed on the mole. "It was necessary," said Nelson, "to show them what an English Man of War can do." One man in the crew was dying and a hundred were down with scurvy.

Goethe once said, "Naples is a paradise, in it every one lives in a sort of intoxicated self-forgetfulness."

"God send us good success," Nelson wrote in his journal. "I believe we carry with us the good wishes of Naples and of Sir William Hamilton and Lady Hamilton in particular which I esteem more than all the rest. Farewell Naples. May those who were kind to me be repaid ten fold. If I am successful I return, if otherwise go to Toulon."

It was otherwise. He had been there five days and he did not return for five years.

CHAPTER TWO

Lady Hamilton's Services

AFTER THIS un-Neapolitan burst of activity, which the shock-headed little Captain had started like a small boy in a rock pool, there was no more peace for the great people of Naples.

The troops who had set out for Toulon happily out of step were brought back miserably defeated. They had arrived just in time to retreat. There had been disasters, desertions, and the dead hand of a divided command. Lord Hood was forced to abandon the city and half the captured French fleet to the Republican army, who celebrated their victory in the blood of the wretched Royalists. The great hope of subduing France was extinguished. The shadow of times to come crossed the sun.

"Were there ever such times, such vertigos, such bedevilments?" Beckford asked Sir William on Christmas Day 1793. "Remember me in your kindest manner to the lovely Emma, whose friendship for me throws a bright ray over my whole existence. I cannot help looking upon her as a sort of superior being—so good, so candid, so ingenuous, that the poor old woman who mistook her in the dawn of the morning for a statue of the holy Virgin need not have been ashamed to have renewed her homage in open daylight."

It was not only the epicene author of *Vathek* who noticed the Madonna-likeness of Lady Hamilton. Her maids would come and beg favors of her because she resembled the Virgin, and the peasants of Ischia knelt before her when she visited their island. A priest who saw her with a shawl over her head burst into tears and cried that God had sent her for a purpose. For what purpose, he did not say. To her classic features, which Sir William happily compared to those of the Apollo Belvedere, she could add such a purity of expression that a nun once told her she was like the marble statues she saw when she was in the world. "I think she flatered me up," said Emma, who had only to open her mouth to ruin the whole impression, "but I was pleased."

"In my life I have never been so completely occupied as for these ten months past," the Chevalier wrote to Sir Joseph Banks in April 1794. "Lord Hood is now battering Bastia with the shells that I procured for him." Captain Nelson had asked for the shells a month before, as he intended to capture the Corsican seaport by himself. "The shells and mortars from Naples are good for nothing," said Captain Duncan, who had to fire them. Bastia fell in May. "I always was of opinion, have ever acted up to it, and never have had reason to alter it that *one Englishman* was equal to three *Frenchmen*," Nelson told Fanny.

On July 12 he was again ashore with his sailors, serving the guns in the siege of Calvi. An enemy shot hit the parapet of the battery where he was standing and a splinter of stone struck his right eye. "It was cut down," he wrote, "but is as far recovered as to be able to distinguish light from darkness, but as to all the purpose of use it is gone. However the blemish is nothing, not to be perceived unless told. The pupil is nearly the size of the blue part, I don't know the name."

At Naples the Court had just come out of mourning for Marie Antoinette when a Jacobin plot was discovered. A group of high-minded young noblemen were planning to murder King Ferdinand and declare a republic. The flickering candle of tolerance was snuffed out. Some eighty of them were imprisoned and eventually three were executed. It is a measure of the relative terrors of royal and republican rule, that three guilty men died in Naples and some six thousand innocent men, women and children were slaughtered in Toulon.

Then, as if in sympathy with the times, Vesuvius erupted. The town of Torre del Greco was obliterated and Naples itself was threatened. The Neapolitans besought the protection of their patron, St. Januarius. The phial containing the saint's congealed blood was brought in procession from the cathedral and held up in the direction of the volcano. The blood liquefied, Vesuvius stopped belching lava, and the city was saved.

"We have had a thumping Eruption of Vesuvius," Sir William wrote to Sir Joseph delightedly, "certainly the greatest in History except those of 79 and 1631. I am convinced having examined the Course of the Lava and the immense rents in the mountain that the combustibles broke out with great difficulty, and supposing it had not got vent this City would have been a heap of ruins." And he quoted a Neapolitan ditty,

31

It is to save you that I shit
I have let three farts and a sneeze.

When the ashes settled, the mountain was seen to have changed shape. The conelike summit was gone and there was a huge jagged crater. The giant had lost a ninth of its height.

If St. Januarius had had the effect on Vesuvius that the people celebrated in song, he overdid the dose. Emma reported to Greville late that summer, "My dear Sir William as had the disorder that we and all Naples have had since the eruption—a violent *diarea* that reduced him to so very low an ebb, that I was very much alarmed for him, notwithstanding I thought I should have gone with him."

In the same letter she congratulated Greville on his appointment as Vice-Chamberlain, which put him in easy circumstances. The absence of a child three years after his uncle's marriage kept him at his task of managing the Welsh estate. However, a child did figure occasionally in his letters to Naples.

"Little Emma" was growing up. In 1794 she was twelve. "Growing and worms more usually affect persons of her age than great sensibility," said the objective Greville. The girl, who was small and plain, was lodged with a family called Blackburn, and the bill was paid by Sir William. Two years later the question of her future arose. Greville thought that a clergyman might marry her, worms and all, for a consideration.

Then he devised the model for a later deception. "I am still uncertain of her history but I believe her to be niece to Mrs. C [Cadogan] and that her parents are alive; this she should know, for her age is now such as to make it proper to give her at least the comfort of knowing, or the certainty that she cannot be the better for receiving the information, neither of which I am able to give, unless Ly. H. will inform you, or communicate to me her wishes." This was written to Sir William, who was in on the secret, but the decision to keep the girl in ignorance of her true parentage was Emma's. She was told that her name was Emma Carew, and that she had no great connections or expectations.

The winter of 1794 was a hectic one for the Hamiltons. British travelers flocked to Naples until one might have said, as the haughty Sarah Goudar did to Casanova, "One cannot put one's foot down without treading on an Englishman." They were led by Prince Augustus, who occupied his room at last, and included the magnificent Lord Bristol. This noble ecclesiastic—he was also Bishop of Derry—made Rome his wash pot and cast his shoe over Naples. He was always dressed in scarlet and white; the

Neapolitans thought he was some great Catholic prince of the church, for he kept a crowd of panders and painters. He was a bishop who had no time for lords and a lord who had no time for bishops. He loved living and Lady Hamilton, and once apostrophized:

> Oh, Emma, who'd ever be wise,
> If madness be loving of thee,

which was not bad for lord or bishop. He had a brutal wit and accused Prince Augustus of braying like an ass when he tried to harmonize with Mrs. Billington in Sir William's drawing room.

Mrs. Billington was the finest soprano in Europe. The composer Bianchi wrote his *Inez di Castro* for her and the première was given at the San Carlo theater in Naples. She made her reputation—two reputations, the other for frailty—at Daly's theater in Dublin and Gallini's opera house in London. The Prince of Wales was her lover. Once when she was applauded for ten minutes after leaving the stage, a critic remarked that she would not be flattered because she knew a clap was contagious. She was a dear friend of Emma Hamilton.

Lord Bristol spared no one. When he had left Naples, he wrote to his ever dearest Emma, "You say nothing of the adorable Queen; I hope she has not forgot me; but as Shakespeare says, 'Who doats, must doubt'; and verily I deem her the very best edition of a woman I ever saw—I mean of such as are not in *folio*, and are to be *had* in *sheets*."

Emma was thicker with the Queen than ever. Sir William suffered from recurrent bilious attacks and was absent from Court for long periods. In the tortuous ways of Neapolitan politics, the back stairs to Maria Carolina's boudoir was the most direct route, and Lady Hamilton could take it regularly without arousing suspicion. "Send me some news, political and private," she wrote to Greville, "for, against my will, *owing to my situation here*, I am got into politicks, and I wish to have news for our dear much-loved Queen, whom I adore. . . . She loves England and is attached to our Ministry, and wishes the continuation of the war as the only means to ruin that abominable French council."

In the summer of 1795 the alliance against France was disintegrating. Prussia, humiliated at Valmy, was ready to withdraw. Charles IV of Spain, under the baleful influence of Godoy, was planning to do the same, and he wrote to his brother Ferdinand telling him of his intention. Maria Carolina filched the letter from her husband's pocket and gave it to Emma to copy for the English government.

In the last codicil to his will Nelson referred to another letter Emma obtained in 1796, in which the King of Spain wrote that he was about to declare war on England. It has, so far, defied discovery. However, it would be ungrateful and unwise to doubt the one document in which a man may be relied on to tell the truth and shame the devil, without the most convincing evidence to the contrary. Lady Hamilton's claim to have done her country some service is borne out by the undeniable fact that she was the link between the governments of Naples and England. It was a new role for her, not Scævola or Regulus, but perhaps Belisarius saving the Two Sicilies from the Goths.

The year 1796 was a disastrous one for the allies. In Paris the Terror had bled itself to death and there was that corpse of a government called the Directory. Idealism and power had passed to the army, which had conquered Holland, Belgium, Savoy, and taken the French frontier to the Rhine. Italy, rich and ripe, was next on the list for the fraternal squeeze. The campaign was entrusted to General Bonaparte. Within a month he had occupied Milan and was marching south. King Ferdinand declared, "He would rather die at the head of his troops than submit to an ignominious Peace," and signed an armistice with the enemy in June.

In August came the treaty between France and Spain in which Charles IV agreed to declare war on England. This was followed by the decision of the British government to withdraw the fleet from the Mediterranean, and the belated advice of the Foreign Secretary Lord Grenville to the Court of Naples to make the best terms they could with Bonaparte. It cost Naples an indemnity of 8,000,000 francs a year to make peace with France. The treaty was signed on November 27. The same month the fleet commanded by Sir John Jervis abandoned the Mediterranean.

It was an impolitic move. Nelson wrote to Sir William, "Till this time it has been usual for the Allies of England to fall from her, but till now she never was known to desert her friends whilst she had the power of supporting them." The Court of Vienna was alienated. Chancellor Thugut blamed the collapse of Austrian armies on the absence of the British fleet. Austria was given something like an excuse to withdraw from the war in the negotiations that ended in the treaty of Campo Formio in April 1797. All Italy lay open to the arms of France.

In the middle of all this adversity, like an actress in the blitz, Emma was on nightly. "We have not time to write to you," she told Greville, "as we have been 3 days and nights writing to send by this courier letters of *consequence* for our government. They ought to be grateful to Sir William and *myself in particular,* as my situation at this Court is very *extraordinary,* and what no person as yet arrived at; but one as no thanks, and I am allmost sick of grandeur."

It was ten years since she had first come to Naples; five since she had married Sir William. In 1796 she was thirty-one and he was sixty-six; as she had bloomed, so he had withered.

Lady Holland was in Naples in 1794. "The Hamiltons were as tiresome as ever; he as amorous, she as vulgar. . . . *Mullady* sang *Nina*, Paisello's music; her vile discordant screaming took off the whole effect of his simple melody."

Now, nobody has an eye like a backbiter. Her ladyship was in Naples again in 1796. "I dined at Caserta with the Hamiltons. I found *Mullady* altered, and Sir William seemed more occupied about his own digestion than in admiring the graceful turn of her head." Lord Bristol was there. "He called old, shrivelled Sir William Hamilton a piece of walking *verd-antique*. . . . He is a great admirer of Lady Hamilton, and conjured Sir William to allow him to call her *Emma*. That he should admire her beauty and her wonderful attitudes is not singular, but that he should like her society certainly is, as it is impossible to go beyond her in vulgarity and coarseness. So much so, that the Austrian Ambassador's sarcasm is excellent. After showing her attitudes, which she does by representing the finest statues and pictures, he asked, 'Et quand est ce qu'elle fera Miledi?' Her vulgarity destroyed the illusion when I saw her once. She had worked one's imagination up to a pitch of enthusiasm in her successive imitations of Niobe, Magdalen, and Cleopatra. Just as she was lying down, with her head reclined upon an Etruscan vase to represent a water-nymph, she exclaimed in her provincial dialect: 'Doun't be afeard, Sir Willum, I'll not crack your *joug*.' I turned away disgusted, and I believe all present shared the sentiment."

Nobody has an eye like a backbiter, except a candid friend. Sir Gilbert Elliot, later Lord Minto, was in Naples when the Hamiltons returned from England in the winter of 1791. "We dined at Caserta yesterday with Sir William and Lady Hamilton. She really behaves as well as possible, and quite wonderfully considering her origin and education. . . . You never saw anything so charming as Lady Hamilton's attitudes. The most graceful statues or pictures do not give you an idea of them. Her dancing the Tarantella is beautiful to a degree."

Elliot was Viceroy of Corsica during the British occupation. When Corsica was evacuated in 1796, he went to Naples and, of course, stayed with the Hamiltons. "She is the most extraordinary compound I ever beheld. Her person is nothing short of monstrous for its enormity, and is

35

growing every day. She tries hard to think size advantageous to her beauty, but is not easy about it. Her face is beautiful; she is all Nature, and yet all Art; that is to say, her manners are perfectly unpolished, of course very easy, though not with the ease of good breeding, but of a barmaid; excessively good humoured and wishing to please and be admired by all ages and sorts of persons that come in her way."

Once again he saw the show. "We had the attitudes a night or two ago by candle-light; they come up to my expectations fully, which is saying everything. They set Lady Hamilton in a very different light from any I had seen her in before; nothing about her, neither her conversation, her manners, nor figure announce the very refined taste which she discovers in this performance, besides the extraordinary talent that is necessary for the execution; and besides all this, says Sir Willum, 'she makes my apple-pies.' "

Emma's conversation was lively and uninhibited. Her accent, "Emma's Dorick dialect," said Lord Bristol, was frankly Liverpudlian. She said *booth* for *both*, *as* for *has*, *ous* for *us*. She spoke out what she thought. Therefore, in English society, with its peculiar obsession with speech, she was called vulgar.

Her manner was frank, open and confident, and her emotions were immediately seen in her face—vulgar. She ate and drank what she liked; she was a big girl, "tall in statue," she said, and she became a large woman—vulgar. She was an amusing, handsome, open-hearted companion, who was easily pleased and did her best to please—and so she was called vulgar. Given the choice of an evening with Emma or one with Lady Holland and her set, Sir William and Nelson are not the only ones who would not hesitate to choose the vulgar Lady Hamilton. There was no one better in the whole hokey-pokey tutti-frutti city of Naples.

"Eating and drinking are the first and most important concern of the populace," Kotzebue wrote in 1805. There were food and lemonade stalls in every street. Macaroni was the staple diet, with plenty of fruit and vegetables. Calves, pigs and chickens foraged everywhere, and milk was supplied from the cow on the doorstep. The bread was tolerable and the wine, the famous Lachryma Christi, sweet. When a Neapolitan family sat down to dinner, twelve dishes were considered a plain meal. At fetes and balls, there was an unending flow of little cakes, sweets and ices, claret cup, madeira and champagne. Kotzebue decided, "The higher classes in Naples are indeed the *savages* of Europe. They eat, drink, sleep, and game."

Gambling was the first occupation of society. Every night there were parties called *conversaziones* where not a word was spoken except to demand a card or place a bet. Faro and rouge et noir were the favorite games. The second occupation was crowding the theaters, where they talked throughout the plays and operas. The third was attending the services at the cathedral and joining the huge religious processions, where the jeweled and painted saints appeared on elaborate portable stages, for all the world like actors in a theater. The fourth, to which they were devoted, was fornication.

All this went on in a city teeming with *lazzaroni*, beggars of every description, artisans working in the streets, lawyers outgesticulating each other on the corners, storytellers acting out the favorite tale of *Rinaldo* on the mole, a kaleidoscope of priests in the colored robes of their various orders, groups of white-robed monks carrying the dead to burial—and the only time the noise stopped and anyone stood still was when a tinkling of bells announced the Host was being hurried through the streets to a dying person. There was no stopping the activities of millions of lice and fleas or the intolerable stench of the place. "You must see Naples and die," was the proud Neapolitan boast. They might have added, "But see it from a distance."

The distant prospect appealed to Sir William in 1797. There was a sort of peace on the Continent and the old Chevalier was tired. He applied to Lord Grenville for permission to go home on leave.

Had the Hamiltons returned to England when Sir William received his *congé* in June 1797, they might have met Nelson—Rear-Admiral Sir Horatio Nelson, with his star of the Bath on one breast and his empty right sleeve across the other. Lady Nelson would have been hanging on his remaining arm, and he would have been in the middle of a crowd because he was famous.

At the battle of St. Vincent on February 14, 1797, he had captured two of the four Spanish prizes taken that day. His country had rewarded him with the red ribbon and a gold medal. Sir John Jervis, who was made Earl St. Vincent for the day's work, rewarded him with the chance to make his fortune by seizing a Spanish treasure ship which was reported to be harboring at Tenerife. There, on the night of July 24, a desperate attack on the town of Santa Cruz had failed miserably. Nelson's right elbow was shattered by a musket ball and, but for the quick thinking of Josiah, he might have bled to death. As it was, he was taken back to his ship and the arm was amputated high up near the shoulder. It was a bad job and the ligature, which ought to have been extracted nine days after the operation, was stuck fast in the raw and suppurating flap of flesh that was pulled over the end of the stump. For three months after his return home, Nelson suffered agonies of pain in his arm and ghostly right hand, until the ligature rotted and fell off early in December 1797. Then he was ready to go to sea again.

He left town toward the end of March 1798 for Portsmouth, where he hoisted his flag on board the *Vanguard*. Fanny went to live at Round Wood, a house they had bought near Ipswich. Nelson's father went with her. The old gentleman was now seventy-five, just seven years older than Sir William Hamilton. Round Wood was a bad choice. The house was damp and Ipswich society, according to Fanny, was damper. She liked Bath, London and Brighton, where she could meet other genteel ladies and tut-tut over the doings of the Prince of Wales; and where there were no spare rooms for Nelson's country nieces. Her great regret was that Josiah had not come home with his stepfather. He was with St. Vincent's fleet at Lisbon. He was eighteen and, through Nelson's influence, already a master and commander.

However, Sir William delayed taking his *congé* until it was too late to take it at all. The Hamiltons stayed in Naples and Nelson came to them again.

The Austrian withdrawal from Lombardy and the British retreat from the Mediterranean undermined the influence and prestige of the Queen of Naples. She further alienated the King by an indiscreet association with a young officer, the Prince of Saxe. Acton, who had supported Maria Carolina's policies, was supposed to have told Ferdinand about this affair, and consequently, by changing sides, he kept his post. This seems strange for Naples, where there were few secrets and many to tell them. The Prince was packed off to Vienna, but at about the same time Acton was talking to Sir William of retiring to his family estate in Shropshire. Sir William did not take him seriously—"He is naturally very chilly even in this warm climate"—and suspected that he was maneuvering to make the King ask him to stay. If this was so, he succeeded, and continued to govern—but not for long.

Impregnated with the martial spirit of Bonaparte, the Republic begat republics. There were already two in Italy, the Ligurian, which was the old city-state of Genoa, and the Cisalpine, which stretched from the Alps to the Papal States. Rome was an irresistible attraction to the conqueror. In February 1798, after a staged incident to provide the pretext, the city was occupied by a French army and the Roman Republic was proclaimed. Pope Pius VI, who was eighty, was driven off into exile in Tuscany. At one swoop Paris obtained the greatest collection of art in Europe.

The Court of Naples was fearful that the next republic would be the

Neapolitan one. It seemed certain when Bonaparte insisted on the removal of Acton from the government. King Ferdinand complied, and the Marquis de Gallo, the Neapolitan Ambassador in Vienna, who had figured in the negotiations at Campo Formio and was known to be pro-French, was recalled to become Prime Minister. Acton, however, still retained his influence and so there was a double government. This made the normal confusion of Neapolitan affairs more confounded than ever. While Gallo tried to keep the peace with France, Acton sent appeals to Vienna for a defensive alliance, and to London for a fleet to return to the Mediterranean. Nothing was done in Naples for the defense of Naples, as they half hoped they would not be attacked, and half feared, if they raised their army, they would.

"As *mezzi termini* or half measures are seldom attended with success," Sir William wrote Lord Grenville on April 15, "this Country, notwithstanding its nominal Peace, by having followed such measures finds itself in a most critical situation—the French are arming at Toulon, Ancona, Genoa and Civita Vecchia." A week earlier the Court had hired a privateer at an enormous fee to carry a letter to Lord St. Vincent imploring his assistance. "They flatter themselves," continued Sir William, "that a British fleet is actually, which I much doubt, on its way to Naples." For once the Court flattered itself with justification. On April 20 a dispatch arrived from Lord Grenville to say that a fleet was indeed on its way. His lordship was a little premature, as the *Vanguard* did not join St. Vincent's command until April 30.

Wars aggravate the conditions they are fought to end. France, swollen with conquest, was a greater threat in 1798 than in 1793. The decision to reestablish a British presence in the Mediterranean was part of a larger project to form a new coalition against the enemy, to revive the old regimes with subsidies and, hopefully, the example of a signal victory. This is why Nelson was chosen to command the powerful detachment from St. Vincent's fleet in preference to senior admirals. Pitt needed a victory to restore his own credit at home and England's credit abroad, and Nelson was the man most likely to achieve it.

Both Lord Spencer, First Lord of the Admiralty, and Lord St. Vincent had a share in the appointment of Nelson. They both denied it in correspondence with Sir John Orde, an influential admiral who had been set aside. George Rose, Treasurer of the Navy, wrote to Orde, "Neither Lord Spencer nor Lord St. Vincent were to blame; whoever made the selection of Lord Nelson had a fair and just Right to do so." As this was written after the victory, it confirms that the appointment aroused a lot of resentment, certainly enough for Rose to continue to shield whoever was to *blame*. The only person who had the *right*, who could be *blamed* and who had no wish to invite the opposition of Orde's friends was William Pitt.

The expedition began on May 2, when Nelson left the fleet off Cadiz with a small force of fast sailing ships to reconnoiter Toulon, where a vast enemy armada was reported to be assembling. Three weeks later this force was scattered in a storm. The *Vanguard* was crippled and Nelson was forced to seek shelter off the island of San Pietro in the south of Sardinia. His frigates, not finding him at the rendezvous, returned to Gibraltar and he was left in company with only two other ships of the line. At the same time, the enemy armada of some 300 ships sailed from Toulon. This was the first of the strokes of misfortune which Nelson had to suffer before his victory.

At the end of May he was off Toulon and learned that the enemy had gone toward the south. He returned to the rendezvous and there, on June 7, he was joined by ten ships of the line, commanded by Captain Thomas Troubridge. Now he had his famous squadron, thirteen 74s, the elite of the navy, the brilliant band of brothers. In company with them, and no less illustrious, were the *Leander* of fifty guns and the *Mutine* brig, Captain Hardy.

St. Vincent's orders were to take, sink, burn and destroy the enemy fleet. The Earl believed, like everyone else, that the French were on their way to invade Naples or Sicily. He had got his letter by the privateer and wrote Nelson, "I am sure your heart will bleed, when I tell you, that the lovely Queen of Naples is in the deepest affliction and distress, and has called upon me personally to fly to her succour, happy you! who have that lot." On a more practical level he ordered the Rear-Admiral to treat any port, Neapolitan and Sicilian included, where he was refused permission to water and provision his squadron, as hostile. He was to force an entry if necessary.

Many reputations were nailed to Nelson's masthead. Pitt's, Spencer's, and the war cabinet's: St. Vincent's—he had two recalcitrant admirals on his hands and a bunch of protesting captains who objected to Troubridge's preferment. "I gave them such a set-down," he wrote, "that if it did not bring them to a stool, certainly made them piss and cry." Nelson's own reputation flew in the wind, and the reputation of the navy, brought low by the recent mutinies at Spithead and the Nore. Above all hung England's reputation.

The squadron turned to the south and sailed after the enemy. On June 14 Nelson sent Troubridge off to Naples in the *Mutine*. Troubridge, "my honoured acquaintance of twenty-five years," was to get answers from Sir William Hamilton to three questions. Where were the enemy? Would the King of Naples send frigates to join the squadron? Were the ports of Naples and Sicily open to the British fleet?

Sir William had been asking the Court the last question ever since he had heard a fleet was on its way. He was a very harassed old gentleman. The British Consul had died in 1795 and had not been replaced, and the proconsul was sick. Though Prince Augustus and the great people had gone off at the first sign of trouble, he had the welfare of the British residents and a shipload of *émigrés* left him by Sir Gilbert Elliot to attend to. He was anxious to leave with his pictures and vases before the French attack, which he and all Naples expected to take place at any minute. Worst of all, he could get no favorable answer to his question.

The Court dreaded that Bonaparte was coming to republicanize them. In May the French Ambassador had been replaced by Garat, the man who had read the death sentence to Louis XVI. They believed the regicide had come to practice his trade among them. When Garat assured Acton that the great expedition was destined for Egypt, where his glorious countrymen would rebuild the ancient city of Berenice and cut a canal across the isthmus of Suez, Acton took it as a glorious French lie. When, early in June, the armada appeared off Trapani in Sicily and Bonaparte sent a message ashore to reassure them, they waited tremulously for the invasion to begin.

On June 10 the *Transfer* sloop, Captain Bowen, brought the news that the squadron under Rear-Admiral Sir Horatio Nelson was sailing to relieve Naples. Naples was not particularly relieved, and Acton remarked without much hope, "I wish that Sir Horace Nelson could run and catch them."

Sir William renewed his demand for an official assurance that the ports of the Two Sicilies would be open to the British fleet. The answer was the same—they were neutral, and the laws governing neutrals allowed only three or four belligerent ships to enter port at any one time. They were not prepared for an open rupture with France. The defensive alliance with Austria had not yet been ratified and, in any event, only provided for assistance if either nation was attacked; it did not allow for a provocation, such as the free use of their harbors by the British fleet. But at the same time as the British Ambassador was being publicly rebuffed by Gallo, he was being privately assured by Acton that the fleet would be supplied with water and provisions when and where they wanted them.

"My dear Admiral," wrote Sir William in a letter dated June 10 and sent off to Nelson in a hired privateer, "How happy Lady Hamilton and I are made by finding that you are the Commander in Chief of the Squadron coming as a guardian angel to protect the remainder of poor Italy. . . . P.S. Emma's most kind love attends you."

Six days later the squadron was sighted from Ischia. Sir William sent another letter in a Maltese sailing boat. In this he described the enemy armament with its cargo of savants, astronomers and mathematicians—"All the ships of war are visibly much incumbered with lumber of all sorts"— and gave the old news that it had appeared off Trapani on June 5. For some reason he failed to mention, what was known in Naples on June 12, that the French were at La Valetta and the Knights of Malta had capitulated to Bonaparte! And for some other reason the Maltese boat failed to reach the squadron! Here was the second stroke of misfortune.

The events of June 17, a fine Sunday, have always been rather difficult to distinguish through the mist of fancy that Lady Hamilton exhaled in her later years, when she was playing Britannia. The account which she gave Harrison is, in short, this.

The *Mutine* arrived at 5 A.M. Sir William got up and had a conference with the King and General Acton, "who, after much deliberation, agreed, that nothing could possibly be done, which might endanger their peace with the French republic." Lady Hamilton, aware that nothing would be done, went to the Queen and obtained an order from her to the governors of the ports in Naples and Sicily to admit the British fleet. The order was sent to Nelson, who used it a month later to gain admission to Syracuse, where the squadron victualed before returning to Egypt and winning the battle of the Nile.

None of the letters written at the time contain a word to substantiate this account.

The *Mutine* certainly came into the harbor early, and, at about the same time, the rest of the squadron anchored far out in the bay, so far that their hulls were not visible from the shore. Sir William was up and he immediately took Troubridge and Hardy to see Acton. Nobody went to see King Ferdinand on business—nobody ever did! Sir William also sent a boat off to the squadron with a letter giving the same information as the one that had gone astray the day before.

He described the meeting with Acton in his dispatch to St. Vincent written the same day. "They were much pleased with the answers given to them by that Minister who still remains all powerful in this Country. Capt. Troubridge having expressed a desire to have an order to the Commanders of all the Ports in Sicily to supply our Ships with provisions and in case of an action to be permitted to land the sick and wounded in those Ports, the

General was so good as to give him such a written order in the name of His Sicilian Majesty, signed by himself and addressed to the several Governors of the different Ports in Sicily. Capt. Troubridge was perfectly satisfied with this." The order in Acton's handwriting, stating in Italian exactly what Sir William said it did, is still in existence.

Troubridge, who now knew that the enemy was at Malta, hired pilots to take the squadron through the Straits of Messina. After being ashore two hours, he returned to the *Mutine* and sailed to rejoin the squadron.

In the meantime, Lady Hamilton had been to see the Queen, and she gave Troubridge this letter to take to Nelson.

Dear Admiral, I write in a hurry as Capt. T cannot stay a moment. God bless you and send you victorious Oh that I will see you bring back buonaparte with you—pray send Capt. Hardy out to us. Yes I shall have a fever with anxiety. The Queen desires me to say everything that's kind and bids me say with her whole heart and soul She wishes you victory. God bless you my dear Sir, I will not say how glad I shall be to see you indeed I cannot describe to you my feelings on your being so near us. Ever ever dear Sir, Your obliged and grateful, Emma Hamilton.

Nelson was waiting impatiently aboard the *Vanguard*. He dashed off a note to St. Vincent: "My Lord, I have only to assure you I will bring the French Fleet to action the moment I can lay my hands on them. Till then adieu." He wrote to Sir William to urge his need for frigates on the Court: "The King of Naples may now have part of the glory in destroying those pests of the human race." Both letters were sent ashore in the boat that had gone out that morning.

Once the *Mutine* had sailed, Sir William returned to his office and wrote a report of the morning's business for Nelson. He added, "Emma writes to you herself and sends a charming letter she has just received from the Queen of Naples—such an Original letter will give you pleasure, and I desired her to send it you as it will prove to you what they are at heart here and how sensible they are that you have saved them from ruin."

Emma wrote, "Dear Sir, I send you a Letter I have received this moment from the Queen *kiss it* and send it me back by Bowen as I am bound not to give any of her Letters, Ever your Emma."

Captain Bowen took these letters out in the *Transfer* and returned with Nelson's answer. It was dated "17th May 6 PM." This is an obvious mistake and it was first noticed by Dr. Pettigrew, one of Nelson's many biographers. It is unusual to find a mistake in the month of a date, but the contents of the letter show unquestionably that it must have been written on June 17.

> My Dear Lady Hamilton, I have kissed the Queen's letter, pray say I hope for the honor of kissing her hand when no fears will intervene, assure her Majesty that no person has her felicity more at heart than myself, and that the sufferings of her family will be a Tower of Strength on the day of Battle, fear not the event, God is with us, God bless You and Sir William, pray say I cannot stay to answer his letter, Ever Yours faithfully, Horatio Nelson.

On the bottom of this note, and this is the basis of her claim to a share of the glory and rewards of the Nile, Emma Hamilton wrote later, "This letter I receved after I had sent the Queen's letter for receving our ships into their ports—for the Queen had decided to act in opposition to the King who would not then break with France, and our fleet must have gone down to Gibraltar to have watered, and the battle of the Nile would not have been fought for the french fleet would have got back to Toulon."

Everything is wrong about this. Sir William mentioned a charming letter, not one about receiving ships into ports. The King was not involved, except that Acton had signed an order in his name exactly the same as the one supposed to have been sent by the Queen. The conclusion is wrong, because Nelson had orders to force an entry into any port where he was refused permission to victual his ships.

Emma's claim could be dismissed as the delusion of an overblown Britannia, or the sprat of a lie to catch the mackerel of a pension, if it had not been endorsed by Nelson, never specifically, but in general terms that admit of no misunderstanding.

What was the Queen's letter? Was it a charming letter, or a letter of vital importance? What was Maria Carolina's part in these events, queen or pawn? There is a letter, undated as were most of her letters to Lady Hamilton, but which, from the contents and the reference to Troubridge, could only have been written on June 17, 1798. It answers all the questions.

> My dear Miledi, I am affected even to tears by the true delicacy of the just English—our circumstances, or rather those of the other great powers, prevent our opening our ports and our arms entirely to our brave defenders, but our gratitude is none the less. I hope events will so occur that we shall see that squadron again,

with its brave officers crowned with new victories, and that I and all my dear family may go on board to drink to the health of a nation that possesses all my esteem and gratitude. I should have much wished to see the brave Trowbridge, but they said it would not be prudent. . . .

This is the letter that Nelson kissed.

The squadron sailed on the evening of June 17, fully expecting to fall in with the enemy off Malta. In a note to Sir William the next day, in which he again referred to the two subjects that bedeviled him, frigates and supplies, Nelson used a phrase that often occurred to him before battle. "Pray present my best respects to Lady Hamilton. Tell her I hope to be presented to her crowned with Laurel or Cypress, but God is good and to him do I commit myself and our cause."

They were off the Faro of Messina on June 20. The Admiral complained, "On the arrival of the King's Fleet I find plenty of goodwill towards us, with every hatred towards the French, but no assistance for us, no hostility to the French, on the contrary the French minister is allowed to send off Vessels to inform the Fleet of my arrival, force and destination." He emphasized "*No co-operation.*" As his letter was carried to Naples by the British Consul who had escaped from Malta, there was no need for the duplicity that has been attributed to all Nelson's comments on the attitude of the Sicilian governors.

Then, as far as Naples was concerned, the squadron disappeared for a month.

They missed the enemy at Malta, the third stroke of misfortune, and crossed their path on the night of June 22; so close were the two fleets that the French could hear the signal guns of the British ships. They missed them again at Alexandria, the fourth stroke, quitting the coast only a few hours before the enemy reached it. They stretched around the eastern shores of the Mediterranean without finding a single clue to Bonaparte's destination.

Anxiety and frustration made Nelson sick with what he called a breaking heart. After two months at sea, his ships needed water and fresh provisions. When Syracuse came in sight on July 19, he was in no mood to trifle with governors or engage in the finesse of Neapolitan diplomacy.

For those in Naples it was a month of increasing despair. As the days passed without news of a battle, their former fears crept back to chill the fever of expectation. Garat regained confidence and began to threaten the Court with terrible retribution. As a sop, he was allowed to send corn to the French garrison in Malta, and the political prisoners, who had been in jail since the plot of 1794, were released. The negotiations with Austria were dragging. "The Emperor does not oblige himself to go to war and break his peace with the French *if we are not attacked by them*," Acton told Sir William on June 25.

The British Ambassador was ready to quit Naples. His collections of pictures and vases were packed. He believed the kingdom was doomed by the unwillingness of the Court to commit themselves to war with France. Nelson had left them and might leave the Mediterranean. Austria remained stubbornly aloof. A French army was reported to be marching into Italy. At this conjuncture he proposed a plan of action which he considered the only one that could save the Two Sicilies. Naples must throw off the mask of neutrality, raise the army and attack the French garrisons in the Roman Republic.

The merits of Sir William's plan need not be discussed, as it was eventually carried out and can be judged from the results. What is fascinating is that, at the age of sixty-eight and after a lifetime of planning nothing more momentous than a trip to Vesuvius, he should have a plan at all. He had lived at Naples for thirty-four years—the Neapolitans did not have a plan. What had happened to make the Chevalier a general?

The answer is Nelson. A hero is like a magnet which attracts the steel within its field, charging it with its own electricity. Sir William knew all about the dead heroes on his vases—here was a living one, one he had met, one who was going about being heroic. Nelson was not a polite hero who won his battles at a distance, but a blood and muscle hero, for all his littleness, who fought and conquered sword in hand. He was mutilated like a hero. He was modest like a hero, only his heroism kept breaking through his modesty. There was no one quite like him even before his great victory. For Sir William, with his passion for collecting heroes, there was no one quite like him at all. It is not anticipating later events to say that Nelson's presence charged the old gentleman with something of Nelson's spirit. It was a match compared to a lighthouse, but it does him credit.

On June 27 four British frigates, one of them the *Bonne Citoyenne* commanded by Captain Josiah Nisbet, came to Naples looking for the squadron. Lady Hamilton gave Captain Hope of the *Alcmene* a letter for the Admiral.

> Dear Sir, I take the opportunity of Capt. Hope to write a few lines to you and thank you for your kind letter by Capt. Bowen. The Queen was much pleased as I translated it for her and charges

me to thank you and say she prayes for your Honner and safety—
Victory she is sure you will have. We have stil the Regicide Minister here *Garat* the most impudent insolent dog making the most
infamous demands every day and I see plainly the Court of Naples
must declare war if they mean to save their Country. *Her Majesty*
sees and feels all you said in your letter to Sir Wm. dated off the
Faro de Messina in its true Light, so does General Acton, but alas
their first minister *Gallo* is a frivolous ignorant self conceited coxcomb that thinks of nothing but his fine embroidered coat ring
and snuff box and half Naples thinks him half a frenchman.
. . . The jacobins have all been lately declared innocent after suffering 4 years imprisonment, and I know they all deserved to be
hanged long ago, and since Garat as been here and through his
insolent letters to Gallo these pretty gentlemen that had planned
the death of their Majestys are to be let out on Society again.

In short I am afraid all is lost here and I am grieved to the
heart for our dear charming Queen who deserves a better fate. I
write to you my dear Sir in confidence and in a hurry. I hope you
will not quit the Mediterranean without taking *us*. We have our
leave and every thing ready at a day's notice to go, but yet I trust
in God and you that we shall destroy those monsters before we go
from hence, surely their reign cannot last long. If you have any
oportunity write to us pray do—you do not know how your letters comfort us.

Shortly after this, Garat left for Rome. Naples waited listlessly for him
to return at the head of an army. "We can do no more," Sir William wrote
Nelson, "than pray sincerely as we do for your success and Emma ever since
you appeared off our Bay wears a ribbon on which is embroidered in gold
God prosper Nelson."

On July 20 Nelson brought his whole squadron into Syracuse. They
had chased 600 leagues in twenty-seven days without finding the enemy; he
was ready to chase another 600 leagues and would brook no delays. As the
fighting ships anchored, they were surrounded by dozens of country craft
filled with fruit and vegetables. The boats were lowered to carry the water
casks ashore to be filled and to collect live bullocks and fuel. At half past
ten the Admiral went ashore to see the Governor, Brigadier Don Giuseppe
della Torre.

Now, whether or not the Brigadier respected Acton's order, or any
other orders he had received from Naples, and winked at the breach of
neutrality committed by Nelson is anybody's guess. Nelson's letters from
Syracuse are of no use as evidence, as he believed they would probably be

opened and read by the French minister, and he wrote different things in different letters and sometimes different things in the same letter. But whether the Brigadier winked or whether he protested, it made no difference. The squadron was already in the harbor and the Sicilians, who hated the French, were busy supplying their wants. Nelson never allowed a situation to develop where he would have to depend on Acton's order, or any other order. This is important in judging the value of his support of Lady Hamilton's claim to have been the sole cause of the victualing of the squadron at Syracuse, and therefore, indirectly, of the victory of the Nile.

Her part in the business was not broadcast until the winter of 1800, when they all returned to England. She had rehearsed it so often by then that she had come to believe it, and by then Nelson had his own reasons for believing it.

On July 20 Nelson told Fanny of his wretchedness at missing the enemy. "I yet live in hopes of meeting these scoundrels but it would have been my delight to have tried Buonaparte on a wind; for he commands the fleet as well as the army." He wrote a note for St. Vincent. "We are watering and getting such refreshments as the place affords and shall get to sea by the 25th." There was also a long letter to Sir William about the chase. "It is an old saying the Devil's children have the Devil's luck . . . here I am, as ignorant of the situation of the Enemy as I was twenty seven days ago."

On July 22 he wrote again:

> I have had so much said about the King of Naples' orders only to admit 3 or 4 of the Ships of our Fleet into his Ports that I am astonished. I understood that private Orders at least would have been given for our free admission. If we are to be refused supplies pray send me by many vessels an account that I may in good time take the King's Fleet to Gibraltar. Our treatment is scandalous for a great Nation to put up with and the King's flag is insulted at every friendly Port we look at. . . . P.S. I do not complain of the want of attention in individuals, for all classes of people are remarkably attentive to us.

Sir William showed this letter to Acton, "abuse and all," and Acton apologized for the behavior of the Governor of Syracuse. Sir William also wrote to St. Vincent and Lord Grenville to explain that Sir Horatio's "heavy complaints" were the result of the Court's reluctance to commit themselves until the treaty with Austria was ratified. This was done on July 16 and he was advised on July 31 that the Sicilian ports were open without limitation. He thought the news so important that he sent Captain Bowen to tell Nelson about it!

When Lady Hamilton got her hands on Nelson's letter book, she wrote above the letter of July 22, "The Queens letter privately got by me got him and his fleet victualed and watered in a few days Emma Hamilton."

She had a letter from the Admiral that day, too:

> I am so much distressed at not having had any account of the French fleet and so much hurt at the treatment we receive from the power we came to assist and fight for, that I am hardly in a situation to write a letter to an elegant body; therefore you must on this occasion forgive my want of those attentions which I am ever ambitious to show you. I wish to know your and Sir William's plans for going down the Medn. for if we are to be kicked in every port of the Sicilian dominions the sooner we are gone the better. Good God! how sensibly I feel our treatment. I have only to pray I may find the French and throw all my vengeance on them.

Finally, there was an odd little note presumably written late that evening, or early the next morning. (Day aboard ship began at noon and ended at noon.) "My dear Friends, Thanks to your exertions we have victualled and watered, and surely watering at the Fountain of Arethusa, we must have victory. We shall sail with the first breeze, and be assured I shall return either crowned with laurel or covered with cypress." It goes with another note to Sir William dated July 23. "The fleet is unmoored and the moment the wind comes off the land shall go out of this delightful harbour, where our present wants have been most amply supplied, and where every attention has been paid to us; but I have been tormented by no private orders being given to the Governor for our admission."

What a muddle! But then life is a muddle, and if it is written like geometry it is not life. God knows why people do half the things they do, they may not know themselves, and other people can only guess.

To say upon a guess that Emma lied and Nelson abetted it is to say that someone else might guess she told the truth and he confirmed it. What did he say?

> First, that she obtained the King of Spain's letter in 1796, to his brother the King of Naples, acquainting him of his intention to declare war against England; from which letter the ministry sent out orders to the then Sir John Jervis, to strike a stroke, if op-

portunity offered, against either the arsenals of Spain or her fleets: that neither of these was done, is not the fault of Lady Hamilton; the opportunity might have been offered.

Secondly, the British fleet under my command could never have returned the second time to Egypt, had not Lady Hamilton's influence with the Queen of Naples caused letters to be wrote to the Governor of Syracuse, that he was to encourage the fleet being supplied with everything, should they put into any port in Sicily. We put into Syracuse, and received every supply; went to Egypt, and destroyed the French fleet.

The last sentence is true.

CHAPTER THREE

The Flight from Naples

Arise Arise Britannia's sons arise
And join in the shouts of the Patriotic throng.
Arise Arise Britannia's sons arise
And let the Heavens echo with your song.
For the Genius of Albion victory proclaiming
Forth to the World our rights and deeds maintaining.
And the Battle of the Nile shall be foremost of the file.
And the Battle of the Nile shall be foremost of the file.
And Nelson gallant Nelson's name applauded shall be.
Then huzza huzza huzza huzza huzza boys.
Mars guards for us what freedom did by charter gain.
Huzza huzza huzza huzza boys.
Britannia still Britannia rules the waves.
—From Lady Hamilton's Song Book

THE BATTLE was fought and won on the night of August 1, 1798. Eleven out of thirteen enemy ships of the line were captured or destroyed. Two out of four enemy frigates were destroyed. Not one British ship suffered irreparable damage. A Frenchman at Rosetta, shaken by the enormity of the victory, wrote, "that the first of August had broken the fabric of the power and glory of France; that, destroying her fleet, it had bestowed the empire of the Mediterranean on her enemies."

Nelson was wounded at the height of the battle. A fragment of iron gashed his forehead above his blind eye. He fell and said to his Captain, Edward Berry, "I am killed. Remember me to my wife." It was some time before he was persuaded he was not dying. Then he went down to the hold of the *Vanguard* and began to write his public dispatch. "Almighty God has blessed His Majesty's arms in the late battle by a great victory over the

Fleet of the Enemy. . . ." "The beginning of Rodney's was pretty much the same," said Admiral Cornwallis, "which he said was for the *bench of Bishops.*"

On August 6 Berry sailed in the *Leander* to carry the dispatch to England. Unluckily, the ship fell in with *Le Généreux,* one of the fugitives from the Nile, and was captured after a brave and unequal struggle. On August 10 Sir James Saumarez left the Bay of Aboukir with six prizes and six of the squadron for Gibraltar. Nelson sent a packet of intercepted letters to Lord Spencer with the comment "Buonaparte has differed with his generals here, and he did want—and if I understand his meaning does want and will strive to be, the Washington of France."

The frigates that had been chasing the Admiral around the Mediterranean finally found him on August 13. They brought an order from St. Vincent, who knew nothing of what had passed, for the squadron to sail to support an assault on Minorca. Josiah handed his stepfather a devastating report from the Commander in Chief. "It would be a breach of friendship," wrote St. Vincent, "to conceal from you that he loves drink and low company, is thoroughly ignorant of all forms of service, inattentive, obstinate, and wrong-headed beyond measure, and had he not been your son-in-law must have been annihilated months ago. With all this, he is honest and truth telling, and, I dare say, will, if you ask him, subscribe to every word I have written." These were hard words, even from an admiral who never used soft ones.

Nelson had had the boy under his eye since the day the *Agamemnon* sailed from Portsmouth in 1793. He had always referred to him affectionately in his letters to Fanny. At Santa Cruz, Josiah had saved his life, and Nelson's first letter written with his left hand recommended Josiah for promotion. He must have been insensible not to have loved the boy and cared deeply about his future—and Nelson had one of the most sensible and susceptible hearts that ever beat. Josiah was Fanny, the marriage, the child they had never had, Nelson's link with home and the past, and his hope for the future. But if Josiah was a disgrace to the Service, if he showed carelessness and ingratitude, he could no longer belong to Nelson.

For a long time Nelson defended Josiah against St. Vincent's charges and later ones. He, who never had to blush for his own actions, swallowed the shame of his stepson's, and it turned to bitterness inside him. St. Vincent's letter, coming at the moment of victory, was the first blow to the foundation of Nelson's marriage.

The next ship to leave the bay was the *Mutine.* Hardy went into the *Vanguard* and was replaced by young William Hoste, one of Nelson's *élèves.* The *Mutine* sailed for Naples with Captain Capel, who was to travel through Germany to England with news of the victory. The Admiral sent letters to Sir William to say he was coming to Naples to refit the ships that had suffered most damage, and to Lady Hamilton, acknowledging her letter sent with Captain Hope, and urging, "Why will not Naples act with vigor, these scoundrels only need to be faced like men, and what are they." She wrote on the bottom, "In consequence of this note we made Naples act with vigor." Capel also carried the sword of the French Admiral Blanquet to be presented to the City of London, and a line from Nelson to Fanny to say he was as well as could be expected and would probably be home in November.

On August 19 Nelson left the scene of his victory in the *Vanguard* and, accompanied by Troubridge in the *Culloden*, Ball in the *Alexander*, and the *Bonne Citoyenne*, sailed for Naples. They made slow progress. The *Vanguard's* masts were tottering, and the *Culloden*, which had run aground before the battle, had a sail wrapped round her hull to stop the leaks.

Nelson was in his cot, sick with a fever and a racking cough that he blamed on the fever of anxiety he had endured since the middle of June. He nursed his sore head and wrote his letters.

To Lord Minto in England he reported, "We have saved Sicily in spite of Neapolitan Councils, that Marquis de Gallo is a wretch who minds nothing but fine Cloaths, his Snuff Box and Ring, this is the best I can say of him. I am on my way to Naples to put matters in a fair train for the advantage of Italy and ourselves. . . . Now a word for myself, I doubt if I ought to stay here, my brain is in such a state that rest of mind, if that is possible for me, is, the Doctors say, absolutely necessary." This is revealing, because he had never met Gallo and passed on Emma's opinion as his own, almost word for word. Similarly, his idea of what was to the advantage of Italy was Sir William's plan for a march on Rome.

He answered St. Vincent's letter about Josiah. "I am glad to think you are a little mistaken in Nisbet. He is young but I find a great knowledge of the Service in him, and none that I see as I see as so good a Seaman in any Ship. He may have lived too long in Lisbon." He continued to press the Earl and Lord Spencer for Josiah to be made post.

As the crippled ships slowly approached Naples, the problems of his command crowded in on Nelson and took his mind off his illness. He had to maintain the blockade of Alexandria to prevent the French transports there from escaping. There were French garrisons on Corfu and Malta to be reduced. A Portuguese squadron had appeared to help him, and he had to find a place where their help would do the least harm. He sent the *Bonne Citoyenne* ahead with a note for Sir William. "For myself, I hope not to be more than four or five days at Naples, for these times are not for idleness."

He had no idea of what was happening at Naples, of what had been happening since the arrival of the *Mutine* on September 3. He had no idea, until the *Mutine* came out to join him on September 14. Emma sent him a letter.

Naples Sepr 8th 1798.

My dear dear Sir how shall I begin what shall I say to you— tis impossible I can write for since last monday I am delerious with joy and assure you I have a fevour caus'd by agitation and pleasure. Good God what a victory—never never has their been any thing half so glorious so compleat. I fainted when I heard the joyfull news and fell on my side and am hurt but what of that—I should feil it a glory to die in such a cause—no I would not like to die till I see and embrace the *victor of the Nile*. How shall I describe to you the transports of Maria Carolina—tis not possible— she fainted cried kiss'd her Husband her children walked frantic with pleasure about the room cried kiss'd and embraced every person near her exclaiming *oh brave nelson oh God bless and protect our Brave deliverer oh nelson nelson what do we not owe to you oh victor savour of itali oh that my swoln heart could now tell him personally what we owe to him.* You may judge my dear sir of the rest but my head will not permit me to tell you half of the rejoicing. The Neapolitans are mad and if you was here now you would be kill'd with kindness—sonets on sonets illuminations rejoicing —not a french dog dare show his face. How I glory in the Honor of my Country and my *Countryman*—I walk and tread in air with pride, feiling I was born on the same land with the victor nelson and his gallant band. But no more—I cannot dare not trust myself for I am not well. . . .

We are preparing your apartment against you come, I hope it will not be long for Sir William and I am so impatient to see and embrace you. I wish you could have seen our house the 3 nights of illuminations tis was cover'd with your glorious name—their were 3 thousand lamps and their should have been 3 millions if we had had time. All the english vied with each other in celebrating this most gallant and ever memerable victory. Sir William is ten years younger since the happy news and he now onely wishes to see his friend to be compleatly happy—how he glories in you when your name is mention'd he cannot contain his joy. For Gods sake

54

come to naples soon. We receve so many sonets and Letters of congratulation I send you some of them to shew you how your success is felt here. How I felt for poor Troubridge—he must have been so angry on the Sand Bank—so brave an officer. In short I pitty all those who were not in the Battle. I would have been rather an english powder monkey or a swab in that great victory than an emperor out of it. . . .

My dress from head to foot is alla nelson—ask Hoste—even my shawl is Blue with gold anchors all over, my ear rings are nelsons anchors, in short we are beNelson'd all over.

She sent her mother's love, and two letters from the Queen. "She bids me say that she longs more to see you than any woman with child can long for anything she may take a fancy too."

Maria Carolina's letters were almost as impetuous. *"Ma chere Miledy quel Bonheur quelle Gloire quelle Consolation pour set unique Grande et illustre Nation que Je vous suis obligé recconoissante. J'ai pleuré rié embrasse mes enfans mon mary"*—and so on—*"si jamais on fait un portrait du Brave Nelson Je le veux avoir dans ma chambre . . . hype hype ma chere Miledy Je suis folle de joye."* Emma's hip hips were catching. The Queen's second letter ended, *"Faites un hip hip hip en mon nom chantez God Saeve die King et puis God Saeve Nelson et marine Britanique adieu."*

Sir William was more than his usual phlegmatic self. "History either ancient or modern," he wrote, "does not record an action that does more honor to the Heroes that gained the Victory than the late one of the first of August. You have now completely made yourself, My Dear Nelson, *Immortal,* God be praised! and may you live long to enjoy the sweet Satisfaction of having added such Glory to our Country and most probably put an end to the Confusion and Misery in which all Europe would soon have been involved. You may well conceive, my dear Sir, how happy Emma and I are in the reflection that it is *you, Nelson, our bosom Friend,* that has done such wonderous good in having humbled these proud robbers and vain boasters."

In his letter, Acton exhausted his little command of English and congratulated the Admiral and the officers and men, "who have under your direction so unanimously and admirably careered to the most surprising victory."

In the cabin of the *Vanguard* the hero clutched his aching head. Sir William had offered his house, "A pleasant apartment is ready for you in my House, and Emma is looking out for the softest pillows to repose the few wearied limbs you have left." Nelson replied, "With your permission and good Lady Hamilton's, I had better be at a hotel. . . ." It was like trying to stop a tidal wave with a paddle.

On September 18 the *Bonne Citoyenne* came into the Bay of Naples, and the three ships of the line were visible in the distance with the frigate *Thalia* which had joined them. It seems likely that Sir William advised Nelson that it would be a compliment to King Ferdinand to delay his entry until September 22, the anniversary of the King's coronation. Otherwise, the *Vanguard* took four days to reach her anchorage, which, though her jury mast had fallen and she was being towed by the *Thalia*, seems rather long. In any event, Captains Thomas Troubridge and Alexander Ball took the first wave of Neapolitan gratitude.

Out went dozens of boats to meet them. The King was in his barge, the Hamiltons were in theirs, and there was another full of musicians playing "God Save the King" and "Rule Britannia." When Sir William reached the *Alexander*, he pointed out the royal barge and shouted, "My lads! that is the king, whom you have saved, with his family and kingdom." "Very glad of it, sir—very glad of it," came the answer.

The two warships were towed away to the dockyard at Castellammare. In the Palazzo Sessa Emma flirted with Ball, who called her "the best friend and patroness of the Navy." Troubridge would have none of it and went off to see his ship careened.

Naples was awake early on Saturday, September 22. But not a Frenchman stirred, not a French dog was taken for its morning walk. The mole, the quayside, the sea-front, were soon covered with a jostling mass of people, pointing out to the bay, gesticulating and cheering. The Hamiltons were out in their barge, Emma in white muslin and anchors looming over the prow like a splendid figurehead. Sir William treasuring his emotions in the stern, and his guests Lady Knight and her daughter Cornelia, who chronicled the occasion, peering over the gunwales as the view ahead was blocked: in their wake came the Ambassador's band, fiddling away over the waves. Not far behind surged the royal barge, with King Ferdinand urging on his rowers, and probably regretting that the solemnity of the occasion prevented him from doing a spot of fishing on the way. Then came the barges of the nobles and their musicians, and some five hundred boats of all shapes and sizes, aflutter with flags and colors. The whole bay was alive like a fairground, and moving toward the dark hulk of a solitary warship.

On his quarter-deck, the Admiral was in his best frock coat with the star of the Bath on the breast and his gold medal glittering on the red sash. He was no bigger than one of his own midshipmen, his hair was properly powdered, but it was his lined and haggard features and the scar burned on his forehead that showed what he had undergone. He was still shaken by a dry feverish cough, and agitated his stump, a sign of excitement or irritability with him. He had given two orders that morning, for a twenty-one-gun salute for the King, and, "The Ships of the Squadron at this place are to use all possible dispatch in victualling and fitting for sea and report to me the moment they are ready." He waited to see his friends, his bosom friends, whom he had seen for five days five years ago.

Alongside came the Ambassador's barge. There were the sounds of female plaints and male exertions, and up flew Lady Hamilton, took one look at the hero, cried, "*Oh God is it possible*," and fell on him, weeping. He held her in his arm. Sir William came up, resplendent in his star and sash, to relieve and embrace him. The two stars pressed together, and they were from that moment, indissolubly, the *Tria Juncta in Uno*.

A few moments later King Ferdinand was aboard and, taking Nelson by the hand, called him "*Nostra Liberatore*." There were tears in the royal eyes, and in the hero's eyes, Emma cried openly, and Sir William took a little snuff to cover his emotion.

Soon the *Vanguard* was swarming with the great people of Naples. The boats bobbed about, and the bands played "Rule Britannia" and "See the Conquering Hero Comes." Parties toured the ship, and more than one person noticed a small bird hopping about in the Admiral's cabin. It had flown on board the evening before the battle, a bird of good omen. "It flew away, I believe," said Miss Knight, "soon after the ship reached Naples."

Three hours later the King went ashore to the thunder of the guns. Nelson and the Hamiltons followed, and they drove to the Palazzo Sessa in Sir William's open carriage through streets filled with cheering *lazzaroni*, and under loaded balconies and a canopy of birds caught and released specially for the occasion. In the afternoon Nelson was taken by Emma to see the Queen, and was received with all the imperious affection with which Maria Carolina's matronly bosom was filled.

When Nelson came to describe the day's events, he tried to explain his feelings. "If God knows my heart," he wrote Lord Spencer, "it is amongst the most humble of the creation, full of thankfulness and gratitude." And he told his father, "I am placed by providence in that situation that all my caution will be necessary to prevent Vanity from shewing itself superior to my gratitude and thankfulness."

Vanity, then, was the danger. But vanity makes heroes. Nelson's life was the struggle to be what his vanity told him he could be. Vanity demands the highest standards and greatest exertions. It is the most godlike characteristic of man. Vanity was no danger, on the contrary. Vanity is purely selfish, it seals up the generous emotion of love. The vain man is happiest alone. Nelson was in danger, in love, when his gratitude and thankfulness proved superior to his vanity.

He had been three days in the palazzo, and Emma had been bathing his head and giving him asses' milk and gazing at him angelically. "She is one of the very best women in this world," he wrote home to Fanny. "How few could have made the turn she has. She is an honour to her sex and a proof that even reputation may be regained, but I own it requires a great soul. Her kindness with Sir William to me is more than I can express. I am in their house, and I may now tell you it required all the kindness of my friends to set me up. Her ladyship if Josiah was to stay would make something of him and with all his bluntness I am sure he likes Lady Hamilton more than any female. She would fashion him in 6 months in spite of himself." Poor Fanny, who had not seen her son for nearly six years, would hardly have relished that!

Though Nelson was the center of attention in the Hamilton household, in the streets, and at Court, he was not distracted from his main purpose, which was to down the French wherever they might be. He hoped to recapture Malta as soon as his ships were ready for sea. The inhabitants were pleased to be rid of the alien and overbearing knights, and made little resistance to the French garrison until they began looting the churches; then they rose, drove the French into the citadel of La Valetta, and sent urgent messages to Naples for support. The Court sent back promises.

Naturally, Nelson was an ardent supporter of Sir William's plan. There was a rumor that the old Pope was going to Spain. "Now is the moment for a Religious War," Sir William told Acton. "The Pope will be no use in Spain, bring him here, put him in a litter and let him march at the head of the army with his Cardinals."

It was not a bad plan (except for the Curia!). Bonaparte and his army were stranded in Egypt and a concerted attack by the Neapolitan and Austrian armies would probably have forced the French to quit Italy then, as they did later. Unfortunately, the Austrian Chancellor Thugut was unwilling to commit his country to a new war. His problem was Prussia, pro-French, predatory and unscrupulous. Austria could not move until an alliance with Russia, brought about by Pitt, neutralized the Prussians. So the answers from Vienna were evasive, and the answers of Gallo and Acton were evasive. Sir William grumbled, Nelson swore—and Emma swore, too.

On Saturday, September 29, there was a great dinner and ball at the Palazzo Sessa in honor of Sir Horatio's fortieth birthday. Eighty officers of the squadron and English residents dined off plates emblazoned with the motto *H.N. Glorious 1st August.* Afterward, 1,700 Neapolitan guests arrived for the ball and were given *Nelson* ribbons and buttons. In the ballroom, under a canopy, there was a column adorned with trophies of the battle and inscribed *Nelson. Veni Vidi Vici.* There was supper for 800 . . . by which time Josiah was drunk and had to be taken out by Troubridge and another officer.

The whole splendid affair was the climax of Sir William's career at Naples, a career that had been brought to a triumphant conclusion by Nelson's victory. It seemed likely that the Admiral would soon return to England, and the Chevalier intended to go with him and be the Chevalier no longer, but a retired English gentleman with his clubs, societies and collection. And if he did come back to Naples, he would have a minister under him to do the work. These were Sir William's intentions, as he stood with his guests and sang Miss Knight's new verse to the National Anthem.

> *Join we great Nelson's name*
> *First on the roll of fame*
> *Him let us sing.*
> *Spread we his praise around*
> *Honour of British ground*
> *Who made Nile's shores resound*
> *God Save the King.*

Nelson's intentions were also to leave Naples at the first opportunity. The morning after the party he wrote to St. Vincent, "I trust my Lord in a week we shall all be at Sea. I am very unwell and the miserable conduct of this Court is not likely to cool my irritable temper. It is a Country of fiddlers and poets, whores and scoundrels."

England expected Nelson to return. The capture of the *Leander* delayed the arrival of the dispatch announcing the victory until Capel reached London two months after it had been won. There were rumors that an action had been fought, which appeared in the papers as early as the third week in August, and which tormented Fanny. On September 11 the last letter she had received from her husband was dated May 24, telling her about the storm off Sardinia, though some thoughtful person had written on the wafer that Sir Horatio was well on July 22. As the days passed, there were rumors on rumors, until the nerves of all concerned were stretched under the load of expectancy.

Captain Capel arrived at the Admiralty at 11 A.M. on October 2. When he was told the news, Lord Spencer fell flat on his face! That afternoon the dispatch was published in a *London Gazette Extraordinary*, guns were fired from the Tower and in the Park, and a mob gathered outside the

Admiralty and made every passerby pull off his hat. Workmen were employed in putting up illuminations on public buildings, and the stage-coaches were being painted with the words *Nelson* and *Victory* to carry the news to the country. In the evening, the audience at the Drury Lane Theatre kept calling for the song "Britons Strike Home." Someone shouted, "Why, damn it, they have haven't they!"

The next day all the papers carried the story of the battle, which, the *Times* said, "claims a pre-eminence over every past achievement on that element which is now the undisputed scene of British superiority," and added the verse:

> *Nelson! thy name from shore to shore shall ring.*
> *Joy to the Nation! Joy to England's King!*
> *Such prowess every tribute justly craves,*
> *E'en Arabs shout "Britannia rules the waves!"*

Mr. Pitt suggested to the Dean of Winchester that the text for his next sermon should be "And the Lord smote the Egyptians in the hinder parts."

On October 3 the City of London accepted the sword of Admiral Blanquet and voted Nelson, who was already a freeman, a sword worth 200 guineas. On October 6 the London *Gazette* announced that Nelson had been created Baron Nelson of the Nile and of Burnham Thorpe in the County of Norfolk. There was an immediate outcry. St. Vincent had been made an earl and Duncan a viscount for victories which put together could not compare with the Nile. Fanny was mortified; Maurice, Nelson's eldest brother who was a clerk in the Navy Office, said he would have refused it; William, the next brother, who was a clergyman, hoped that, whatever the title was, the pension would be the same as St. Vincent's and Duncan's.

All over the country the bells were ringing, and the bonfires were blazing, the bands were playing and people were dancing to "Lady Nelson's Fancy." The last two Sundays in October were designated as days of national prayer and thanksgiving. At the opening of Parliament on November 20 the King's speech dwelt on the victory, and later both houses voted their thanks to Lord Nelson and the officers and seamen serving under him. Pitt explained away the meager reward of a barony by saying that, as Nelson had won the greatest naval victory on record, no one would consider whether he had been created baron, viscount, or earl. The real reason was that he was not a commander in chief and, as a second, had to put up with second-class honors. The same applied to his pension. He was voted £2,000 a year for life and for the lives of his next two heirs. St. Vincent and Duncan had that, but they also had £1,000 a year from the Irish Parliament. Nelson got the thanks of the Irish, but none of their money.

Among the mass of tributes paid to the victory of the Nile, the speeches, prints, plays, eulogies public and private, there was one solid one which the hero prized because he could wear it. The King had already announced the award of a gold medal to the captains who had taken part in the battle, when the financier Alexander Davison capped it with the presentation of a medal to every man in the squadron, gold for the captains, silver for the warrant officers, gilt for the petty officers, and copper for the seamen and marines.

Davison could well afford the £2,000 this gesture cost him, as, through Nelson's influence with his captains, he had been appointed sole agent for the prizes taken in the battle. This was an unusual business and caused a lot of resentment from other agents, from Nelson's own agent in England, William Marsh of Marsh & Creed, from one he had appointed in the Mediterranean, George Purvis, who was Jervis's secretary, and at first from brother Maurice. Nelson had met Davison in Quebec in 1782, and he may have been grateful to him for talking him out of an affair with a girl that was in danger of becoming serious. However, there is no sign that Davison was in 1798 the very close and intimate friend he became later.

Nelson was secretive about the appointment, he would not write down his reasons for choosing Davison to handle the vast amount of money involved—Davison's estimate was £177,440 (Nelson's share was £1,774, much less than his agent's!). He told Marsh that he would satisfy him in five minutes' conversation, and Maurice that he would never forget his family, though he had made a point of instructing Davison that Maurice was not to be associated with the agency. This suggests that the two had done business together before, that Nelson did not want it to appear that he was favoring his brother, and that there was some arrangement whereby Maurice benefited secretly. He certainly had £3,000 later, as he offered it to one of the commissioners to the Navy Board to retire in his favor. Nelson often claimed to despise money. When he had it, he was generous with it, but there was always a certain country parsonage caution in his dealings. He wrote to Emma once, when she had lost a few hundred pounds through carelessness, "Whilst I have 6 pence you shall not want for five pence of it, but you have bought your experience that there is no friendship in money concerns and your good sence will make you profit of it." By then he was so much in love he would have believed anything.

Davison was one of many who urged Nelson to return to England.

"Your object now," he wrote, "ought to be that of contributing to the Tranquility and Comfort of your Inestimable Wife."

On October 1 Nelson wrote to his inestimable wife.

> Our time here is busily employed and between business and what is called pleasure I am not my own master for 5 minutes. The continued kind attention of Sir William and Lady Hamilton must ever make you and I love them and they are deserving of the love and admiration of all the world. . . . The Grand Signior has ordered me a rich jewel if it was worth a million my pleasure will be to see it in your possession. My pride is being your husband, the son of my dear father and in having Sir William and Lady Hamilton for my friends. While those approve of my conduct I shall not feel or regard the envy of thousands.

The Neapolitan Court was eternally in council. Under the rococo ceiling of the council room Maria Carolina, now in her middle forties, handsome and imperious, sat between the elegant Gallo, whom she hated, and the elderly Acton, whom she no longer loved. The Chevalier and the Admiral were invited to enter and the conference began in a mixture of French, German, Italian, and English for Nelson. What was the latest news from Vienna? There had been a sort of promise of support and the famous General Mack was coming to command the Neapolitan army. General who? Mack. "Allowed to be one of the best generals in Europe," said Sir William. When will the campaign begin? The vanguard of the army will march toward Bologna. "I do not mean the *Vanguard*," Acton explained, "the ship now mounted by the brave Admiral Nelson." There was an exchange of courtesies. Gallo got up and bowed. "An excellent Petit Maitre was spoiled when he was made a minister," said Nelson. When will the vanguard march? Some time after the arrival of General Mack. . . .

Up jumped the Admiral. "I trust that the arrival of General Mack will insure this Government not to lose any more of the favourable time which Providence has put in their hands, for if they do, and wait for an attack in this Country instead of carrying the war out of it, it requires no gift of prophecy to pronounce that these kingdoms will be ruined, and the monarchy destroyed." Gallo examined his rings, Acton looked inquiringly at Sir William, who smoothed the words into Italian, and the Queen gazed at Nelson with shining eyes. "May the words of the great William Pitt Earl of Chatham be instilled in the Chemistry of this Country, *The Boldest measures are the safest*." The conference went on for hours. Nothing was decided.

Back in the Palazzo Sessa Nelson was writing, with Emma looking down on him amiably from the other side of the table. Sir William was down at the quay supervising the loading of his crates of treasures aboard the *Colossus* storeship bound for England. "I am writing opposite Lady Hamilton," Nelson reported to St. Vincent, "therefore you will not be surprised at the glorious jumble of this letter, was your lordship in my place I much doubt if you could write so well, our hearts and our hands must be all in a flutter. Naples is a dangerous place, and we must keep clear of it."

On October 9 the famous General arrived. Nelson found him out after one meeting (it took everyone else two disastrous campaigns), and said, "General Mack cannot move without five carriages—I have formed my opinion and I heartily pray I may be mistaken." The Court had moved to Caserta for the lying-in of the Princess Royal, and they met before dinner in the huge barrack-like palace. King Ferdinand beamed, Emma and Sir William stood by to interpret, and the Queen introduced one of the world's worst soldiers to the world's best sailor with the exhortation "General, be to us by land what my hero Nelson has been by sea."

At this time Nelson resolved to leave Naples for good once his ships were ready for sea. He wrote to Lord Spencer that he would go to Malta, where he had already sent Ball to take over the blockade of La Valetta from the Portuguese Marquis de Niza, and then to Egypt to try to find a Turkish fleet that was supposed to have relieved his ships there and which had not yet arrived. But his resolve could not last as long as he followed the weather vane of Neapolitan politics, particularly when it pointed in the direction advocated by Sir William and his statuesque lady. Mack's arrival stirred the Court into something like activity. More plans were made. Acton announced the army would march. When? As soon as the Admiral and his ships returned to Naples. Nelson was drawn into a promise to be back in the first week of November. Maria Carolina and Emma, made anxious by the prospect of his departure, exchanged happy smiles.

On October 15, after three weeks ashore, Nelson went aboard the *Vanguard*. After giving King Ferdinand and his friends breakfast, he sent them ashore and sailed with the ships of his squadron for Malta.

The Queen sent a note to Miledy. "I guess how much you are affected at the departure of the brave and valorous Admiral . . . but we will have the happiness of seeing him again soon."

Emma's letters followed Nelson.

> Caserta, October 20th. Oh how we feil our loss! Could you but know how miserable we were for some days, but now hopes of your return revives us. We are oblidged to be here now till her Royal Highness squaling is over and thank God her Belly is full, so

all the Ladies in the pallace say—I know nothing about it. Yesterday we heard talk of nothing but the *pancia caduta* which is a sign she will soon bring forth, then we go to Naples. . . . I hope your doctor is satisfied with your health, how do you do for your cook? Perhaps your stomach is better with John Bull's roast and boil than the italian spoil stomach sauce of a dirty Neapolitan. God bless you. How *we* abused Gallo yesterday—how *she* hates him—he won't reign long, so much the better. Write to me and come soon for you are *wanted at Court*. All their nodles are not worth yours. Ever ever yours, Emma.

October 26th. We have just had another letter. The Grand Signior has written to the King of England to beg his permission that you may wear the order or feather that he took out of his own turban to decorate you and which is a sign of sovranity. I do not exactly know how many thousand piastres it's worth but unprecedented is the present. *Vivo il Turco* says *Emma*. If I was King of England I would make you the most noble puisant *Duke Nelson, Marquis Nile, Earl Alexander, Viscount Pyramid, Baron Crocodile and Prince Victory*, that posterity might have you in all forms.

Caserta, October 27th. Your present is a pelicia of Gibelini with a feather for your hat of dymonds large and most magnificent and 2 thousand sechins for the wounded men and a letter to you from the Grand Signior God bless him. Their is a frigate sent of a purpose, we expect it here. I must see the present. How I shall look at it, smel it, taste it and touch it, put the pelice over my own shoulders, look in the glass and say Vivo il Turk; and by express desire of his Imperial Majesty you are to wear these Badges of Honner, so we think it is an order he gives you for you are particularly desired to wear them; and his thanks to be given to all the officers. God bless, or Mahomet bless, the old Turk—I say no longer Turk but good Christian. The Queen says that after the English she loves the Turks and she as reason, for as to Viena the ministers deserve to be hanged, and if Naples is saved no thanks to the Emperor, for he is kindly leaving his father in the lurch. . . .

their arrived here Sunday last 2 couriers, one from London, one from Viena. The first with the comforting news of a fleet to remain in the Meditn. a treaty made of the most flattering kind for Naples, in short everything amicable, friendly and was truly Honerable. T'other from their dear son and daughter, cold, unfriendly, mistrustfull, frenchified, and saying plainly—help yourselves. How the dear Maria Carolina cried for joy at the one and rage at the other, but Mack is gone to the army to prepare to march directly, and I flatter myself I did much, for whilst the passions of the Queen were up and agitated, I got up, put out my left arm like you, spoke the language of truth to her, painted the drooping situation of this fine Country, her friends sacrificed, her husband, children and herself led to the block, and eternal dishoner to her memory after, for not having been active in doing her duty in fighting bravely to the last to save her Country, her Religion, from the hands of the rapacious murderers of her sister and the Royal family of France.

3 o'clock. The Emperor as thought better and will wish then the war to be declared Religious. . . . We are tied by the feet here. The Princess is got well after being in pain all one night, and us all dress'd in galla 24 hours, so we must wait with patience. The King says it will not be these ten days (*How should he know?*) . . . oh do you know I sing now nothing but The Conquering Hero—I send it to you altered by myself. . . .

May you live long long long for the sake of your Country, your King, your familly, all Europe, Asia, Affrica and America, and for the scorge of france, but particularly for the happiness of Sir William and self . . . your statue ought to be made of pure gold and placed in the middle of London. . . . I told her Majesty we only wanted Lady Nelson to be the female *tria juncta in uno* for we all love you and yet all three differently and yet all equally— if you can make this out. Sir William laughs at us, but he owns women have great souls, at least his has. . . . I would not be a luke warm friend for the world—I am no ones enimy and unfortunately am difficult and cannot make friendship with all, but the few friends I have, I would die for them and I assure you now, if things take an unfortunate turn here and the Queen dies at her post, I will remain with her . . . thank God the first week in November is near. . . . Love Sir William and myself for we love you dearly. He is the best husband, friend, I wish I could say father allso, but I should be too happy if I had the blessing of having children, so must be content.

Emma's verse

NELSON'S ARRIVAL FROM EGYPT AS CONQUEROR

See the conquering Hero comes
Sound the Trumpet beat the drums
Sports prepare the Laurel bring
Songs of Triumph to him sing

See our gallant Nelson comes
Sound the Trumpet beat the Drums
Sports prepare the Laurel bring
Songs of Triumph Emma sings
Myrtle wreaths and roses twine
To deck the Hero's brow divine.

Caserta, November 2nd. The Princess not brought to bed—
oh dear what can the matter be.

Emma's letters tell more about her than a whole glossary of adjectives.
They are quite innocent of punctuation and scrawled at a tremendous rate,
very long and packed with trivialities. But even in the orderliness of print
they leap about like a can-can dancer in a corset. They are frank, flamboy-
ant, vivacious, gleeful, entertaining. "Your letters are so interesting," wrote
Nelson from Malta, "that I am gratified beyond belief at receiving them,
and your whole conduct has ever been to me so very much above my deserts
that I am absolutely at a loss how to express myself."

He was back at Naples on October 31, anticipating—well, anticipating
his promise by a day. The French garrison was secure in the citadel of La
Valetta. There were some 5,000 soldiers, well supplied with food and arms.
The Maltese were pitiably short of both, and for all the promises of support
from Naples and Sicily, the only aid that had arrived was one elderly and
palsied general. The British and Portuguese had landed what muskets they
could spare, but there was little hope of capturing the citadel or three Nile
fugitives, the *Guillaume Tell* and two frigates, harboring under the guns.
The Admiral had received the surrender of the little island of Gozo before
he sailed for Naples, leaving Ball to blockade La Valetta.

Nelson was ill again. Four days at sea had brought back his coughing
spasms. They were in Sir William's house at Caserta, waiting for the Princess to have her baby so that the campaign could begin. Emma cornered
him with jugs of asses' milk, smoothed his hair forward over his scarred
brow, wrote his letters, carried his messages to the Queen, chatted, praised
him, danced for him, sang "See the Conquering Hero Comes," and generally made herself indispensable. And when he was busy, she turned to Josiah and tried to make herself pleasant to the scowling boy and teach him
how to dance. And when he balked at it, she wrote to Lady Nelson and
sent her poems in her husband's honor and a present of some heroically
decorated fan mounts.

How could he fail to admire her? She made herself his right hand.

66

What's more, Nelson was a lover of women and no confirmed celibate when away from his wife. He had a whore at Leghorn, his friends knew that, and there is good reason to believe that Emma knew it too. His friends knew Emma. St. Vincent warned them both. "Pray, do not let your fascinating Neapolitan Dames approach too near him; for he is made of flesh and blood, and cannot resist their temptations," he wrote her. "I thank God that your health is restored and that the luscious Neapolitan Dames have not impaired it," he wrote him.

Emma was luscious, with a lovely girlish face on a full woman's body barely concealed by the thin muslin dresses she wore. No drawers or stays or petticoat—they were uncomfortable and unfashionable. She was always on the move and God knows that Nelson must have caught his breath more than once. He never thought her vulgar, as Lord Minto and Lady Holland did. Why should he? He was not like Lord Minto or Lady Holland. There was no great social gap between them. Burnham Thorpe was not much grander than Nesse. She could speak French and Italian (Italian better than Sir William) and sing and play the piano. Her past never worried him, on the contrary, her overcoming of it was a proof of her great goodness. He was a Christian "with a heart replete with every moral and religious Virtue," as his father said, and Christianity then precluded neither hatred nor love.

And what of her? She had loved Charles Greville, she loved Sir William, but she adored and possessed Nelson. He was so dependent—physically as a sick, one-armed man depends on his nurse, and emotionally as a lonely man depends on a woman who shows him kindness. ("Except from you my dearest Fanny, did I ever before experience friendship?" he wrote at this time.) Emma loved to touch and help people. "Tell him to keep his head clean," she wrote to Nelson about one of his mids, "and when he comes back I will be his mother as much as I can, comb, wash, and cut his nails, for with pleasure I could do it all for him." Nelson had the tugging appeal of a mangled body attached to his looks, which, if they were not handsome, were sensitive and melancholy.

Much more attractive than that was his lodestar magnetism as a hero. Emma had the highest sense of the drama of her situation, so much so that it overshadowed her sense of its reality. She was the friend and confidante of the Queen of Naples. She was Great Britain's representative at the great moment of British triumph. She was the companion and collaborator of Britain's hero and Italy's savior. She was controlling the movements of armies and navies, hand in hand with Nelson. So she embraced her hero and, in the larger sense, his wife and family and everything about him, his officers and ships and seamen, his patriotism—she was a sort of oceanic Boadicea, and rehearsing her next role of Britannia.

Sir William caught the same fire, only at sixty-eight and being naturally rather damp it burned dimmer. "So fine a character," he said, "I realy never met with in the course of my life." Nelson's achievement was of such classic proportions that, even had he not loved the man for himself, he would have loved him for his victory. He likened it to the church of St. Peter's at Rome: "It strikes you at first sight from its magnitude but the more you examine into its dimensions and details the more wonderful it appears." But Nelson came to Naples like a breath of English air, with the tang of salt and gunpowder, and the old Chevalier, who had snuffed up nothing but the incense of flattery and corruption for so long, was inspired. He was proud to be British and he began to collect sea captains at his table. The Admiral was always his most honored guest.

In his turn, Nelson loved and respected the intelligent and entertaining old gentleman for being kind to him. And so it went on, and there seemed to be no reason on earth why they should not live happily together, until the parting that then, of course, appeared inevitable.

In the second week of November the Princess Royal gave birth and the war could begin. On November 14 Nelson and Sir William were summoned to the camp at San Germano below Monte Cassino to watch General Mack command the army on maneuvers. Mack called his 32,000 men *"la plus belle d'armie d'Europe,"* according to Nelson, who agreed "that a finer *army* cannot be." He had no reason to alter his opinion of the General, as, during a mock battle, Mack managed to get his force entirely surrounded by the enemy.

That evening there was a consultation where it was decided that while King Ferdinand led the army to Rome, Nelson's ships should carry 5,000 men to Leghorn to take the enemy in the rear. "Thus I went to bed last night," the Admiral wrote Lord Spencer, "and at 6 this morning came to take leave of their Majesties. I found them in great distress, the Courier who left London on the 4th has not brought any assurance of support from the Emperor. Mr. Turget [Thugut] is evasive and wishes he *says* the French to be the aggressors. . . . I ventured to tell his Majesty directly that one of the following things must happen to the King and he had his choice, either to advance trusting to God for his blessing on a just cause, or die l'epee a la main, or remain quiet and be kicked out of your kingdom. The King replied he would go on and trust in God." It was a splendid moment, but those who trust in God and nothing else are liable to find themselves with him fairly soon.

Nelson was back in Naples on the 16th, reading his letters from England. "My Dear Madam," he wrote to Emma, tactfully advising her of his new condition, "I honor and respect you and my Dear friend Sir Willm. Hamilton and believe me ever your faithful and affectionate, Nelson." She wrote underneath, "The first letter written by our gallant and immortal Nelson after his dignity to the peerage. May God bless and preserve him and long may he live to enjoy the Honners he so deservedly won, prays his true friend, Emma Hamilton." Of one of the honors, Sir William wrote, "Ly. Hamilton is delighted that by a glance of her eye the City of London give you a fine sword in return for the one she spit upon."

The Ambassador's letters from London were more than encouraging. There was an opportunity, instructed Lord Grenville, for the King of Naples to rescue himself and his kingdom by a vigorous exertion. "You will omit no occasion of expressing His Majesty's fervent hope that the opportunity thus offered will not be suffered to be lost." The English government was in favor of any action that would reopen hostilities on the Continent. On November 19 the *Times*, which was a government paper, announced, "We cannot speak in terms of sufficient praise of the magnanimous conduct of the King of Naples, who with fewer means than some other Sovereigns of Europe takes the lead in pointing out to them the duty they owe to themselves and to their people." And that was three days before the campaign began!

The Neapolitan army crossed the Roman frontier on November 22, and Nelson's expedition to Leghorn sailed the same day. In order not to appear the aggressors, the Court did not declare war on the French Republic. Instead, King Ferdinand proclaimed that he was going at the head of his army to restore religion and order peacefully to the Roman states.

Lord Nelson's destination was a secret. "I would sooner have my flesh torn off by red hot pinchers sooner than betray my trust," Emma told him in words to set his imagination running riot. Unfortunately, nobody let the Neapolitan General Naselli into the secret; he thought he was going to Malta, and sulked when he found the ships pointing in the opposite direction. They ran into a storm and the Portuguese ships with the squadron were blown off course. The *Bonne Citoyenne* turned back to Naples. Emma took the opportunity to write to Nelson, "How unhappy we are at the bad weather how are you toss'd about why did you not come back? Pray keep your self well for our sakes and *do not go on shore at Leghorn* their is no comfort their for you." Presumably she knew what comfort there had been there once for him. "We have got Josiah how glad I was to see him." Nelson was not glad. "Pray do you have no occasion to *go on shore at Leghorn.*"

The expedition straggled into the Tuscan seaport on November 28. Nelson, already angry at the delay, was enraged when Naselli insisted that he alone was entitled to summon Leghorn to surrender. "I am certain that I was never more hurt in my life," fumed the Admiral, "being clearly considered by the General as a nothing, as a Master of Transport." Now he sulked.

The summons was taken to Florence and presented to the Grand Duke Ferdinand, who was surprised to find Lord Nelson and a Neapolitan force come to seize his port. He sent the British Ambassador, William Wyndham, to Leghorn to protest that Tuscany was neutral. Wyndham went and protested. Nelson answered that he had come to protect the Grand Duke's neutrality with his life's blood. Wyndham said that the Grand Duke would undoubtedly be flattered to be under his lordship's protection, but the summons had come from a Neapolitan General, and he was not at all sure the G.D. trusted the protection of his father-in-law the King of Naples. So Nelson summoned Leghorn and it was given up. And now Naselli sulked again.

The troops were landed and Nelson sent Troubridge to take possession of some twenty French privateers and seventy Genoese merchant ships in the harbor. Naselli protested that this would be unlawful, as Naples was not at war with France . . . and Nelson gave up and sailed in the *Vanguard*, leaving Troubridge to sort it out. And Wyndham sulked because he had promised to bring the hero to Florence to meet the Grand Duke and he had disappeared!

The Roman campaign was conducted with the same imbecilic courtesy to the enemy. General Mack was in regular communication with the French General Championnet, advising him of his movements so that the French outposts could be withdrawn and a clash, which the Austrian Court might call aggression, avoided. Championnet, outnumbered six to one, obligingly pulled back his forces and concentrated them at Civita Castellana, thirty miles north of Rome. He left 500 men to hold the fortress of San Angelo as a sign that he intended to return.

So King Ferdinand entered the Eternal City at the head of his hurdy-gurdy army. Accompanied by Mack and Acton, and a glittering crowd of generals, nobles and priests, he rode through the wildly cheering populace to his own Farnese Palace.

On the very next day, November 30, Mack marched his columns out of the city to the north. Championnet waited. At the first brush with the enemy at Terni, a Neapolitan general abandoned his column: at the second brush, at Civita Castellana, the column abandoned its general. That was the end of the campaign. The officers went over to the enemy wholesale, the soldiers threw down their arms and ran away. Among the carriages and carts clattering back the way they had come was the royal coach, with Ferdinand rolling inside, clutching his stomach with fear.

On December 6 the Directory declared war on Naples. Championnet reoccupied Rome and began his march south. Mack pulled together what forces he could from the fleeing mass and pushed them into Capua to block the road to Naples.

The *Vanguard* sailed back into the bay on December 5. Nelson, who said he felt his strength failing daily, was at once beset with a host of problems. Ball had written from Malta for slops and bedding for his ships. Captain Hood at Alexandria wanted to know when the Turks were coming to relieve him. Troubridge complained from Leghorn that Naselli, "such an old woman for a General I never saw before," would not move, except to perform "the *true Neapolitan shuffle* on all occasions." Josiah was in trouble with Troubridge for taking a French ship out of a neutral port and refusing the order to give it up. And overshadowing all the little problems there was the great problem. "If Mack is defeated," Nelson wrote Lord Spencer, "this Country in 14 days is lost, for the Emperor has not yet moved his army and if the Emperor will not march the Country has not the power of resisting the French."

Nelson worked at his table in the palazzo near a window overlooking the bay from early morning until noon, when Emma made him go out for an hour before dinner. "What can I say of her and Sir William's goodness to me," he asked Fanny on December 11. "They are in fact with the exception of you and my dear father the dearest friends I have in this world. I live as Sir William's son in the house and my glory is as dear to them as their own. In short I am under such obligations that I can never repay but with my eternal gratitude."

There were hurried and agonized notes from the Queen, as the news of the disasters was brought back by the men who had fled from them. Maria Carolina was losing her nerve and already heard tumbrils rolling along the Via Toledo and the champ of the guillotine in the square outside her palace. These people she saw swarming about in the streets were not honest Austrians, but fickle Neapolitans, as cowardly as rabbits and as treacherous as snakes.

There was Josiah, forgiven again, getting his daily lesson in manners. Nelson's letter goes on, "The improvement made in Josiah by Lady Hamilton is wonderful. She seems the only person he minds, and his faults are not omitted to be told him but in such a way as pleases him, and his, your and my obligations are infinite on that score. Not but dear Josiah's heart is as good and as humane as ever was covered by human breast, but his manners are so rough, but God bless him I love him dearly with all his roughness." (Fanny took her pencil years later and wrote underneath, "My son did not like the Hamiltons and would not dance— No reflections on any people are proper.")

There was an irksome incident that stung Nelson's vanity. Minorca had been captured by General Stuart and a junior naval officer, Commodore Duckworth, and he had not even been told the expedition had sailed. "Lord St. Vincent is in no hurry to oblige me *now*," he continued. "I am got he fancies too near him in reputation. In short I am the envied man, but better that than the pitied one." He ended with a promise, if matters were favorable, to return to England in the spring.

It is an interesting letter, and the last in which his love for the Hamiltons and home is evenly balanced. It was written on the eve of the great adventure that, almost literally, flung Nelson and Emma Hamilton into each other's arms.

There is one other incident to be noticed, which, though totally unconnected with everything that had gone before, nearly ended the affair before it had started. On December 11 Sir Sidney Smith arrived at Malta in the *Tigre* and informed Nelson that he was going to Constantinople with full powers to act as Minister in conjunction with his brother John Spencer Smith. There were two sentences in his letter which burned in Nelson's head like fuses in a barrel of gunpowder. "My instructions from Lord Grenville do not go to the communication of them to your Lordship." "I presume I am at liberty to dispose of the force I find in the Levant (the Captains of H.M. Ships there being junior to me)." Nelson exploded, but not until it was safe.

On December 14 a large fugitive in ill-fitting plain clothes, which he had got in exchange for his splendid uniform, hurried out of his coach into his palace. "The King is returned here," the Admiral wrote Troubridge, "and everything is as bad as possible." He ordered Troubridge to come to Naples as soon as possible, leaving a frigate at Leghorn for the Grand Duke's escape. He sent to Ball for the *Goliath*, adding, "The situation of this Country is very critical, nearly all in it are Traitors or Cowards." On the same day he advised Sir William that three transports in the bay were ready to take on board the effects of the English residents with as little bustle and as much secrecy as possible.

The question of whether or not the royal family should quit their capital did not arise, only those of how and when. How was decided by Nelson and Prince Belmonte of the royal household; when, by King Ferdinand, who insisted on taking all his movable treasure with him.

Yet there was no revolution in the sense that the streets were filled with people clamoring for change. The mass of the people—and that does not mean workers, who were a nineteenth-century phenomenon, but artisans, small shopkeepers, tenant farmers, serfs, and the peculiarly Neapolitan body of non-workers, the *lazzaroni*—were opposed to change. They were illiterate, superstitious and loyal.

There were revolutionaries—Jacobin lawyers, Republican nobility, patriotic intellectuals, altruistic priests—who detested the oligarchy of feudal barons who ruled Naples from the Council of State. The officers of the army, demoralized by defeat, welcomed the opportunity to shift their disgrace on to the King. The seamen of the navy, the best organized and most intelligent of the lower orders in Naples as elsewhere, played a leading part. But all they could do was to betray Naples treacherously, not overthrow the government openly.

Finally, there was the small and influential group of merchants, bankers, doctors, professors, administrators and civil servants, who supported the ruling authority whatever it happened to be; who feared the mob more than anything, and were ready to bribe a court official, or a French officer, as long as they were allowed to enjoy their privileges.

If a revolution is likened to a man changing his clothes, then Naples changed its hat. The crown fell off and the French put on the red cap of liberty.

King Ferdinand fled, not from a revolution, but from 5,000 French soldiers and from his loyal subjects who wanted him to stay and fight them. He was, no doubt, helped on his way by his wailing Queen and Acton, who shared her deep mistrust of the Neapolitans. "You know as well as myself," the Minister wrote Sir William on December 15, "the Nature of this mollifyed people since ages and ages, and of their being without any *caracter*, but ready to follow any leader even against their own advantage . . . can we begin to load tomorrow night?"

The royal treasure began to arrive at the Palazzo Sessa after dark on the 16th. "There were between 6 and 700 casks, half ankers, filled with silver, and a great many others with gold," an eyewitness reported to the *Times*. Lady Hamilton received the casks, labeled them "Stores for Nelson," and sent them down to the quayside where the *Vanguard*'s boats were waiting. Each consignment from the royal palace was accompanied by a note from Maria Carolina. "I venture to send you this evening," she wrote on the 17th, "all our savings, the King's and mine, amounting to 60,000 ducats in gold . . . the Diamonds of all the family, men and women, will come tomorrow evening to be consigned to Lord Admiral Nelson. The General [Acton] will have already spoken to him about our money for paying the troops and seamen." "Here are three more coffers and a little trunk," she wrote on the 18th, "in the first three, a little linen for my children and some clothes; in the trunk, small-clothes." There were more boxes and trunks the next evening. "I have, unfortunately," wrote the Queen, "an immense family."

Nelson was in good spirits. While Hardy was aboard the *Vanguard* supervising the stowing of the treasure and the preparation of the cabins for the royal family, he was arranging a plan with Prince Belmonte to pluck them out from under the noses of their loyal subjects. He took a moment on December 18 to write Lord Spencer. "There is an old saying that when things are at the worst they must mend—now the mind of man cannot fancy things worse than they are here, but thank God my health is better, my mind never firmer and my heart in the right trim, to comfort, relieve and protect those who it is my Duty to afford assistance to."

It was impossible to conceal the movement of so many casks and cases to and from the palazzo from the *lazzaroni*, whose kingdom was the streets, or the spies of the Republicans. Nelson was watched whenever he went out, and he believed there was even a plot to seize him and the Hamiltons and hand them over to the French. Emma was busy with her mother packing up their own linen and household goods in crates, while Sir William wandered unhappily through his empty galleries and the echoing chambers of his elegant house. His place at Caserta and the Villa Emma at Posilipo had to be abandoned entirely, together with his horses and carriages. There were so many memories that could not be laid decently by a graceful retirement but were being dragged out by the roots—Catherine's piano, Emma learning to play, Prince Augustus braying like an ass, and Lord Bristol, now a prisoner in Milan but still Lord Bristol. "If Sir William does not contrive to send me my passport," he had threatened Emma, "I will—I will—excommunicate him and send him to the Devill before his time." What use was a passport, a contract between a gentleman and his country, when gentlemen and countries were being swept aside?

The mob was out. On the 16th there had been a great service at the cathedral and St. Januarius had been invoked to protect his people. But the saint's blood had been slow to liquefy and the people glanced sideways at strangers whose blood might prove a better omen. They milled around the palace, calling for the King, begging him not to abandon them, but to point out the traitors so that they could show their loyalty. They were so clamorous on the 20th that Ferdinand and Maria Carolina went out onto a balcony to quiet them by showing that they were still there.

The embarkation was fixed for that night. Mack had written to say he could no longer hold Capua. Emma scrawled notes to the English residents warning them to be ready. The hours slipped by in high excitement—then some more treasure was discovered and everything had to wait while it was loaded!

On December 21 the rabble on the quayside saw a man in an embroidered coat climbing into a boat. They sauntered over. Who was he? Where was he going? His name was Ferreri. A Frenchman! Alessandro Ferreri, an émigré, a Royalist. A Frenchman! A spy! They pulled him out of the boat, tore his coat, and buffeted and kicked him until he was dead. They tied a rope around his leg and dragged him off, over the huge cobbles of the old streets of Naples, to lay him before the King. The rabble swelled into a vast howling mob outside the palace. Maria Carolina fainted. Ferdinand, looking down on the bloody corpse and ferocious faces of his followers, would not have spent another night in Naples for all the treasures of Peru.

That evening Nelson, the Hamiltons and Mrs. Cadogan left the Palazzo Sessa for the last time and went to a reception given by Kelim Effendi, the emissary of the Grand Signior who had arrived with the Admiral's presents on December 16. The elderly Turk must have been astonished at his guests' behavior. Having dismissed their servants and ordered the carriage to return in two hours to take them home to supper, they walked off on foot, leaving him bowing on the steps of his residence. They hurried down to the quay where Nelson's barge was waiting and were rowed out to the *Vanguard*.

Nelson returned at nine o'clock, with Captain Hope and a boat from the *Alcmene* full of armed seamen. He landed at the Molesiglio and was met by Count Thurn, an officer of the Neapolitan navy who was in the plot. The seamen drew their cutlasses and took up positions guarding the approaches to the quay. The Count gave the password. "All goes right and well" (had it not been going right and well, he would have said, "All is wrong you may go back"). Then he led the Admiral into the palace and through a secret passage that took them up the dark staircase that Emma knew to the Queen's room. There they found the King and Queen, the Hereditary Prince and Princess with their baby daughter and her nurse, two young princes, Leopold and Albert, three princesses, Acton, Prince Belmonte, Prince and Princess Castelcicala, and the Duke de Gravina. They all hurried back along the passage to the Molesiglio, climbed into the boats, and were taken off to the *Vanguard*.

A second journey brought off twenty-two attendants, the Austrian Ambassador Prince d'Esterhazy, and the Russian Count Mushkin Pushkin.

There was a heavy swell in the bay and the flagship was in confusion—boxes of treasure were in the cabins, boxes of linen were in the hold. Young princes and princesses, who had never before seen a commoner except from a safe distance, stumbled about peering at those unusual creatures, British sailors, until Emma herded them back into the Admiral's cabin and pushed them into their cots. The Queen sat distraught in Nelson's chair, the Princess Royal lay moaning on his couch, the nurse suckled the baby—Acton looked in and was shocked: "A sucking child makes a most dreadful spectacle to the Eyes of the servant women and in the rest of the family." Emma got out her own sheets—in the wardroom Mrs. Cadogan was making up the King's bed.

Ferdinand was the least concerned of the party. He was up on deck chatting to Sir William. There would be good hunting in the woods around Palermo. "We shall have plenty of woodcocks, Cavaliere; the wind will bring them, it is just the season and we shall have rare sport, you must get your *cannone* ready. . . ."

The next morning Naples awoke to find the palace windows shuttered and the royal family gone. Out in the bay the royal standard flapped above the *Vanguard*. Nelson's mids scurried about calling up the English and shepherding them down to the quay where they were taken aboard the ships of the Portuguese squadron that had returned from Leghorn. The mole was piled with baggage and crowded with frantic Neapolitans bargaining for berths on the twenty or so merchant ships in the bay. The French *émigrés* embarked on two polacres hired for them by Sir William. More than two thousand people quitted Naples. There were two unlucky latecomers; they were the Mesdames of France, Adelaide and Victoire, the daughters of Louis XV. The two old ladies had been living at Caserta and had been forgotten. They eventually traveled overland to Manfredonia and escaped to Trieste, where they expired, the last of the *ancien régime.*

The city was in turmoil as the news spread that the King had announced that he was going to Palermo and had signed an edict appointing General Francesco Pignatelli, an elderly lawyer, Governor and Mack Commander in Chief in his absence. Dozens of boats set out for the *Vanguard*, full of people clamoring for Ferdinand to come back to them. Only one person was allowed aboard, Cardinal Zurlo, Archbishop of Naples, and the King told him, somewhat enigmatically, that he would return with pleasure when he saw that his subjects did their duty. Perhaps he got the phrase from Nelson.

The Admiral was busy with his final arrangements. British crews were sent to man two Neapolitan warships, the *Archimedes* and the *Samnite*, as half their men had deserted and the rest were mistrusted. Francesco Caraccioli, who commanded the *Samnite*, was bitterly offended because the King chose to sail in a British ship and at this second affront. The rest of the navy, six hulks unfit for sea, were towed out into the bay and left in the charge of the Marquis de Niza, with orders to burn them when the French entered Naples.

At the last moment Mack paid a fleeting visit to the *Vanguard*. "My heart bleeds for him," said Nelson, "he is worn to a shadow." The news was bad. On December 23 they sailed.

That night the wind blew up a storm and the next day a tempest of giant waves and screaming squalls that ripped the sails and cracked the masts. The seamen hung on the rigging with axes ready to cut away the masts if they fell. Nelson, who said he had never seen such a day in all his life at sea, strained an anxious eye aloft—he had two and a half millions and a whole branch of the Bourbons beneath his feet.

Below, the Neapolitans were on their knees with their hearts and stomachs in their mouths, the royals vomiting and praying with the rest. Emma alone fought her way with bowls and towels from one to the other.

She looked into a small cabin and found Sir William sitting calmly with a pistol in each hand. He had no wish, he said, to die with the guggle-guggle-guggle of salt water in his throat and the moment he felt the ship sinking he was going to shoot himself.

A disheveled white-faced figure struggled up on deck and, taking a last look at his gold snuffbox adorned with the picture of a naked lady, hurled it overboard. Prince d'Esterhazy was making his peace with the gods by sacrificing his mistress's portrait.

As night fell so did the wind—it was Christmas Day.

"My Dear Lady Hamilton," Nelson sent a note, "I shall most certainly expect the happiness of seeing you Sir Wm. and Mrs. Cadogan at dinner. Come and let us have as merry a Xmas as circumstances will admit and believe me ever, Yours most truly, Nelson."

At 3 P.M. there was a cry from the watch. Palermo was in sight. In the Admiral's cabin, little Prince Albert, six years old, was writhing in convulsions before the eyes of his despairing mother. The Queen's women stood by helplessly. Emma nursed the little boy, and he died in her arms that evening.

The ship, burdened with treasure and grief, came into the harbor of Palermo at 2 A.M. on December 26. Maria Carolina immediately went ashore. At 9 A.M., when a great crowd of people had assembled, King Ferdinand left the *Vanguard* in the Admiral's barge to the firing of the guns and the welcoming cheers of his Sicilian subjects.

On the quarter-deck Lord Nelson stood with Lady Hamilton, exhausted but undefeated.

CHAPTER FOUR

Rumor and Reality

It was snowing at Palermo. The old city, which rivaled Naples in the splendor of its setting and exceeded it in the charm of its architecture, took on a strange, pure beauty. It was unappreciated by the fugitives, who were more concerned that there were no fireplaces in the palaces, than that their domes and towers were unspoiled by chimney pots.

In the villa of Montalbo near the Flora Reale, where they had taken up temporary residence, Nelson and the Hamiltons shivered with the rest. Sir William, wrapped in a quilt, sat sipping James's powders to ward off a bilious attack. He bore his losses philosophically and consoled himself that his vases were safe in the *Colossus* and some of his best pictures were coming from Naples in one of Nelson's transports. But he felt his years shaking him and promised himself that he would go to England as soon as he decently could, in the spring.

Emma was shaken with weeping. She was worn out with anxiety and fatigue and wept copiously at the smallest provocation. Her dear adorable Queen wept and she wept with her. She wept that she would soon be leaving her. She wept for Naples, *dear dear Naples*, for Sir William who suddenly looked so old, and for Nelson who was being agitated in a corner.

The Admiral was shaking with anger as much as anything else. Now he had time to think, he could think of nothing but Sir Sidney Smith's brash and offensive letter. The great S.S.S., Knight of the Order of the Elephant of Sweden, had an unfortunate reputation as a braggart. Nelson knew him from Toulon, where his attempt to burn the enemy fleet before the place was evacuated only half succeeded. "Great talkers do the least we see," said Nelson. And here he was, with the authority of the great men at home, come to take over a part of his command!

Nelson wrote privately to St. Vincent:

I do feel for I am a Man that it is impossible for me to serve in these Seas with a Squadron under a Junior Officer could I have thought it *and from Earl Spencer*. Never never was I so astonished as your letter made me. As soon as I can get hold of Troubridge I shall send him to Egypt to endeavour to destroy the Ships in Alexandria, if it can be done Troubridge will do it, and the Swedish Knight writes Sir Wm. Hamilton that he shall go to Egypt and take Capt. Hood and his Squadron under his Command. The Knight forgets the respect due to his Superior Officer. He has no orders from you to take my Ships away from my Command, but it is all of a piece. Is it to be *borne*. Pray grant me your permission to retire and I hope the *Vanguard* will be allowed to convey me and my friends Sir Wm. and Ly. Hamilton to England.

He sent a similar request in more restrained terms to Lord Spencer and wrote Fanny to buy "a neat house in London near Hyde Park, but on no account on the other side of Portman Square. I detest Baker Street."

When she heard of the possibility of Nelson's departure, the Queen wrote in a panicky note to Emma, "I demand on your humanity to prevent our being sacrificed." She feared the Sicilians, if anything, more than the Neapolitans. She was "the most unhappy of Queens, mothers and women." The whole blame for the Emperor's non-cooperation and the subsequent disaster fell on her. The King avoided her and Acton once again changed sides. She confided her wretchedness to Gallo, who had returned to Vienna, hoping to touch the hearts of her daughter and son-in-law. She leaned heavily on Emma and, through Emma, on Nelson.

Ferdinand was the only one who was enjoying himself. "He feels nothing but self love," said the Queen, "and he hardly feels that." He barged into his second kingdom with the clumsy gusto of an overgrown schoolboy. The royal estates were reserved for his sport. He took a little country house and began building and farming, doing many of the simpler operations himself. He attended the theaters and masquerades at Palermo and played a new game of his own invention, spotting Jacobins by the length of their whiskers or, the female variety, the shortness of their hair. A man who appeared in public unpowdered, without a pigtail, and with sideburns growing below his ears, was liable to be seized, shaved, and even imprisoned. A lady who followed the *directoire* line and wore her hair *à la Brutus* dared the King's displeasure. It was not as absurd as it sounds. Fashion is the flag of society. The rebels of every age run up their own opposing colors.

The Queen was not alone in fearing that the fires now burning in

Naples might spread to Sicily. The revolution had come, precipitated by the flight of the royal family, and it was a revolution of the upper classes against the rule of the mob.

The sudden departure of the Court left Naples without a government. Old General Pignatelli was one of the respectable people who feared the mob more than the enemy, and when the *lazzaroni* demanded arms with which to defend the city, he ordered the arsenal and naval storehouse to be burned rather than put weapons into their hands. In the confusion the navy's gunboats were set on fire and Commodore Campbell of the Portuguese squadron burned the Neapolitan navy in the bay. Having done nothing but arouse the resentment of the *lazzaroni*, Pignatelli hurried to Capua in an equally absurd attempt to placate the French.

Championnet had no intention of advancing on Naples. He had not yet taken Capua and was even then on the point of opening negotiations with Mack, when Pignatelli came begging for an armistice. The Frenchman promptly stipulated that Capua should be given up, that all ports should be closed to British ships, and that Naples should pay an indemnity of ten million francs, in return for a two months' armistice.

When they learned of this betrayal, the *lazzaroni* took over the city, breaking open the prisons to swell their bands with thieves and murderers, and occupying the forts of Nuovo and del Ovo and the castle of St. Elmo. The troops returning from Leghorn were disarmed, and a body of *lazzaroni* marched out to Capua to persuade the soldiers to join them, and to seize General Mack, who was accused, most unfairly, of being a traitor. Mack went over to the French. Championnet gave him a passport, but he was arrested in Rome and sent a prisoner to Paris. He was released in good time to lose the battle of Ulm.

On January 16 Pignatelli fled to Sicily, where he was imprisoned. In Naples the *lazzaroni* would have killed him. When the French commissioners came to collect the indemnity they had to run for their lives. The mob started looting and burning, first the houses of known Republicans, then those of suspected ones, then any house that looked promising and was not too well defended. The revolutionaries were already calling for Championnet to enter the city; now the nobles and doctors, priests and lawyers, the merchants and all reasonable men joined in the plea.

Championnet answered that he would not come while the *lazzaroni* occupied St. Elmo, which dominated Naples and was built to resist a siege. The clever revolutionaries used the religious fervor of the masses against them. The Archbishop announced a day of prayer, the cathedral bells rang out, the blood of St. Januarius was held up and the saint's protection invoked, the *lazzaroni* flocked to the cathedral to witness the miracle, and the Republicans walked into St. Elmo.

The French did not steal Naples so easily. There were three days of bloody street fighting before the *lazzaroni* decided it was enough. They left the barricades and took time to plunder the royal palace, respectfully limiting themselves to three hours' depredation before disappearing in their holes and hovels. On January 22 the Parthenopean Republic was declared. Championnet made his due obeisance to St. Januarius, but the French were never safe in Naples. The *lazzaroni* decided that Januarius was a Republican and called quietly on his rival, St. Anthony, when they stabbed solitary French soldiers in the dark streets.

In spite of the Court's fears, there was little chance of such a revolution spreading far from Naples, and none at all of its coming to Sicily. The Sicilians hated the French so ferociously that Sir William's *émigrés* were not allowed to land and had to be sent off to Trieste. When, on January 20, a French ship, carrying 140 sick and wounded men from Alexandria, put into Augusta, the inhabitants rose up and killed eighty-seven of them, and, the story goes, roasted and ate their livers. The trouble in Sicily was that the Court were *foreigners*.

Nelson summed up Sicily in a letter to Lord Minto. "The state of the Country is this, *hate the French, love the English, discontented with the present Government, as Neapolitan Councillors take the lead* to the entire exclusion of the Sicilians." Mind you, when two Sicilians, Prince Luzzi and Count Trabia, were brought into the Council, they were more inefficient and corrupt than the Neapolitans. After merely touching at Palermo, Troubridge exploded, "It is high time this rascally Italian gang should be annihilated."

The Captain came from Leghorn in a formidable mood. It seems probable that he wrote to Nelson officially, accusing Josiah of refusing to obey his orders while under his command: not surprisingly, the letter he refers to has not been found. "My Lord," Troubridge wrote about this time, "I wish to withdraw my letter respecting Captain Nisbet; but after pointing out to him his *ingratitude* to you and *strange* and *insulting conduct* to me and that so publickly, I could obtain no promise of any change. The only answer I could procure was that he knew it would happen, that you had no business to bring him to Sea, that he had told you so often, and that it was all your fault. I again pointed out to him in the strongest language his black ingratitude to you by making use of such speeches; no arguments I could make use of would induce him to alter his language, I therefore have no alternative as your Lordship will see. I am convinced he has a bad set about him. I therefore again take the liberty of intreating your Lordship not to permit him to take any followers from the sloop."

Troubridge left Palermo on January 7 and sailed for Alexandria, as Nelson had promised in his letter to St. Vincent. On the same day Josiah was sent off in the *Bonne Citoyenne* to take Kelim Effendi back to Constantinople. On the 17th Nelson wrote Fanny, "I wish I could say much to your and my satisfaction about Josiah but I am sorry to say and with real grief, that he has nothing good about him, he must sooner or later be broke, but I am sure neither you or I can help it, I have done with the subject it is an ungrateful one."

Tears are the true currency of love. Sadness, discomfort, despair, sickness, loneliness, hopelessness—all afflictions—drive one person to look for consolation in the arms of another.

Toward the end of January Nelson and the Hamiltons moved from the villa into the Palazzo Palagonia near the mole. The Admiral needed a room for his business, and the Ambassador found himself obliged to accommodate some of his English friends who had fled from Naples. There was only one inn at Palermo and that was full, the city was overflowing with exiles. In this cold palace Nelson and Emma went to bed together.

Sometimes the easiest things to find are those that people have taken the greatest trouble to conceal. The very absence of evidence is evidence itself. A closed door can tell as much as an open one, but it helps if there is a keyhole. The keyhole through which the present can peep at the past is in a letter Nelson wrote on February 17, 1801. It shows no more than a keyhole normally shows. "Ah my dear friend"—this is to Emma, of course—"I did remember well the 12th February, and also the two months afterwards. I shall never forget them, and never be sorry for the consequences."

There were only two February 12s they could remember together, those of 1799 and 1800. On February 12, 1800, Nelson sailed from Palermo for Malta, in company with Lord Keith, and did not return until March 16. Hardly memorable!

Among the English who came from Naples there were a traveling aristocrat, Lord Montgomery, and his companion, Major Gordon. Gordon, who would have got on very well with Lady Holland, remembered their reception at the palazzo.

When we had sat a few minutes, and had given all our details of Naples, which we thought were received with great *sang-froid,* the Cavaliere retired, but shortly returned, entering by a *porte-*

battante, and on his arm, or rather his shoulder, was leaning the interesting Melpomene, her raven tresses floating round her expansive form and full bosom. What a model for a Roman matron! but alas! poor Emma was indisposed, "dying," she said, "of chagrin for the loss of her beloved Naples," yet the roses on her cheek prevailed over the lilies, and gave hope that her grief would not prove mortal. [Naturally, Gordon remarked Emma's accent, "a *mélange* of Lancashire and Italian," and the coarseness of her conversation.]

The hero of the Nile now came forth from a corner where he had been writing. . . . After a few trifling queries about the burning of the gun-boats, Lord Nelson said to me—"Pray, Sir, have you heard of the battle of the Nile? . . . *That* battle, Sir, was the most extraordinary one that was ever fought, and it is *unique*, Sir, for three reasons; first, for its having been fought at night; secondly, for its having been fought at anchor; and thirdly, for its having been gained by an admiral with one arm." To each of these reasons I made a profound bow; but had the speech been made after dinner, I should have imagined the hero had imbibed an extra dose of champagne.

Gordon was invited to a dinner given by Sir William in honor of the captain of a Turkish frigate, who had brought a letter and a magnificent gold and diamond snuffbox from the Emperor of Russia to Nelson. Gordon recalled that Emma had made the hero dress up in his pelisse and diamond aigrette to receive the Turk, who had, quite properly, fallen on his face in a grand salaam.

At dinner, the Turk got drunk and boasted, through an interpreter, of his exploits. "With this weapon," said he, in his vile jargon, and drawing his shabola, "I cut off the heads of twenty French prisoners in one day! Look, there is their blood remaining on it." The speech being translated, her Ladyship's eye beamed with delight, and she said, "Oh let me see the sword that did the glorious deed!" It was presented to her; she took it into her fair hand covered with rings, and looking at the encrusted Jacobin blood, kissed it and handed it to the hero of the Nile!

Gordon goes on and elaborates his story with a fainting lady, cries of "Shame," and Nelson hanging his head. But the incident rings true. If Emma spat on Admiral Blanquet's sword, she probably kissed the Turk's.

He tells another good story, worth repeating, about Emma.

On one occasion, being desirous to astonish a gentleman who had just arrived, and had not heard of her ladyship's attitudinal celebrity, she dropped from her chair on the carpet, when sitting at table after dinner. The comb which fastened her superabundant locks had been removed (like Caesar she had fallen gracefully), and nothing could have been more classical or imposing than this prostrate position. Sir William started up to open a little of the curtain in order to admit the proper light, while the stranger flew to the sideboard for water, with which he plentifully sprinkled the fainting dame, before he discovered it was a *scena* (and not a fit as he thought) which had been got up.— "You have spoiled, my good friend," said the Knight, "one of the most perfect attitudes that Emma ever executed—how unlucky!"

Gordon took his stories back to England. The flight from Naples was reported in the *Times* on January 28, and on February 6 this item of news appeared: "We are informed from a very respectable authority that the Queen owed her safety much to the address of Lady Hamilton, who assisted in her getting away." How delighted society must have been to learn that Emma was no heroine, but the same coarse creature they had always thought her. Gordon's opinion was favorite.

Lady Hamilton could bear no rival near her, and flattery was as necessary to her as the air she breathed. She had also the art of flattering others with great success; and there can be no doubt but she persuaded poor Nelson that she was actually in love with him, not as a Mars but as an Adonis! Queen Caroline knowing this, made her the tool of all the projects she wished to accomplish by means of the British admiral; being fully aware of the influence that such a woman, devoted to her by bribes and flattery, would have over such a man. As to Sir William, he was a perfect Neapolitan both in mind and manners. The little consequence he retained as an ambassador was derived from his wife's intrigues; but as long as he could keep his situation, draw his salary, and collect vases, he cared little about politics; he left the management of that to her ladyship.

Before following the *tria juncta in uno* into the very abyss of depression in that late Palermitan spring, it might be as well to point to two future references to a creature, which help to fix the relationship between two of them at that time. It is like taking a bearing on two landmarks to find out where one is.

On March 14, 1801, Nelson was on his way to the Baltic. He was in a strange tormented mood, torn between visions of Glory and Emma, which had not yet fused into the single vision of Glory and Emma of his last years. "For these two nights," he wrote her, "I have done nothing but dream of you, the first I saw your tears as plain as possible on your left cheek, and waking with anguish I had lost your picture the Hair had broke, last night I thought that poor *Mira* was alive and between us, what can this mean time can discover."

On May 19, 1799, Nelson left Palermo after living in intimacy with the Hamiltons since the beginning of the year. He wrote Emma, "You and good Sir William have spoiled me for any place but with you. I love Mrs. Cadogan. You cannot conceive what I feel when I recall you all to my remembrance. Even to Mira do not forget your faithful and affectionate, Nelson."

Both references suggest that Mira was a pet of some kind. Nelson and Emma loved dogs, and she may have belonged to the same clan as another Emma and Nilus. They also suggest that Nelson, tossing in his cot in the North Sea, dreamt of another cot and its contents that he had known in Palermo. Of course, there is no lack of suggestions from the people who knew them at Palermo, or of the plain corroboration of the lovers themselves later, but Mira is an odd little indication that the affair began when the rumors began—perhaps she was a pointer?

Nelson was having trouble with his bowels, and his teeth, but his bowels were worse. "I send Troya with the '*Machine de la Douge,*'" wrote Maria Carolina, "and shall think myself happy if it should relieve my great hero Nelson." Troya must have taken liberties, as she wrote again, "I send Troya not to tease my Lord but only to show how the machine is to be placed."

He was deskbound. "With more writing than two hands could get through," he told Fanny, "you must take a line for a page and a page for a sheet of paper." His letters were short and irritable. "Josiah has got a commission for *Thalia* I wish he may deserve it. However he has had more done for him than any young man in the Service and made I fear the worst use of his advantages. We are here as badly situated as heart can wish but I have no permission to quit my post and of course I must remain." This one was dated February 2; the next, March 21. "Nothing worth relating has occurred since I wrote you last. We go dragging an existence from day to day. How matters will end God only knows."

Josiah returned from the East and was packed off to Malta. Ball was still there, struggling to keep the islanders alive with the meager supplies sent from Sicily. Only the constant badgering of the Court by Nelson and the Queen by Emma got anything sent at all.

The Turkish and Russian squadrons, which lumbered about like two bears, uneasy together but suspicious apart, had taken Corfu. Yet they would not go where Nelson wanted them, the Russians to Malta and the Turks to Egypt, and stuck at Corfu waiting for each other to move.

Egypt was a nagging problem. The business with Sir Sidney Smith was settled decisively in Nelson's favor. "There must have been some very great misunderstanding," wrote Lord Spencer, "as it never was our intention here that he should consider himself as a Commander in Chief." St. Vincent ordered "this Hero of Romance" to put himself immediately under Nelson's command. When Troubridge returned on March 16, unsuccessful, as the mortars on the bomb ships he had taken to Alexandria had burst, Nelson ordered S.S.S. to blockade the port and not to allow a single ship or Frenchman to escape. Shortly afterward, French ships were captured carrying passports from Sir Sidney. Nelson sent a three-line-whip of an order. Sir Sidney ignored it, but by then he had captured Bonaparte's siege train and was happily throwing stones at the great General from the walls of Acre.

There was trouble in Tuscany. The King of Sardinia escaped in one of Nelson's frigates, and added another gold and diamond box to the Admiral's collection. The ancient Pope did not escape, and suffered the indignity, and agony, of brutal Frenchmen ripping off his bandages to make sure he was really dying before being sent off to die in France. Wyndham fled to Palermo, and at Sir William's dinners collected enough scandal to dine out on when he returned to Florence.

Another gossip was Lord Keith, St. Vincent's second at Cadiz. The Earl was ill and worried about leaving Nelson under Keith: "It would revolt his feelings." Keith received a different impression. "It is here reported Lord Nelson is to go home immediately," he wrote his sister on April 10. "Lord St. Vincent says he shall not go in the *Vanguard*. The world says he is making himself ridiculous with Lady Hamilton and idling his time at Palermo when he *should* have been *elsewhere*—so says G. Hope and the officers who are come thence to me." He wrote again on April 19. "A ship from Palermo brings the most wretched account of Sicily—the King despised and insulted by the people, squeezing money off the public to hoard up and carry off to Trieste, the Queen, Lady Hamilton, General Acton and Lord N——n cutting the most absurd figure possible for folly and vanity."

Poor Nelson, who had written to St. Vincent, "At present I cannot move, would the Court but let me I should be better, for here I am writing from morn to eve." At least Sicily was safe. They had made him a citizen of

87

Palermo. And General Stuart had brought two regiments from Minorca to garrison Messina. But Naples . . . "I see but gloomy prospects look which way I will. In short my dear Lord everything makes me sick to see things go to the devil and not to have the means of prevention."

So if he walked with Emma in the woods, or went in a carriage with her along the Marina, where the band played at midnight and no torches were allowed to spoil the pleasure, or if he stole an hour with her in the palazzo after dinner, for everyone was awake all hours of the night, it was not because he was happy but because he was miserable. She was good and she was virtuous, yes virtuous; Sir William was good and virtuous; and so, of course, was Nelson.

Well, he was Nelson and he was in love, and he was a bit of a sinner. "Doctor," he said dying, "I have *not* been a *great* sinner." But he never sinned against *bienséance*, which he would have done by taking Emma out of Sir William's house. He would not have been forgiven that, least of all by Sir William. While avoiding generalizations of a doubtful nature, it is possible to realize something of the morality of that day from the morality of this. They were marching into the shadow of the sanctity of marriage as we are marching out of it. Lord Chesterfield, the arbiter of the fashionable morals of the day, judged, "It is possible for a woman to be virtuous though not strictly chaste." It is the commonplace judgment of the modern divorce court.

Sir William was lamenting the loss of his vases. On December 10 the *Colossus* had been wrecked on the Scillies. "All the brave crew were saved," said the *Times*, "except one Quarter Master who fell overboard in heaving the lead." The tars salvaged one box which they had been told contained treasure. Instead they found the corpse of Admiral Shuldham being shipped home for burial.

"Damn his body," wrote Sir William to Charles Greville on March 22, "it can be of no use but to the Wormes, but my Collection would have given information to the most learned and convinced every intelligent Being that there is but one Truth and that God Almighty has never made himself known to the miserable atoms that inhabit this globe otherwise than bidding them to increase and multiply and to leave the rest to Him." It was a bitter blow to his fortune. He already owed his bankers £15,000, and that over and above his losses at Naples and his expenses at Palermo. He wanted to go home. "And now Lord Nelson who lives with us and has done so ever since he returned from Egypt says he cannot do without Emma's and my assistance, not having any language but his own. How I shall get out of this scrape I know not, but as I mean to leave him my

Secretary as Interpreter and I have made him well known to Genl. Acton and the Prince Belmonte who both speak English, and that Charles Lock who came here as Neapolitan Consul and may carry on the correspondence with Lord Grenville's office, I still hope to be with you some time in June or July."

He ended the letter, "I need not tell you that Emma goes on perfectly well and plays a very conspicuous part in the Political Line as she is and has long been the true friend and Confidential one of the Queen of Naples, and is realy of great use to us all."

He continued to grumble, to complain that while he longed to go to England, Lord Nelson needed him at Palermo. "You may judge, my dear Charles," he wrote on April 8, "what it is to keep a table for all the poor British emigrants from Naples, who have none, and for all the officers of the fleet, as Lord Nelson lives in the house with us, and all the business, which is immense, is transacted in our house." Perhaps he would get to England, "but if unfortunately the business should drag on the summer, it would not be prudent for me to dash into a London fog at once, and I must wait next Spring, and God knows I have little time to lose, for I feel old age coming on fast. . . . I love Lord Nelson more and more—his activity is wonderful, and he loves us sincerely."

By April 28 all hope of going home that year was gone. Events were taking place at Naples that might lead to a negotiation between the King and the Jacobins, "Besides, Lord Nelson, for want of languages and experience of this Court and Country, without Emma and me, would be at the greatest loss every moment. Considering all this, although I have rheumatism in my hip, and am tired and worn out almost, I will not abandon their Sicilian Majesties in so very interesting a moment."

What sort of crisis was concealed beneath all these apologies? What kept Nelson ashore at Palermo and the Hamiltons with him?

"Good Sir William, Lady Hamilton, and myself, are the mainsprings of the machine, which manage what is going on in this country," the Admiral told his wife, adding, because she had written half in earnest to say she would like to join him, "We are all bound to England when we can quit our posts with propriety." Acton confirmed the complete dependence of the Court on Nelson in his own droll way. "Unhappiness and disappointment seem to be still our lot, and if your Lordship and Squadron did not keep up hopes and expectations of a better situation I am afraid that the confusion and uncertainty in every plan and operation of our own would bring to the Sovereigns further and even more disagreeable consequences."

However, the council chamber of a foreign court was hardly the place for a British admiral. Nelson knew that, and made the importunity of the Queen his reason for staying in Palermo. Maria Carolina's intermediary on all occasions was, of course, Emma Hamilton. So Nelson stayed with Emma, and while she stayed, so did Sir William.

They were joined by an increasing dependence on each other. They really were *tria juncta in uno*, or, as Emma said once, "three hearts in one body." Had it not been for the three-sided nature of the relationship, it must have collapsed, or ended in separation and disaster for one or more of them. To prove the theorem, join Emma and Nelson in love; join Emma to Sir William in gratitude; join Nelson to Sir William in friendship; join Sir William to Emma in comfort and companionship in his last years; join Sir William to Nelson in love and admiration; add the riders of Emma's past history, Sir William's philosophy, and Nelson's susceptibility; and Q.E.D. This is the simplest expression of the relationship, the pattern in the carpet. It makes one assumption—that Sir William knew of the affair and put up with it, for his own sake, for their sakes, and for the sake of *bienséance*.

In March 1799 Pitt's second coalition of great powers was completed and an Austro-Russian army marched into northern Italy, driving the French back without much difficulty.

Malta was part of the price of the Russian alliance. The Emperor Paul had had himself elected Grand Master of the Order of St. John, and insisted that the island, when recaptured, should be returned to the Order. The capturing was supposed to be done by a combined force of British, Russian and Neapolitan troops. This was not one of the Emperor's caprices, but a part of the continuing Russian policy of having access to, and bases in, the Mediterranean. It was a thoroughly bad arrangement, and stemmed from the ignorance of the English government. The Maltese hated the Order as much as the French, and King Ferdinand, who had a good claim to Malta, stopped the trickle of aid from Sicily once he knew he was not going to get it. Ball was left to blockade La Valetta and to keep up the spirits of the Maltese as best he could—he could do little for their bodies.

Josiah was at Malta. On April 1 he took command of the *Thalia*. St. Vincent gave him a good officer, Lieutenant Colquit, as first lieutenant, and Ball gave him Lieutenant Quarrel from the *Alexander* as second. "I shall endeavour," said Ball, "to make him feel his very fortunate situation." But it was not fortunate for Josiah, who knew his officers were there to watch him and advise him, or for the officers who, with the best intentions, were bound to irritate any captain, let alone one of Josiah's temper. However, all seemed well at first. "I have now determined," Josiah wrote his stepfather, "to do every thing in my power to deserve the unmerited pro-motion which you have given me, and hope my endeavours for the future will always meet with your approbation, as you are the only person on earth who has my interest truly at heart, and I trust and hope my future conduct will effectually do away my former folly." Nelson wrote Fanny, "He has sent to say that he is sensible of his youthful follies, and that he shall alter his whole conduct. I sincerely wish he may, both for his and your sake."

The allied successes in the north of Italy hastened the end of the Parthenopean Republic. It was bound to fail, as any government of poets, professors, lawyers, and idealists, is bound to fail. Government is the business of practical men. It is ridiculous to expect men who could not run a sweetshop to run a country. Power should be kept from intellectuals as matches from children—they will not be happy until they have set the house on fire and burnt themselves and everyone else in it. The least government is the best government.

The Parthenopean Republic was a republic of paper: newspaper, white paper, paper promulgations, paper proclamations, paper laws, paper reforms and paper taxes. While the self-styled "patriots" were papering Naples, the French were coolly stripping it of art and treasure. Championnet was sacked for protesting to the Directory of the plunder of palaces, galleries and museums by the civil commissioners, and replaced by Macdonald, who had no such qualms. Macdonald was a cynical and brutal soldier, whose remedies for unrest were the gallows and the firing squad. He was encouraged by the "patriots," who, like all radicals, would stretch a man's neck to improve his stature. He abandoned them to their fate the moment it suited him.

The liberal infection in the head of Naples was resisted by the body of the kingdom and eventually cured, rather drastically, by removing the brains. There were three separate operations.

The first was in the city. "The French at Naples are scarcely 6,000," wrote the Queen, "and every night some are massacred in the brothels they enter, in which way more than 450 of them have been already slaughtered and thrown into the sea." The brothels claimed more victims. Acton reported, "About 1,000 French at Naples very ill in the venereal disease sent off to the Camp at Capua." An army of occupation destroys itself. When Macdonald withdrew early in May to prevent himself from being cut off from France by the Austro-Russian campaign, the *lazzaroni* took a more open part which culminated in the bloody crisis in June.

The second operation began in the provinces. Early in February Cardinal Ruffo returned to the mainland from Sicily with the King's appointment as Vicar General and eight companions. Ruffo was a Neapolitan noble with great estates in Calabria; he was a man of sixty, once the secretary of Pius VI, and as ambitious as a politician. He knew his Calabrians, promised them relief from taxes and the chance to steal from their compatriots, and within a month he raised a host of 17,000 ruffians, which he sanctified with the title of the Christian Army of the Holy Faith. As Ruffo advanced slowly, he was joined by 450 Russian marines and 80 Turks landed from the squadrons at Manfredonia. The Christian Army came in sight of the capital early in June. To the north, a second band of irregulars under a ferocious brigand called the Gran Diavolo was besieging Gaeta.

The third operation took place in the Bay of Naples. At the end of March Nelson sent Troubridge with a squadron to blockade Naples. Within a few days Troubridge was in possession of the islands of Ischia and Procida. He had thirty-five Republicans as prisoners and was shouting for a judge. "The villains increase so fast on my hands eight or ten of them must be hung." Nelson answered, "Just come from the Queen and Acton, send me word some proper heads are taken off this alone will comfort me." By the middle of April, Troubridge had "organised Capri" and was demanding flour for his islands and another judge. "The judge appears to me to be the poorest creature I ever saw, frightened out of his senses, says seventy families are concerned, and talks of it being necessary to have a Bishop to degrade the priests before he can execute them. I told him to hang them first and if he did not think the degradation of hanging sufficient I would piss on the D——d Jacobins carcass."

So the situation at the beginning of May was that the *lazzaroni* were spoiling for a fight in Naples, while Ruffo's rabble were ravaging their way toward the city and Troubridge was jesting in the bay and promising the Republicans short shrift.

At this interesting moment, as they used to say, news arrived from St. Vincent that brought Nelson out of the palazzo onto the quarter-deck of the *Vanguard*. The French fleet from Brest, which had been at sea giving the Admiralty palpitations since the beginning of the year, was off the coast of Portugal. May 12—Nelson answered he would send at least eight warships to act with Duckworth at Minorca. The French fleet had joined the Spanish fleet at Cadiz and swept through the Straits of Gibraltar. May 14—Nelson wrote he would collect his squadron at Maritimo, west of Sicily, and he hoped that Duckworth would join him. The odds were that Admiral Bruix and his forty-three ships of the line were coming to relieve Malta before sailing to Egypt to rescue Bonaparte and the army. Nelson, now incidentally Rear-Admiral of the Red, called for Troubridge and Ball—if they arrived in time, he would have eight 74s and three Portuguese warships.

"What a state I am in," he complained to St. Vincent, "if I go I risk and more than risk Sicily and what is now safe on the continent, for we know from experience that more depends on *opinion* than in acts themselves. As I stay my heart is breaking and to mend the matter I am seriously ill."

On May 19 he left his friends to join Troubridge, who was passing Palermo on his way to Maritimo. He wrote Emma, "To tell you how dreary and uncomfortable the *Vanguard* appears is only telling you what it is to go from the pleasantest society to a solitary cell, or from the dearest friends to no friends. I am now perfectly the *great man*, not a creature near me. From my heart I wish myself the little man again. You and good Sir William have spoiled me for any place but with you. . . ."

Maria Carolina consoled her dear friend. "That God accompanies our brave and virtuous Admiral there are my sincerest vows, believe that I lament exceedingly the grief which you have suffered and I will see you with great pleasure tomorrow, try to sleep and rest yourself . . . I suffer myself also from the departure of our dear virtuous Admiral."

Nelson did not sleep well either. When he arrived off Maritimo the next day, there was no sign of Duckworth or Ball. He waited impatiently, in the growing belief that he was going to be left to his fate. Sir William read, "I will stand or fall with their Majesties and you and Lady Hamilton, nothing shall swerve me from this determination." On the 23rd one of his Nile captains, Benjamin Hallowell, sent him a present, a coffin made from the mainmast of *L'Orient*, the French flagship that blew up in the battle. Nelson kept it behind his chair as a reminder of his business, until his servant Tom Allen insisted on it being taken below.

Nelson was never gloomy before a battle, quite the contrary, the prospect of death or victory lifted his spirits out of their normal low and rather melancholy plane. On the 25th he added a codicil to his will—everything was going to Fanny and, if she died before him or intestate, there was £10,000 for Josiah—leaving a diamond box given him by the Grand Signior's mother to Emma, "as token of regard and respect for her very eminent virtues," and 50 guineas to Sir William to buy a ring. And on the same day he wrote resolutely to Miss Knight, "I hope the ships from Malta will join me tomorrow as I think they have been seen from Mt. Pelligrino, then although we shall not be strong enough to seek a battle yet *as we are* we shall not run away." But he did run on, "I agree with you that the World cannot say enough of the goodness of Lady Hamilton, we know it well, and where our Pen or Voice can reach, there it shall be known, for a more Pure, Noble and Generous heart does not fill the human breast."

Three days more waiting. Ball did not arrive, but neither did the French. Nelson turned for Palermo. "To fight is nothing," he wrote Sir William, "but to be continually on the stretch for news and events of the greatest importance is what I find my shattered carcass very unequal to." On May 29 he was once again at Palermo. Ball, who had struggled round from Malta against foul winds, turned around and sailed back again.

Bruix had sailed for Toulon, followed sluggishly by St. Vincent's fleet of thirty-one ships of the line. The Earl was ill and went ashore at Port Mahon, leaving the command at sea to Lord Keith. On hearing that the enemy were in the Gulf of Genoa, Keith pressed after them, came in sight of their advanced ship, and then turned back to Minorca. "Very much in the dumps I assure you all of us," said Collingwood, "for having missed the fairest opportunity that ever offered of terminating at least the Naval war." "You may prepare to hear me abused because I have been unlucky," Keith wrote his sister on June 8. He had disobeyed orders in going as far as Genoa. "Here we were overtaken by a strong east wind which obliged me to return to cover Minorca, in obedience to my positive orders." The shooting of Admiral Byng for the loss of Minorca, so far from encouraging the others, actually discouraged them!

At Palermo the Court was in gala for the celebration of George III's sixty-first birthday on June 4. The Ambassador was giving a dinner for the English, "and a great bore it will be," said Consul Lock. There was a motive for the Court's courtesy. Acton was trying to persuade the Admiral to carry a body of troops to Naples to keep order once the city had fallen to Cardinal Ruffo. Nelson was uncertain. Duckworth had arrived with three 74s and a new flagship, the *Foudroyant*, the finest two-decker afloat, but without any news of the enemy fleet. Nelson learned that St. Vincent was ill and likely to retire, and wrote him, "If you are sick I will fag for you, and our dear Lady Hamilton will nurse you with the most affectionate attention. Good Sir William will make you laugh with his wit and inexhaustible pleasantry." He did not relish the thought of serving under Keith.

On June 10 there was a laboriously written letter from King Ferdinand, entreating Nelson to take charge of the expedition to Naples and giving him full power to treat with the French garrison left in St. Elmo and even, if necessary, with the rebels. The clincher came two days later. "I have been with the Queen this evening," wrote Emma, "she is very miserable and says that although the people of Naples are for them in general, yet they will not be brought to that state of quietness and subordination till the fleet of Lord Nelson appears *off Naples*. She therefore begs, intreats, and conjures you my dear Lord if it is possible, to arrange matters so as to be able to go to Naples. Sir William is waiting for General Acton's answer. For Gods sake consider it and do. We will go with you if you will come to fetch us. Sir Wm. is ill, I am ill, it will do us good. God bless you, ever ever yours sincerely."

The next morning Sir William, Acton and the Hereditary Prince, the spirit of royal authority, Nelson was the substance, boarded the *Foudroyant*, and 1,700 soldiers were distributed through the squadron. They sailed that afternoon. The next day, June 14, the squadron was met by two ships of the line sent by Keith to say the enemy was off the Italian coast and he had gone back to Minorca. There was also an unconfirmed report of a fleet sighted off Trapani in the west of Sicily. Nelson put back to Palermo, disembarked his passengers, and headed once again for Maritimo.

He was on his station west of Sicily anxiously looking out for news of the enemy from Keith or for reinforcements to enable him to go off in search of them. He now had sixteen ships, including the Portuguese, and had summoned Ball with his two ships from Malta. But he was on the rack, for while he had turned his back on Naples and the confused rumors that the Cardinal had compounded with the Republicans, he was not strong enough to face the enemy fleet with the certainty of beating them, even though Keith's information was that Bruix had parted from the Spaniards and had twenty-two ships of the line.

On June 18, with Ball in sight, Nelson wrote to the Hamiltons. Naturally, his letter to Emma is the most interesting.

> As to my feelings my Dear Lady I know not how to express them, but I know how to feel them for they have made me very unwell. Jefferson wants to give me castor oil but that will not smooth my anxious mind. I long to be at the French fleet as much as ever a Miss longed for a husband, but prudence stops me. Ought I to risk giving the cursed French a chance of being mistress of the Medn. for one hour? I must have reinforcements very soon. Ah Lord Keith, you have placed me in a situation to lower me in the Eyes of Europe, they will say "this cried up Nelson is afraid with 18 Ships to attack 22," the thought kills me. I know what I am equal to and what Ships and men can do and I declare to God if no more Ships could join me that I would instantly search out the French fleet and fight them, for believe me I have no fear but that of being lowered in the Opinion of those I love and esteem.

The Adl. [Niza], Troubridge and Campbell dined here yesterday. They all love you and Sir William and charge me to say so. Martin came after dinner and amongst them they told such things of Palermo Ladies that I was all astonishment; that one who is a Lady we saw oddly lifted up on the quarter deck of the *Principe Reale* [Niza's flagship] gives herself up for money, price named a great deal more I am sure than she is worth. In short, we of your house know nothing of the Infamy of C - - - n, P - t - r - and a Lady who's with Child was not spared. Where have I been not to have known as much as these Gentlemen? Living in a house of Virtue and Goodness. These anecdotes I only catched as they flew, for I was thinking of other things much more interesting to me.

He asked her to send him his new plain hat that Allen had left behind, and sent her some washing and compliments to Mrs. Cadogan, Mrs. Graefer and her children, Gibbs and Noble. These were merchants from Naples who were living in the palazzo.

Emma is very well and growing fat and saucy, she goes to all parts of the Ship at the different meal times, she seems to prefer Roast Goose to all other things. To the Queen you will I am sure say everything which is proper, answer for my attachment and that I will fight in defence of her Crown and dominions, and that the damn'd French shall not get Sicily with their fleet but through my heart's blood. May the God of heaven bless you and be assured I am your faithful and affectionate friend.

In the letter to Sir William, he added an invitation to join him at sea: "I will come to Palermo for you and if I am to go away to fight I will promise to land you from some frigate."

On June 19 there was a diversion when the squadron picked up five French vessels going from Jaffa to Toulon. On board were a group of Turkish prisoners, among them a chief, Hadji Osman Agha. The release of this important gentleman resulted in the award of Nelson's second star, the Order of the Crescent.

The 19th also brought news of Naples and of his friends. Cardinal Ruffo's army had entered the city on the 14th, the French were quiet in St. Elmo, but the Republicans were defending the forts of Nuovo and dell' Ovo against the mob. Again there was the story that Ruffo was making terms with the rebels. Sir William wrote, "*His Eminency was resolved to conquer Naples himself.*" He continued:

Poor Emma is unwell and low spirited with fanthoms in her fertile brain, that torment her, in short she has no other fault than that of too much sensibility, and that at least is a fault of the right side, if any . . . I am but in a weak situation of health no stomach —great goings out and nothing getting in, but I am going to my old remedy Sea Bathing and Bark. I hope you are not fretting your guts to fiddle strings. It is a strange world but let us make the best of it.

That night Nelson was torn between his duty and desire to go in search of the enemy fleet and his duty and desire to return to Palermo for Emma and Sir William and go on to Naples to capture a capital. He decided to go after the enemy. His state of mind is evident in the note he sent Sir William the next day. "I am agitated, but my resolution is fixed. For Heaven's sake suffer not anyone to oppose it. I shall not be gone eight days. No harm can come to Sicily. I send my lady and you Lord St. Vincent's letter. I am full of grief and anxiety. I must go. It will finish the war. It will give a sprig of laurel to your affectionate friend."

Then his decision was suddenly reversed. He received a dispatch from Keith saying that St. Vincent had retired, that Keith was now Commander in Chief, and that Lord Gardner was at Gibraltar with a fleet of sixteen ships of the line. His relief was immense and he turned his head toward Palermo, where an old gentleman was writing, "I am sorry you have been ill, Emma is much better today and so am I, but we both miss your Lordship heavily."

Every good story, no matter how badly told, should have a villain. Charles Lock, at first sight, seems scarcely important enough to fill the part. He was a young man of moderate circumstances, and even more moderate talents, who had married above himself. His wife, Cecilia, was the daughter of the Duchess of Leinster by her second husband, the half-sister of the Irish rebel Lord Edward Fitzgerald who was hanged for treason, and, more important, the cousin of Charles James Fox. So Lock was allied to a family which had strong Republican sympathies.

As he had failed at everything else, the Leinster connections had Lock appointed Consul General to Naples, an unimportant position which St. Vincent, who recommended Mrs. Lock to Lady Hamilton's protection, thought would make it difficult to bring her forward. However, when the Locks came to Palermo at the end of January, Emma found them a house, had them to dinner and introduced them at Court. Sir William went so far as to suggest making Lock his chargé d'affaires should he leave Palermo.

Lock was neither grateful nor gracious. In great company he was hot-

97

headed and belligerent, he felt his position as a man of a superior and liberal intellect, a connection of Mr. Fox, a better man than a decrepit ambassador or a half-blind admiral. This would not have mattered, he would have been no more than a minor irritant, a loud voice in a corner, if he had not written long letters home which, because of their scabrous comments, gained a wide circulation among those who were pleased to attack the government by attacking its servants.

He began his campaign of denigration on June 30 in a letter to his father.

> Sir William and Lady Hamilton embarked with great secrecy for Naples about ten days ago, in the *Foudroyant* which came singly for them off the Harbour with Lord Nelson on board. I underwent a severe mortification in not being invited to accompany Sir William or receiving any intimation of their designs, which I relied on as Sir William had repeatedly promised I should attend him when he went. . . . But for this I may thank that superficial, grasping and vulgar minded woman whose wish to retain her husband in a situation his age and disinclination render him unfit for, has made her use every endeavour to keep me in the dark, and to make it difficult for Sir William to give up his employment at this moment. . . . Sir William has ever showed a forwardness to give me an insight into the politicks of this Court, and of the mode of conducting business, but the unbounded power her Ladyship possesses over him, and Lord Nelson, with her taking the whole drudgery of it upon herself, has easily prevented his intention. The extravagant love of the latter has made him the laughing stock of the whole fleet and the total dereliction of power and the dignity of his diplomatic character, has made the friends of the former regret that he retains the title of a situation, of which he has resigned the functions.

There is no gentility in Lock at all. He was going to Naples. He said, "My object in going to Naples, is to obtain a house and to *accrocher* a little of the loads of furniture which the plunder of the wretched Jacobins has occasioned to be sold as cheap as dirt."

The rumors from Naples were the merest murmur on the edge of the storm that was raging in that city.

On June 14, believing that the expedition from Palermo would arrive in a day or two, Cardinal Ruffo let his Christian Army loose on Naples.

Within hours they were treating the place as if they had conquered it, and it was the French capital and not their King's. Bands of *lazzaroni* were already prowling the streets, seizing any decent-looking person and dragging them off to the main square before the palace, where they were beheaded or worse.

"The *lazzaroni* roasted men in the streets and begged money of the passers by to purchase bread to their roast meat. Many of them carried in their pockets fingers, ears etc. which they had cut off; and when they met a person whom they looked upon as a patriot, they triumphantly exhibited their bloody spoils." So wrote Kotzebue, who talked to people who would never forget those bloody days in Naples. "The women were the most outrageous; it was sufficient to be pointed out by one of these furies as a jacobin to be instantly sacrificed. All who wore cropped hair were devoted victims. False tails were procured, but the deception being perceived, the people ran behind everyone that passed, pulling him by the tail, and if it came off, it was all over with the wearer."

As it grew dark, the slaughter went on, lit by the flames from buildings pillaged and set on fire, or burning from the bombs shot from the forts of Nuovo and dell' Ovo, where the last of the Republicans were fighting for their lives. The French garrison in St. Elmo, where the desperate "patriots" had been refused refuge, was quiet. The vengeance of the mob on those who had hoped, however ineffectually, to better their lot, was none of their concern.

The hideous gaiety of this festival of blood screamed out as fresh batches of victims were herded from their houses to be sacrificed in the streets. The men had their clothes torn from them and were hacked and stabbed and dragged off to the ghastly banquets, or, if they were luckier, to the granaries by the Maddalena Bridge which served as prisons. The women were stripped and tortured and, if they fell into the hands of the Turks rampaging through Naples, raped. This last atrocity was the one least committed in the peculiar, almost religious, ritual of the counterrevolution in the sultry days of June.

At his headquarters near the Maddalena Bridge, Cardinal Ruffo saw with abhorrence the tide of destruction released on his city. His ruffians hauled their prisoners before him, naked, wounded, pleading for mercy. Some were shot at once, the rest were dragged away and thrust into the granaries, broken and bleeding to die among the straw. Ruffo had repeated orders from the King and Queen not to treat with the rebels; the French could have terms, but not their subjects. "As a Christian I pardon every-

99

body," said Ferdinand, "but as he whom God appointed, I must be a strict avenger of the offences committed against Him." "Rebellious Naples and her ungrateful citizens may make no terms," said Maria Carolina.

The ungrateful citizens were not a danger, it was the grateful ones who were destroying the city. When the report came that Nelson had turned back and the expedition was not coming from Palermo, the Cardinal sent General Micheroux, the liaison officer with the Russian marines, to negotiate a truce with the Republican chiefs in Nuovo. He explained his action to the King on June 17.

> There is no going on with what your Majesty commands which, though very just, is not proper for the present moment, when the object should be to be put a stop to anarchy which is without bounds. The people become as cruel as Tygers and neither mind laws or Edicts. . . . I must then make use of equivocal means or Naples will be a mass of stones. I have then offered to the garrisons that the French should be embarked at your Majesty's expence for France, and to those who are not French and will follow them, they must go at their own expence, without harming Rebels. I have done all to conclude and they showed the best disposition, but in one moment they have changed and broken all Treaty, first by facts then by writing. I fear yesterday 16th they had notice of the French and Spanish Fleets.

New terms were proposed and accepted by the Republicans, and on June 19 a treaty was signed between them and the Cardinal, Micheroux, and the Turkish and Russian commanders. The main provision was that the Republicans were to leave the forts with the honors of war, and were given the option of returning to their homes or of being taken by sea to Toulon at the King's expense. The treaty was approved by General Méjean, commander of the garrison of St. Elmo, and was then sent to Captain Foote of the *Seahorse* frigate, the only British ship in the bay.

Foote, who had been left by Troubridge to cooperate with the Cardinal, realized the immediate advantage of a cessation of hostilities. However, he had no orders for such a contingency and hesitated; the Cardinal pressed him, saying that the French and rebels refused to capitulate to a priest and that, in any event, the Russians were responsible for the treaty. Left to himself and without any advice that the fleet was on its way to Naples, Foote signed the treaty on June 23, adding a qualification that he was not bound by anything in it that might be contrary to the rights of the British King and nation.

Flags of truce flew from the castles and from the *Seahorse*. The vampire saturnalia exhausted, some sort of order was restored in Naples. Boats were being prepared to take those Republicans who chose to Toulon. Others left the forts and went to their homes. All, it seemed, was over.

Then, on June 24, the *Foudroyant* sailed into the bay with the fleet, and with the Hamiltons and Lord Nelson on the quarter-deck. They came to break whatever truce or treaty had been arranged. This is clear from a note written by the Admiral that day. "All armistices signify that either party may renew hostilities, giving a certain notice fixed upon by the contracting parties . . . and I fancy the question need not be asked whether, if the French fleet arrived this day in the Bay of Naples, whether the French and rebels would adhere one moment to the armistice." All their advice from Palermo was that the Cardinal had, at the best, overstepped his authority, and at the worst, become involved in some plot to shelter the rebels.

The last of Nelson's eighteen warships came to anchor in line, threatening the city, at 2 P.M. on June 25. Troubridge and Ball had already been sent ashore with a letter for Cardinal Ruffo expressing the Admiral's disapproval of the terms allowed the rebels, and his determination to intervene on the King's behalf. Poor Foote, who had borne the brunt of the Admiral's anger for an hour, had rowed back to the *Seahorse* and hauled down the flag of truce. The good citizens of Naples, who had opened their shutters and put out their royal flags, closed their shutters, though they left the flags flying.

That evening the cabin of the *Foudroyant* was the scene of the meeting between Nelson and Ruffo. Through the elegant bay window that stretched the width of the ship, the lights of Naples twinkled in the summery night air; the lamps of dozens of boats bobbed about the battleships; from the barges of the nobility, on which the blue-red-yellow tricolor of the Republic had been miraculously replaced by the white crested standard of the Bourbons, came the strains of "Rule Britannia," which the fiddlers knew by heart; and from the rough floats of the fishermen arose the more heartfelt cries of "*Viva il Re, Viva il Re.*"

The Admiral walked up and down, working his fin and occasionally stopping to thump his left hand on the table. (Nelson had a considerable advantage in being able to stand upright in his own cabin, anyone a few inches taller had to stoop or bang their heads on the beams of the deck above; Hardy, who was over six foot, sloped about the ship and earned the nickname of "the Ghost.") The Cardinal sat, guardedly, at one end of the table. Sir William cleared his throat. Emma dashed about, in constant danger of knocking out her beautiful brains, peering out of the window, waving when she fancied she saw the faces of friends in the boats below, and rushing back to the table whenever she heard the Queen's name mentioned. She was Maria Carolina's special agent, her deputy, come to form the Queen's party once again in Naples.

The conference began with Nelson's plain opinion that the treaty was infamous, that rebels could not have terms, but must surrender unconditionally and throw themselves on the mercy of their sovereign. Sir William translated. The Cardinal replied that he had already given *his* sovereign his reasons for making the treaty, but if the Lord Admiral Nelson had orders from *his* sovereign, he was under no engagement and might do as he thought best. Sir William translated. But, continued the Cardinal, from what he had signed he could not depart, and he still believed that what he had done was the best that could be done. Sir William translated. Nelson shouted. Before the fleet arrived! The arrival of the fleet ends the armistice and the treaty! Sir William coughed. I annul the treaty! The Cardinal shrugged. With the King's authority! And the Queen's, said Emma. . . .

The trouble was that Acton, jealous of his position, had filled Nelson's head with so much suspicion of Ruffo that any sort of communication between them was sparked with atmospherics of mistrust. "An admiral is no match in talking with a Cardinal," was Nelson's opinion. "A little of my phlegm was necessary between the Cardinal and Lord Nelson or all would have blown up the very first day," was Sir William's, and, on another occasion, "Lord N is so accustomed to dealings fair and open that he has no patience when he meets with the contrary, which one must always expect when one has to deal with Italians, and perhaps his Eminency is the very quintessence of Italian finesse."

The conference ended with Nelson giving Ruffo a written declaration that the treaty could not be carried into effect without the consent of His Sicilian Majesty, and there it rested.

There was another visitor to the *Foudroyant* that night. "Having the head of the Lazaronys an old friend," Emma wrote Charles Greville, "he came in the night of our arrival. He told me he had 90 thousand Lazaronis ready at the holding up of his finger, but only twenty with arms. Lord Nelson to whom I enterprated got a large supply of arms for the rest and they were deported with this man. In the meantime the Calabrese were comitting murders, the bombs we sent into St. Elmo were returned, and the Citty in confusion." Things were back where they started. "As Lord Nelson is now telling Lady Hamilton what he wishes to say to the Queen, you will probably know from the Queen more than I do of Lord Nelson's intentions," the Ambassador wrote to Acton before going to bed.

Early the next morning Sir William persuaded Nelson to allow him to write to the Cardinal to assure him, in Sir William's words, "that he would not do anything that could break the Armistice which His Eminence had thought proper to make with the Rebels in the Castles of Ovo and Nuovo, and that his Lordship was ready to give him any assistance that the Fleet under his command could afford. . . ." Now, that appeared to put matters to rights. Later in the day Troubridge and Ball settled with the Cardinal that the rebels should embark on the boats prepared for them that evening, while 500 marines should occupy the castles.

It was done. The rebels came out, the marines landed, the people cheered and the city was illuminated. Troubridge took a party to the square in front of the royal palace, which had been covered by the guns of Nuovo, to cut down the Tree of Liberty and take the red cap off the head of a huge ill-hewn statue of Jupiter, affectionately called "the Giant."

However, in the midst of all the good will there was a fatal misunderstanding. The Republicans came out believing that they were protected by the treaty they had signed. Nelson believed they came out because he had agreed to respect the armistice or truce, and that the validity of the treaty depended on the King. Of course, the fatal part of the fatal misunderstanding fell on the Republicans. It did not matter to Nelson whether they came out willingly, or were bombed out, or starved out, he was quite clear that they came out without the honors of war and in submission to the mercy of the King.

On the morning of June 28 letters arrived from the Court at Palermo giving Nelson full powers to overrule the Cardinal and, if necessary, arrest him and send him to Palermo. In her letter to Emma the Queen wrote, "I recommend Lord Nelson to treat Naples as if it were an Irish town in rebellion similarly placed." The British had a good reputation in these matters.

Nelson responded by ordering the boats with the rebels on board to be hauled out under the guns of the warships. Some of the leaders were taken out of the boats and put in irons. He also issued a proclamation summoning the people who had left the forts during the truce to give themselves up on pain of death. The Cardinal protested. "It was a toss up yesterday," said Nelson, "whether the Cardinal would not have been arrested." Sir William advised against it, the Cardinal's conscience turned a somersault, the Republicans were lost.

That day Troubridge went ashore with 1,300 marines, about 120 men from each warship, to besiege St. Elmo, in company with the Russians and Ruffo's irregulars. "I rather hope for a capitulation without coming to blows," Sir William wrote Acton. "However your Excellency knows that if Troubridge is once irritated he will spare no pains to carry his point."

Among the prisoners brought on board the *Foudroyant*, though he had left the castles before the capitulation, was Francesco Caraccioli, the Neapolitan naval commander. He had returned to Naples early in March, with the King's permission, to prevent the confiscation of his estates. Before long there were reports that he was serving the Republic. Orders were issued in his name as Commander of the Marine, and he took part in a gunboat attack on the *Seahorse* and the Neapolitan frigate *Minerva* toward the end of May. Now, whether Caraccioli turned Republican out of conviction, spite or necessity is of as little consequence now as it was then. The facts were inescapable and Sir William wrote, two days before his trial, "Caraccioli will probably be seen hanging at the yard arm of the *Minerva* Neapolitan frigate from daybreak to sunset for such an example is necessary for the future marine service of H.S. Majesty."

Caraccioli was tried by a court-martial composed of Neapolitan officers under Count Thurn. Nelson signed the death sentence before dinner on June 29. Caraccioli was hanged from the yardarm of the *Minerva* after dinner. "It was usual to give 24 hours for the care of the soul," said Sir William. "Lord N's manner of acting must be as his conscience and honor dictate, and I believe his determination will be found best at last." The corpse was cut down and sunk in the bay with a double-headed shot fastened to each foot. The Neapolitans who had rowed out to look thought they had seen the last of it.

"I have received with infinite gratitude your dear obliging letters," the Queen wrote Emma on July 2, "three of Saturday and one of the previous day, together with the list of the Jacobins arrested, who are some of the worst villains we have had. I have also noted the sad but merited end of the unfortunate, crazy, Caracciolo. I am deeply conscious of all that your excellent heart must have suffered, and this increases my gratitude."

Maria Carolina was in constant communication with her deputy, the more so when King Ferdinand decided to visit his erring capital without her. "I am relegated to Palermo," she wrote. "No one wanted me." Emma was touched and scrawled impulsively on the envelope, "This from my friend whom I love and adore. Yes I will serve her with my heart and soul. My blood if necessary shall flow for her. Emma will prove to Maria Carolina that an humble-born Englishwoman can serve a Queen with zeal and true love, even at the risk of her life." (This, written for no one but herself, is a splendid example of how she saw herself as the heroine of whatever drama was being enacted. The only danger she risked was falling overboard while making an exit!)

Her suffering, however, was real, and her power over Nelson greater than ever; both appeared in the case of John Jolly. Troubridge was up outside St. Elmo, working himself into a fury with the Neapolitans: "I am really making the best I can out of the *Degenerated race* I have to *deal* with." And catching Jacobins: "I have got a packed jury, Darby at their head for fear justice should not reach the villains." On July 6 one of his marines, John Jolly, was court-martialed for striking a lieutenant and condemned to death. Jolly petitioned Lady Hamilton, "Oh Madam . . . your interest might save me from an early grave . . . Lord Nelson will pardon, if you apply for mercy."

A pardon was a tediously difficult thing to get, as it had to be signed by the King. Nevertheless, John Jolly got one. Troubridge protested, "So great a villain does not exist in the Fleet." The marines were getting out of hand, looting and drinking instead of digging trenches under fire from St. Elmo. Nelson was adamant. "You will in obedience to my Orders prepare everything for the execution of the Sentence of the Court-Martial held on John Jolly . . . but not execute him." *Amor vincit omnia!*

No one, except Troubridge, was keen to approach the walls of St. Elmo. Apart from the chance of getting shot on the eve of the King's arrival when rewards might be expected, several noble hostages, sent in during the truce, were still inside. Troubridge favored blowing the place up. "I am a strong advocate, if we can accomplish that, to send them, *Hostages and all to Hell* without notice and surprize old Satan with a group of *Nobility* and *Republicans*." The affair was settled by the ubiquitous Micheroux, whose brother was one of the hostages, and a bribe of 150,000 ducats to General Méjean. The French marched out honorably and were shipped to Toulon. The General obligingly stood in the gate and pointed out some wretched "patriots" who were trying to escape in French uniforms. The haggling took longer than expected and the royal standard did not float from the battlements until July 12, two days after King Ferdinand's arrival in the bay.

The King sailed in with Acton and his suite aboard his ship *La Sirène*. The first thing that greeted him was the corpse of Caraccioli, upright, staring, half out of the water, bobbing like a cork. The royal hair prickled in the royal scalp, until some acute courtier quickly explained that it was a most auspicious omen, the traitor had risen from the bottom of the sea to implore His Majesty's pardon. Some fishermen towed the poor corpse ashore, where it was hurriedly buried in the sand. Years later, when Ferdinand was execrated and Caraccioli was a hero, it found a decent resting place.

The King established his Court aboard the *Foudroyant*, sleeping in the Admiral's cabin, holding levees on the quarter-deck, fishing and shooting sea gulls, and being entertained in the warm evenings by Lady Hamilton, resplendent on the poop, singing "Rule Britannia." The swelling notes filled the hearts of King, and Admiral, and Ambassador; they rang across the bay and stirred the seamen in their hammocks; they reached the unhappy Republicans, crammed in their floating prisons.

> *When Britain first, at heaven's command,*
> *Arose from out the azure main,*
> *This was the charter of the land,*
> *And guardian angels sung this strain . . .*

"I have a letter from Lord Nelson, got into Naples," Keith wrote his sister. "He is absurd with Lady Hamilton and vanity. I wish he would go home and her too."

Keith was off Majorca following the enemy. "Swan hopping," said Nelson. "They did what they pleased," said Collingwood, "and having done it, they went where they liked, and we followed them."

At the end of June Admiral Bruix and his fleet were off Cartagena, and Keith was following them, and, as Commander in Chief, he wrote to Nelson asking him to send part of his squadron to Minorca. Nelson had anticipated some such request and had already made up his mind to refuse it. As Keith sailed toward Gibraltar in the wake of the enemy, the request became an order, and the order for a part of the squadron to repair to Minorca became a firm order for the whole squadron to go there, which was repeated.

Nelson received the order to quit Naples on July 13. It was the same day that Troubridge and his army of marines, Russians and Calabrians marched off to besiege Capua and Gaeta, to clear the kingdom of the last French garrisons. Nelson could not obey without bringing the marines back to their ships, and would not obey because he believed that the *actual* situation of the Kingdom of Naples required the presence of the squadron more than the *supposed* situation of Minorca. He wrote Lord Spencer, "I am fully aware of the act I have committed; but sensible of my loyal intentions I am prepared for any fate which may await my disobedience. . . . It will be my consolation that I have gained a kingdom, seated a faithful ally of His Majesty firmly on his throne, and restored happiness to millions."

Then he waited morosely for the Admiralty's sentence. Nelson was rather morose these days.

The *Thalia* had arrived in the bay on July 5 and anchored alongside the *Foudroyant*. Not for long. On the 10th the Admiral sent Captain Nisbet off with Captain Foote to Leghorn, recently occupied by the Russians. Josiah, who could not do anything right, ended up in Civita Vecchia with a sprung mainmast. He promptly summoned the French garrison there and was rebuffed. "I am persuaded," Nelson wrote wearily, "it was done for the best."

Even the news that the East India Company had voted him the tremendous sum of £10,000 for his victory failed to raise his spirits. "I never regarded money or wanted it for my own use," he told Fanny, and instructed her to give £500 each to his father, brothers and sisters. His brother Suckling, never much more than a suckling, had died. "Three are now dead younger than myself. . . . My situation here is not to be described but suffice it to say I am endeavouring to work for good."

The burden on his mind was the fate of those he called "Rebels, Jacobins and Fools." Every day brought a sheaf of petitions from the prisons and boats, either to him or to Emma. They ranged from harrowing pleas for mercy to dignified protests.

> Excellency, The individuals in Felucca No. 5 have the honour to represent to Your Excellency, how they have capitulated and put their faith in the loyalty of the English nation, with the full power of His Eminence Cardinal Ruffo, Vicar-General of His Majesty the King of the Two Sicilies, and the good faith of the Russian and other powers.
> The aforesaid individuals now see themselves treated worse than slaves. They implore the humanity and the faith of Your Excellency for the treaty to be observed, and that they be treated as prisoners of war, and not as criminals. They hope everything from the generosity of the English and the justice of the worthy Admiral.

The story of one of these unfortunates must serve for them all. Dr. Domenico Cirillo was an elderly and renowned biologist, a Fellow of the Royal Society, and Sir William's friend. He was known to have served in the Republican government, he came out of the forts with the others, and was put in irons on one of the Portuguese ships. On July 3, a few days after his capture, Cirillo wrote Emma, "I hope you won't take it ill, if I take this liberty to trouble you with a few lines, in order to make you recollect that nobody in this world can protect and save a miserable and innocent being, but you." He continued, with the same dignity, to describe how he had refused to accept office under Championnet and the Parthenopean Republic four times; how he had finally been threatened and forced to accept a place on the legislative commission; how he had never taken an oath or spoken against the King; how he had avoided public ceremonies and never been paid, except for 100 ducats which he had given to the poor; how the few laws passed in his time were beneficial; and how he had protected the English garden and Mrs. Graefer's children. "Procure for me," he ended his petition, "a full pardon from our merciful King."

Now, Cirillo was hanged in October. Nelson had nothing to do with that, but years later (February 10, 1803), he wrote in his notes on a violently Republican account of the events of 1799, "Cirillo—strange to say would *not* be saved, he refused Sir William and Lady H's entreatys on the quarter deck of the *Foudroyant* when brought up for trial and, asked who he was, answered, in the Reign of the Tyrant I was a Physician, in the time of the Republic I was a Patriot, and now I am a Victim."

Martyrs have recanted and burned the hand that signed the recantation, but can this be the same man? In the same notes Nelson wrote, "Capt. Foote capitulation, though not approved, yet most religiously adhered to," and "Capitulation not closed but negociation broke off by Ld. Nelson." Both statements are palpably untrue.

The trials and executions that began while the King was at Naples were continued under a Supreme Junta that became notorious for its corruption and injustice. Of some 8,000 prisoners, 105 were executed, 6 were reprieved, 222 were sentenced to life imprisonment and 322 to shorter terms, 355 were deported and exiled, and the rest were released. The business went on for a year and shocked European society. Nelson and the Hamiltons came in for their full share of censure.

"Lord Nelson has brought back the fugitive monarch to his capital," wrote Lady Holland, who was not one to miss an opportunity, "and Naples now exhibits a scene of revenge, more bloody than the Sicilian vespers. The hearts of Frenchmen are brought as trophies to a cruel people, who crouched in a senile subjection when they were too abject to fight their own cause. Lady Hamilton has not been remiss in adding her quota to the barbarity which enflames every breast."

Her ladyship was not there, of course, but she got her information from a reliable source, no less than the Consul General, Mr. Lock. On July 13 Lock wrote home, "You will hear with grief of the infraction of the articles convented with the Neapolitan Jacobins and of the stab our English honour has received in being employed to decoy these people, who relied upon our faith, into the most deplorable situation. I have no time to enlarge as Sylvester the Messenger is going in a few hours, but the sentiment of abhorrence expressed by the whole fleet will I hope exonerate the nation from an imputation so disgraceful, and charge it where it should lie, upon the shoulders of one or two."

Injustice is not the prerogative of Royalists or Republicans, admirals, consuls, or ladies of fashion with political leanings. Inhumanity does not belong to one age or another. Indifference to suffering is no less in modern cities than in ancient encampments. These things are constants. It is people not politics, individuals not eras, men not environments, that count.

Nelson was a just, humane and sensible man. That means that in balance, justice outweighed injustice, humanity inhumanity, sensibility indifference, not that all the desirable qualities were present all of the time, and none of the undesirable qualities were present any of the time. He was a human being, you could go up and prod him and he would turn and ask you what the hell you thought you were doing! He had a human pride and stubbornness, and once he had gone in and put aside the treaty he could not interfere, one way or the other, without admitting he had been wrong. And he was not the man to do that. He was morose instead.

As for Emma, she was so busy with her letters backward and forward to the Queen, deciding which ladies should be received and which dismissed, that she could write to Greville, "If I can judge, it may turn out fortunate that the Neapolitans had a dose of Republicanism." She did not see the condemned poetess Eleonora Pimentel brought by her executioners into the Piazza del Mercato; she did not see the gallows and the coffin with four of the white-robed brethren sitting on it, the crowds gnawing their handkerchiefs with excitement, the mob spitting its pips and befouling the cobbles; she did not see the hangman placing the rope about her neck, and coaxing her up the ladder after him; fastening the rope to the crossbeam, and then throwing her down from the ladder and leaping on her shoulders, riding her, while his ragged assistant hung on her feet, swinging about like children in a playground; she did not hear the shout of jubilation that shook the crows off the rooftops, or see the thin dead carcass, stretched a foot beyond endurance, dangling like a plucked fowl from a butcher's hook. She did not see that, or she would not have said what she did.

And as for Sir William, he wanted to go home. "We mean to profit of the first ship that Lord Nelson sends downwards," he wrote Lord Grenville on July 14, "after that their Sicilian Majesties shall have been happily reinstated on their throne of Naples, having had, as your Lordship knows, in my pocket for more than two years the King's gracious permission to return home for a short time to look after my private concerns." In his letter of the same date to his nephew Charles, he added, "You will find me much worn and am little more than skin and bone, as I have very little stomach. . . . No one are I believe more popular in the navy at this moment than Emma and I. It will be heart breaking to the Queen of Naples when we go; she has realy no female friends but her, and Emma has been of infinite use in our late very critical business. Lord Nelson and I could not have done without her."

Emma wrote Charles Greville one of her Ulyssean letters, a mile long and not a stop from start to finish, telling how she had arranged matters for the Queen.

She is not to see on her arrival any of her former evil counsellers, nor the women of *fashion* alltho Ladys of the bedchamber formerly her friends and companions and who did her dishonor by their desolute life. *All all* is changed. She has been very *unfortunate* but she is a great woman and has sense enough to proffit of her *past unhappiness* and will make for the future *amende honorable* for the *past*.

I have not been on shore but once, the King give us leave to go as far as St. Elmo to see the effect of the Bombs. I saw at a distance our despoiled house in town and Villa Emma that have been plundered, and Sir Wm new appartment—a Bomb burst in it—but it made me so low spirited I don't desire to go again.

[She really had turned diplomat.] We shall, as soon as the government is fixed, return to Palermo and bring back the Royal family, for I foresee not any permanent government till that event takes place: nor would it be political, after the hospitality the King and Queen received at Palermo, to carry them off in a hury, so you see their is great management required. I am quite worn out, for I am enterpreter to Lord Nelson, the King, Queen, and all together feil quite shattered, but as things go on well that keeps me up. And we dine now every day with the King at 12 o'clock; dinner is over by one; his Majesty goes to sleep and we sit down to write. In this heat and on board you may guess what we suffer. My mother is at Palermo, but I have an English Lady with me [probably Miss Knight] who is of use to me in writing and helping to keep papers and things in order. We have given the King all the upper cabbin, all but one room that we write in and receive the Ladies who come to the King. Sir Wm and I have an appartment below in the ward room and as to Lord Nelson, he is here and there and everywhere, I never saw such zeal and activity in my life as in this wonderful man.

The Admiral was on his quarter-deck on the evening of July 23 when he was approached by Charles Lock. The Consul had been soliciting for the exclusive privilege of supplying the fleet with fresh beef, wine, bread and provisions while they were at Naples. This privilege was considered the main perquisite of a Consul, but since there had not been one before Lock, the pursers of the ships were dealing directly with the merchants in the city. Nelson had intimated through his secretary John Tyson that he had no intention of interfering with this arrangement.

Lock walked up and down with the Admiral and told him that he had seen a bill which proved that one of the pursers was cheating the government. He hastened to add that he did not know the purser's name, nor could he produce the bill as evidence. He was just advising the Admiral so that he might be on his guard. (All this was in a letter Lock wrote home on July 27.)

Nelson stopped and looked up at Lock. "By God I will sift this matter to the bottom. Here Hardy—here's Mr. Lock tells me, as there's the most scandalous abuses in providing the fleet; and tells me I don't know what Pursers has cheated, I'll find it out! Put it into public orders; that whereas I have received information that the most gross abuses exist in the purchase of fresh beef, wine, &c. for the purpose of the fleet, it is my directions that the Captains do look more narrowly into the Pursers' accounts and do sign no vouchers which are not attested by respectable merchants."

Lock suddenly realized he had gone too far. Raising his voice to match Nelson's, he said he could not prove his charge, he had only given it as his personal opinion . . . and he became so agitated, waving his arms about, that Nelson called to Hardy, "Here! take him off from me, by God, he'll strike me!" He walked off, leaving Lock with Hardy.

Hardy was bigger than Lock, but the Consul badgered him, jostled him, stood in his way, trying to get the order rescinded. The Captain answered shortly that every word spoken on a quarter-deck was irredeemable. Lock behaved so badly that the rumor spread afterward that he was drunk.

The unlucky man hurried off to see Sir William in his cabin under the poop. The old Ambassador, whose only knowledge of fresh beef was that it upset his stomach, could not help. On his way out, Lock saw Nelson again and begged him to withdraw the order, or at least not to mention his name.

The answer was that nothing could be done, the captains and pursers would undoubtedly want to know who had made the charge and Hardy could not be off telling them.

The next morning, the order was published. The captains examined the accounts and found them in order and the pursers demanded an apology from Lock. He replied that he was not responsible for the improper use of information given in a private conversation. This infuriated Nelson, who promptly referred the whole matter to the Commissioners for Victualling in London. Lock begged his father to recruit his influential friends in his defense. He went to see Sir William again.

"His wife is at the bottom of all the mischief," he wrote on July 30. "I can paint nothing so black and detestable as that woman; there are not five dissenting voices amongst our many countrymen here with regard to her."

Now this was unforgivable. Lock was disappointed because Sir William would not go home and he blamed, probably with some justification, Emma's influence. He was apprehensive about the results of his stupidity in challenging the Admiral on his quarter-deck. But he had no right to turn on Emma, who knew no more of the incident than she knew of anything outside her own immediate interest.

"Pray do not neglect to apprise Lord Grenville of the state of the case," he continued, "as I think it would be right that the King were informed of it. But I know my dear father will neglect nothing for my interest."

So the stories of Nelson's infatuation, Emma's scheming and Sir William's decrepitude were insinuated into the highest places, to justify the asinine blundering of this fathead.

By the end of July Capua and Gaeta had surrendered to Troubridge, and he was marching onward to Civita Vecchia. Now that he felt free to do so, Nelson sent Duckworth back to Minorca with five of the squadron; two more sailed for Genoa, to cooperate with old Suwarrow who was marching there from Leghorn; Louis and Hallowell went to blockade Civita Vecchia, where Louis was imposed on by the French commander and received this advice from Nelson: "There is no way of dealing with a Frenchman but to knock him down. To be civil to them is only to be laughed at, when they are enemies."

Having disposed of the squadron and made Troubridge a commodore in command at Naples, Nelson was ready to return to Palermo. King Ferdinand wanted to leave his unhappy capital for his happy one. Cardinal Ruffo, too powerful to be dispossessed, was appointed Captain-General of the Realm, the realm stripped of treasure, ravaged by friend and foe, and steaming with guilt and corruption.

Naples was still Naples, and put on the most elegant tribute to the victor on August 1, the anniversary of the victory. Ferdinand dined with Nelson in state, and, when he drank the hero's health, a royal salute was fired from the *Foudroyant,* and the warships in the bay, and answered from all the castles.

In the evening the city was illuminated. A cavalcade of boats rode on the bay, led by a Roman galley; there were lamps fixed to the oars, which rose and fell with every stroke, in the center stood a rostral column emblazoned with the name of Nelson, and in the stern two gilded angels supported Nelson's picture. "In short the beauty of the thing was beyond my powers of description," said Nelson, describing it for Fanny's benefit.

> More than 2,000 variegated lamps were fixed round the vessel, an orchestra was fitted up and filled with the very best musicians and singers. The piece of music was in great measure my praises, describing their distress, but Nelson comes, the invincible Nelson and we are safe and happy again. Thus you must not make you think me vain so very far from it and I relate it more from gratitude than vanity.

In the darkness the King found himself next to Emma. "He calls me his *grande Maîtresse,*" she told Greville. "I was near taking him at his word, but as I have had seven long years of service at Court I am waiting to get quiet, I am not ambitious of more honners, il est bonne d'etre chez le Roi mais mieux d'etre chez *soit.*" She found herself next to Nelson.

On the night of August 5 the *Foudroyant* sailed from Naples. "Their is great preparations *for our return,*" she went on, "the Queen comes out with all Palermo to meet us, a landing place is made, Balls, Suppers, Illuminations, all ready; the Queen has prepared my cloaths; in short if I have fag'd I am more than repaid."

In short if they all had fagged they were all more than repaid.

CHAPTER FIVE

Discreditable Occupations

PALERMO WAS a beautiful place, but oh so hot in summer. The sun seemed fixed directly overhead all day. The wind, when it came, was hot from the oven of Africa, stirring the dust and fleas and whipping the clouds of flies into devils. The air was heavy with the spice of oranges, figs and pomegranates, jessamine, cassia and cloves, and the stench of ordure and corruption that lingered lovingly about palaces and hovels alike. If the days were unbearable, the nights closed down like the lid of a coffin with holes pierced for stars.

The city sat on the bay in a circle of mountains. The Saracens had built it in a square, the Normans cut a cross with two great streets, and the Sicilians filled up the four quarters with top-heavy houses that leaned toward each other, making tunnels of the sewer-alleys below. It was small, about a mile across, but nobody except the meanest beggars walked—that was a crime worse than adultery. The Sicilians were as proud as Spaniards. The dead were carried to the grave in sedan chairs; the living were dragged along in two-wheeled carriages by old and spavined horses, of that pathetic race of rheumy-eyed creatures, all skin and bone, that haunt the streets of southern cities.

The place was full of nuns. There were twenty-two nunneries, but they spilled out of those and filled up the houses, peering through windows and bursting out on balconies. All the girls in Palermo were brought up in the nunneries until they were marriageable, at the age of thirteen or fourteen; they were grandmothers by the time they were thirty, and retired to the nunneries.

There were some splendid buildings that formed a square where the two great streets crossed in the middle of the city, and the symmetry of the whole was enriched by the oddity of the parts, a Saracen cathedral, and a

Norman chapel. However, the most pleasant place was the Marina, the promenade between the city wall and the sea, where every night there was a concert which began at midnight and ended at two. During the day the Marina was deserted, except, of course, on great occasions, like the triumphant return of King Ferdinand on August 8, 1799.

"All Palermo is astir," wrote the Queen, "and hoping for this happy return, me more than anyone, to embrace you and thank you for all you have done. Oh how much, how much, my dear Emma, I have to say to you and about which you will answer. . . ." She was the first person aboard the *Foudroyant* and, after receiving the King's offhand embrace, she turned to Emma, raised her in her arms, and placed a gold chain carrying her portrait set with diamonds and inscribed *"Eterna Gratitudine"* on her shoulders.

All Palermo shouted and cheered as the royal party came ashore in Nelson's barge, and drove in procession to the cathedral to attend a *Te Deum,* that must have made the French knights lying there clank in their chain mail. That night and the next two nights the city was illuminated, showered with fireworks, and kept awake with the drums and bagpipes of impromptu processions.

In the Palazzo Palagonia it was like Christmas. The Queen sent Emma her picture and hair set with diamonds in a bracelet, earrings of pearl and diamonds, an aigrette of her cypher in diamonds, a complete dress of the finest point lace, baskets of gloves, "in short," as Sir William wrote his old friend Sir Joseph Banks, "just such a present as such a fine Woman as Emma, for except for being a little fatter she is as you saw her eight years ago, could desire." The King sent her "as fine a Medallion with His Picture set with Large Diamonds as is ever given to a foreign Minister."

Sir William got "a thumping yellow diamond set round with Diamonds in a ring." Every captain who had been in the Bay of Naples received a ring or snuffbox with the royal cypher or portrait. There were 2,300 ounces of silver to be divided among Nelson's servants and the crew of the *Foudroyant.* And Nelson?

On August 13 the Duke of Ascoli, one of the Gentlemen of the Bedchamber, brought him the King's own sword of gold with the hilt and blade set with diamonds; this sword, which Ferdinand had been given by Charles III as a token of his duty to defend his kingdom, was the one that Louis XIV gave his grandson Philip V on succeeding to the throne of Spain. It was a royal present. On the same day Prince Luzzi wrote to Nelson to inform him of his creation as Duke of Bronte, with an estate at the foot of Etna worth 18,000 ducats (£3,000) a year. This was more than royal, it was appropriate. Bronte was the cyclops who lived inside Etna, forging Jove's thunder. It was a munificent and gracious gift, the more so as the King, knowing Nelson had no children, allowed the reversion to go to any of his most distant relations.

Nelson offered Ferdinand his gratitude beyond words and, out of courtesy, began signing himself Bronte Nelson. He wrote to his father, offering him £500 a year from the estate, though, partly due to the mismanagement of John Graefer, whom he appointed agent, and partly due to his own sincere wish to make Bronte the happiest place on earth, he got no income from it for several years. He was a duke in Sicily, but not in England, and he had to wait an unconscionable time until January 1801 for George III to recognize the title. He tried to keep signing himself Nelson on official documents, but the Bronte kept creeping in.

"I find," wrote Acton, "with the usual and admirable way of thinking of your Lordship on the present events, and the necessity of forwarding the true and real Business that the *Fêtes* and rejoicings while the work is not *all* performed cannot suit your just manner of seeing things: you are certainly in the right. These rejoicings are an odd and pious ceremony used every year, to which the low people is much attached."

He was talking about the Feast of St. Rosalia. The preparations were occupying even the little time that the Court usually gave to business.

Nelson was concerned as usual with Malta and sent the *Foudroyant* to support Ball, hoisting his own flag on a transport in the bay. Later the King of Sardinia wanted to be taken back to Leghorn and the *Foudroyant* had to go and fetch him. And there was General Suwarrow, sitting on his *chaise percée* outside Genoa asking for ships, but the *Foudroyant* did not go there, because there were four Russian warships at Palermo which would not go anywhere.

In the palazzo they were all suffering from bilious attacks and the heat, and the glare of the sun got into Nelson's good eye and he complained of blindness, and on August 16 the Feast began.

Wooden arches, covered with flowers and lamps, were erected over the streets, and pyramids in the squares. There were horse races up and down the Corso, and firework displays in a different place each evening. Throughout the whole time, all day and most of the night, carriages and crowds crammed the streets, parading up and down, until everyone had greeted everyone else a dozen times. The Archbishop's palace, the Viceroy's palace, and the King's palace, all had their day, and the climax was reserved for the saint herself and her palace, the cathedral.

There was a huge triumphal car, seventy feet long, thirty wide and eighty feet high, that towered over the houses. The base was shaped like a galley, with bandstand on top, then a dome supported by columns and surmounted by a giant silver statue of St. Rosalia. This was dragged about by fifty-six mules, up and down, blocking the way, and crushing people good-humoredly together. On the fourth day it arrived at the cathedral, with everyone else in Palermo.

Inside the cathedral every inch of the stonework was covered with mirrors, 20,000 tapers were alight and glittering, reflected a myriad times, so that the people knew what it was like inside a diamond. During the service a great silver casket containing the bones of St. Rosalia was brought forward and carried in procession with the car and the people and the orchestras and choirs, around the square and back again, out of the torchlight and into the sparkling carapace of the cathedral. That was the Feast of St. Rosalia, and the city was, hopefully, safe for another year.

The Admiral did not give a damn for Rosalia. The affair with Emma kept him hanging about Palermo, stifling in the heat, and drained with what Sir William called, "great goings out and nothing coming in." His letters were full of excuses why he was obliged to stay; the King's minister had demanded it, he told Fanny. Indeed, he had to stay in the Mediterranean. Since Keith's departure, following the French fleet back to Brest, he was the senior officer, with a station stretching from Cadiz to Alexandria. But it was love that kept him lingering at Palermo.

Emma stayed, naturally, because she would lose her lord in London. And Sir William, well, he needed Emma more than ever.

"Sir William's health is very much broken," wrote Lock, "and his frame is so feeble that even a slight attack of bile, to severe fits of which he has lately been subject, may carry him off." The old Chevalier wrote to Banks on September 13, "I am nearly worn out . . . this thick air and sciroccos of Palermo do not agree with any of us, Lord Nelson, Emma and myself having been frequently attacked with bilious complaints, but from these attacks owing to my age I do not recover so soon as they do." He looked forward to next spring, "when alive or dead I shall come home, for at my first wife's particular desire I am to lye by her in Slebeck Church when I am dead and we shall roll soon together into Milford Haven for the sea is undermining that church very fast."

They were gloomily anticipating another fete to celebrate the anniversary of the arrival of the news of Nelson's victory at Naples on September 3. Dispatches arrived from S.S.S. reporting, with no little flourish, Bonaparte's retreat from Acre. "Adieu Mr. Bonaparte," wrote Nelson, and sent Smith his congratulations. The bay was suddenly filled with strange ships, and the alleys with baggy-trousered Turks and round-faced Russians, as England's allies arrived, in the wrong place as usual. Troubridge was writing from Naples, "Knavery and villainy is beginning to rear its head."

> Today *departed this Life Princes, Dukes, Commoners and Ladys,* to the amount of Eleven some by the *Axe* and others by the *halter,* I sincerely hope they will soon *finish,* on a *Great Scale,* and then pass an Act of Oblivion . . . *Death* is a *trifle* to the *Prisons.*

Troubridge was a marvelous friend, an honest man and a great captain. He did Nelson's dirty work with glee, and was really concerned about his chief. Nelson did him full justice with the Admiralty, but did not appreciate his advice. "I dread all the feasting &c. at Palermo," wrote Troubridge. "I am sure your health will suffer, if so all their Saints will be D——d by all here, I mean the Navy. . . . Everything gives way to their cursed pleasures, so trifling a Character as a Neapolitan I never before met with. . . . I have forwarded four large cases of Mineral water for Her Majesty, very necessary after so much Feasting."

Josiah was in trouble again, and Troubridge advised Nelson, "With great concern I learn Captain Nesbit has given great offence to the Austrian General at Leghorn by seizing one of his Privateers and breaking her up for fire wood . . . better to get Captain Nesbit to make some slight apology and some recompense. Complaints of this sort does a young Officer harm at the Admiralty." Josiah was ashore at Leghorn, reported to be sick, and the *Thalia* had gone off to Genoa without him. The matter must have been settled as no more was heard of it.

The *fête champêtre* of September 3 was the last and most splendid of the Court's tributes to Nelson and the Hamiltons. Nelson did not describe it himself, as he usually did when the occasion was in his honor, but sent a copy of Miss Knight's long and eloquent description to his brother Maurice to be inserted in the newspapers. It appeared in the *Times* on October 23, and did nothing but harm, as it gave a picture of an English admiral involved in a very un-English situation.

The scene was the garden of the royal palace at evening, lit with fairy lights. There was a select company of courtiers, foreign ministers and their suites, officers from the British, Turkish and Russian navies, and the principal nobility of Naples and Palermo. On arrival, they were greeted by the King and Queen and young Prince Leopold, who did the honors of the evening dressed in his midshipman's uniform. The three royal princesses and the Hereditary Princess were in white, with garlands of laurel on their heads and shoulders, and headbands embroidered "Long live the King and

Queen," which was rather charming. Nelson was wearing his new sword, Sir William his diamond, and Emma—she was wearing everything; the portraits, earrings, aigrette, bracelet, gloves, and, if she could have brought the basket they came in, doubtless she would have done so, because it was all out of gratitude to her friend and benefactress, Maria Carolina.

The entertainment began with a magnificent display of fireworks representing the battle of the Nile, and ending in the blowing up of the French flagship *L'Orient* and the burning of the tricolor. The Queen watched from a balcony with Emma and the Admiral, and Admirals Ouschakoff and Cadir Bey. "On this day," she said, "we received from dear Lady Hamilton intelligence of this great man's victory, which not only saved your country and ours, but all Europe." Cadir Bey, to whom this was addressed, seemed highly delighted.

The second part of the entertainment was the performance of a cantata.

> *Long live the British Hero!*
> *Long live great Nelson!*
> *It is he who drove far from us all affliction.*
> *It is he who gave peace to our troubled hearts.*

Then the guests partook of ices and sweetmeats in the garden to fortify themselves for the climax of the evening. Led by the royal party, they approached a part of the garden brighter than the rest. They passed between two pavilions, one dedicated to the English and Portuguese, the other to the Turks and Russians. Then before them they saw the most elegant Greek temple, magnificently illuminated. There was a flight of steps leading up to a vestibule supported by columns; and there in the vestibule were three figures, in wax and as large as life, Lord Nelson and Sir William and Lady Hamilton. The Admiral was in full dress, the Ambassador in the Windsor uniform, and her Ladyship in white with a blue shawl embroidered with the names of all the captains who took part in the battle.

Beyond the vestibule, inside the temple, there was an altar surmounted by the allegorical figure of Glory, and right in the middle, in a chariot, stood the figure of King Ferdinand, looking every bit as impressive as Ferdinand himself, who was advancing with the others to pay his respects to himself. Around the inside of the temple shone the inevitable words "Rule Britannia Britannia rules the waves."

At the steps of the temple the royal party paused and an orchestra played "God Save the King." Little Prince Leopold climbed up the steps and stood on tiptoe to place a laurel wreath on the figure of Nelson, and the orchestra played "Rule Britannia." Then there was an entirely unexpected incident. Nelson suddenly ran forward up the steps and knelt to kiss the Prince's hand, and the boy threw his arms around his neck and hugged and embraced him. There were tears.

He was so slight and haggard, with one arm and one good eye, and he had done so much for them, and he knelt before the boy. That one moment, which gave life to the wax and meaning to the meaningless adulation, was not recorded in the columns of the *Times*.

The company dispersed to wander in the gardens, where there were monuments to every captain, including Troubridge, and they retired at midnight.

In the first week of September the Russian Admiral was persuaded to take his squadron to Naples. The city was seething with rival factions. The nobles intrigued to regain their feudal authority, the *lazzaroni* kept their weapons and mastery of the streets, and the upright people of the center strove to engross the estates and positions of the fallen Republicans. The only hope of stability lay in a general pardon and the return of the Court, and King Ferdinand was too vindictive, fearful and self-indulgent to allow either to happen.

No sooner had the Russians gone than the Turks were involved in a desperate affray with the Palermitans. Ever since their arrival, the good citizens of Palermo had stared at them with the hatred of centuries and cheated and insulted them in the markets. The Turks had responded by swaggering through the streets in bands, monopolizing the brothels and offering their services to the Palermitan women wherever they met them. In the grueling heat it only needed a spark to ignite the atmosphere.

Lock reported:

> A little boy came up to a Turk who was bargaining at a stall and whipped his legs; the Turk was going to chastise him when he was prevented by a man who took the boy's part, on which the Turk drew a pistol out of his girdle and shot the man dead. The report was immediately spread that the Infidels were murdering the Christians, and they were attacked with sticks and stones wherever they were found; a hundred and twenty were killed and eighty desperately wounded, amongst them the Turkish Admiral's nephew; fifteen of the Palermitans fell in this massacre and a number were wounded.

The Turks retired to their ships and turned their guns toward the city. The *Times* report (December 9) accused Lady Hamilton of interfering and procuring a free pardon for the Turk who fired the first shot, thus aggravating the riot. As Lock does not mention this, and he would not have missed the chance, it is an example of the acceptance of any story that served to vilify her.

Lock continued:

> A Council was held at which the Russian minister Italinsky assisted. Italinsky proposed to execute upon the Marina in sight of the fleet, ten of the condemned Jacobins, who the Turks would believe were some of the murderers—a most sensible proposition, but it was rejected, from a prejudice one should have thought had not existed at the close of the eighteenth century, because it should not be said that a Christian life had been sacrificed for that of a Turk. The Admiral with his fleet got under weigh next morning for Constantinople, in a great rage, vowing he would sink the first Neapolitan vessel he met.

Cadir Bey was the victim rather than the villain, because a mutiny broke out which he overcame with difficulty, and even then two of his frigates refused to obey his orders. When last seen, these two frigates were off the south of Italy being pursued by the rest of the Turkish fleet.

In the third week of September Nelson received a large packet of letters from the Admiralty. They were dated around August 20, and included the official notification that he was now senior officer (not Commander in Chief because St. Vincent kept the title though he was in England). Lord Spencer wrote that the recapture of Naples had pleased everybody, and that Troubridge was now Sir Thomas, a baronet for his efforts; he hinted gently that Nelson was "at liberty to attend to some other points where the assistance of the fleet will probably be very essential to the cause of His Majesty and his allies."

The letter that Nelson had been anticipating since his disobedience to Keith's orders was there too. "Their Lordships by no means approve of the Seamen being landed to form a part of an army to be employed in operations at a distance from the coast . . . there was no justification for disobeying orders and leaving Minorca unprotected."

Under the circumstances this was a mild censure. "I suppose that the mentioned disaprobations are a formal system relative to the disciplinary methods," was Acton's comment. But Nelson was depressed into gloomy forebodings, broken by angry outbursts. He wrote Davison:

> Ah my dear friend, if I have a morsel of bread and cheese in comfort, it is all I ask of kind heaven, until I reach the Estate

of 6 feet by 2, which I am fast approaching. I had the full tide of honor but little real comfort. If the war goes on I shall be knocked off by a Ball or killed with *Chagrin*, my conduct is measured by the Admiralty by the narrow rule of Law, when I think it should have been done by that of Common Sence. I restored a faithful ally by breach of Orders. Lord Keith lost a fleet by obedience, against his own sence, yet as one is censored, the other must be approved, such things are.

"To serve my King," he wrote the Duke of Clarence, an old acquaintance who became king himself as William IV, "and to destroy the French I consider as the great order of all, from which the little ones spring; and if one of these little ones militate against it (for who can tell exactly at a distance) I go back to obey the order and object, to *down down* with the damned French villains."

Gloom pervaded the palazzo. Fanny heard that her husband hoped to rub through the winter. He never set foot outside his writing room, except now and then in an evening with Sir William and Lady Hamilton to the palace. Sir William told Lord Minto that he would not be surprised to end his career at Palermo—Minto was continuing his as Ambassador at Vienna. "The Queen of Naples is also ill and worn out, talking of dying, and what is more extraordinary Emma who looks as well and as blooming as ever talks of death every day. I believe it is the heat and scirocco winds that depress us all for Lord Nelson complains too."

Even the news that Troubridge had captured Rome failed to raise their spirits. This event, unique in British naval history, came about after Sir Thomas had sailed to Civita Vecchia on September 7 to negotiate the surrender of the French garrison there. He found himself talking to General Garnier, who commanded both the garrisons at the seaport and at Rome. Neapolitan troops were already on the outskirts of Rome and the Austrians were marching to take possession from the north. On September 26 Garnier signed the capitulation of both places. The Neapolitans occupied the city, and the Austrian general was so furious that he attacked the French troops as they marched toward Civita Vecchia to be embarked for Toulon. Nearly all the treasures stolen from Naples were recovered. There was one shadow on Troubridge's quarter-deck, the elongated and tremulous one of General Naselli, come to command at Rome. "The Court has nobody better," said Nelson, "you may think they can have nobody worse."

Of course, opinions of people are shaped by prejudice. For example, Charles Greville wrote to Sir William about Emma, "I spoke to many and all admire her conduct, and the Prince of Wales particularly, of his own accord, told me that after the Queen of Naples' account of Ly H conduct to her, she might be assured that all would be made pleasing to her when she arrived again in England." And the Duchess of Leinster wrote about Emma, "This Lady Hamilton was a Dolly Sir William Hamilton married, and had she been nothing worse it would not have signified, but she is artful, malicious, envious and detracting; has every bad quality and more spiteful to my Cissy than can be conceived." Her Cissy was Cecilia Lock.

By the same mark, Miss Knight wrote, "Admiral Nelson is little, and not remarkable in his person either way; but he has great animation of countenance, and activity in his appearance: his manners are unaffectedly simple and modest." Whereas Lord Elgin's opinion was, "He looks very old, has lost his upper teeth, sees ill of one eye, and has a film coming over both of them. He has pains pretty constantly from his late wound in the head. His figure is mean, and in general his countenance is without animation."

The Elgins stayed at Palermo on their way to Constantinople, where Lord Elgin was going as Ambassador, in October 1799. Lady Elgin had made up her mind before she arrived: "They say there never was a man turned so *vainglorious* (that's the phrase) in the world as Lord Nelson. He is now completely managed by Lady Hamilton."

When she did arrive, and Emma pressed her to accept an apartment in the palazzo, she did not have the least scruple (her words) in refusing. She could hardly refuse to dine with the Hamiltons. "She looked very handsome at dinner, quite in an undress;—my Father would say, 'There is a fine Woman for you, good flesh and blood.' She is indeed a Whapper! and I think her manner very vulgar. It is really humiliating to see Lord Nelson, he seems quite dying and yet as if he had no other thought than her. He told Elgin privately that he had lived a year in the house with her and that her beauty was nothing in comparison to the goodness of her heart."

Nothing escaped Lady Elgin, even Mrs. Cadogan was spotted and pinned down as "the housekeeper in a white bed gown and black petticoat." In fact, Emma's mother, *La Signora Madre dell'Ambasciatrice*, was very much more than the housekeeper. She was well known at Palermo, had her own rooms in the palazzo and dined with the family. On great occasions, like the visit of Lady Elgin, she retired to her apartment, where she entertained the friends she preferred instead of those she was obliged to see.

But they were all butterflies in the Elgin collection. "Sir William," said Emma one morning, "we shall not go to the country today, you must dress yourself and go to Court after breakfast." "Why?" "Oh I will tell you presently." And at Court: "You never saw anything equal the fuss the Queen made with Lady Hamilton, and Lord Nelson wherever she moved was always by her side. . . . I never never saw three people made such thorough dupes of as Lady Hamilton, Sir William and Lord Nelson."

Emma had her revenge. They were going to Court one day. "Lady Hamilton told me the evening before, that she should go quite in a common morning dress and that nobody would think of dressing till afterwards, instead of which, when I arrived I found her in a fine gold and coloured silk worked gown and diamonds; the Queen and Princesses in fine dresses with pearls and diamonds. . . . I find it is a constant trick of Lady Hamilton to make everybody she can go undressed." But Lady Elgin won in the end. "I was introduced to Mrs. Lock. She has almost quite lost her affectation. I took her up and left Lady Hamilton."

While the Elgins were at Palermo, Nelson went to sea. "At the Queen's ball," said Lady Elgin, "I heard people laying bets that he would not go." The *Foudroyant* had been away taking Charles Emmanuel, King of Sardinia, back to Leghorn. Hardy brought her back on October 4 and Nelson sailed the next day for Gibraltar. There were reports of an enemy fleet off the coast of Portugal and of a squadron of supply ships at sea bound from Toulon to Malta. The Admiral was also hoping to persuade General Erskine, commanding the troops at Minorca, to send some regiments to Malta to break the interminable deadlock there.

"You cannot conceive how melancholy we are without you," wrote Sir William, "And we dare say you are not very merry—but we are going to the Colli to try a change of air." The Elgins were leaving. "Lord Elgin was here this morning and told me he intended to sail tonight for Constantinople. His Excy. does not appear to me to be so wise and have so much penetration as I was made to expect and I find his scavants and followers are not very fond of him." So much for the collector of marbles. Naturally, Lady Elgin had the last word. "We dined at Sir William's yesterday and only think of Elgin being so scandalous as to drink 'Lord Nelson' upon which my Lady actually GREETED. For she loves him better than a brother!"

The Colli was a mountainous wooded district west of Palermo, where the King had his country house, kept his cows and made butter *a l'Inglese*. The Queen had her retreat at Bagaiva the other side of the city, but she provided the accommodation: "Not to Lady Hamilton but to my dear friend Emma, the house of Verdura at Colli is at your service." If that was not suitable, "there is one quite close to the casino of the King, if I were there, I should entreat you to take it, that we might see one another continually—I wish we were nearer each other, for you are my friend in every thing, affairs of state, politicks, and the Heart."

On the way to Gibraltar the *Foudroyant* fell in with the *Bulldog*, bringing Sir Edward Berry from England to replace Hardy. Nelson learned that the ships reported off Portugal had put into Ferrol, and, sadly, that one of his young nephews coming out in the *Bulldog* as a midshipman had died on the voyage. He turned for Minorca.

Off Port Mahon on October 14 he found the *Thalia*; Josiah, true to form, had quarreled with one of his officers. Nelson, perplexed and sorrowful, sent him down to Duckworth. "I wish I could say anything in her praise inside or out," he wrote about the ship, "you will receive an order for holding a court martial on the Lieutenant of Marines, perhaps you will be able to make something of Capt. Nisbet, he has by his conduct almost broke my heart." He added later, "There are two women in the *Thalia*'s Gun Room who do no good and I wish were out of her, excuse my plaguing you with this, but I cannot help being interested for this young man and my wish is only that he would let me be kind to him."

Nelson stayed at Port Mahon four days, trying without success to talk General Sir James St. Clair Erskine into parting with some troops for Malta. The General was polite but immovable. He had no orders, he was about to be relieved by General Fox, he would not allow even the garrison of Messina to go to Malta. *"Is His Majesty's Service to stand still for an instant?"* cried Nelson. Yes, said the General, taking a page or two to say so.

"Emma is tired of the Colli," wrote Sir William after a week in the country, "and we come back to Palermo tomorrow—for God's sake come back as soon as you can." He wrote again on October 19, "Your appartment is clean and prepared and we are all with open arms ready to receive you at the Mole." He was writing to his wife's lover—what matter? He was writing to his friend.

Sir William had been an amateur, which then meant an enthusiast, at love affairs. Could he have seen less than Consul Lock or Lady Elgin? It is likely he saw more. Emma had come to him from Charles Greville for her own good, and as a token of friendship. Why then should she not go to Nelson for the same reasons? Because she was his wife and not his mistress. But Sir William knew, and said as much, when he married her, that when he was old she would be in full bloom. What extraordinary luck that she was in love with the man he loved!

There is no other answer that does not rely on one of two very doubtful propositions: either that everyone who saw them, friend and enemy, told lies and they were not in love; or they told the truth, and Sir William was so old and stupid that he did not see what was obvious to everyone else.

To be in love does not necessarily mean to be in bed; though for a man of forty-one and a woman of thirty-four it would be surprising if the idea had not occurred to them. But Nelson's life was devoted to the principle that the thought was the action. "I am fitter by far," he said, "to do the thing than describe it." And Emma never had a thought that was not immediately expressed physically. To deny that these two hearts grappled each other is to drain them of life and blood.

Nelson was with the Hamiltons on the evening of October 22. He told Lord Minto on the 24th, "We are the real tria juncta in uno."

The Admiral's sea trip did nothing to alleviate his gloom. On the contrary, his lack of success seemed to impress him with the feeling that he was unappreciated, even persecuted. He wrote Fanny on November 7.

> My task here is still arduous for I cannot get the General at Minorca to give me some troops for the service of Malta and I have not force enough to attack it. This and other things have half broke my heart but I trust that one day or other, I shall rest from all my labours. I still find it good to serve near home. There a man's fag and services are easily seen. Next to that is writing a famous account of your own actions. [He is referring to S.S.S.] I could not do justice to those of my friends who rescued the Kingdom of Naples from the French and therefore Parliament does not think of them.
>
> I have just received from the Grand Signor a diamond star with a crescent in the centre which I wear above that of the Bath. But these jewels give not money meat or drink and from the various circumstances of my having much more expenses than any commander in chief without any one profit it has been a heavy money campaign to me. I will mention the circumstance to Lord Spencer but I doubt if he will do anything for me. I trust the war will very soon be over.

The star was Nelson's reward for his kindness to Hadji Osman on June 19. It was designed by Spencer Smith in Constantinople, who suggested that it might serve as the insignia of a new order. "I have called myself first Knight of the Order of the Crescent," Nelson told Ball.

Stars and medals fascinated Bronte Nelson. It was as if he wanted to have his victories about him, not from any lack of self-confidence, but as a sort of trademark, like Napoleon's gray coat, or Wellington's plain cocked hat. They were immediately distinguishable among the glittering uniforms of their officers: Nelson glittered among the plain uniforms of his.

Diamonds had little attraction for him. When the island of Zante sent him a sword and cane, apologizing that they could not find enough diamonds in Zante to make more than one band of them around the cane, he answered that the letter and sentiments accompanying the present were "valuable ten thousand times more than any gold and diamonds."

He wanted an order for Emma and solicited first Sir Charles Whitworth, the British Ambassador at St. Petersburg, and then the Emperor Paul himself, for the Order of Malta for her and for Ball. Ball's claim was sound, he had been there over a year and ruled the island. Emma's was dubious, but she had entertained a party of deputies who came to beg for food for their compatriots, and persuaded the Queen to part with 7,000 ounces of her own. Nelson begged, almost on his knees, for money for the islanders on his return to Palermo. The crisis at Malta came at the end of the year.

Nelson's expenses were the subject of considerable scandal. Mr. Rushout was one of the tribe of society gossips who could make a pound of lies out of half an ounce of truth. This gentleman reminisced, "Nelson and the Hamiltons all lived together in a house of which he bore the expense, which was enormous, and where every sort of gaming went on half the night. Nelson used to sit with large parcels of gold before him and generally go to sleep, Lady Hamilton taking from the heap without counting and playing with his money to the amount of 500£ a night. Her rage is play, and Sir William says when he is dead she will be a beggar. However, she has about 30,000£ worth of diamonds from the royal family in presents. She sits at the Councils and rules everything and everybody."

The tissue of lies may be removed. Nelson did not pay for the house, Sir William did. There were no large parcels of gold, for where would they have come from? Lady Hamilton did not count the money and yet played for £500 a night. The inference is that she lost regularly, in which event Nelson would have been ruined in a week. The total value of her diamonds, when she told them, was enough to furnish a house. Nelson reckoned the cost between 3,000 and 4,000 pounds. Lady H. never sat on a Council and ruled nobody and nothing. What is left? Oh yes—they played cards half the night.

Troubridge was worried. He had come to Palermo via Port Mahon in November with the news that General Fox had at last arrived and had given permission for the two regiments at Messina to go to Malta. Nelson gave him the job of taking them there. On December 5 Troubridge was at Messina grumbling, "The people here are the most imposing villains you ever knew; *beat Palermo and Naples,* they have added 200 per cent on all articles since we arrived—so much for serving Vagabonds." He worked furiously, and five days later the regiments, now commanded by General Graham, landed on Malta. On December 15 he wrote Nelson a letter which no one but him would have dared write.

> I see by your lordship's last letter your Eyes are bad, I beseech, I intreat you do not keep such horrid hours, you will destroy your constitution. Lady Hamilton is accustomed to it for years, but I saw the bad effects of it in her the other day, she could not keep her eyes open, yawning and uncomfortable all day; the multiplicity of business which your lordship has to perform must with the total want of rest destroy you, pardon me my Lord it is my sincere esteem for you that makes me mention it: I know you can have no pleasure sitting up all night at Cards why then sacrifice your health, comfort, purse, ease, everything to the Customs of a Country where your stay cannot be long, I again beg pardon. If you knew my feelings you would I am sure not be displeased with me.

He even prevailed on Ball to add his voice to the campaign to save Nelson. "I feel infinite concern that your Grace has a complaint in your Eye—I am afraid Sir William's late hours do not agree with it. I shall lay the fault to her Ladyship, because if she were to go to bed early, Sir William would soon follow." This was a bit naïve. The picture was not of Nelson and Sir William waiting for Emma to go to bed, but of Nelson and Emma waiting for Sir William to go to bed.

Nelson ignored the advice, but answered on the 22nd that he was undergoing a course of electricity to improve the sight of his good eye and restore that of his blind one.

Troubridge was quick to reply:

> I trust and hope the Electrifying will restore your sight, pray keep good hours, if you knew what your Friends feel for you I am sure you would cut all *Nocturnal* partys, the gambling of the people at Palermo is publickly talked of every where. I beseech your Lordship leave off, I wish my pen could tell you my feelings I am sure you would oblige me. Lady H—— Character will suffer, nothing can prevent people from talking, a gambling Woman in the Eye of an Englishman is lost, to say they can leave it off when they

Lord Nelson, by Sir William Beechey

Reverend Edmund Nelson, by Sir William Beechey

Lady Nelson, by R. Cosway

A COGNOCENTI contemplating ỹ Beauties of ỹ Antique.

Sir William Hamilton, by an unknown artist
Reproduced by permission of the Trustees of the National Portrait Gallery

Lady Hamilton at Dresden, by J. H. Schmidt

Maria Carolina,
Queen of Naples:
a miniature by
an unknown artist

Ferdinand,
King of Naples:
a miniature by
an unknown artist

Lady Hamilton
as Thalia:
an engraving from
a portrait by
Angelica Kauffmann
*Reproduced by permission of
the Trustees of the
National Maritime Museum*

Lady Hamilton
at Prayer,
by George Romney
*Reproduced by permission of
the Greater London Council,
Trustee of the
Iveagh Bequest, Kenwood*

Lady Hamilton, by George Romney

Lady Hamilton as a Vestal,
after Romney

A LYONESS.

Lady Hamilton as a Lyoness:
a caricature by J. Gillray

Horatia Nelson: a drawing by Baxter

Lady Hamilton and [?]
later Lady [?]

Lady Hamilton in an
"attitude" — (? by Flaxman)

SKETCHES MADE AT MERTON BY BAXTER

OPPOSITE PAGE, TOP: Merton After the Improvements; OPPOSITE PAGE, BOTTOM: *Upper left,* Lady Hamilton; *upper right,* Lady Hamilton and Charlotte; *lower left,* Horatia; *lower right,* Lady Hamilton in an Attitude.

THIS PAGE: Frequent visitors at Merton were Nelson's relatives the Matchams, the William Nelsons and the Boltons, Nelson's niece Charlotte and Emma's cousins the Connors, two of whom acted as governesses for Mrs. Cadogan and Horatia. *Top sketch,* Lady Hamilton and one of the girls; *center left,* a group with Lady Hamilton and Nelson's young nephew Horace, who was designed by Nelson to marry Horatia if both survived, but who died early; *center right,* Lady Charlotte before her marriage; *lower sketch,* Lady Hamilton, Charlotte, Horace, the Matcham or Bolton girls and perhaps one of the Connors, around Nelson's table at Merton, playing cards.

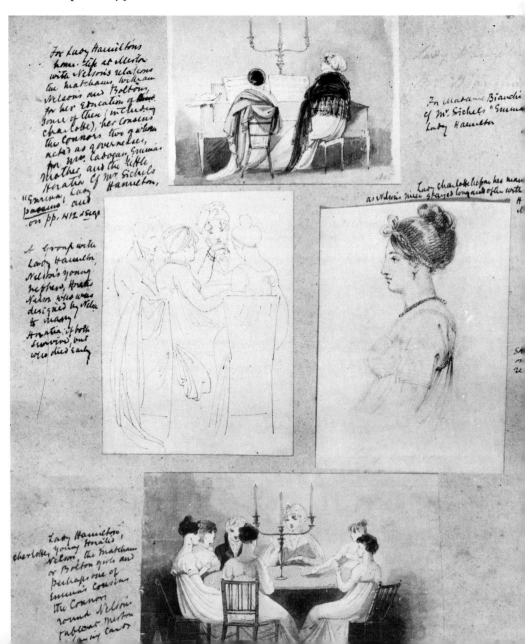

ABOVE: Nelson Falling at Trafalgar, by D. Dighton

LEFT: The Battle of Trafalgar, by G. Chambers after Stanfield

Lord Nelson:
a drawing by
L. F. Abbott

Jack and Poll at Portsmouth
After the
Battle of Trafalgar:
an engraving by Argus

please, might amuse a School Boy, but people who has seen the World know better, you will be surprized when I tell you I hear in all Companys the sums won and lost on a Card in Sir Wm's house, it furnishes matter for a letter constantly, both to Minorca, Naples, Messina &c. &c. and finally in England. I trust your Lordship will pardon me.

Now this was plain speaking with a vengeance. The warning was clear and they heard it. The card parties were stopped. On January 14, 1800, Sir Thomas thanked Emma. "I am duly favoured with your Ladyship's letter of the 8th inst, and feel most completely happy at your promise to play no more. Be assured I have not written to you from any impertinent interference, but from a wish to warn you of the ideas that were going about, which you could not hear of, as no person can be indifferent to the construction put on things which may appear to your Ladyship innocent, and I make no doubt done with the best intentions—still your enemies will, and do give things a different colouring." Was he just talking about cards?

The burden of running the Mediterranean with a few ships weighed Nelson down. Apart from Malta, which hung around his neck like a millstone, he had to think of keeping the French army in Egypt, of assisting the blockade of Genoa and the defense of Minorca, of protecting the trade from the pirates of North Africa and the privateers of Cadiz—over and above the self-imposed task of Councillor and Secretary of State of the Kingdom of the Two Sicilies. He was not, remember, Commander in Chief, and this irked him no end. When he received a severe set-down from the Admiralty for not writing by a particular ship sent to England, he protested that he had written to them twice that day the ship sailed. "Do not let my dear Lord," he begged Spencer, "let the Admiralty write harshly to me; my generous soul cannot bear it, being conscious it is entirely unmerited." He confided to Duckworth, "The Admiralty wish to show I am unfit for this command."

Nelson hated to be put in the wrong. He longed to be recognized for what he knew he was. This is why the blatant flattery and adulation of the Neapolitans, including the Hamiltons, never revolted him. Later in his life, after his second great victory, he seemed to mature and gain confidence in this respect. At this time, however, when he felt he was being belittled, he either resorted to specious pleading, or lashed out in scarcely controlled rage.

Early in November 1799 the Admiral heard that Mr. Lock was boasting that the Victualing Board had thanked him for saving the government 40 per cent on the purchase of fresh beef in Naples. Without pausing to consider what he already knew, that Lock was quite capable of speaking without thinking himself, Nelson dashed off a letter to the Board.

"If it is true, which I cannot believe, that you have wrote Mr. Lock any Letters on the subject, I desire to say, and not to be misunderstood, that the conduct of the Board is very reprehensible and Scandalous in its treatment to me, the Commanding Officer of H.M's Fleet in the Mediterranean." This was bad enough, but he went on, "I defy any insinuation against my honor, Nelson is as far from doing a scandalous or mean action as the Heavens are above the Earth." And he accused Lock of being malicious and scandalous and wanting the monopoly of supplying the fleet. He sent a copy of the letter to Lock. Hardy, who was going home overland, was ordered to take the matter up with the board on his arrival.

On November 30 Lock replied sensibly enough that he had received no official letters respecting the victualing of the fleet, but he could not let Nelson alone. A few days later he bragged that he had received private letters saying the board was grateful to him; this was followed by an assertion that he considered himself wholly independent of Nelson's authority in his civil capacity of Consul; and then he wrote accusing Nelson of making false statements to the Board.

Once again Lock had gone too far. Nelson replied that he was sending the whole correspondence to the Admiralty, "that they may either support the dignity of the Admiral they have entrusted with the Command of the Mediterranean Fleet, or remove him." The Consul hurried to the palazzo to see Sir William and found him with the Admiral. "As I have resolved," said Nelson, "to quit the Service should the Lords of the Admiralty reflect so far upon me as to deem your conduct not worthy of condemnation, so in *justice* shall I insist upon no less a mark of their disapprobation of you than the privation of your office."

Sir William intervened, and prevailed upon Lock to write an apology, and upon Nelson to accept the roundabout apology that Lock wrote.

The Consul wrote home:

> We shook hands, and have since dined at Sir William's, at whose house Lord Nelson when on shore always lives and indeed discharges three fourths of the expenses, and they have dined with me. Lady Hamilton has taken the whole credit of this reconciliation. She has informed all Palermo that my submissions, aided by her entreaties, have averted Lord Nelson's anger and my ruin.

Eventually, Hardy confirmed that the Victualing Board had not written to Lock, and the board rebuked Nelson for the tone of his letter. This was really a trifling matter, but Lock, who reckoned he was £4,000 out of pocket through Nelson's animosity and had lost the chance of being chargé d'affaires through Lady Hamilton's malice, continued his campaign of denigration with a flow of half-truths and false accusations. He was lately championing the cause of the Maltese. "They have expended their all in maintaining the struggle for their freedom and they are now suffered to starve."

Who was suffering them to starve? Not Nelson. Not Troubridge. It was the short-sighted decision of the British Cabinet to give the island back to the Order, which meant to Russia, that alienated the Court of the Two Sicilies and made it practically impossible to procure supplies for the Maltese.

There were some 200,000 inhabitants on the island; 30,000 of them lived in La Valetta, where the French garrison of between 6,000 and 7,000 men were holding out in the citadel. The harvest of 1799 was poor, it was the same all over Europe, there was a serious shortage of grain in every country. In Malta, which in good times depended on Sicily for its supplies, the effect was disastrous. Not only did their own crop fail, but the Court banned the export of grain from Sicily and refused money to purchase supplies elsewhere.

On December 23 Troubridge begged Nelson to have the order banning exports from Sicily lifted. "I beseech your lordship press them for a *yes* or *no* the crys of hunger are now too great to admit of the common evasive answers usually given by the Sicilian Government." A week later he wrote again. "We are *dying off* fast for want. I learn by letters from Messina that Sir Willm. Hamilton says Prince Luzzi refused corn some time ago and he does not think it *worth while* making *another application*. If this is the case, I wish he commanded at the distressing scene instead of me."

He saw a plot and had his own idea who was behind it. "I foresee much mischief brewing, *trust not the Court of Palermo particularly the female part*." It was the end of the year, the end of the century. "Many happy returns of the day to you, I never spent so miserable a one, I am not *very tender* hearted, but really the distress here would if he could see it move a Neapolitan."

By January 5 the situation was desperate. Sir Thomas stripped his ships of provisions. "I have this day saved 30,000 people from dying, but with this day my ability ceases, as the King of Naples or rather the Queen and her party are bent on starving us." There was grain at Girgenti, a port in the south of Sicily, and he had scraped together money to pay for it, but the Governor refused to allow it to be sold. "Such is the fever in my brain this minute *that I assure you on my Honor* if the Palermo traitors was here I would shoot them first and then myself."

He wrote again that day, "200,000 people will not quietly starve." He expected the Maltese to approach the French General Vaubois and beg for bread. "I have taken some strong measures if they do not succeed the game is up. . . . I trust your lordship will bear me out of this scrape." He had sent a sloop to Girgenti with money on board to buy grain. If the Governor again refused his permission, the captain was to seize enough grain to meet the immediate need. *"Hunger knows no Law."*

Two vessels carrying grain were taken out of Girgenti, with the Governor protesting but no violence. On January 8 Nelson ordered Troubridge to do what had already been done, so taking the onus of responsibility on himself. The Admiral was no less concerned than his Commodore, he was prepared to pledge Bronte for money, and to press Sir William formally and with success to draw £4,540 on his own risk, in order to alleviate the distress at Malta. Nelson's problem was his involvement with the Court. "I really think it dangerous at present to trust the Queen," Troubridge advised. "Women never could keep a secret or ever should be trusted with one."

It was too late for secrets. On November 14 the *Times* printed the first public reference to the relationship between Nelson and Emma Hamilton.

> Lord Keith is going out immediately to take the command in the Mediterranean. Upon his Lordship's arrival, Lord Nelson will return to England.

Perfidium ridens Venus & Cupido!

> These perfidious Gods have in all time spread their smiling snares for the first of mankind. Heroes and Conquerors are subdued in their turn. Mark Anthony followed Cleopatra *into the Nile,* when he should have fought with Octavius! and laid down his laurels and his power, to sail down the *Cyndnus* with her in the dress, the character and the *attitudes* of Venus. What will not the eye effect in the bosom of a Hero?

No reader would have missed the association of the attitudes. They turned up again on November 28. "By a false point in one of the morning Papers, the admirable attitudes of Lady HAM-T-N are called *Admiral-attitudes*."

Nelson, who had to endure a ton of this heavy raillery from what Cobbett called "the leaden prints," was upset. Acton tried to reassure him: "You cannot my lord enjoy the praises and honourable rewards in the esteem of every nation and of all belovers of glory without being exposed to these necessary consequences of base detraction from miserable and envious a party." But Nelson was as much upset by the news that Keith was returning as Commander in Chief as he was by the bad pun.

A few weeks after the Admiralty decided to send Keith to supersede Nelson, Lord Grenville wrote in vague terms to Sir William, "Your long and faithful service, and particularly your conduct at the difficult close of it have unquestionably well intitled you to His Majesty's favor on your retreat, and I have His Majesty's gracious permission to assure you of it." The Secretary of State failed to add that Arthur Paget, Lord Uxbridge's young son, was being appointed Ambassador in Sir William's place. The old Chevalier had to read that in a newspaper! However, Lord Grenville was particularly occupied that winter.

In October General Bonaparte was welcomed in France as if he had won an empire instead of having lost an army. "God knows," said Nelson, "I thought he must have *Bit the Dust* in Egypt long ago." On November 9 the Directory was swept away, leaving nothing behind but a nice line in furniture and fashion. Shortly afterward the General appeared in his civil capacity as First Consul offering peace, and Grenville had the task of finding reasons to reject the offer without binding the government to the principle of the restoration of the Bourbons, or apparently any principle for the continuation of the war. He resorted to the abuse of Bonaparte, which was not difficult, but which ended the chance of making peace on the most favorable terms that had existed since the beginning of the war.

Lord Keith was at Gibraltar on December 6, 1799. He found the *Thalia* there. The court-martial had not been held, because Duckworth's squadron had been called away to watch the enemy in Ferrol, and he sent Josiah to Minorca for it to be conducted by Captain Louis. Keith, as Commander in Chief, ordered Nelson to put himself under his command, and sent him on his letters from England.

There was one of Fanny's fortnightly chatty epistles, and she was talking about leaving England for the winter, indeed her physician had ordered her to Lisbon. "Whatever any physicians may say about Lisbon," answered her husband, "I can have no idea that the most dirty place in Europe covered with fog can be ever wholesome; to old débauchés who must lead a more regular life from the want of any decent society, it may be of benefit on that account, but I will answer on no other. . . . I shall never go to Lisbon for if I can get that far, Portsmouth will be the place to find me."

He expanded his ideas about Bronte and described his position as the Duke: "I am absolute in church and state." Josiah was expected. "I hope he will yet make a good man, his abilities are equal to any thing, he was too much spoilt by me in his younger days." In fact he had received encouraging reports about the boy from Duckworth and the Commissioner at Gibraltar. The letter ended sharply: "Lady Hamilton has never received from you the scrap of a pen or any prints." Poor Fanny, she was wrapped up in two suits of flannel to keep out the cold, but nothing could keep out the coldness of his tone.

On January 16 Nelson sailed from Palermo to Leghorn to pay his respects to Keith. He had no small vessel with him so there were no letters back to Palermo. Josiah was at Leghorn, the court-martial over and the marine lieutenant gone, but he was in trouble again for having broken the quarantine regulations on entering the port. Nelson's name still protected him and Keith wrote, "Now my good lord for God's sake let the young man write a letter of apology to the Grand Duke (His Senate) because you know if it comes to me in form what must be done and it may end ill for him." Never did an officer get away with so much as Josiah.

"Lord Nelson is arrived," Keith told his sister, "I am much employed. Of course he brings me no news." While it annoyed Nelson, Keith's return took the whole burden of the Mediterranean off his shoulders. Though he complained, he brightened up perceptibly, particularly when he was kept a mere five days at Leghorn, and on January 25 the *Foudroyant* in company with Keith's flagship, the *Queen Charlotte*, sailed back again to Palermo.

Sir William was feeling better too. Riding and asses' milk, with occasionally a little bark and rhubarb, had cured his diarrhea and he was putting on a little flesh. "I must own," he wrote Greville, "that I am a little tired of keeping open house so long as I have, and which I realy could not do without Emma's doing the honors so well as she does, yet I must own that I have made some very valuable acquaintances among the officers of the fleet." He was about to make another, though he could not appreciate the value of Lord Keith.

The warships anchored in the Bay of Palermo on February 3. Nelson was anxious to get ashore and sent Tom Allen to the palazzo with a note. "Having a Commander in Chief I cannot come on shore till I have made my *manners* to him, times are changed, but if he does not come on shore directly I will not wait." Keith did go on shore and put up at the Hamiltons', and made up his mind he was not going to like it. His sister heard, "Notwithstanding every attention this life does not suit me. Business and pleasure go ill together." That was on the first evening!

One of the things that annoyed him was that all communications with the Court, invitations and arrangements, naturally went through Lady Hamilton, and she was far more concerned with getting the royal family on board the Queen Charlotte for dinner, and entertaining the C. in C. with balls and operas, than with business. It was only Lock who accused her of engrossing the business of the embassy, whereas she really engrossed the pleasures. She was doing her best.

"I was sick of Palermo and all its alurements," Keith wrote later, "and much as I was made up to (their hours are beyond belief) I went to bed at ten, and never entered a door but the Palace and men in office—of course you may guess the reflection!" And again: "The whole was a scene of fulsome Vanity and Absurdity all the *long* eight days I was at Palermo." For all his early nights, he achieved very little there. King Ferdinand promised to send some troops to Malta and that was all. However, everyone who came from England had heard so much of the blandishments of Palermo that they were determined not to enjoy them.

Keith sailed for Malta on February 12, taking Nelson with him. The hero was not happy to be going; his commander told him nothing, not even that he was sending a boat ashore. "I feel all," Emma read, "and notwithstanding my desire to be as humble as the lowest midshipman, perhaps, I cannot submit to be much lower, I am used to have attention paid me from his superiors." When Keith did tell him something, it was not intended to please him: "Palermo being in a remote corner, I have ordered Syracuse, in future, to be the rendezvous of the ships &c. employed in the blockade of Malta."

Six days out of Palermo, and off Cape Passaro, Nelson's squadron ran in with an enemy squadron bent on reaching La Valetta. The *Foudroyant* chased the French flagship. In his cabin Nelson wrote Emma, "I feel anxious to get up with these ships and shall be unhappy not to take them myself, for first my greatest happiness is to serve my gracious King and Country, and I am envious only of glory; for if it be a sin to covet glory I am the most offending soul alive. *But here I am* in a heavy sea and thick fog—Oh God the wind subsided—but I trust to Providence I shall have them. 18th in the evening. I have got her—*Le Genereux*—thank God. Twelve out of thirteen, only the *Guillaume Tell* remaining; I am after the others." He had *Le Généreux* and a large storeship. *Guillaume Tell*, the last of the French fleet at the battle of the Nile was still safe at La Valetta.

Nelson went on board the Queen Charlotte to report his success, and described his reception to Emma. "Had you seen the Peer receive me I know not what you would have done, but I can guess. But never mind. I told him that I had made a vow if I took the *Genereux* by myself it was my intention to strike my Flag, to which he made no answer." Keith's stony silence was caused by his anger that Nelson had chased off without orders, and even more anger that he had captured the prize. In his dispatch he congratulated Nelson on his skill in comprehending his signals. "Lord Keith received my account and myself like a philosopher (but very unlike you)," Nelson told Sir William, "it did not, that I could perceive, cause a pleasing muscle in his face."

On February 24 Keith left his unpleasing subordinate at Malta, in charge of the blockade, and sailed north again for Genoa. The city was now besieged by the Austrians alone, as the two Emperors had quarreled and Paul of Russia had withdrawn his army, General Suwarrow, commode and all. No sooner was the *Queen Charlotte* out of sight than Nelson wrote his C. in C., "Without some rest I am gone. I must therefore whenever I find the service will admit of it, request your permission to go to my friends at Palermo for a few weeks, and leave the command here to Commodore Troubridge. Nothing but necessity obliges me to write this letter." Keith cannot be entirely without sympathy. In the meantime Nelson stayed at his post.

Strange things were happening in Palermo. "Emma has just let me into the secret that she sends her dispatches to your Lp. tonight to Girgenti," wrote Sir William soon after Nelson's departure.

However as I now find that Lord Keith is really in the place of Lord St. Vincent established Commander in Chief in the Mediterranean, I have now not a doubt but we shall have the extreme satisfaction of returning home with our dearest friend Lord Nelson, for your Lp. will have known from Emma that I have either (after 36 years service at this Court) been either kicked up or down out of my Post and Mr. Paget, Lord Uxbridge's son, is named Envoy Extry. and Plenipotentiary to the King of the Two Sicilies and is on his way here in a frigate. I have not had the least hint of such an intention from England, Public or private, but Lord Grenville has a letter of mine the beginning of the year 1798 authorizing his Lp. to dispose of my place to whom he pleased if he would ensure me an annuity for life of clear *Two Thousand Pounds Sterling*, not a *nominal pension*, as I would rather continue all my life at Naples than retire for life.

I suppose it is a Cabinet job wishing to provide for Paget and they could do it no other way than by satisfying me. I see it gives much uneasiness at this Court and poor Emma is in the greatest distress, but let me get hence and settle my affairs and she and the Queen may dispose of my old Carcass as they please.

Adieu my very dear Lord. Emma will tell you that Acton is a rascal—you must not quite mind what Women say in passions but I allow he is of the rascally tribe of animals called Cabinet Ministers, and we know what such unfeeling animals are in our Country—but God be thanked your Lp. and I that go straight honorably and honestly can never be realy hurt or affected by such insects.

Adieu get yourself well and come to your sincere and hearty friends and let us go home together, but Emma swears she will, like a true Chevr. of Malta, make one caravan to Malta before she goes home, that will depend on your Lp.

The old gentleman was happy enough for all his bad news. Whatever Acton had done to make them angry, he was shortly to do something to make them laugh. And Emma had got her order—Dame Petit Croix de l'Ordre de St. Jean de Jerusalem. Ball was an honorary commander.

Sir William's next letter was in the same lighthearted strain, in spite of the nature of its subject. "I hope you took vomit as you intended and that it has had the desired effect. Emma is getting better daily having at last submitted to that necessary operation. . . . It is as much as I can do to keep Emma in any bounds with respect to your Lp's situation . . . both you and I are of the same opinion of not sacrificing the Service for private satisfaction, therefore we must have a little patience and do nothing precipitately and as my Lady would be most inclined to do. Take care of your health the first of all blessings and bid the Cabinet kiss your ———— fiddle. PS. Emma because I am not so violent as her, swears I am a rank Scotsman and that we all hang together." Lord Keith was a Scotsman.

On February 18 came the strangest event of all. There was a masquerade at the palace that evening, one of King Ferdinand's favorite occasions.

Emma went as "Favorite Sultana" and in her party there were Miss Knight as a Negro Sultana, two Moorish Ladies, a Grecian Lady, Turks of Quality, Moors of Quality, Slaves white and black; parts for Nelson's secretary, chaplain and surgeon, and any other gentlemen eager to attend on her ladyship.

Sir William described the events of the evening of February 18 to Nelson.

We have had our Royal masquerade and Mr. Lock has got into a worse scrape than ever, but Emma is generously employed to get him out of it. I could never persuade him to cut off his wiskers, and to be sure without powder his appearance is generally very Jacobinical. In the midst of well dressed masks at Court, in comes Mr. Lock with a flannel grey night cap, a checked shirt, red silk handkerchief round his neck, and a striped blue and white flannel waist coat and looking in every respect, except the red bonnet, an enraged sans culotte. The King called to Emma— "Look at Mr. Lock, turn him out Miledy or I must do it myself." Emma called me and I was realy shocked at his dirty appearance in so brilliant an assembly and told him it was not decent. He said he meant no offence but represented the Character of a Thames fisherman. He went away and I went to make the best excuse I could to the King, but his Majesty was outrageous and said, "No —*he is a jacobin and I know it better than you do.*"

Lock is now much frightened and has thrown himself on the mercy of Emma and me and we have negociated and are to carry him on Sunday to the Queen to try if by her means we can pacify the King and prevent the ruin that hangs over him and his poor family.

In his own account of the disaster, for it might well have meant his expulsion from Palermo, Lock told the same story, adding that his wife had gone as a Peruvian with three other ladies representing the four quarters of the world, and he had spared no expense in her dress; that the King had stood on a bench to make sure he left the room; and that the Queen had said, "It was not necessary for Mr. Lock to come here to brave us dressed as a sans culotte in order to demonstrate his principles." He also recorded an interview with Acton, who was furious. "It was observed that since the edict for shaving men's whiskers *mine* had increased in length, to demonstrate the contempt I entertained for Royal institutions. The truth is I had worn mine precisely as I had always done, that is on a line with my ear, which I since learnt was the line of demarcation they were not to exceed in the ordinance passed by His Majesty himself . . . the penalty is three months imprisonment. I shaved, you may imagine, immediately, as close and as high as I could."

Lock could not accept a favor gracefully. "Lady Hamilton wrote the Queen a letter which I understand from numbers of people she showed it to, was written in the greatest earnestness in my favour, so well does this artful woman know how to create herself a merit." They really should have left him to his fate. A stupid man is caught by a stupid law.

Maria Carolina had the last word. "The affair of Mr. Lock is a *sotise* which merits neither trouble or attention, but I tremble for the muddle that these people will make for us with their stupidity when you my dear and good friends go away."

The next odd thing that happened at Palermo was that Acton married his niece. There were two ceremonies, one conducted by Nelson's chaplain, Mr. Comyns, in Sir William's house, and the other, a Roman Catholic ceremony in the Queen's apartments. The oddness was that the groom was sixty-seven and the bride not yet fourteen. "So you hear," said Nelson, "it is never too late to do well."

Acton wrote to Nelson on February 27, to thank him for sending the flag of *Le Généreux* to Prince Leopold, a thoughtful and gracious gesture. "You have made Happy all the Royal Family and it is not certainly the first occasion of the many and most essential Feelings which they have been beneficated with from your loyalty and attachment."

All in all they were hectic days, full of folly, as if Nelson's service, which had flowered so brilliantly, was running to seed in strange and grotesque patterns. "Patience my dear Lord," wrote Sir William, "and come back to us as soon as you can and if possible let us go home together— Home I must go, but a short time will suffice for my arranging my business, and at my time of life the question is where I shall chuse to go and die, for living is nearly out of the question with me. Therefore I shall leave Emma to decide that question." "At Palermo we swear by Nelson alone and so it will be to the end of the chapter. . . . Come back to *your Family* here."

Emma did not want to go to England. And if she had to go, she did not want to stay. She wrote to Charles Greville:

> We go on more united and comfortable than ever in spite of the infamous jacobin papers, jealous of Lord Nelson's Glory and Sir William's and mine, but we do not mind them. Lord N is a truly virtuous and great man and because we have been fagging and ruining our healths and sacrificing every comfort in the cause of loyalty, our private characters are to be stabbed in the dark. First it was said Sir Wm. and Lord N fought, then that we played and lost: first Sir W and Lord N lives like brothers, next Lord N never plays, and this I give you my word of Honner, so I beg you will contradict any of these vile reports. Not that Sir Wm. and Lord N minds it and I get scolded by the Queen and all of them for having suffered one day's uneasiness. . . .
>
> I have had a letter from the Emperor of Russia with the Cross of Malta. Sir Wm. has sent his I.M. letter to Lord Grenville to get me the permission to receive it . . . if the King will give me leave to wear it abroad it is of use to me. The Q——n is

having the order set in dymonds for me, but the one the Emperor sent is gold. I tell you this little history of it that you may be *au fait*. Ball has it allso, but I am the first English Woman that ever had it. Sir Wm is pleased *so I am happy.* We are coming home and I am miserable to leave my dearest friend the Q. She cannot be consoled. We have sworn to be back in six months and I will not quit her til Sir William binds himself to come back.

In the meantime, Lord N. was fretting at Malta. He was ill, he said; he had fallen over with a pain in his heart; he felt he was being treated like a schoolboy; if the French ships in La Valetta did not come out, his health would require a fortnight's rest at Palermo. On March 10, in spite of Troubridge's earnest pleas for him to stay (and Troubridge was sick and spitting blood), Nelson sailed in the *Foudroyant* back to Palermo. He had a long voyage, six days, and—oh so luckily!—sent his flagship back directly to Malta under Sir Edward Berry.

On the morning of March 30, at the very moment of the *Foudroyant's* return, the French ship of the line and last survivor of the Nile, the *Guillaume Tell*, made a bold bid to escape from La Valetta. It was only the presence of Nelson's flagship that prevented her—it was the *Foudroyant* which captured her. Nelson was already being criticized in England. In February Charles James Fox collected his notes, based on the letters of Mr. Lock, and made a speech in Parliament accusing Nelson of having broken faith with the Neapolitan Jacobins in his dealings in the Bay of Naples in June 1799. Rumor had had time to return to Palermo. "I am fully persuaded," wrote Fanny, "many are jealous of your character." "They say here you are Rinaldo in the arms of Armida," said Admiral Goodall. And old friend, Mr. Bulkeley, wrote more specifically.

> One part of the many things said of you, you may have some reason to be vain, for it has begot you the prayers and praises of the fair sex, who *all* impatiently await your return, each hoping that she may be the one of the select few who are to become slaves to your amorous passion. I mention this that you may come back to us, determined to gratify your own countrywomen as much as you have by all accounts others in *your* Italian States.

Lord Minto added his squeak to the chorus.

> I have letters from Nelson and Lady Hamilton. It does not seem clear that he will go home. I hope he will not for his own sake, and he will at least, I hope, take Malta first. He does not

seem at all conscious of the sort of discredit he has fallen into, or the cause of it, for he writes still, not wisely, about Lady Hamilton and all that. But it is hard to condemn and use ill a hero, as he is in his own element, for being foolish about a woman who has art enough to make fools of many wiser than an admiral. He tells me of his having got the Cross of Malta for *her*, and Sir William sends home to Lord Grenville the Emperor of Russia's letter to Lady Hamilton on the occasion. All this is against them all, but they do not seem conscious.

If, on top of all this, the *Guillaume Tell* had escaped while Nelson was resting at Palermo, heaven knows what an outcry would have been raised. As it was, Nelson was given the chance to end his tour of service on a high note.

He had been grumbling at Palermo about his heart. He told Keith, "On the 18th, I had near died with the swelling of some of the vessels of the heart. I know the anxiety of my mind on coming back to Syracuse in 1798 was the first cause, and more people perhaps die of broken hearts than we are aware of." He said the same to Troubridge; his heart was broken, "which on any extraordinary anxiety now shews itself, be that feeling *pain* or *pleasure*." Both gentlemen thought there was nothing wrong with Nelson's heart which a little proper attachment to his wife might not cure.

That diagnosis was wrong and the heart was cured effectively by the capture of the *Guillaume Tell*. The orders of the great Earl St. Vincent to annihilate the French fleet were fulfilled. "My task is done," he wrote Minto, "my health lost, and I have wrote to Lord Keith for my retreat. May all orders be as punctually obeyed but never again an officer at the close. . . ." Emma snatched the pen and wrote, "But he forgets to tell you he has got the *William Tell* the last of the Egyptian fleet . . ." Nelson snatched it back again: ". . . of what I must without being thought vain (for such I am represented by my Enemies) call a Glorious Career, be so treated. I go with our dear friends Sir Wm and Lady Hamilton but weither by water or land depends on the will of Lord Keith."

He raved to Lord Spencer of his children of the *Foudroyant*. "I love her as a fond father a darling child and glory in her deeds. I am vain enough to feel the effects of my school." He gloried in his darling children to Keith, who was praying, whether by land or water, to be rid of his annoyingly fortunate junior.

Keith was unfortunate. On March 17, while he was ashore at Leghorn, the *Queen Charlotte* caught fire and blew up, taking 600 of the crew with her. It was a calamity more costly than a great battle. Then he became the channel of a series of contradictory orders from the Cabinet concerning a treaty made between the Sublime Porte and General Kleber and the army Bonaparte had left him with in Egypt.

On January 24, with the cooperation of S.S.S., who had the authority, the Turks and French concluded the Convention of El Arish, which allowed for the French army to be taken back to France by sea. At first the Convention was approved; Lord Elgin took great credit for it. Then, in February, it was decided that the French could leave Egypt only as prisoners of war; Lord Elgin said that Sir Sidney had overstepped his authority. Finally, Keith was obliged to write that if the French were met at sea they would be captured. S.S.S. complained that England would be accused of acting perfidiously, and showed the letter to Kleber. The General accused the English, as expected, and vented his anger on the Turks, who on March 20 were attacked and massacred wholesale. In the meantime, an English army under General Abercrombie wandered into the Mediterranean and sat down in Minorca. Nelson was again lucky to be out of all this.

The only fly in Nelson's ointment was Josiah. Even since the court-martial the *Thalia* had been sailing about with the Captain at odds with all his officers. It was as if Josiah had made up his mind to have himself sent home, while every senior officer in the Mediterranean was equally determined that he should be spared the disgrace on the account of his stepfather. On the *Thalia* Lieutenant Colquit was accused of treating Captain Nisbet badly, the surgeon was under arrest and demanding a court-martial, and the master was complaining bitterly to the Navy Board that the Captain had told him to jump overboard. The only officer Josiah had not yet argued openly with was Lieutenant Quarrel. Keith packed the whole lot off to Madeira for a month or two to decide who was to be court-martialed, and, almost incidentally, to protect the trade from privateers.

"I hear from your billet, my dear Sir, the arrival on horse-back at Palermo of Mr. Paget," Acton wrote Sir William on April 9. "If I do not mistake, I found him riding yesterday with Mr. Lock."

Paget, who was not very well advised, had gone directly to Naples at the end of March, and had then been obliged to wait a week for a ship to take him to Palermo. Once there, he kept himself at a distance from Sir William and accepted a room in the house the Queen had provided for Mr. Lock. This was unfortunate, because, though Paget came determined to discover apathy and folly, he had no opportunity of discovering anything else. His immediate alliance with Lock aggravated the feelings of dislike only to be expected from an elderly Ambassador to his young successor, whose arrival was sudden and, apart from an article in the *Morning Chronicle* of January 9, unexpected.

Sir William stood on his dignity. When, after two or three days, Paget called on him and suggested that he was prepared to present his credential letters to the Court as soon as the Ambassador had presented his recredential letters, the answer was that the Ambassador, who had received no intimation that an immediate change was required, had no intention of remaining in Palermo as a private individual; he was going on a trip with his friends shortly and would do his business then. Paget blamed Lady Hamilton. Lock's words can be read in this extract from his letter to Lord Grenville dated May 13.

> It is not to be told the pains that were taken by Lady Hamilton to set the King and Queen and the whole Court against me, even before I arrived. I was represented as a Jacobin and coxcomb, a person sent to bully and to carry them *bon gré mal gré* back to Naples. . . . Her Ladyship's language in general has been extremely indiscreet, representing Sir William as an ill-used man &c &c. She has however persuaded herself and others that I am only sent here for an interval and that Sir William will resume his situation at Naples next winter. On the other hand Sir William says that nothing shall induce him to accept it again unless a sort of second Minister is sent under him to do the business and represent.
>
> I am sorry to say that Lord Nelson has given more or less into all this nonsense. His Lordship's health is I fear sadly impaired, and I am assured that his fortune is fallen into the same state in consequence of great losses which both his Lordship and Lady Hamilton have sustained at Faro and other Games of Hazard.

In point of fact, while Emma could have no love for Paget, it was Sir William's own decision to withhold his resignation to the last moment. This appears from an exchange of notes he had with Acton, which ended twenty years of friendship and cooperation. It began on April 15 with Sir William's demand.

> Have you or have you not received in private Mr. Paget and allowed him to talk to your Excellency His Sicilian Majesty's Prime Minister, upon affairs relative to our two Courts? A simple yes or no must decide whether your Excy. has or has not betrayed your old and very sincere friend and at the same time offered the

grossest insult to His Britannic Majesty's Envoy Extraordinary and Plenipotentiary accredited at this Court now upwards of thirty-six years.

On the following day he wrote again.

Instead of an answer I received by an Ordenanza an official cover with your Excy's own seal and under that cover I found nothing more than two sheets of blank paper and a pencilled drawing of a Landscape and a Temple. I now very seriously address myself to your Excy. once more for an answer to my billet of yesterday and if I do not receive one before Ten o'clock to-morrow morning I shall go to His Sicilian Majesty and lay what I think my just complaint at His Majesty's feet.

Acton answered the same day.

I never sent you any letter last night. I shall inquire immediately on this business and any person guilty of that strange blunder shall be conveniently punished.

As to your demand whether or no I have seen Mr. Paget . . . to a peremptory question made to His Sicilian Majesty's Minister, who may see, receive, and entertain any Person of any nation, and upon any subject and matter without being answerable to any one but to his Sovereign, I shall dispense myself to make even any answer. Your billet of this night confirms me in this determination.

Now there were two elderly gentlemen standing on their dignities.

The Queen, who was the person most likely to be affected by Emma's opinions, did not consider Paget a Jacobin or coxcomb; that was Lock. Paget was "absolutely one of those young people who run with the hare and chase with the fox." She once called him "the fatal Paget," but that was because his arrival meant the departure of her dear Emma.

Sir William presented his recredential letters on April 21. He told Greville, "My taking leave at Court yesterday was certainly a moving scene, and does me honour. Mr. Paget has shewn great impatience to present his credential letters. I have certainly been friendly and open to him, but his behaviour to me has been cold and reserved from the moment of his arrival, nor has he asked me any questions relative to this Court or Country, and of which I must certainly know more of than he can, having been Minister at Naples before he was born."

That day the *Foudroyant* came into the harbor bearing the scars of her battle with the *Guillaume Tell*. Three days later Nelson and the Hamiltons went aboard with Miss Knight, whose mother had died some time past and who now lived in the palazzo, Count Mushkin Pushkin, and another English couple whose name nobody bothered to record. They were going on holiday to see Bronte, Syracuse, and Emma's island, Malta.

The disappearance of Lord Nelson for a month and more—the *Foudroyant* did not return to Palermo until June 1—baffled Lord Keith and the Admiralty. Keith was at Genoa blockading the harbor while the Austrians besieged the city. General Masséna, who commanded the French garrison, was less worried by the Austrians than Keith, who had to endure being kissed by them. "It is a vile Austrian custom," he complained. Once he had received Nelson's request for permission to go home, Keith kept writing to offer him a frigate, and then to cancel it and suggest the *Culloden*, or perhaps a frigate, but not the *Foudroyant*, which Nelson wanted, but perhaps a storeship for Sir William's collection of pictures, and so on, and getting no reply.

Lord Spencer was also writing to Nelson. On April 25: "If the Enemy should come into the Mediterranean, and whenever they do it will be suddenly, I should be much concerned to hear that you learnt of their arrival in that sea either on shore or in a transport at Palermo." And more severely on May 9: "It is by no means my wish or intention to call you away from Service, but having observed that you have been under the necessity of quitting your station off Malta on account of the state of your health, which I am persuaded you could not have thought of doing without such necessity, it appeared to me much more advisable for you to come home at once than to be obliged to remain inactive at Palermo while active Service was going on in other parts of the station. . . . You will be more likely to recover your health and strength in England, than in an inactive situation at a foreign Court, however pleasing the Respect and gratitude shewn to you for your Services may be." And Lord Spencer got no answer either.

The disappearance of the Hamiltons for the same length of time allowed Mr. Paget to settle down to his business, to exchange knowing letters with Lord Elgin and Mr. Wyndham about the intrigues against him. "It is what I expected," said Mr. Wyndham. "I know the Characters well." As to his real business of moving the King to Naples, he might as easily have moved Monte Pelegrino. Acton told him Ferdinand would rather abdicate than return to Naples with his wife. Moreover, the Hereditary Princess was pregnant. Had Paget had the courtesy to have asked Sir William's advice, he would have learned that nothing would happen until the Princess was

145

brought to bed. Instead, he annoyed the King by considering his daughter-in-law's condition as no excuse for staying in Palermo; he argued with Acton, he offended the Queen, and he blamed his lack of success on Lady Hamilton. He also heard nothing from Malta. "Malta," he wrote Keith, "is I understand to hold out three or four months longer, unless Lady Hamilton means to take it by storm."

Song addressed to Lady Hamilton on her Birthday, April the 26th 1800, on board the *Foudroyant*, in a gale of wind, by Miss E. C. Knight.

> *Come cheer up, fair Emma, forget all thy grief,*
> *For thy shipmates are brave, and a hero's their Chief;*
> *Look around on these trophies,* the pride of the main,*
> *They were snatched by their valour from Gallia and Spain.*
> > Chorus: *Hearts of Oak &c.*

> *Behold yonder fragment, 'tis sacred to fame:*
> *'Mid the waves of old Nile it was sav'd from the flame:*
> *The flame that destroy'd all the glories of France,*
> *When Providence vanquish'd the friends of blind Chance.*
> > Chorus *&c.*

> *Those arms the St. Joseph once claim'd as her own,*
> *Ere NELSON and Britons her pride had o'erthrown:*
> *That plume there evinces that still they excell:*
> *It was torn from the cap of the fam'd William Tell.*
> > Chorus *&c.*

> *Then, cheer up, fair Emma! remember thou'rt free,*
> *And ploughing Britannia's old Empire—the Sea:*
> *How many in Albion each sorrow would check,*
> *Could they kiss but one plank of this conquering deck.*
> > Chorus *&c.*

On April 30 they came to Syracuse, where they spent two days visiting the city. They had passed Bronte. There is no evidence that Nelson ever visited his estate, though it would be strange if he had not done so. He talked about the chestnut trees there once. The two days visiting at Syracuse comes from Miss Knight's autobiography, which was written years later. Perhaps they went to Bronte on the way? The *Foudroyant* went there

* The Cabin of the *Foudroyant* is ornamented with the flagstaff of *l'Orient*, arms of the *St. Joseph*, and plume of the *William Tell*.

once in December 1799, because Graefer complained that as soon as the ship was out of sight the local Basilican friars began bullying him for a contribution.

There was a town of 8,000 inhabitants there, with eight churches, the Basilican monastery, three convents of one sort and another, and a fourth for Benedictine nuns. Graefer said the estate was approached by a road that got worse as one went along it and finally disappeared. There were sixty tenant farmers and 12,000 hungry vassals. He chose one of the farms for Nelson and sent him a list of the seeds and implements he needed. He also discovered a plot to assassinate him—he was right in the middle of the honored society. The estate had previously belonged to the Great Hospital at Palermo, which had been concerned only with the rents. Graefer was not concerned with rents. "They were informed that his Lordship's wish was that they should all be equal," so none of them paid anything. It must have been a pleasant place in spring, with pastures, orchards, vines, olives and mulberries. Perhaps they went there?

For sure on May 4 the *Foudroyant* anchored in St. Paul's Bay and the party went ashore to meet Captain Ball. They stayed there a week. Then they sailed to Marsa Scirocco Bay and stayed there a week. There was a pretty house and a safe pony and nothing to do but enjoy themselves . . . no letters, so no information! except that Nelson had toothache.

Much has been made of the trip to Malta, because nine months later a child appeared which Nelson believed was his. This only suggests that the opportunities offered in the pretty house at Marsa Scirocco were no less than those taken in the Palazzo Palagonia.

However, the only subjects known to have arisen during the holiday were the projected journey of Maria Carolina to Vienna, Fox's speech in Parliament, and Lord St. Vincent's claim to the lion's share of some rich Spanish frigates captured in the Mediterranean while he was convalescing in England.

On May 12 Nelson wrote Keith that he intended to bring the Queen to Leghorn in the *Foudroyant,* with the *Alexander* in company. On May 9 he answered Davison, whose letter had contained the news of the other matters. On the speech, he stated his belief that the rebels came out of the castles "as *they ought* and as I hope all those who are false to their King and Country will, *to be hanged* or otherwise disposed of as their Sovereign thought proper." On the claim, which he believed devolved on himself, he said, "No Admiral ever yet received Prize money going for the benefit of his health from a foreign station," and he instructed Davison to fight the Earl at law if necessary.

The *Foudroyant* was under sail on May 20, passed to the west of Sicily, and arrived at Palermo on June 1.

"It is so long I have heard of you that I write at you and not to you," Keith complained. Genoa capitulated on June 4, but Bonaparte was already across Switzerland at the start of the brilliant campaign that ended in the battle of Marengo ten days later. When he received Nelson's letter of May 12, Keith complained again, "It is no time for a Queen to be making visits," and followed this with a positive order for the *Foudroyant* and *Alexander* to return to Malta. It arrived after the party had sailed. "I hear they are to sail," he grumbled later, "but there has been an infatuation prevalent in Palermo which seems to me Absurd and Criminal."

Maria Carolina's decision to travel with her family to Vienna was the result of Ferdinand's attitude. "I think I am neither necessary nor agreeable to him," she said, somewhat understating the situation. She took the Princesses and Prince Leopold with her because she could not bear to be without them. "The highest felicity on earth," she told Kotzebue, "is the happiness of being a mother. I have had seventeen living children; they were my only joy. Nature made me a mother; the queen is only a gala-dress which I put off and on."

The last week in Palermo was spent in fitting up the *Foudroyant* for the reception of the royal family and thirty attendants, over and above the Hamiltons and their party, Mrs. Cadogan, Miss Knight, and the servants, including the black girl called Fatima, Nelson's present to Emma. Another twenty-four attendants were to go aboard the *Alexander*, with a vast amount of baggage, Sir William's pictures, and the Queen's library, which she was obliged to take with her though she had never read more than a few of the titles.

Nelson, who had returned from a month's holiday exhausted—"I am so tired fagged and worn out," he told Davison, "that the Nelson you know is gone, and but a shadow remains"—strove with the Court to have his captains rewarded before he left. Troubridge's efforts earned him a pension of £500 a year (unpaid); Ball did rather better with £500 cash for his expenses. Prize money of £60,000 was agreed for the capture of Rome and Civita Vecchia. A new Order of St. Ferdinand and Merit was established and, as it cost the King only a little gold and ribbon, received eventually. Nelson was made the first Knight after the royal family, with the privilege of wearing his hat in the King's presence. Troubridge, Hood, and Hallowell were made commanders of the order, without such a distinction.

The Admiral was an extraordinary sight now, with three stars on his jacket and three medals around his neck; sick, worn and thin. He was signing himself "Bronte Nelson of the Nile," as if to compensate for the contraction of his situation by the expansion of his title. The Ambassador, ex-Ambassador, had that delicate and fragile look which characterizes the very old, like something preserved in a bottle. The Beauty, ex-Beauty, was big and unhappy. She wore the little cross on her bosom, which made it seem littler than ever. Of the three, home had the least attraction for her, and she talked constantly of coming back.

But to what? The Court at Palermo without Maria Carolina was no place for Emma. Naples was lying uneasily under a royal amnesty that solved nothing because it damned guilty and innocent alike as rebels, forbidden to hold office or appear at Court. Her enemies were all busy with their detractions, and no sooner had she gone than Lock wrote, "This Government is informed of the bribes she has received from several families to save certain members of them involved in the late Revolution. Some of which, notwithstanding, have been executed, and the share she pretended to in all affairs has given great and deserved disgust." She had her memories, and memories are best left in the past. A place revisited is a place of disillusionment.

On June 10 the farewells were made, the barges rowed out to the *Foudroyant*, the rigging was manned, the seamen cheered, the guns fired, the great people went on board, the ships sailed. It was two years bar a few days since Nelson had come to the Bay of Naples for the second time. Now, the *tria juncta in uno* left the Two Sicilies for good.

CHAPTER SIX

The Journey Home

THE EVENTS of the next month were calculated to confirm the worst opinions of Nelson and the Hamiltons, entertained by Lord Keith, Wyndham, Paget, Lord Minto and many others who wrote about them with pity and contempt.

On June 14, 1800, the *Foudroyant* and the ships in company arrived at Leghorn in foul weather. The royal party were obliged to wait two days until the waters of the bay were calm enough for the boats to be lowered to take them ashore. They were the days when 6,000 Austrian dead were counted on the battlefield of Marengo. In the armistice that followed, Bonaparte gained all the Italian provinces west of the Mincio, including Genoa. This frightening news was not known in Leghorn for several days; the first reports of the battle spoke of an Austrian victory.

On landing, the Queen and her family and attendants were greeted by the Governor and conducted to the cathedral for a service of thanksgiving. Then the royals went to the palace of the Grand Duke and the English to the house of Consul Udney, an old friend and admirer of the Admiral's. It seemed certain that they would soon go their separate ways, the Queen on to Vienna by land, Nelson and his friends on to England by sea. Maria Carolina sent her farewell presents: to Sir William, a gold snuffbox with portraits of the King and Queen set in diamonds; to Emma, a diamond necklace with the cyphers of all the royal children wound around with their hair; to Nelson, a portrait of Ferdinand in a rich setting, on the reverse the initials MC in diamonds in a border of oak and laurel leaves in diamonds and emeralds; to the company of the *Foudroyant*, 2,500 Sicilian crowns.

Until June 20 the situation was uncertain, as Bronte Nelson of the Nile wrote Fanny, "We are detained by the situation of the armies but a few days will I hope enable Her Majesty to prosecute her intended journey to Vienna, when Lord Keith I think must allow the *Foudroyant* to carry me and my party to England for she cannot be refitted in the Mediterranean.

"My health at times is better but a quiet mind and to live content is necessary for me. A very difficult thing for me to enjoy I could say much but it would only distress me and be useless." This was an odd thing to write, in no way designed to enlighten or comfort Fanny. What could he say much about? Lord Keith perhaps, or Josiah—he was in the news again. Duckworth wrote:

> The near connection Capt. Nisbet bears to your Lordship must ever make me interested that no disgrace should attach itself to him. I therefore felt great concern to find on his arrival that he and his officers were at daggers drawn. The surgeon above three months under an arrest writing for a court martial on his Captain, the first lieutenant with a string of complaints which he signified his intention of sending to your Lordship, that must, to say the least of them, quite destroy Capt. Nisbet's reputation; though on my honour I view much of them as invidious and watching every indiscretion of a young man of his years, when summed up in the aggregate few of us could bear, and his being in disrepute has encouraged those around him to take liberties they would not dared to have done with others, which being naturally resented but with an ill regulated warmth, has produced this dilemma, to which your Lordship's kind intentions may have a little aided, by authorising the first lieutenant to give him advice, which probably from his youth (for he otherwise seems a very good young man) may have been so dictatorial as for his Captain to spurn at, a kind of pride I cannot condemn entirely and true it is there is much of human nature in it. In consequence from viewing the errors on both sides I thought a publick investigation best avoided and after some labour brought it to a compromise and all is buried in oblivion and the surgeon cleared: but there can't be a second opinion of the necessity of the parties being divided, and if I might suggest I think (as the State of Ship must cause her to be paid off) a few months with Lady Nelson would *now* correct his foibles.

Keith kept the *Thalia* under his command until he discovered that Josiah had broken the accepted rule of the service and was acting as his own agent, instead of appointing a proper agent, if not the Commander in Chief's secretary. Keith felt himself insulted and the *Thalia* was sent home, arriving in October. That ended Josiah's career at sea, probably as much to his satisfaction as to everyone else's.

Leghorn began to fill rapidly with refugees fleeing from the advancing

French army, and on June 21 the whole story of the battle and the armistice was known. The Queen, who on a previous evening at the theater had called out the applauding crowd, "Death to Bonaparte," was frightened out of her wits. "I very nearly died," she said. "A congestion, an apoplectic fit, almost carried me off."

Keith was aboard the *Minotaur* at Genoa when the news came that, instead of occupying the city, he had to evacuate it. There was some talk of bringing troops from Minorca to garrison the place, but Troubridge, who was there on his way home, wrote, "General Fox was so undecided, and completely worn out, that it is a misery to have anything to do with him."

Keith was already annoyed with Nelson for using the *Foudroyant* and *Alexander* to bring the Queen to Leghorn, and he peremptorily refused a request to use them to take her back to Palermo again. "It is not matter of capprice," he wrote, "but of actual Duty and necessity which has obliged me to send the order which I must desire to be final. Her Majesty is too just and too well informed to place anything like neglect to me, with Her good understanding I am sure to stand acquitted." He ordered the *Alexander* to Genoa to assist the evacuation, and the *Foudroyant* to Minorca for a refit. He offered a frigate and all the Neapolitan vessels in the vicinity to take the royal family to Palermo or anywhere away from him.

Nelson demurred. In the meantime, Keith wrote to Paget to warn him that the Hamiltons might reappear. "I must go to Leghorn to land the Wretched Fugitives and to be Bored by Lord Nelson for permission to take the Queen to Palermo, and Princes and Princesses to all parts of the Globe, to every request I have said my Duty to the Nation forbids it, God knows it is true." He begged Nelson again, "My dear Lord, get the Queen to Naples in the Neapolitans or to Palermo if Her My. does *not* go to Vienna during the *armistice* which I recommend most strongly." He had no wish, in the midst of all his worries, to have to cope with a hysterical Queen and her stubborn Knight Errant.

In Leghorn, which from the number of refugees was taking on the appearance and discomfort of a beleaguered city, Nelson remained steadfast by the Queen. "I should feel myself a beast," he said, "could I have a thought for anything but her comfort." He gave up hope of returning to England in the *Foudroyant*, though not of a sea journey home once the royal family were safe somewhere. Maria Carolina was in a sad state of nerves, begging for the warship to be reserved for her in the event of an emergency, and crying out against Keith's lack of respect for her rank and position.

The Commander in Chief appeared in person on June 26. He resisted all appeals, and two days later the *Foudroyant* sailed for Port Mahon with all the luggage still aboard, with Tyson to forward it to England, with Nelson's barge crew who had begged to be allowed to stay with him, and with Prince and Princess Castelcicala, on their way to England, where the Prince was to be Ambassador. Nelson hoisted his flag in the *Alexander* and watched with the Hamiltons as the ship which had shared many of their experiences sailed away.

On July 1 General Abercrombie, with General John Moore in attendance, arrive at Leghorn with part of his expeditionary force. This added to the general confusion, as there was nowhere for the troops to go. Naturally, the Queen thought they should go to Naples, but she had no influence with these people. She raged, "Keith, that is to say England, assumes a tone I did not know, and I am disgusted for ever with their words and behaviour. . . . The rest of Europe may be on fire, Thugut Emperor and Fox King of England, but even so I would not be drawn from a permanent system of neutrality or, to be more precise, of nullity."

Keith was equally disgusted with the Queen. He wrote Minto on July 6.

The visit of that Lady has been most inconvenient and no determination is taken when it is to finish. Lord Nelson took a part of the Squadron from Malta which could ill be spared and without my consent for H.M.'s escort and of which conduct I am obliged to disapprove. He goes to England so soon as Her Majesty is disposed of by way of Vienna if the road is open, and you my friend will forgive me when I write that yesterday the Queen sent for me and read her letters, then talked of a Squadron to take her to Trieste, then about our troops and the defence of Naples &c. One Ship I offered to convoy the Neapolitan frigates, she was angry and wept, and stated Nelson's conduct, and my responsibility in terms of respect and affection to the August family, she taxed me with knowledge of the Convention [the Armistice], I was displeased and read a part of your letter to speak for its contents, she talked in an odd strain of you and Paget, I lost temper and said Madame when you see Lord M you will find his Character and Manners so different that I am convinced you will despise the authors of vile falsehood and I am not ignorant whence it comes. I am determined the King's Squadron shall no longer be under the Direction of Lady H——n which it has too long &c if these people come forward I think it right you should be on your guard for the Queen is plausible, the former cunning and interested, such might ill impress the ears of some of the Court and do harm.

What was Emma up to? Some sinister intrigue against the English ambassadors at Palermo and Vienna? Some outrageous plot to divide the allies and discredit their representatives? Not at all. She simply did not want to go to England by sea. Miss Knight knew. "Lady Hamilton cannot bear the thought of going by sea; and, therefore, nothing but impracticability will prevent our going to Vienna. Lord Nelson is well, and keeps up his spirits amazingly. Sir William appears broken, distressed and harassed." Emma wanted to accompany the Queen to Vienna and then to visit the different Courts of Germany. It would give her some months more of Nelson's company. The intrigue was to persuade the Queen to travel by land to Vienna, and to take Nelson, who disapproved, preferring his own element, and Sir William, who expected to die on the way, with her. It was a plot for pleasure.

See what happened on July 9. The French were at Lucca, a day's march from Leghorn. The Livornese became panicky, broke into the arsenal, seized arms, and milled around the palace. What they were doing, or intended to do, no one seemed to know. Miss Knight said they wanted Nelson to lead them against the French. Emma said that too (to Harrison) and added that a riot was only averted by her appearance on a balcony and a bold speech she made, remonstrating with them on their violence to an amiable and illustrious Queen, and threatening them that, if they did not return their arms to the arsenal, Lord Nelson would certainly not lead them. Whether he would lead them without arms or not occurred neither to her nor them. The upshot of it was that the Queen and her children hurried aboard the *Alexander* with every intention of sailing for Trieste.

"We are again afloat," Nelson wrote Berry on July 9, "bound to Trieste but in what a different Ship to the dear *Foudroyant*, and I have not the least thing for comfort of any kind or sort. . . . Leghorn is in a little alarm the people are strongly against the French and have seized the arms in order to defend the Town, but it does not appear to me they will be supported."

Once aboard, however, all the old doubts returned. On July 11 Nelson sent Keith a note to ask, if they went back to Palermo, whether the *Seahorse* could collect him and take him to England, stopping at Port Mahon for his laundry: "I have only six shirts and not a table-cloth." Then he wrote again, on the same day, "It is now determined that the Queen goes by land to Ancona, pray God send us a good voyage, a pleasant one is not to be expected, with your permission the *Alexander* will salute the Queen on her leaving the Ship and if you chuse the other Ships can follow her example, this landing is to be at one o'clock."

What on earth had happened? "I can tell you in confidence," Paget told Keith on July 31, "that the whole of the Queen's conduct, since her departure from hence is highly disapproved here. Perhaps you do not know that Lady Hamilton persuaded her that the crew of the *Alexander* were all Jacobins, and that it was not safe for them to remain in that Ship, was ever anything so monstrous."

This was the stuff of comic opera. John Moore put it in his diary.

> Sir William and Lady Hamilton were there attending the Queen of Naples. Lord Nelson was there attending upon Lady Hamilton. He is covered with stars, ribbons, and medals, more like the Prince of an Opera than the Conqueror of the Nile. It is really melancholy to see a brave and good man, who has deserved well of his Country, cutting so pitiful a figure.

There was a great sigh of relief in high places when Nelson struck his flag on July 13. Early the next morning the Queen, her family and attendants set off on the road to Florence. Nelson, the Hamiltons and their party, followed the next day. The whole convoy consisted of fourteen carriages and three large baggage wagons.

So Emma had her way, but at the expense of making them all look ridiculous. Keith wrote to Minto, "Your old friend I believe a good natured weak man in bad hands, the good old Gentleman felt his situation and did not fail to complain of it to me, all three were implicitly governed by Vulgarity." Nelson a good-natured weak man! But there was worse: "His zeal for the public service seems entirely lost in his love and vanity, and they all sit and flatter each other all day long."

The road from Leghorn to Florence followed the course of the Arno, and the royal party made good time to the Tuscan capital. There was some need for urgency, as the French army was marching south to reoccupy the territories ceded to France by the armistice; nevertheless, two days were spent at Florence in calls and courtesies.

They set out again for Arezzo, passing within two miles of the French outposts. At Castel San Giovanni the wheel of Sir William's traveling coach broke, the coach overturned, and the occupants were tumbled over each other. They were obliged to wait, glancing anxiously back along the road, for the wheel to be repaired. It broke again at Arezzo. The *tria* took the second coach, leaving Mrs. Cadogan and Miss Knight to wait for a new wheel. The prospect of being captured pleased neither the old lady nor the young one, and Miss Knight particularly was a little aggrieved at being considered of so small a consequence. The whole party was reunited a few days later at Ancona.

The Court of Vienna had sent the *Bellona* warship to carry the Queen and her family to Trieste. The cabins were fitted with silk hangings and eighty beds had been set up on the gun deck, leaving room for only twenty-four guns. Nelson, who preferred things the other way around, advised the Queen to go aboard one of three Russian frigates in the harbor. He and the Hamiltons were received on the *Cazanski Bogorodets* by Captain Messer, who had once served under Lord Howe. The squadron sailed and came into the roads of Trieste on August 1. The *Bellona* was captured by privateers in the Gulf of Venice.

The second anniversary of the battle of the Nile produced an elegant letter to Nelson, signed by the three princesses, Prince Leopold his true friend, and Maria Carolina, on behalf of Ferdinand, the Hereditary Prince and Princess, and herself. The Queen was not well, Sir William was very ill, and there was a wait of about a fortnight at Trieste before the party could proceed. Then, leaving on three successive days to spare the post horses, they trundled northward through the romantic scenery of southern Austria, and past little groups of peasants come to stare for a moment at the hero whose fame had spread to such unlikely places as Klagenfurt and Knittelfeld. On August 21 the last of the coaches arrived at the capital of the German Empire.

While the spirits of the Court were subdued by the defeat in Italy, there was as yet no talk of a permanent peace with France and hopes were canvassed of better fortune with their armies on their own soil. The Queen of Naples was received with spontaneous pleasure by her daughter and son-in-law. Her English friends joined the family circle as soon as they arrived. "The Empress would see us yesterday evening," Nelson told Minto on August 22, "and we had the noise of five fine healthy children for an hour."

There was a gala for the Queen on August 27, and then she retired to the palace of Schönbrunn. It was not long before Nelson and Emma were urging Minto to visit "the neglected Queen of Naples." The daughter of Maria Theresa was an embarrassment to a Court that was struggling to reconcile past greatness with present feebleness. Minto had no wish to see the Queen, who had appropriated the whole of a British subsidy for the defense of Naples for her own personal use while at Vienna.

All the town wanted to see Nelson. Lady Minto wrote:

> You can have no notion of the anxiety and curiosity to see him. The door of his house is always crowded with people, and even the street, whenever his carriage is at the door; and when he went to the play he was applauded, a thing which rarely happens here. On the road it was the same. The common people brought

their children to *touch* him. One he took up in his arms, and when he gave it back to the mother she cried for joy, and said it would be lucky through life. I don't think him altered in the least. He has the same shock head, and the same honest simple manners; but he is devoted to *Emma;* he thinks her quite an *angel,* and talks of her as such to her face and behind her back, and she leads him about like a keeper with a bear. She must sit by him at dinner to cut his meat, and he carries her pocket-handkerchief—he is a gig from ribands, orders and stars.

Rumor had been there before them. "It is said that much of the cruelty at Naples is owing to Lady Hamilton, and that if she were to appear there she would be torn to pieces."

Sir William was very ill at Vienna. Lord Minto believed he would not live to see England, and they were obliged to stay a month before he was well enough to continue the journey. It was expensive, and Nelson drew £1,000 and more while they were there. Among other items there figured the hire of a piano and thirty-eight baths, which showed that they were both clean and cultured.

The time was spent in giving sittings to the painter Füger, in attending the various theaters one after another to ensure each had the benefit of a full house when they were there, and in visiting the great houses in and around the city where they were entertained with the profusion and magnificence that can only flourish under the rule of kings and emperors. Charity must be glad it has gone, faith and hope must be disappointed. Equality is no reward for superiority.

Four days passed splendidly at Eisenstadt, where Prince Esterhazy lived in state. Lord Fitzharris was there. "Sunday, grand fireworks. Monday (the *jour de fête*), a very good ball. And yesterday, the *chasse*. Nelson and the Hamiltons were there. We never sat down to supper or dinner less than sixty or seventy persons, in a fine hall superbly illuminated; in short, the whole in a most princely style. Nelson's health was drunk with a flourish of trumpets and firing of cannon. Lady Hamilton is, without exception, the most coarse, ill-mannered, disagreeable woman we met with. The Princess with great kindness has got a number of musicians, and the famous Haydn, who is in their service, to play, knowing Lady H. was fond of music. Instead of attending to them, she sat down to the faro table, played Nelson's cards for him, and won between £300 and £400." Well, perhaps at the age of sixty-eight Haydn was not worth listening to? The composer came off better with Nelson, who gave him a watch in exchange for a pen. Emma used to sing one of his songs, "My Mother Bids Me Bind My Hair."

A day was spent at the Au Gardens, and another on the Danube, where Sir William was well enough to enjoy a little fishing. There were concerts, suppers, balls and dinners, and it was a question whether they were given to honor Nelson, or to display him and his companions to the curiosity of Viennese society. At last, however, the time approached when they must continue their journey. Nelson had to think about London. The thought evidently did not please him. He wrote Davison on September 20.

> As the time of my arrival in England draws near I must request the favor of you and my Brother to take either a house or good lodgings for me, not too large yet one fit for my situation, to be hired by the month, not even which time shall I remain in London, you must consider that I am not rich beyond what you are acquainted with, for all my Sicilian revenue is for 2 years to come laid out in that Country, therefore do not exceed what is right. . . . My health is better but you will see an old Man.

He wrote to Fanny the same day.

> Sir William Hamilton being recovered we set out tomorrow, and shall be in England the 2nd week in October. I have wrote to Davison to take a house or good lodgings for the very short time I shall be in London, to which I shall instantly proceed and hope to meet you in the house.
>
> You must expect to find me a worn out old man. Make my kindest love to my father who I shall see the moment I have been with the King.

The King and attending Court were in his thoughts when he sent this inquiry to Sir Isaac Head at the College of Heralds: "I shall be very much obliged if you will have the goodness to inform me whether I am permitted to wear the Star of the Order of the Bath, which I am allowed to under the King's Sign Manual on my coming abroad, or whether I am to cut it off my coat on my arrival in England, also whether I may wear the Star of the Crescent and the Star of the Order of St. Ferdinand and Merit, all of which at present adorn my coat. It is my wish to be correct in all these points therefore I am this troublesome. A line directed to my Brother at the Navy Office will much oblige." Nelson has been accused of being improperly dressed at Court: it seems strange that, having gone to the lengths of asking for advice, he should have ignored it.

All other business having been arranged, with the assistance of Francis Oliver, a gentleman long known to Sir William, who entered Nelson's employment as secretary and interpreter, there remained only the final parting from the Queen. Maria Carolina was sincerely affected; she hoped for the consolation of seeing them soon in Naples; she would never forget her Emma, dear Emma, her friend and sister; she would always be her constant and sincere Charlotte. Emma said she refused a pension of £1,000 a year from the Queen. Nobody believed her. But it is quite possible the offer was made, perhaps not of pounds but of ounces (she had a way of turning ounces into pounds). It is of little consequence, except to deprive Emma of the grace of a refusal, as, being a Neapolitan pension, it would never have been paid. She certainly did receive a letter from the Queen recommending her strongly to the Queen of England, and made sure that everyone knew about it.

It took almost a week for the party, seventeen in number, to reach Prague, the capital of Bohemia and the home of Maria Carolina's nephew, the Archduke Charles. Charles was the best of the Austrian generals and a popular hero. He knew what was due to heroes, and gave a grand party at his palace on September 29, Nelson's birthday. Prague was illuminated, the hotel where the *tria* were staying was ablaze with lights; the landlord, who also knew what was due, charged for them on the bill.

They journeyed on the next day and left the road at Leitmeritz to embark on the Elbe for Dresden. Two days of leisurely travel through some of the grandest scenery in Europe brought them to the capital of Saxony. They put up at the Great Hotel, where they were soon visited by the English Ambassador, Hugh Elliot, Lord Minto's brother. Staying in Dresden was one of those ubiquitous English ladies who, if they lived to-day, would undoubtedly be writing the gossip columns of the glossier magazines. Mrs. St. George had a very sharp eye.

October 3rd. Dined at Mr. Elliot's with only the Nelson party. It is plain that Lord Nelson thinks of nothing but Lady Hamilton, who is totally occupied by the same object. She is bold, forward, coarse, assuming and vain. Her figure is colossal, but, excepting her feet, which are hideous, well shaped. Her bones are large, and she is exceedingly embonpoint. She resembles the bust of Ariadne; the shape of all her features is fine, as is the form of her head, and particularly her ears; her teeth are a little irregular, but tolerably white; her eyes light blue, with a brown spot in one, which, though a defect, takes nothing away from her beauty of expression. Her eyebrows and hair are dark, and her complexion coarse. Her expression is strongly marked, variable and interesting; her movements in common life ungraceful; her voice loud, yet not disagreeable.

Lord Nelson is a little man without any dignity. . . . Lady Hamilton takes possession of him, and he is a willing captive, the most submissive and devoted I have seen.

Sir William is old, infirm, all admiration of his wife, and never spoke today but to applaud her. Miss Cornelia Knight seems the decided flatterer of the two, and never opens her mouth but to shower forth their praise; and Mrs. Cadogan, Lady Hamilton's mother, is—what one might expect.

She continued her remarks on Emma.

She puffs the incense full in his face; but he receives it with pleasure, and snuffs it up very cordially. The songs all ended in the sailor's way, with "Hip, hip, hip, hurra" and a bumper with the last drop on the nail, a ceremony I had never heard of or seen before.

On October 5 Mrs. St. George was invited by Lady Hamilton, who was obviously not much of a judge of people, to see Nelson dressed for Court. "On his hat he wore the large diamond feather, or ensign of sovereignty, given him by the Grand Signior; on his breast the Order of the Bath, the Order he received as Duke of Bronte, the diamond star including the sun or crescent given him by the Grand Signior, three gold medals obtained by three different victories, and a beautiful present from the King of Naples. In short, Lord Nelson was a perfect constellation of stars and orders."

Two days later, she saw the attitudes.

Breakfasted with Lady Hamilton, and saw her represent in succession the best statues and paintings extant. She assumes their attitude, expression, and drapery with great facility, swiftness and accuracy. Several Indian shawls, a chair, some antique vases, a wreath of roses, a tambourine, and a few children are her whole apparatus. She stands at one end of the room with a strong light to her left, and every other window closed. Her hair (which by the bye is never clean) is short, dressed like an antique, and her gown a simple calico chemise, very easy, with loose sleeves to the wrist. She disposes the shawls so as to form Grecian, Turkish, and other drapery, as well as a variety of turbans. Her arrangement of the turbans is absolutely sleight of hand, she does it so quickly, so easily and so well. It is a beautiful performance, amusing to the ignorant, and highly interesting to the lovers of art. The chief of her imitations are from the antique. Each representation lasts about ten minutes. It is remarkable that, though coarse and ungraceful in common life, she becomes highly graceful and even beautiful, during this performance. It is also singular that, in spite of the accuracy of her imitation of the finest ancient draperies, her usual dress is tasteless, vulgar, loaded and unbecoming. She has borrowed several of my gowns, and much admires my dress; which cannot flatter as her own is so frightful. Her waist is absolutely between her shoulders.

Emma was ahead of the fashion with her high waist and Grecian curls. She presumably kept the hair she had cut off and wore it as a wig, because she was later reported to be wearing it down to her heels.

There was another evening at the Elliots', with eating, singing and card playing. "Her voice is good and very strong, but she is frequently out of tune. . . . I think her bold, daring, vain even to folly, and stamped with the manners of her first situation much more strongly than one would suppose, after having represented Majesty, and lived in good company fifteen years. Her ruling passions seem to me vanity, avarice, and love for the pleasures of the table."

Hugh Elliot was not behindhand in exercising his wit at the expense of his guests. He referred to the lovers as "Antony and Moll Cleopatra," and said of Emma, prophetically, "She will captivate the Prince of Wales, whose mind is as vulgar as her own, and play a great part in England."

The part she was going to play was the great subject of discussion in the Elliot drawing room one evening after Nelson and the Hamiltons had returned to their hotel. Though the Admiral had gone to Court to pay his respects to the Elector of Saxony, Mr. Elliot had received a hint that Lady Hamilton would be unwelcome there, and she had not been presented to the Electress. It was, as Mrs. St. George stated plainly, "on account of her former dissolute life." It could not be put to Lady Hamilton quite like that, and, to her repeated requests to be presented, Mrs. Elliot had quietly replied that it would not amuse her as the Elector never gave dinners or suppers. "What?" cried Emma. "No guttling!" Nelson had taken the matter up with Mr. Elliot, saying, "Sir, if there is any difficulty of that sort, Lady Hamilton will knock the Elector down." But there was difficulty, and they agreed in the drawing room that there would be even more difficulty in England.

After a week in Dresden the party were ready to continue their journey by water. In this place, as elsewhere, there was always a crowd of people straining to get a glimpse of Nelson. When the Dresden Gallery was opened for the hero, there were so many ladies there to see him that he hardly saw the porcelain. One observer was disappointed.

"Nelson is one of the most insignificant looking figures I ever saw in my life. His weight cannot be more than seventy pounds. A more miserable collection of bones and wizened frame I have never yet come across. His bold nose, the steady eye and the solid worth revealed in his whole face betray in some measure the great conqueror. He speaks little and then only English and he hardly ever smiles." As for Lady Hamilton, "She behaved like a loving sister towards Nelson; led him, often took hold of his hand, whispered something into his ear, and he twisted his mouth into the faint resemblance of a smile."

On the last evening at the Elliots', Mrs. St. George recorded, "Lady Hamilton, who declared she was passionately fond of champagne, took such a portion of it as astonished me. Lord Nelson was not behindhand, called more vociferously than usual for songs in his own praise, and after many bumpers proposed the Queen of Naples, adding 'She is *my* Queen: she is Queen to the backbone.'" Even Sir William let his hair down and "performed feats of activity, hopping round the room on his backbone, his arms, legs, star and ribbon all flying about in the air."

The next morning the baggage, Sir William's traveling coach, the maids and manservants were got aboard two large boats on the Elbe. The Ambassador's family went down to see Nelson and the Hamiltons embark. Mrs. St. G. fired her parting shot. "The moment they were on board, there was an end of the fine arts, of the attitudes, of the acting, the dancing, and the singing. Lady Hamilton's maid began to scold in French about some provisions which had been forgot, in language quite impossible to repeat . . . Lady Hamilton began bawling for an Irish stew, and her old mother set about washing the potatoes, which she did as cleverly as possible. They were exactly like Hogarth's actresses dressing in a barn."

That evening Mr. Elliot said quietly, "Now don't let us laugh tonight; let us all speak in our turn, and be very very quiet." Emma was penning a note to Mrs. Elliot: "I cannot tell you with what regret we part from you . . ."

From Dresden the Elbe winds gently through Saxony and Anhalt into Prussia. On October 14 the travelers came to Magdeburg, where they landed to be met by a guard of honor sent by the King of Prussia, Frederick William III, and a great crowd of sightseers. They dined at the hotel called the King of Prussia, and the press to watch Lady Hamilton feeding her one-armed hero was so great that the doors of the dining room had to be opened and the landlord charged a fee to look in. Nelson sent out wine and food to the crowd, and Emma went out and told them what a great man he was and that they all ought to hate the French. "The Hamilton," one of them wrote, "must be well on in the thirties, but a woman full of fire, in whom one can clearly see the beauty of youth; she is somewhat stout."

The travelers continued their journey down the Elbe to the free city of Hamburg, where they arrived on October 21. Hamburg was a rich and populous place, with a large number of English residents who were delighted to have an English hero to fete and applaud, so as to increase their own consequence.

The party stayed at Der Koenig von England. The Hamburg packet was the principal channel of communication between England and the Continent; letters, newspapers, dispatches sent overland, travelers, all took the safe route to Yarmouth, and went on by coach to London. Nelson was news, and it was not long before reports of his activities in Hamburg were printed in the London newspapers. The *Morning Chronicle*, November 1, had this piece of information:

> On the 22nd the company of French comedians at Hamburgh, waited upon Lord Nelson, to know what pieces he would please to command for the entertainment of that night, when, at his Lordship's solicitation, Lady Hamilton fixed upon *Richard Coeur de Lion* and *Le Prisonnier*. His Lordship assisted at the performance and was received in the most flattering manner. The health of the Hero of the Nile seems very much impaired and it is hoped that his native air will restore it to its former vigour.
>
> On the 23rd the Noble Admiral honoured the German Theatre with a visit, to see the representation of *Gustavus Vasa* by Kotzebue: he was welcomed by the audience with still greater demonstrations of joy; but two Germans had the audacity to hiss his Lordship; they were, however, immediately silenced. Inebriety is said to be the cause of this offence.

Apart from visiting theaters where he did not understand a word of what was going on, Nelson was kept busy by petitioners for money, recommendations and his signature on Bibles and prayer books; on one occasion, an elderly priest traveled forty miles to obtain this mark of honor on his parish Bible. The Admiral visited Klopstock, "the German Milton," who was so impressed with Emma that he dedicated his ode "The Innocents" to her; on reflection, he withdrew the dedication as inappropriate.

A visitor to their hotel was Dumouriez, the exiled French general, as the *Times* of December 11 reported in a nasty article. "Among the distinguished personages who hastened to pay their respects to Sir William and Lady Hamilton, and Lord Nelson, on their arrival at Hamburgh, was

Dumourier. During their short stay in that City, the ex-General was invited to one of their parties. After supper Lady Hamilton sang 'God Save the King' at the request of Lord Nelson: but when she came to the couplet reflecting on France, she was interrupted by his Lordship. Dumourier, who had listened in ecstacy to the sweet melodies of the delightful warbler, deeply affected by this act of delicacy, and filled with gratitude, burst into tears. Lady Hamilton, fancying she saw tears of a Royalist, of a heart overflowing with love for its country, glistening in his eyes, wept in excess of softness. Lord Nelson began to weep from sympathy, and old Sir William Hamilton went to a distant corner of the room, and wept to keep the rest company. Lady Hamilton, in constant activity, wiped away the tears of the Admiral with her handkerchief fondly: then those of her husband slightly: then those of Dumourier kindly; and then her own delicately; and then Dumourier, falling on his knee, implored as the greatest possible favour, that the charming Lady Hamilton would make him a present of the handkerchief . . . which had the relics of so many great personages." The ridicule implicit in the story is more unpleasant than any direct condemnation of the three. It is clever journalism.

Nelson certainly met Dumouriez, and sent him a set of Shakespeare to improve his English, and was bothered by him with plans for a descent on France under their joint command.

On October 27 the British residents gave a great dinner for the Admiral's party at their house called "The English Bowling Green." After dinner there was a concert, in which Emma sang "Come Cheer Up, Fair Emma," followed by a ball and a supper. Nelson was wearing his diamond sword, and unfortunately a large diamond dropped out of the hilt. In spite of the offer of 500 dollars reward, it could not be found. It was on this occasion that, referring to the previous afternoon when he had gone to Altona on a visit and had returned after 4 P.M. to find the city gates shut, he gave the toast, "May the Hamburghers who shut their gates against their friends be more careful to shut them against their enemies."

Hamburg was an expensive place to stay, and Nelson was obliged to draw more than £1,000 to pay their bills. The whole journey from Leghorn cost about £3,000, and Sir William owed Nelson half of it. This arrangement, which was continued when they lived together later, meant that Nelson met half of Emma's expenses. Of the party of seventeen he and his followers accounted for three. So they were sharing in more ways than one, and Sir William was aware of, if not grateful for, it.

Before they left Hamburg, Nelson went shopping and bought, according to Miss Knight, "a magnificent lace trimming for a Court dress for Lady

Nelson, and a black lace cloak for another lady who, he said, had been very attentive to his wife during his absence." Nothing much seems to have been said of Fanny, though Miss Knight wrote, "I remember his saying, while we were at Leghorn, that he hoped Lady Nelson and himself would be much with Sir William and Lady Hamilton, and that they would all very often dine together, and that when the latter couple went to their musical parties, he and Lady Nelson would go to bed." Well, he may have said that at Leghorn, he may even have meant it, but he did not say it at Hamburg. Miss Knight had her own reasons for wishing people to believe that it was proper for her to have accepted the Hamiltons' hospitality and generosity after her mother's death in June 1799. Her opinion that "There was certainly at that time no impropriety in living under Lady Hamilton's roof" must be taken for what it was, the opinion of a clever and interested young lady.

Nelson had written the Admiralty for a frigate to take him home from Hamburg. When it was apparent that his request was not going to be granted, the *King George* packet was summoned to collect them, and they embarked for Yarmouth on October 31.

Fanny was waiting in London, where she had been, in obedience to her husband's orders, since the second week in October. Davison had not yet rented a house, and she was staying at Nerot's Hotel, Kings Street, St. James's, with her father-in-law, the Reverend Edmund Nelson.

There can be no question but that she knew of the stories about Nelson's relationship with Lady Hamilton; even if her acquaintances were too polite to mention them in her hearing, the hints in the newspapers were clear enough. On December 3, 1799, she wrote to him, "I am fully persuaded many are jealous of your character and your countrymen in general will allow you are deserving of all that has been done but for all the world to acknowledge your great abilities is another thing"; and on January 4, 1800, "I wish my dear Josiah was with you. He never writes, so much the better for he can never be accused of making mischief."

Nelson came in for as much criticism for his public actions as he did for his private ones. As the time of his return approached, so his name appeared more often in the gossip columns. The *Morning Post* of April 1, 1800, had this: "Of all the seeds lately sent home by Lord Nelson, that of 'Love lays bleeding' was sown and gathered at Naples." On April 29 there was a report that he was acting as a lord in waiting to the King of Naples: "Lord Nelson by signing himself *Bronte Nelson* prefers the Neapolitan to the English title." The visit to Vienna was not to be missed; on September 15: "The German State Painter, we are assured, is drawing Lady Hamilton and Lord Nelson at *full length together*. An Irish correspondent hopes the artist will have delicacy enough to put Sir William *between* them."

The *Morning Chronicle*, the leading Whig paper, had more serious accusations to make. The issue of September 11 called for Nelson and the Hamiltons to be taken to account on their return. "There is indeed a terrible scene to be unfolded of what has passed in Naples these last twelvemonths. We can assert, from the best information, that the British name has suffered a reproach on the Continent by the transactions at Naples." On the 19th there was this: "Lord Nelson, it is reported, leads the fashion in Vienna. We do not believe it. We do not know that a British Admiral shews best in drawing rooms. If Lord Nelson is to be 'the glass wherein the noble youth do dress themselves' we hope it will be, as once it was, 'to do brave acts.' "

Emma was also a fascinating subject for the two or three thousand readers of the *Post*. On September 19 it was noticed, "The *Nelson caps* at Vienna, have been introduced by Lady Hamilton, who is there the *Goddess of Fashion*"; and on October 4, "Lady Hamilton will certainly be in London in the course of the present month. She will govern the fashionable world this winter."

The *Chronicle* followed its own line; on September 24: "A certain lady, according to newspaper report, gains many admirers at Vienna. It is well known *what flames* she kindled at Naples!" And answered the *Post* on October 6, "A paper of Saturday tells its readers that Lady Hamilton will lead the fashions of London next winter. This is no great compliment to our ladies of rank; but the news is not true. London is not Naples."

These were only faint rumblings of the storm of publicity that broke over the *tria* on their arrival in London. The newspapers were written for the ten thousand or so people who made up society out of a population of perhaps ten million. For every one person of rank, wealth and education, there were a hundred who had to manage without them. For every one person who laughed at Nelson for his folly, there were a hundred who loved him for his bravery.

Fanny loved her husband. She loved him, his father whom she always called "our father," and Josiah. Apart from Nelson's eldest brother Maurice, she did not have much time for the rest of his family. In 1800 she was an elegant body, aged forty-two, who was by no means overawed by her title and position. Though she was by nature shy and retiring, and her own poor health and constant attendance on the old clergyman forced her further into retirement, she was easy in company and received her friends, rich relations from the West Indies, county acquaintances, and many admirals and captains who came to pay their respects, with composure. She attended Court, and the elegance and taste of her dress were remarked in the papers. She conversed without embarrassment with the Sovereign. "Our gracious King thought it was a long time since I heard from you," she wrote Nelson in March 1800, "and told me the wind was changed therefore he hoped I should hear from you very soon. The Queen always speaks to me, with so much condescension that I like her very much."

In February she had nursed "our father" out of a sickbed that his doctors had feared was a deathbed. As well as her usual colds and coughs, she was suffering from rheumatism that stiffened her legs; there was a little fussiness about her, she fluttered her hands disparagingly at anything like ill manners or extravagance. She managed her little household with economy, saved her husband's money, complained about the cost of living, deprecated the modern fashions—in short, she was just such a careful, anxious, neat, respectable and proper person as ever entered a drawing room without attracting the smallest attention.

She was deeply shocked by the rumors of Nelson's behavior. First of all she wanted to go out to him, and, when this was curtly refused, she put in her letters the wishes of other people, Lord Hood, Sir Peter Parker and his lady, that he would come home. She could not beg him to return, she had enough dignity for that; the most she would allow herself was a prayer to heaven that they would soon meet. She was hurt by his short letters and the reflections on Josiah, but she never taxed Nelson with them. She wrote her fortnightly letters as she had always done, and obeyed him in everything. The prints for Lady Hamilton were sent, she packed them, and when Hardy mentioned that the Admiral would appreciate a little attention to that lady, she sent a cap and kerchief of the latest style, regretting they might be thought too whimsical. Heaven knows what a charade Emma must have made out of them!

When the time came for Lady Nelson's faults to be paraded for the benefit of Emma's party, nothing could be recruited except the bedraggled lie that she did not appreciate Nelson's greatness. Of course she appreciated it. His achievements made her Lady Nelson, Duchess of Bronte, and brought her into the company of the Hoods, the St. Vincents, the Spencers, and the great Norfolk families of Coke and Walpole. She knew Nelson's consequence, and wrote him once about a meeting with Lady Minto, "It is not in her power by her acquaintance to honour your wife." What she did not do was flatter him.

On March 29, 1800, in one of the last letters (of those that have survived) which she wrote Nelson before his return, Fanny said, "I can with safety put my hand on my heart and say it has been my study to please and make you happy, and I still flatter myself we shall meet before very long. I feel most sensibly all your kindnesses to my dear son, and I hope he will add much to our comfort. Our good father has been in good spirits ever since we heard from you. Indeed my spirits were quite worn out, the time had been so long. I thank God for the preservation of my dear husband, and your recent success off Malta. The taking of the *Genereux* seems to give great spirits to all. God bless you my dear husband and grant us a happy meeting." She never wrote an unappreciative or unfeeling line to him in her life. In October, in London, she was waiting for that meeting.

With Fanny at Nerot's Hotel, and, according to Captain Hardy, a good deal more impatient than she was, waited the Reverend Edmund Nelson. "Our father" was seventy-eight, a gentle and mildly selfish old man, who preferred Fanny's company to that of his children. His principal pleasure seemed to be hearing good reports of his famous son, and occasionally writing to his dear Hor, in big shaky characters, homely letters with touches of the pulpit in them. "Though your reputation stands high, very high, yet we all know that the most beautiful building may receive an injury by some accidental event or by a secret Enemy, before it is completely finished." He was not happy to be kept waiting in a London hotel while Horace was enjoying himself in Hamburg, but he probably attributed the delay to the unaccountable will of Providence, and endured it with fortitude. However, he was to show more independence of spirit in the last year of his life than he had before, which suggests, as nothing else does, that Nelson did not get all his fire from his mother.

The Nelsons were undistinguished as a family. Not one of them, before or after, came anywhere near Horatio. They were parsons and their daughters married parsons, or, and this was never happily accepted, into trade. For example, no one was quite sure whether cousin Goulty of Norwich ought to come to the hero's funeral, let alone ride in one of the carriages. However, the Reverend Edmund had married Catherine Suckling, of a wealthy and well-connected family, related to the Walpoles; her brother, Captain Maurice Suckling, was something of a hero himself.

The eldest surviving son of this marriage was Maurice. In 1800 he was forty-seven, and an under-commissary in the Navy Office with a salary of £300 a year. He had a cottage at Laleham, six miles from Windsor, where he lived with Sarah (Sukey) Ford, a lady who was unfortunately blind, and who was generally known as Mrs. Nelson. Maurice was closer to Fanny than any of the rest of the family, and, on important occasions, wrote her rather stiff and formal letters, as if addressing a board. He was Horatio's favorite brother, well, this was natural enough as his eldest brother, and was closely associated with Alexander Davison. Maurice had no wish to succeed as Lord Nelson, he had no children, not much money, and his sole ambition was to be made a commissioner. He evidently disapproved of his brother's relationship with Emma; he had nothing to do with the Hamiltons; and Nelson never sent his letters to her through Maurice. He used Troubridge or Evan Nepean, the Secretary to the Navy, or Davison. There is not a lot to be said about Maurice, except that no one disliked him, and it must be hoped he found some consolation with his dear Sukey for the disappointments of his career.

The eldest daughter was Susanna, who was now forty-five. Twenty years previously she had married Thomas Bolton, a merchant from Norwich, and even the Nelsons did not consider it a favorable match. Later Bolton bought himself a farm at Cranwich, near Brandon in Norfolk; it was said by the family that the farm was too large for him; in any event, he was regularly short of money and borrowed both from Lady Nelson and Lady Hamilton. Fanny thought very little of him. "My maid tells me," she wrote Nelson, "that they say at Ipswich his family is supported from the Gaming Table—true it is that he is always there, so his family says, but they call it—the Coffee House." In February 1800 Bolton visited Fanny in London, "Our Father had him up to ask *how the four kings went on* VERY HIGH PLAY, HIGHER than ever."

Susanna was by no means an insignificant person. She had a good deal of spirit and was sorry for her famous brother's behavior. A family of six, an objectionable husband, dependence on that brother for money to get them out of trouble and to pay for the education of her eldest boy, blunted her finer feelings, and she was obliged to change her loyalty from Nelson's wife to his mistress. In 1800 the first son, Tom, a pleasant but not very bright lad, was at school preparing to be sent to the East Indies. The next son, George, who had a scalt head and could not read at the age of eleven, was the midshipman who died on his way to the Mediterranean. The twins, Catherine (Kitty) and Susanna, were ill-tempered, ill-mannered, ill-washed girls, often at Round Wood with Fanny; their grandfather called them, "True Boltons, I pity the men that marry them, but no man will venture." The two little girls, Anne and Elizabeth, were too young as yet for anyone to say whether they were horrors or not.

The queerest member of the family was William, aged forty-three, and Nelson's elder by eighteen months. He was a clergyman, with the good living of Hilborough in Norfolk worth £700 a year. The family called him the "Rector," as if he was too odd a creature to deserve a Christian name.

In 1786 he had married Sarah Yonge, who was eight years older than himself, and they had two children, Horatio, at Eton, and Charlotte, at a school for young ladies.

The Rector was crude, vulgar and ambitious; a heavy, ill-looking man with an uncouth manner of speech that sometimes frightened his hearers. Fanny thought he was "the roughest mortal surely that ever lived." He was obsessed with the notion that his brother's victories ought to bring him the rewards he was incapable of earning for himself. After the Nile his sister Catherine wrote, "I daresay he thinks the *Mitre* is very near falling upon *his head. Now* he will be *very great* in his own Eyes. Poor fellow he has his good qualities, though he has an odd way of shewing them."

He was continually nagging Fanny to put in a good word for him with the great people she knew. In June 1799 she wrote her husband, "The various passions that torment the Rector discomposes our good father who has been describing them to me. First of all ambition, pride and a selfish disposition." As to the good word, "Some women can say or do anything. I cannot and feel happy it is my disposition by which I never get myself into any scrapes." The dislike of the William Nelsons for Fanny probably stemmed from this reticence.

The Rector was no less importunate with his brother. "What must we think," he wrote him in January 1800, "of the gratitude of Ministers who pass over your Father and Brother almost every day? No longer ago than last week, *Two* Deaneries, and *Two* Prebendal Stalls were disposed of, but the name of *Nelson* is not even mentioned or perhaps thought of by Mr. Pitt."

He and his wife were quick to court any new friend of Nelson's, from whom his sole chance of preferment must come. They were the first to take Emma up, or rather, to be taken up by Emma. She found them willing allies in her campaign against Fanny, and congenial company.

Nelson's youngest sister, Catherine, was thirty-three the year he came home. She was married to George Matcham, an interesting gentleman of means. In twelve years of marriage, they had had eight children and they were to have four more. Catherine, therefore, had little space left in her letters after she had listed who had colds, who had measles, and who had whooping cough. That little space was devoted to praise of Nelson, criticism of Fanny, and a few kind words for Emma.

George Matcham inherited a small fortune in India and traveled back to England overland. He was a restless, curious person, always making plans to move to town when he was in the country, and to the country when he was in town. His large and increasing family seemed to take him by surprise, and he regarded them with both delight and regret. He talked to Nelson, but to no one else in the family. The Matchams were presently living in Bath.

These were the people who found themselves, in that October of 1800, suddenly anticipating the return of their brother, the Hero of the Nile, Lord Nelson.

CHAPTER SEVEN

Scandal in London

ON THURSDAY, November 6, 1800, the *King George* packet arrived at Yarmouth in stormy weather. The pilot came out, and it took a glass of spirits and a few hard words from the Admiral to persuade him to steer them in over the bar. Normally, the passengers went ashore in boats, but Nelson was having none of that.

All Yarmouth was there to greet the hero as he landed, and, as he never quitted a large lady and elderly gentleman, they received the same hearty welcome. The flags were flying and the bells ringing. The horses were taken from their coach and burly fishermen dragged them to the Wrestlers Inn where they were to spend the night. In between being called out on the balcony to receive the salutes of the militia, and being called in to receive the Mayor and Corporation, Nelson managed to write three notes. The first was to the local vicar, saying that he and his friends would attend church the next day to give thanks for mercies vouchsafed. The second was to the Admiralty, begging to acquaint their Lordships of his arrival and his wish to serve immediately. The third was to Fanny, whom he supposed to be at Round Wood, telling her that he and the Hamiltons would be there for Saturday dinner and would stay the night. He had completely forgotten that he had written to her from Vienna asking her to meet him in London.

They rumbled out of Yarmouth the next day, with Sir William's traveling coach leading the way, and an escort of the volunteer cavalry trotting alongside. Ipswich was the next stop, and there they were received with the same vigorous enthusiasm as they were dragged through the town with resounding huzzas.

Round Wood was only a few miles from Ipswich, and they set off about noon. They found the house closed. There was no going back to the town that had just bid them farewell, and they drove on to Colchester. Nelson must have felt aggrieved, and it was an occasion to slight a rival that Emma would not have missed. The welcome at the Essex town was as noisy and exuberant as the others, but it was a pleasure that was wearing thin, and they would have preferred the horses left in the shafts, so that they could reach their inn with time for something to eat before going to bed.

Their tempers could not have been of the best as they set out for London early on Sunday morning.

The first thing to hit London was a freak storm, which began about noon and lasted for twenty minutes. Tiles were blown off in Fleet Street, chimney pots fell in Grosvenor Square, some trees in Kensington Gardens were uprooted, and the north windows of the Foundling Hospital were blown in. Clergymen in their pulpits preached all the harder as the lead was ripped from the roofs over their heads. People and parapets were knocked down by the wind in Lincoln's Inn fields. The storm went as quickly as it had come, and was shortly followed into town by Lord Nelson.

"LORD NELSON OF THE NILE!" announced the *Morning Post* next day.

> *The chamber, where*
> *The GOOD man meets his doom, is privileg'd*
> *Beyond the common walks of life?*
> YOUNG

His Lordship arrived yesterday afternoon at three o'clock at Nerot's Hotel King-street, St. James's, in the German travelling carriage of Sir William Hamilton. In the coach came with his Lordship Sir William and Lady Hamilton and a black female attendant. The noble Admiral, who was dressed in full uniform, with three stars on his breast and two gold medals, was welcomed by repeated huzzas from the crowd which the illustrious tar returned with a low bow. Lord Nelson looked extremely well, but in person is very thin: so is Sir William Hamilton: but Lady Hamilton looks charmingly, and is a very fine woman. . . . The first interview between Lady Nelson, the Admiral and his father, took place in the hall of Nerot's hotel. About ten minutes after their arrival his Grace the Duke of Queensbury paid them a visit, and staid about an hour.

At five o'clock Lord and Lady Nelson, Sir William and Lady Hamilton dined together. At half past seven his Lordship went in a chariot to Earl Spencer, and about half an hour after, Lady Nelson paid a friendly visit to the Countess Spencer, where with a select party they passed the evening.

That the Duke of Queensberry should have visited the new arrivals was a bonus for the newspapers. "Old Q.," at the age of seventy-six, was always good for a snigger. He was related to Sir William, but heaven knows what he was doing there, unless it was leering at Emma. There was a note from Charles Greville. As Vice-Chamberlain, Greville had an ear in the Court, and a shrewd idea of how his uncle and aunt would be received. Emma was not going to be received at all, and Sir William had to see Lord Grenville as soon as possible, to try and repair the damage done by Paget, Lock, and the rest.

The unsatisfactory nature of the public situation of the three was noticed by St. Vincent in a letter to Nepean. "It is evident from Lord Nelson's letter to you on his landing, that he is doubtful of the propriety of his conduct. I have no doubt he is pledged to getting Lady Hamilton received at St. James's and everywhere, and that he will get into much brouillerie about it."

Nelson was pledged to more than that and, though his relationship with Fanny can only be guessed at, the signs of estrangement were soon apparent. In the meantime, he stayed on at Nerot's Hotel, while the Hamiltons went to Beckford's house, 22 Grosvenor Square. Naturally, Mrs. Cadogan and Miss Knight went with them, but the young lady soon left and accepted an invitation to stay with the Nepeans. "Most of my friends," she wrote, "were very urgent with me to drop the acquaintance, but, circumstanced as I had been, I feared the charge of ingratitude, though greatly embarrassed as to what to do, for things became very unpleasant."

Monday, November 10, was the day of the Lord Mayor's Feast, which afforded a favorable opportunity for presenting Nelson with the sword voted him by the City. However, etiquette demanded that the Admiral's first public appearance should be at the levee, which was held on Wednesdays, and he ought to have obtained the King's permission before accepting the Lord Mayor's invitation. Whether he did or not is open to question, but there is some reason to think that if he did, King George was not aware of it.

That morning Nelson, in what was called half-dress, paid his respects at the Admiralty. He was coming with a companion through the Adelphi Buildings and into the Strand when he was recognized and found himself in the middle of a mob. He was in some danger of disappearing beneath his wellwishers, and pushed his way into Somerset House, the home of the Navy Office. When he came out, there was still a crowd waiting, and they followed him down Whitehall to Lord Grenville's residence.

In the afternoon Fanny went with Princess Castelcicala to Somerset House to watch the Lord Mayor's procession going by water to the City. Nelson and Sir William joined the parade at the Tower in Sir William's coach. At the top of Ludgate Hill they were spotted by the crowd, and once again the horses were relieved of their burden, which was willingly taken up as it was downhill all the way to the Mansion House. The hero waved his handkerchief and more than once put his hand out of the window for his grateful countrymen and women to press and kiss.

After dinner, which was a regular gargantuan affair involving much moaning of turtles, lowing of cattle, groaning of boards, and eructating of aldermen, the sword was presented with a lengthy patriotic speech. Nelson made a short patriotic answer. It was a fine sword, cost 200 guineas; the hilt was gold, ornamented with blue enamel and diamonds, and decorated with a crocodile and anchors.

Nelson was showing a disposition to keep clear of Fanny, or at least to avoid her company by being in company. He spent most of Tuesday with the Duke of Clarence, who doubtless bored him, as he did everyone else, with his claim to be Lord High Admiral. Clarence, who had given Fanny away at her wedding, was proud of his friendship with Nelson. He had little else to be proud of, unless it was Mrs. Jordan and the brood of illegitimate children he kept at Bushy House.

Wednesday was given to the levee, and Nelson went with Sir William to St. James's. The Admiral was dressed in full uniform, with the Grand Signior's chelengk in his hat, his three stars on his breast and the King of Naples' portrait around his neck. It seems unlikely that he set out to brave the King's displeasure, or that, having written for advice on the subject, he was ignorant of the proper dress in which to meet his Sovereign. His new orders had not been gazetted, but a word from the King would have been enough to entitle him to wear them. He had dropped the Bronte from his signature in England, and it would have been as easy to have taken two stars off his coat.

His reception by the King was offhand, almost pointedly disapproving. Collingwood said that Nelson had told him, "His Majesty merely asked him if he had recovered his health; and then, without waiting for an answer, turned to General ———, and talked to him near half an hour in great good humour. It could not be about his successes." Another gentleman reported, "He was coldly received by the King, who merely observed that his Lordship had come to Town on Monday and was to hoist his Flag in the Channel Fleet; then turned and spoke to another." The reference to Monday suggests that the King might have taken exception to Nelson's appearance in the City. Most likely the King disapproved of what he had heard about Naples and Palermo. Who knew what went on inside George III's head?

That evening Nelson and Fanny dined at the Spencer's house, which was situated inside the precincts of the Admiralty. The last time they had dined there, in the spring of 1798, Nelson had told Lady Spencer that Fanny was beautiful, accomplished, an angel who had saved his life by her care and attention; he had behaved like a lover, handing her into dinner, sitting by her, refusing to be parted from her. This time, the Countess noted, with something like relish, "he treated her with every mark of dislike, and even of contempt." There were some walnuts she had peeled and put in a glass for him, which he had pushed aside so roughly the glass had broken. Fanny had wept, and in the drawing room had told her everything. What a triumph for the Countess! But other people's wretchedness was always the happiest subject for a conversation.

The Queen's drawing room was held on a Thursday, and Thursday, November 13, was no exception. Society held its breath. Would Queen Charlotte receive Lady Hamilton? Lord and Lady Nelson were there, and Sir William Hamilton, and Captain Hardy with four captains who had been promoted after the battle of the Nile—but no Lady Hamilton. Society breathed until the next Thursday. Emma was the topic of the day, and the *Morning Herald* gave this sketch of her for the benefit of its readers.

> Her Ladyship is in her 49th year, rather taller than the common height, still displaying a superior graceful animation of figure, now a little on the wane, from too great a propensity to the *en bon point*. Her *attitudinarian graces*, so varying in their style, and captivating in their effect, are declining also, under this unfortunate personal extension. Her teeth are lovely, and her hair is of the darkest brown, immensely thick, and trails to the ground. Her eyes are black, and possess the most fascinating attraction, but her nose is rather too short for the Grecian *contour* of her face, which, notwithstanding, is singularly expressive; and her *conversazione*, if not solid and argumentative, are at least sprightly and unceasing. Such, after ransacking Herculaneum and Pompeia, for thirty-eight years, is the Chief curiosity, with which that celebrated *antiquarian* Sir William Hamilton, has returned to his native Country.

The *Morning Post* came to her defense the next day. "A paper of yesterday makes Lady Hamilton 49 years of age—Monstrous! This is adding *ten* at least, rather than deducting a few as common politeness would." The *Post* also mentioned her long hair. "Lady Hamilton must appear as *rara avis* among our fashionable croppies. Her Ladyship's hair is so long that it touches the ground." The portrait by Schmidt painted at Dresden, confirms Mrs. St. George's description, so it seems certain that she wore a wig. She knew how to make herself noticed. That she should want to be noticed is a different matter. The reference to the "unfortunate personal extension," which the *Herald* pursued later, suggests she was pregnant. It is a subject that must be reserved for a fuller discussion.

After the drawing room Sir William and Emma went to dine with Queensberry. Nelson, who was sitting for his portrait, sent a note. "My dear Lady Hamilton, I have had but a very indifferent night, but from Sir William Beechey's will come to you to know weither it is fixed for me to dine with the Duke of Queensberry, to say the truth I am not fond of meeting strangers."

If he meant the last remark, he could hardly have enjoyed the days that followed, in which he devoted himself to meeting as many strangers as possible. He visited the Royal Exchange, India House and the offices of the Turkey Company, where he received a great silver bowl, a masterpiece of craftsmanship by Paul Storr. In the evenings he joined large parties at the theater.

The theater then had little of the formal dreariness it has since acquired. While a performance was always something of an occasion, the audience did not feel it necessary to submit dumbly to whatever was put before them. They were quite capable of laughing at a tragedy and weeping at a farce; of applauding a good speech and hissing a bad one; of joining in a chorus; in short, of enjoying themselves immoderately, which would not be tolerated today.

There was a wealth of talent, and the two great rivals, Covent Garden and Drury Lane, presented opera, ballet, and spectacular battle pieces, as well as the rather dim romances and dimmer farces that appealed to the taste of the time. Sheridan survives, all the rest have gone. However, there was as much doing in the boxes and the pit as on the stage; whether it was the lunatic Hadfield taking a potshot at George III—in one of his more lovable moments, George turned to Queen Charlotte, who was about to throw a fit, and said, "Only a squib, a squib; they are firing squibs"—or whether it was the appearance of Lord Nelson in a box between Lady Nelson and Lady Hamilton.

On November 17 the hero was supposed to have gone to Drury Lane. "The splendors of *Pizarro* will not prove more attractive than his Lordship, whose appearance occasioned the theatre to overflow *thirteen* times at Vienna," said the *Chronicle*. The *Post* was better informed. Nelson had gone to Old Bannister's benefit at the Theatre Royal Haymarket, which used to be called the Little Theatre. "The whole audience rose to salute him in an ecstacy of joy, clapping, huzzaing, and waving their hats. His Lordship seemed much affected; and never was enthusiasm more warm and prolonged than that with which he was received." Young Bannister appeared in *Ways and Means* and Old Bannister did his imitation of Garrick. The *Chronicle* got its own back. "A foreign journal remarks with truth, that Lord Nelson's shattered arm, and his eye lost in his country's service, are more honourable marks of distinction than the innumerable ribbons &c. which are the perpetual ornaments of his person."

The next evening belonged to Covent Garden, where the comedy *Life* was playing, followed by the spectacle of *The Mouth of the Nile* with a representation of the Glorious First of August. The theater was full to bursting, and when Nelson appeared in his box, on the left near the stage, the audience burst into applause, louder and longer than anyone could remember. Nelson bowed deeply, and again, and kept on bowing. Old Reverend Edmund, who had been persuaded to come along, burst into tears. Then the cast sang "Rule Britannia" and Nelson sat down with Fanny on his left, and Emma on his right. "Lady Hamilton," somebody remarked, "sat on that side of Lord Nelson on which he is *disarmed*." Next morning's *Herald* described their dresses.

> Lady Nelson appeared in white with a violet satin head-dress and small white feather. Her Ladyship's person is of a very pleasing description, her features are handsome and exceedingly interesting: and her general appearance is at once prepossessing and elegant. Lady Hamilton is rather *en bon point* but her person is nevertheless highly graceful, and her face extremely pretty. She wore a blue satin gown and head-dress, with a fine plume of feathers.

Sir William, Nelson's father, and Captain Hardy sat behind. The comedy went off with a bang. Then Munden came forward and sang a song by young Dibdin.

> *May Peace be the end of the strife we maintain,*
> *For our Freedom, our King, and our right to the main!*

178

We're content to shake hands; if they won't, why, what then!
We must send out brave Nelson to thresh 'em again.

And up came the applause louder than before, and up jumped Nelson to bow his thanks. It took another chorus of "Rule Britannia" to get the house in order for the next piece. *The Mouth of the Nile* naturally could not fail to bring the audience to their feet, and Nelson and his party left to cheers and huzzas that followed them out into the Garden.

That was a great evening and it was finished off at Lady Elcho's, where Emma sang and the Nelsons listened, at least one of them rapturously.

The most significant evening at the theater, and the last time Fanny and her husband appeared together in public, was on November 24, when they went to Drury Lane to see *Pizarro*.

Kotzebue's turgid melodrama had been dressed up by Sheridan with some fancy language, and was a great hit in London. Pizarro hats were in fashion for a whole season. It would be an imposition to relate the plot, which was contrived to draw a tear a line; the play is a monument to the fashionable emotion of sensibility, which, metaphorically, enabled a young lady to swoon over a dying violet while watching a public execution.

The Nelsons, Hamiltons, Reverend Edmund, and Princess Castelcicala, were in a box together. The house was crowded and they had been greeted with cheers and "Rule Britannia." To Lady Hamilton's regret, Mrs. Siddons was not playing the part of Elvira, but Mrs. Powell was doing very well; "forcibly impressive," said a critic, "and her acting drew many tears from the blaze of beauty around."

At the end of Act Three the jealous and inhuman Pizarro, having resisted the entreaties of his love Elvira for the life of the youth Alonzo, stalked off with the words "He dies at sunrise!" Elvira wound herself up: "'Tis well! 'tis just I should be humbled. . . . Fall, fall, ye few reluctant drops of weakness—the last these eyes shall ever shed. How a woman can love, Pizarro, thou hast known too well—how she can hate, thou hast yet to learn. Yes, thou undaunted!—thou, whom yet no mortal hazard has appalled—thou, who on Panama's brow . . ." and she began to pile it on . . . "raging elements . . . horrid night . . . the crashing thunder's drift . . . the red volcano's mouth!—thou, who when battling on the sea . . . bestride a fragment of the smoking wreck . . . wave thy glittering sword above thy head, as thou wouldst defy the world in that extremity!" She hit the top: "Come, fearless man! now meet the last and fellest peril of

179

thy life; meet and survive—an injured woman's fury, if thou canst." There was a shriek from the box and Lady Nelson fainted!

The curtain fell, but instead of applause there were murmurings, people looked up to where the hero sat immobile. After a few moments his wife recovered and was helped out by Lady Hamilton and old Mr. Nelson. Soon afterward they left the theater. But Nelson, as reported by the *Morning Post*, stayed where he was to the end.

Fanny was an injured woman. She was reminded of it every day by the innuendoes in the press and by Nelson's studied indifference. Sometime about November 24 they had moved to a furnished house, 17 Dover Street. He had blamed her, of course, for not having a house ready for him on his return, though the fault was Davison's. The guilty make a point of blaming those they have injured. In the first week of December he dined out at least the four times reported in the newspapers. His father wrote Mrs. Matcham, "Your Bro is so constantly on the wing that I can but get a short glimpse myself."

Fanny was a gentlewoman. It is not credible that she started any broils such as Emma claimed drove Nelson out into the streets to wander half the night before coming to Grosvenor Square and flinging himself on her bed in despair. Nelson could be intolerable in a mood of self-pity, but not Fanny. She had given too much of her life to other people to be accused of that. She was as proud as her birth and situation demanded, but if her eyes showed her reproach, her letters showed only her concern.

In the meantime, Nelson was as wretched as his dearest friend could have wished him. "This place of London," he wrote to an old acquaintance, "but ill suits my disposition, however, till the War is finished I shall not be much from my proper Element." He was anxious to go to sea again, not only to escape from his domestic problems, but also to solve his financial ones.

At the end of November his account with Marsh & Creed stood at just over £16,000 in stocks of various kinds. He was obliged to sell half his holdings to pay his debts incurred at Palermo and on the journey home. £4,000 of what was left had been brought to him by Fanny, and he was determined not to touch it. By selling his shares, he halved his income from them, which together with his pensions and half-pay as Rear-Admiral, was all he had to live on. The expenses of a London house could not be supported for long.

His main hope for improving his income, apart from curtailing his expenditure by going to sea, was an impending court case with Lord St. Vincent. In October 1799 the *Alcmene* had captured two Spanish frigates, and the Commander in Chief's share of the prize money was £14,000. This had been paid to St. Vincent, who was then in England convalescing. Nelson claimed that as he was the senior officer in the Mediterranean, and the captures had been made while the *Alcmene* was under his command, the C. in C.'s share should have come to him. Nelson's case was being handled by William Haslewood, his solicitor. "God forbid I should deprive you of a farthing," St. Vincent wrote Nelson from Tor Abbey where he was staying, and then added several pages of reasons why he should.

On November 20 the noble Admiral was introduced in the House of Lords between Lords Romney and Grenville; he went to Court again; he sat to Mrs. Damer, who was making a bust for the Guildhall and who complained he never kept his head still; he sat to Lemuel Abbott, who was touching up the portrait he had painted in 1798 and adding the new stars and medals, in, as Nelson said, "an attempt to adonize it."

He dined at the Priory, the home of the Earl of Abercorn, Sir William's relation, where the Hamiltons were spending a weekend. He dined with Davison in St. James's Square, where the company included the Prince of Wales, Earls Chatham and Spencer, Mr. Pitt and his cabinet, Sir William, and Admiral Payne (Emma's downfall!). There were three gentlemen who had slept with Emma at the table, and one who wanted to.

He and Sir William dined with the Scottish Corporation on St. Andrew's Day, and with the directors of the East India Company the day after. He was out so much that St. Vincent, who did not want to lose his best officer through a sweat, warned him against "going out of smoking hot rooms into the damp putrid air of London streets." But he was not out quite so much as the papers suggested, because the managers of every entertainment in town, from Mr. Pidcock's zoo to Sans Souci in Leicester Square, had discovered they could ensure a full house by mentioning that Admiral Nelson might drop in that evening.

Following in the train of his meteoric friend, Sir William Hamilton was gloomily contemplating his old debts while inevitably incurring new ones. His estate was mortgaged for £13,000 and he owed his bankers, Ross & Ogilvie, £7,000. His income from the estate was limited by Greville's expenditure on a great plan that neither of them (nor anyone else for 150 years) would live to see finished. Milford Haven was to become a harbor to rival Liverpool and Bristol in importance. It was a better natural harbor than either, and there was only one drawback, it was stuck out on the nose of Wales, miles from anywhere. However, Greville got the consent of Parliament for his plan, and spent his uncle's money on works that are still his monument—a dry dock.

The old gentleman's hopes for a competence on which to finish his life in comfort were pinned on Lord Grenville. He was claiming compensation for his losses at Naples and expenses at Palermo. A pension of £2,000 a year he hoped would come as a matter of course. Nelson helped him work out his claim, which amounted to £10,000 for his furniture, carriages, etc., left behind at Naples, and £13,213 for the bills drawn at Palermo. Nothing stuck to Lord Grenville, except the pensions he took for himself and his wife, and Sir William did not receive even the courtesy of an answer. He was very upset. "I cannot think," he said, "that the King has forgot that my Mother reared us, and the same nurse suckled us." The King was not to blame. The claim was lodged in the bowels of the Treasury.

In spite of his debts, Sir William entertained expansively at Grosvenor Square and bought the lease of 23 Piccadilly, a house opposite Green Park. There were several reasons why he gave his musical parties and why he needed an elegant residence in town. He had a position to maintain as an ex-Ambassador, and a gentleman of taste and learning; he had recently been elected to the Council of the Royal Society. He intended to sell his collection of pictures and vases, and knew the world well enough to realize he would get a better price if the buyers believed he did not want the money. He needed influential friends to forward his claims and knew a *quid* required a *pro quo*. Of course, Emma figured largely in his plans, and she was not to be put off with a cottage in the country or anything west of Bond Street. There was another reason, though how far it influenced Sir William is difficult to say. Emma and Nelson thought it important.

Shortly after his return Sir William was approached by Beckford with a plan to solve his financial difficulties while gratifying Beckford's main ambition. Beckford was a lot of things, a genius, a millionaire, a pederast, and he wanted to be a peer. He suggested that Sir William should apply for a peerage. His long service and boyhood friendship with the King deserved no less. On Sir William's death, the remainder must go to Beckford; in return, Beckford would pay Sir William £2,000 a year until that time, and Emma £500 a year thereafter. It was an odd plan that never hatched, though Emma and her lover brooded on it occasionally. It might have persuaded the old Knight to spread himself a bit.

The trouble was that the fashionable people who went to Lady Hamilton's drawing room were those least likely to be heard in government or at Court. Prince Augustus and his morganatic wife Lady Augusta Murray, Old Q., Lord William Gordon, the Abercorns . . . Sir William's powerful relations, the Hamiltons and Warwicks, were pleased enough to see him, but not Emma. Emma had not been received at Court and everything stopped there.

The saga of "will she, won't she?" was followed by the newspapers and their readers with all the enthusiasm that is usually devoted to trivial questions of this kind.

The *Times* led off on November 18 with this canard: "Lady Hamilton, who is one of the Ladies of the Bed Chamber to the Queen of Naples, is to be presented at the next Drawing-room." When that proved a lame duck they followed it on the 29th with a report that emanated from Emma herself. "Lady Hamilton brought with her a letter from the Queen of Naples to the Queen of England, in which the former expresses how much she was obliged in common with the whole Court to Lady Hamilton, for the services rendered by her ladyship. It was principally owing to her exertions and activity which her conduct inspired, while our fleet was provisioning at Syracuse, that Lord Nelson was enabled to reach Aboukir so soon after the French army had landed."

The *Morning Post*, the fashionable paper, was more interested in Emma's complexion, "a most beautiful *tawny tinge*," and her attitudes. "Lady Hamilton is fitting up a room for the purpose of displaying her *attitudes* and in a short time she will give large *attitude parties*. *Attitudes* it is thought will be much more in vogue this winter than *shape* or *feature*." The reference to shape was no accident. The opportunity for another dig offered by the *Times*'s story was not to be missed. On December 1 there was this pretty obvious hint. "Lady Hamilton has arrived in the very nick of time in this country. It was owing to her Ladyship's activity that Lord Nelson's fleet was so soon *victualled* at Syracuse."

The *Morning Herald* was fascinated by Emma's past and was prepared to change the color of her cheeks to make its point. "Lady Hamilton's countenance is of so rosy and blooming a description that, as Dr. Graham would say, she appears so far a perfect '*Goddess of Health*'!" They agreed as to her condition. "Lady Hamilton has been a very fine woman; but she has acquired so much *en bon point*, and her figure is so swoln, that her features and form have lost almost all their original beauty. It was her figure for which she was particularly celebrated and in consequence of which her reputation commenced. She served for a model in the Academy of Painting and Sculpture. She was then Miss Hart. It was then doubtless that she acquired this taste and talent for fine attitudes and antique positions, in which she has displayed so much skill." On November 29 the paper referred to the Bed Chamber story. "It has been proposed in a certain elevated quarter, that Lady Hamilton should be introduced at Court as *Maid of Honour* to the Queen of Naples; but this has not yet been acceded to, from some doubtful principle of *etiquette,* not altogether of the *Courtly* kind." This was followed by a report that the Queen of Naples' letter had not been answered, which was confirmed on January 5, 1801. "Lady Hamilton has received no answer whatever to the recommendatory letter which the Queen of Naples wrote to our Queen in her favour, although a Great Personage received it at the Levee from Sir W.H. and was himself the bearer of this courtly epistle to his Royal Consort."

The *Morning Chronicle* confined itself to contradicting all the others. "The Papers have stated that Lady Hamilton has not been at Court, because she has received no answer to the Letter of Recommendation she brought from the Queen of Naples to her Britannick Majesty. We are told that the letter which Lady Hamilton brought from the Queen of Naples contained nothing respecting her Ladyship."

At best these papers are of value in providing a commentary on what was passing; their statements of facts are always slightly suspect, and if several said the same thing it was, as often as not, because they copied each other. The laws of libel barely existed compared to today, but, on the whole, the proprieties were observed. In the fashionable coterie a wink was as good as a nod, and when the *Post* wrote that Lady Hamilton had arrived in the very nick of time, the knowing ones knew for what.

So Emma's condition was sufficiently advanced to be noticed. She was evidently determined to brave it out in London with the help of her complaisant husband. Society would take its attitude from Sir William. This was one of the rules. Charles Greville wrote it down when he was advising his uncle on *bienséance.* "People who do not live with us are as indifferent to us as we to them, and, unless we make ourselves purposely the subject of general observation, that class leave us to ourselves. Those who know us take us with more discretion, if they are in confidence and we only open on a subject guardedly and in general terms, they will have discretion not to renew enquiry; those who are not in intimacy cannot take the liberty, and if they do, remain unsatisfied."

This is most civilized. This is the true freedom of the Englishman, impinged on by the church in the last century and the state in this, until it has almost gone. This is the inviolable right to turn around to anyone and say, "Mind your own business."

As long as Emma stood on her two feet and Sir William stood by her, no one would be so impolite as to ask when the happy event would take place. It was certainly an inconvenience for the old gentleman, and required all his indifference. Perhaps that was why Emma made a great sacrifice and sold her diamonds to help him pay for the furnishing of their new house. They needed everything—furniture, plate, crockery, linen, a coach, wine, a French cook . . . Nelson reckoned it out at about £2,500, over and above the £1,000 for the lease. Lady readers will appreciate the extent of Emma's sacrifice; gentlemen will perhaps agree that Sir William deserved it.

The *tria juncta in uno* were united again under the same roof at Christmas. William Beckford invited them to Fonthill, his estate near Salisbury. The rift between Nelson and Fanny was now so wide that he could go off with his friends, leaving her and "our father" to a lonely Christmas in Dover Street. The Matchams were in Bath, where Catherine was having yet another child. The Boltons were at Cranwich. Maurice was eating his turkey with Old Blindy at Laleham. Only the William Nelsons were in town, and they were shifting with the wind of Lord Nelson's inclination toward the Hamiltons.

Beckford's guests set off on December 19 and spent the night at the Star & Garter at Andover. The next morning, they drove on to Salisbury. On the borders of Wiltshire they were met by some gentlemen of the Yeoman Cavalry and escorted into the town through crowds who cheered them all the way to the Council House. The Mayor and Corporation were waiting, the hero was presented with the freedom of Salisbury in an oak box, and they all sat down to a cold collation. These freedoms were not free, and Nelson always left something for the poor, this time it was £20.

Outside the town hall the crowd was milling around the carriage. The little Admiral appeared on the steps, looked about with his good eye, and spotted two sailors, who were happily prepared for just such a distinction. One had lost his right arm at the Nile, the other claimed to have been present at his lordship's amputation and waved a bit of lace from his lordship's shirt to prove it. Both were rewarded with guineas. Nelson was good in crowds, as a correspondent of the *Gentleman's Magazine* noticed. "Lord Nelson unites a feeling and generous heart, a quick discernment of occasion, and popularity of manners." He was ready to give his hand to anyone, he was unashamed to let the tears show in his eyes, he was sincere and unaffected, he had the touch to take hearts.

They drove on toward Fonthill, and as they reached the neighborhood of that strange place, the fog rolled down, appropriately clouding their arrival in a mysterious gloom.

Their approach was awfully quiet; the comforting sounds of raucous carriage wheels and hoofs briskly striking the road were muffled on a mat of wet leaves. Then, through the somber darkness with its gray shroud of mist, they caught the faint orange light of flambeaux on the glistening stone arch of a Gothic gateway. An ill-assorted party of the Fonthill volunteers were waiting in the shadows, and fired a ragged and unconvincing *feu de joie*, before drifting away like disturbed spirits. The coach clattered across the cobbles beneath the arch and was then engulfed in the silence of the drive beneath a dripping canopy of trees.

They came upon the mansion suddenly. This was a solid modern structure, some distance from the Abbey, and they were reassured by the apparently normal appearance of their host on the steps.

William Beckford was then forty-one, with the look of a dissolute choirboy. He was married and had two girls, one of whom became Duchess of Hamilton, which was as near as Beckford ever go to a peerage. He had a fortune and the imagination to spend it; he created the fantastic *Vathek* when he was twenty-one, and devoted the rest of his life to emulating his hero. His palace was to be the most turreted, gabled, mullion-windowed, battlemented palace ever built. His tower was to be Vathek's tower: "He cast his eyes below, and beheld men not larger than pismires; mountains, than shells; and cities, than bee-hives." His collection was to be the world's museum. The reality was as insubstantial as the dream. The palace was demolished, the tower collapsed, the collection was discovered to be of the curious, the glittering, the trivial, the childish, and the least valuable. Beckford's saving grace was his humor, often at his own expense. Anyone who thinks him a fool should read the last pages of *Vathek*, the description of the Hall of Eblis where the caliph meets his doom with its terrible final judgment: "The condition of man upon earth is to be—humble and ignorant." Beckford was a tremendous romantic.

There was a large company at the mansion. In the mornings they looked over the house and wandered through the galleries and in the library. When the weather allowed, they went for excursions in the surrounding countryside. Dinner took up the afternoons, and in the evenings there were cards, conversation and music. Emma naturally sang "Rule Britannia" and "God Save the King," and performed duets with Banti, the Italian prima donna. The Abbey, which was in construction, was reserved for a special occasion.

After dinner on December 23 the company entered their carriages and set off through the darkening woods. Lanterns hung from the branches led them toward the Abbey. As they came in sight of the massive pile, an orchestra struck up a solemn march. The crenellated walls and half-erected tower looked as much as if they were falling down as building up; as if they were the ruins of a cathedral and not the foundations of a new structure.

Once past the great door they found themselves in a hall so high that the light barely reached the groined ceiling. They walked on into the Cardinal's Parlor, a room hung with purple damask and lit by silver sconces, where servants in hooded gowns silently took their cloaks and hats. Then they passed into the library. The immensity of the chamber was compensated by the richness of its decoration. Here the hangings were yellow, and in between the shelves of books there were candlelit shrines containing religious statues and reliquaries. Solemn music was playing from the gallery. The guests sat down at a vast refectory table covered with golden baskets of fruit and sweetmeats and flagons of spiced wine. But where was Emma, who was seldom absent when there was eating and drinking to be done?

She appeared like a ghost from the far end of the room, wearing a simple white robe and carrying a golden urn. "Agrippina," whispered Sir William to Nelson, who had not the slightest idea of what was going on, "bearing the ashes of Germanicus." Whether the Admiral was any the wiser or not, doubtless he looked as intelligent as the rest of the company as Emma went into her performance. Alternately supplicating and demanding, sorrowing and scorning, proud, angry, pathetic, and triumphant, Agrippina excited the Romans to revenge the death of her husband, and Emma excited tears from her audience. One critic claimed she was entitled to be rated "with the greatest actresses of the English stage."

As an encore Emma returned with two young ladies from among the guests and impersonated an abbess receiving two nuns into a convent. The critics said she performed her character "with the greatest truth and propriety," so it cannot have been so hilarious as it sounds. The performance ended at 11 P.M. and the company returned to the mansion.

Beckford's house and a party that consisted of scholars, poetasters, opera singers and journalists was an odd place to find a sailor, though no odder than an Italian palazzo. Nelson detested poets, fiddlers, whores and scoundrels, and there are no better words to describe the company Emma kept. She led him into strange waters.

The driest comment on the visit, which ended on Boxing Day, was made in the *Oracle* of January 9, 1801. "Notwithstanding all the accomplishments which Lady H acquired in *Italy*, the gentleman with whom she was lately on a visit to at *Font-Hill* is supposed to have a knowledge of *Italian manners* to which *that* Charming Lady must ever remain a *stranger!*"

At the turn of the year Mr. Pitt's chickens came home to roost, bringing with them a vulture or two. Politicians, who generally take the credit for the good acts of God, must expect to take the blame for the bad ones.

There was no relief from the near famine in the country that winter, unless one counts the flour saved by King George when he gave up eating soup and pastry. The poor had no resource except to gather in the streets in futile demonstrations, which ended in charges by the local cavalry, rick-burning, and savage sentences by outraged magistrates. Earnest gentlemen wrote monographs on the merits of rice and potatoes. The government suspended habeas corpus and put up the taxes.

January 1, 1801, was the date of the union between Great Britain and Ireland. This was meant to solve the problems of that tormented place by bringing them to Westminster from Dublin. It resulted in the Union Jack, and a short season of union balls where the ladies wore union caps. The problems were not reduced by being brought to London, but it was easier to ignore them there.

On the Continent the armistice after the battle of Marengo led to a congress at Lunéville, which was supposed to establish terms for peace. Nelson's old bogey, Thugut, had resigned and the Austrian delegation was led by Count Cobentzel. England had no seat at the congress and Bonaparte's price of admission was a naval armistice. In a desperate attempt to keep the struggle going, Pitt supported the war party in Vienna with a subsidy of £2½ millions. The Austrians renewed hostilities, and were decisively beaten by Moreau at Hohenlinden (December 3). There was a second armistice, and Cobentzel returned to Lunéville in the humiliating role of a defeated aggressor.

The last of Mr. Pitt's chickens, and the one that hatched the biggest egg, was Malta. The French garrison in La Valetta finally surrendered on September 5. The shortsighted policy of promising the island to the Order and its Grand Master, the Emperor Paul of Russia, ran the British government into the ridiculous position of being obliged to hand it over to a potential enemy. Paul had withdrawn from the coalition and was flirting with Bonaparte, whom he admired exceedingly. To add to the embarrassment of Mr. Pitt and Lord Grenville, Bonaparte mischievously ceded Malta to Russia.

There was no going on in that direction, and the government executed a smart about-turn. Paul had never been elected Grand Master. Paul had none of the qualifications to be Grand Master; for one thing, he belonged to the wrong religion; and for another, he had never been a knight of the Order, or lived in a state of celibacy, or waged perpetual war against the Turks. In short, there was no Grand Master and so the island might as well remain British. Pitt put on dark glasses to cure his myopia.

Paul was angered into active hostility. More than 200 British merchant ships were detained in Russian ports and the crews imprisoned. This was followed by a confederation of northern states. Russia, Sweden, Denmark and Prussia leagued themselves together to resist the British dominion of the sea. Sweden and Denmark were in the Russian sphere of influence and had no option but to join the confederacy. Prussia had no maritime interests, but coveted King George's Hanoverian territories and saw a chance to grab them.

This was a resurrection of the old armed neutrality of the American War of Independence. Britannia really did rule the waves. In wartime the British navy claimed the right to stop and search all neutral shipping, and to confiscate any cargoes destined for an enemy port. This was the way Great Britain engrossed much of the world's trade.

Nations protested, but individually were unable to resist the overwhelming strength of the British navy. In 1780, during the American war, the Empress Catherine the Great declared an armed neutrality, a union of neutral nations pledged to resist the right of search. It was completely ineffective, as Great Britain immediately retaliated by picking on the Dutch, smashing their fleet and seizing their colonies, and no other nation was prepared to risk such awful retribution.

In 1800 circumstances might be supposed to be more favorable to a confederacy of this sort, ostensibly neutral, but committed to resist aggression. The Russian navy boasted sixty-eight ships of the line and thirty frigates. The Swedish and Danish navies could produce perhaps half as many. Together they comprised a threat from the north of alarming proportions.

On December 31 Lords Nelson and Hood conducted the King to the throne in the House of Lords. In his speech His Majesty referred to the detention of British ships in Russia, and continued, "If it shall become necessary to maintain, against any combination, the honour and independence of the British Empire, and those maritime rights and interests on which both our prosperity and our security must always essentially depend, I entertain no doubt either of the success of those means which in such an event I shall be enabled to exert, or of the determination of my Parliament and my people to afford me a support proportioned to the importance of the interests which we have to maintain."

On the first day of the new year Nelson was promoted to Vice-Admiral of the Blue. He already knew that his flagship was to be the *San Josef*, one of the prizes he had taken at the battle of St. Vincent, and Hardy was down at Plymouth getting her ready.

Two days later he attended the funeral in Kent of his old captain, William Locker. He wrote to Emma, "Believe me when I say that I regret that I am not the person to be attended *upon* at this funeral, for, although I have had my days of Glory, yet I find this world is full of jealousy and envy, that I see but a very faint gleam of future comfort. I shall come to Grosvenor Square on my return from this melancholy procession, and hope to find in the smiles of my friends some alleviation from the cold looks and cruel words of my enemies."

Who were his enemies? His gentle wife and elderly father?

Nelson's last few days in London were spent in preparing his furniture, plate, provisions, crockery and clothes, to be carried down to his new ship. From his later correspondence it seems likely that he quarreled with Fanny. They were days he looked back on with hatred. The only record of words between them was made by Haslewood more than forty years later. He said that he had been at breakfast in their house and Nelson had been talking about "dear Lady Hamilton." Fanny stood up and said vehemently, "I am sick of hearing of dear Lady Hamilton and am resolved that you shall give up either her or me." Nelson answered calmly, "Take care, Fanny, what you say. I love you sincerely. But I cannot forget my obligations to Lady Hamilton or speak of her otherwise than with affection and admiration." Whereupon Fanny walked out. It might have happened, though it reverses their temperaments. Nelson was the vehement, Fanny the calm one. Certainly, nothing was settled between them before he left London, and neither realized they were seeing the other for the last time.

On January 7 Nelson went to the levee to kiss hands on his promotion. On the 9th he was at the Admiralty, where he received his orders to proceed to Plymouth. He asked for, and was refused, full pay from the time he had struck his flag in Leghorn. The days to the 13th, when he left town with his brother William, are empty of any recorded word or incident. It can only be assumed that his farewells were fonder at Grosvenor Square than they were at Dover Street.

CHAPTER EIGHT

Mrs. Thompson's Friend

THE POST CHAISE carrying Lord Nelson and his brother the Rector to the west country arrived at Southampton late in the evening of January 13, 1801. The Admiral scrawled a note to his wife to say they had arrived heartily tired, as if nothing had happened to make such a considerateness surprising.

The next morning they drove on to Cuffnells, the Hampshire residence of George Rose, the Secretary to the Treasury. The King sometimes stayed at Cuffnells on his way to Weymouth. Nelson went there to introduce his brother to the Secretary, in the hope that the Rector's appearance might forward his claim to a prebendary, or even a deanery. However, William's clerical charms were not exercised, as Mr. Rose had left for London. The brothers climbed back into their carriage and were taken on to Axminster. It was an eventful ride, as Nelson wrote Emma that evening. "Anxiety for friends left and various workings of my imagination gave me one of those severe pains of the heart, that all the Windows were obliged to be put down, the Carriage stop'd, and the perspiration was so strong that I never was wetter, and yet dead with Cold; however it is gone off. . . . I find the same Crowds and applause that you for ever join in—make my best regards to Sir Wm. the Duke, Mr. Beckford, and tell Lord W. Gordon his last verses are perfectly *true*." Lord William's verses have not descended to posterity. They were something to do with "Henry's anchors fixed in——'s heart."

After a night at Axminster they traveled on, stopping at Honiton for a friendly visit to the family of a captain who had been killed at the Nile. Nelson discovered that Mrs. Westcott had not received her son's gold medal and took his own from his neck to give to her. In the afternoon they arrived at Tor Abbey near Dartmouth, where Lord St. Vincent had his headquarters.

Though Nelson was at law with the Earl, not a word was said about it. St. Vincent, however, did not spare his protégé in a letter to Nepean. "Poor man! he is devoured with vanity, weakness and folly; was strung with ribbons, medals &c. and yet pretended that he wished to avoid the honour and ceremonies he everywhere met with upon the road." He did not notice that one medal was missing.

Nelson arrived at Plymouth on the 16th and dropped another friendly note to Fanny. He went aboard the *San Josef,* and as his flag was hoisted to the masthead, a cheer went up from the ships of the fleet. Whatever those on land might think of him, Nelson was welcomed back to the sea. And there he will be left for the moment, living in Hardy's cabin because his own smelled of paint, and sorting out his luggage which had followed him down in two wagons. He had promised Emma never to go ashore into mixed company and he remained a willing prisoner aboard ship. He knew the time of her confinement was approaching and suffered the double torment of absent lover and expectant father. He lived on letters. They had devised a scheme to enable them to correspond freely without arousing the suspicions of inquisitive clerks in the post office—she was to write on behalf of a Mrs. Thomson (or Thompson) who was expecting the child of her lover, a sailor aboard Nelson's ship, and he was to answer in that guise. So there he was, the little Vice-Admiral, waiting alone in a misery of anxiety for the first letter in Emma's familiar scrawl over an unfamiliar name.

Round Wood was to be sold and the house in Dover Street given up. The Reverend Edmund went to stay with the Matchams in Bath. For the first time since her marriage, Fanny was on her own. She decided to go to Brighton and tried to persuade Mrs. William Nelson to go with her. "I am sure," she wrote her on January 22, "I need not repeat my constant desire to do anything in my power to serve or accommodate my dear Lord's family." The answer was not agreeable and she left London alone two days later.

A seaside resort in the gray of January is as good a place as any to nurse a suffering heart. As Fanny sat over her parlor fire with her friend Miss Locker, she could compare her husband's faithlessness with the cold wind, and Lady Hamilton's insincere professions of friendship with the candle that gave light but no warmth. Perhaps she recounted the days she had waited for her lord's return. The humiliation of his coldness to her, his open preference for that woman's company, and that woman's very obvious condition were not to be recalled without pain. Yet Fanny taxed herself with the failure of her marriage, and waited to hear from Nelson, and when she did hear, she offered to go to him.

Josiah was around. He had returned to England in the *Thalia* in October and, after a spell of convoy duty, had come ashore on half-pay. In fact, Nelson was trying to have him reappointed to the *Thalia*. Josiah and his mother were strangers. After an absence of seven years, he found a faded, rather nervous lady, who gently scolded him for not listening to his stepfather. She had once written him, "There is an admiral who has got himself much laughed at in wishing to defame my Lord's understanding," and warned him that stories of his misbehavior were current among her naval acquaintances. She found a cocksure young captain, not yet twenty-one, who felt not grateful but hard done by, and who was determined to steer his own course in future. She knew, as every mother knows, that her son could succeed in his profession if he would only try. He knew he could not.

The Hamiltons opened their new house on Twelfth Night. The sale of Emma's diamonds allowed Sir William to live in the manner to which he was accustomed, and he acknowledged his debt by making out a deed of gift returning all the furniture and elegant fittings to her on his death. The household was numerous and included Mrs. Cadogan, Oliver, Emma's maids Fatima, Julia and Marianne, Sir William's valet Gaetano, his Neapolitan butler, the French cook, the coachman and all the other bodies essential to a gentleman's residence. And there was Nelson's dog Nile, until he ran away. The *Morning Chronicle* of January 20 advertised:

> Lost, a Black Tanned TERRIER DOG, with a yellow spot over each eye, cropped to blunt Fox ears, of a square make and middle size.—Whoever brings him to No. 23 facing the middle of the Green Park in Piccadilly shall have One Guinea Reward. No Greater Reward will be offered.

Poor Nile, who had a famous master for a few days and was only worth a guinea.

It is inconceivable that the fact that the lady of the house was going to have a baby was not known to everyone in it. This has been the story propagated from a doubtful principle of propriety, as if the cuckolding of Sir William was somehow more decent if he knew nothing of it; in other words, if he was a fool as well as a cuckold. His story has shown him to be anything but a fool. He was, as always, consulting his own interest in deciding to ignore what was passing. He had managed to ignore "little Emma," so why should he not ignore little Horace or whoever it was coming. Emma would retire to a sickroom for a few days, the child would disappear, and the present moment would be enjoyed, as he always had enjoyed it, by making the best of it. In the meantime, he went to Court regularly, frequented his clubs and societies, and accepted invitations to dinner.

The *Morning Herald* of February 2 reported, "The Duke of Norfolk yesterday gave a grand dinner at his house in St. James's Square, to Sir William and Lady Hamilton, the Duke of Queensbury, and several persons of distinction. There was a very brilliant concert in the evening, which afforded a delicious treat to numerous Amateurs that his Grace had assembled on the occasion. Madame Banti, Viganoni, Rovedino &c assisted, and his Royal Highness the Prince of Wales honoured the assembly with his presence."

On February 7 the report was amended. "Lady Hamilton did not dine at the Duke of Norfolk's last Sunday, as mentioned in this paper of Monday; we are concerned to find her ladyship was indisposed."

She was indeed indisposed and, just about that time, the cause of her indisposition was being disposed of.

Sir William was not often in company with the Prince of Wales and it was very likely on this occasion that the Prince made the request to hear Emma sing; the request that, when he heard of it, drove Nelson to distraction. Princes are not often refused their wish and, we may suppose, they are never refused by elderly gentlemen waiting on a pension. It is probably not necessary to add that this Prince was a notorious fornicator, a collector of women whose mere visit to a house was enough to label it a brothel.

There is not a scrap of writing from Emma at this crucial period of her life that has yielded to the researches of a hundred years and more. One reason for this is that Nelson carefully destroyed all the letters that might compromise her, just as she carelessly kept the letters that compromised him. Another reason is that, after his death, some hand, intent on giving his reputation the sterility of perfect goodness, went through his correspondence scratching out, and very likely tearing up, every reference to his child.

However, much of what she wrote can be gathered from his answers to her letters. One thing can be said with some confidence—Emma was not playing a part as she lay in her closed room in Piccadilly. She was desperately anxious about her future. She had committed herself to Nelson and was ready to use any means to keep him attached to her. The child, his insane jealousy (it nearly drove him insane though he may have had good reason for it), her pretended jealousy that exacted his promise never to go into the company of another woman, her abuse of Tom Tit (her cruel nickname for Fanny), her alliance with the Rector and his wife against the rest of the family—these were her weapons, or rather her chains to keep him bound to her. She underestimated the strength of his passion and almost drove him mad with her intrigues.

Nelson was already in a bad temper. Fanny's heart had not been in her packing. "All my things are now breaking open," he complained in a letter dated January 20, "for only one key can be found." He was in a mood to exaggerate—there was nothing to make him comfortable except two chairs, and he knew she was aware they were a present from Lady Hamilton. The next day he wrote irritably that half his wardrobe had been left behind, that all the wrong things had been ordered, that he was obliged to send out to buy even a little tea. He niggled, "In short I find myself without any thing comfortable or convenient." He flung about petulantly, "It is now too late to send my half wardrobe, as I know not what is to become of me, nor do I care." William was with him and probably egged him on.

This was the "letter of truth" he told Emma that he had written Fanny. Emma, of course, was perfect. He had a word for poor Nile: "Active dogs will not do for the house"; well, he should have thought of that when he bought him. He hoped that her very serious cold would soon be better. "I delivered to Mr. ———, Mrs. Thomson's message and note and he desires me, poor fellow, to say he is more scrupulous than if Mrs. T. was present. He says he does not write letters at this moment, as the object of his affections may be unwell and others may open them, not that he cares only for her sake." He had refused to dine with Lady Louisa Lennox, "although she is 65 and very much the looks of a *Gentleman*." She had been a beauty in her day.

Perhaps it is too much to expect lovers to have a sense of humor and the absence of that saving grace is the most tedious thing about them. Love may laugh at locksmiths, and so may theft, but that is all love laughs at.

On January 22 Nelson was at Exeter, where, with the usual bustle and ceremony, he received the freedom of the city. Then he went on a second visit to the Earl at Tor Abbey. There was much to talk about. The government had placed an embargo on the ships of the northern confederacy in British ports. An expedition to the Baltic was under discussion. The last dispatches to the Court of St. Petersburg had been returned full of holes where they had apparently been stabbed with a penknife. The Emperor Paul had issued a challenge to the rulers of Europe to come to his capital with their ministers and generals and settle their differences in single combat. He was mad, of course, but such madness commands respect. There were rumors that Mr. Pitt might resign over the King's refusal to agree to the repeal of the Test and Corporation Acts, which debarred Catholics from office and so made a nonsense of the union with Ireland, and the Earl had heard whispers that, in a new government, he might go to the Admiralty . . . but the small anxious-looking Vice-Admiral was leaving, perhaps there was a letter actually waiting for him on board the *San Josef?*

There were letters and rumors that he did not like. "There are nonsensical reports here that you are going to buy a fine house for me," he wrote Davison on the 24th. "I do not believe Lady Nelson can have desired any such thing, for where am I to get the money and if I should ever have so much I should not think of a House at this time, the best thing for Lady N. when she is in Town, is good Lodgings, next to that to hire a very small ready furnished house." He had business he could not trust to the post and asked Davison to come and see him. His anxiety was such that he mentioned only casually that he was going to receive the freedom of Plymouth that day.

Perhaps Emma had also heard the rumors, because he reassured her the next day. "Where friendship is of so strong a cast as ours it is no easy matter to shake it—mine is as fixed as Mount Etna, and as warm in the inside as that mountain." As to Fanny, "Let her go to Briton or where she pleases, I care not; she is a great fool and thank God you are not the least bit like her." There had been a note from Mrs. Thomson to her lover. "He appears to me to feel very much her situation; he is so agitated, and will be so for 2 or 3 days, that he says he cannot write, and that I must send his kind love and affectionate regards."

It was January 26—and we must go from day to day in these dramatic times. The date reminded Nelson of another red-letter day. "When I consider that this day nine months was your birthday and that we had a gale of wind, yet I was happy and sang *Come Cheer up Fair Emma* &c. Even the thought compared with this day makes me melancholy, my heart somehow is sunk within me." Well, more was sown than the wind that day.

Then there was this, so the Prince of Wales must have been in the offing before the Duke of Norfolk's party: "I own I wonder that Sir Wm. should have a wish for the Prince of Wales to come under your roof," then Sir William was the villain, "no good can come from it, but every harm. You are too beautiful not to have enemies, and even one visit will stamp you as his Chère amie, and we know he is dotingly fond of such women as yourself, and is without one [spark] of honour in those respects, and would leave you to bewail your folly. But, my dear friend, I know you too well not to be convinced you cannot be seduced by any prince in Europe. You are, in my opinion, the pattern of perfection."

It was an odd thing for a lover to write to his mistress when she was about to become the mother of his illegitimate child. "Why beholdest thou the mote that is in thy brother's eye, but considerest not the beam that is in thine own eye?" How blind was this Nelson?

Physically, he was almost completely blind. Dr. Trotter said he had ophthalmia. Nelson wrote Emma on the 28th, "He has directed me not to write (and yet I am forced this day to write Lord Spencer, St. Vincent, Davison about my law suit, Troubridge, Mr. Locker &c. but you are the only female I write to), not to eat anything but the most simple food, not to touch wine or *porter*, to sit in a dark room, to have green shades for my eyes. Will you my Dear Friend make me one or two, nobody else shall, and to bathe them in cold water every hour. I fear it is the writing has brought this Complaint. My eye is like blood and the film so extended that I only see from the corner farthest from my nose."

Spiritually he seems equally blind. Here he is the next day, answering one of her letters that must have been full of gossip. "My Dear Lady, Old Daton is a chattering old fool, what would the World say if you flirted it away with every coxcomb, all would despise you as they now envy you; for what can they say, only that you are kind and good to an old friend with one arm, a broken head, and no teeth, the good must love you and I trust I am amongst the foremost if not the very first." He advised her to take no notice of Princess Castelcicala, who had significantly dropped her. Then he went on about Fanny. "As for t'other proud —— she is ignorant of anything like good manners. I go to the *watering place*—if I do without your consent may God inflict his punishment. I cannot serve God and Mammon. I long to get to Bronte, for believe me this England is a shocking place; a walk under the chestnut trees, although you may be shot by a Banditti, is better than to have our reputations stabbed in this Country." There was, as usual, a little letter for Mrs. Thomson. "What a hard case these poor people's is, but between your unparalleled goodness and my attention, I hope they will yet be happy and comfortable. In my opinion neither of them can be happy as they are."

On the last day of January the *San Josef* sailed from Plymouth to Torbay.

Alexander Davison was hurt by Nelson's reference to the fine house for Fanny. "I could never be such an egregious fool," he replied, "as to go and do that which I knew would be diametrically opposed to your wish and intention, and which the frequent conversations we have had on the subject must have fully made me acquainted with." In fact, Fanny had no intention of coming to town. She was in Brighton, and very likely in tears over her husband's ill-tempered letters.

At the house in Piccadilly, in the last days of January, Emma's child was born. The writer of *Lady Hamilton's Memoires*, published after her death, who was not very accurate but who knew more about this event than most, recorded, "As soon as the patient was capable of moving about, which owing to her remarkable constitution was tolerably early, the infant was conveyed by her in a large muff, and in her own carriage, to the house of the person who had been provided to take charge of it in Little Titchfield Street. On this occasion her Ladyship was accompanied by Lord Nelson's confidential agent, Mr. Oliver." The house was Number 9 and the person was Mrs. Gibson.

Very many years later the infant, then a married lady, asked her brother-in-law to find Mrs. Gibson's daughter, and to discover what were her recollections of the event. "Lady Hamilton brought you to her mother in a hackney coach one night and placed you under her charge telling her that she should be handsomely remunerated. She was unattended and did not give the nurse any information as to your parents, the nurse declared at that time you were no more than eight days old."

The first piece of concrete evidence is a note from Emma to Mrs. Gibson, postmarked February 7, 1801. "Dear Madame, my cold has been so bad I could not go out today, but tomorrow will call on you. Write me by the penny post how the dear little Miss Horatia is—ever your sincere friend, E.H."

Not too much need be made of how the infant was taken to Mrs. Gibson's house in that poor quarter of London north of Oxford Street. As the infant was openly brought to 23 Piccadilly within a few days, there seems to be no reason why Emma should have risked going alone in a hackney carriage at night. The daughter's memory is suspect, as she was certain it happened at the beginning of January.

Mrs. Thomson's letter to her lover, telling him he was the father of a girl, was probably written on January 29. Nelson answered it from Torbay on February 1. "I believe poor dear Mrs. Thomson's friend will go mad with joy. He cries, prays, and performs all tricks, yet dare not shew all or any of his feelings, but he has only me to consult with. He swears he will drink your health this day in a bumper, and damn me if I don't join him in spite of all the doctors in Europe, for none regard you with truer affection than myself. You are a dear, good creature, and your kindness and attention to poor Mrs. T. stamps you higher than ever in my mind. I cannot write, I am so agitated by this young man at my elbow. I believe he is foolish; he does nothing but rave about you and her. I own I participate of his joy and cannot write anything."

In matters of emotion, writing is a poor second to saying, and saying is a lap behind doing. Poor Nelson could not do anything, except cavort about his cabin on his own. He could not say anything, though perhaps his company at dinner wondered at his rare smiles and unaccustomed bumpers. He could only write of the joy, the hope, the purpose this child brought into his life. And as long as his letters went by post, he had to write in the third person.

On February 3 he told Mrs. Thomson, "Your good and dear friend does not think it proper at present to write with his own hand but he hopes the time may not be far distant when he may be united for ever to the object of his wishes, his only, *only* love. He swears before heaven that he will marry you as soon as it is possible, which he fervently prays may be soon. He charges me to say how dear you are to him, and that you must, every opportunity, kiss and bless for him his dear little girl, which he wishes to be called Emma, out of gratitude to our dear, good Lady Hamilton; but weither its from Lord N. he says, or Lady H. he leaves to your judgement and choice. I have given Lord N. a hundred pounds this morning for which he will give Lady Hamilton an order on his agent; and I beg that you will distribute it amongst those who have been useful to you on the late occasion; and your friend, my dear Mrs. Thomson, may be sure of my care of him and his interest, which I consider as dearly as my own." Not surprisingly, he got mixed up with *he* and *I*. Happiness is best shared, if only with an imaginary companion.

Emma was writing too, good and kind letters. He cut two lines from one of them and swore never to part with them. Fanny wrote as well to say that the bad packing was not her fault, and that started him off on a string of complaints about nails driven into his mahogany table and decanter stands without decanters to fit them. But he was still her affectionate Nelson.

He would not be so for long. The birth of this child completed the separation between Nelson and his wife. There remained only a financial settlement and that had to wait until Davison came down to see him. And a last letter had to be written. There was no question of a divorce. The sole prospect of a marriage with Emma lay in their surviving their respective spouses. This seemed certain with regard to Sir William, but hardly so with regard to Fanny. That is why she became, more than ever, the object of their hatred.

"Who doats," quoted Lord Bristol, "must doubt." Nelson's doubts as to Emma's power of resisting the advances of the Prince of Wales are quite extraordinary. "I know his aim is to have you for a mistress," he wrote her on the 4th. "The thought so agitates me that I cannot write. I had wrote a few lines last night, but I am in tears. I cannot bear it. Tell Mrs. T. her friend is grateful for her goodness, and with my kindest regards to Mrs. Jenkins and Horatia. . . ." Mrs. Jenkins? He *was* upset, or Emma's handwriting was more unreadable than usual. Of course, she provoked him with the Prince and teased him with her high prospects—this is in his letters—but he shows none of the "fixed as fate" Nelson of the dealings with Fanny at this time.

He is unbalanced and he becomes hysterical in his jealous outbursts. He is evidently under huge pressures—the separation from a wife after fourteen years of marriage, the birth and survival of a child, the scandal and gossip. At no other time in his life does he reveal this tormented, sensitive, almost feminine side of himself, as much as in these wretched days. In January he received the King's permission to adopt his title as Duke of Bronte, and began signing himself Nelson & Bronte. At times, he really does appear as two people, the parson's heroic son and the highly strung Italianate *cicisbeo*.

When Nelson began to think of altering his will in order to provide for the future of the child, he found two difficulties. The first was in the wording of his bequests to Emma to prevent Sir William or his heirs getting the money. The second was, in a semi-public document, in giving a reason that could not be challenged by his own heirs for leaving her so much.

On February 5 he wrote a memorandum which he sent Emma for her approval. In it he referred to Lady Hamilton as "the great cause of my performing those services which have gained me honours and rewards." This was to be his reason for leaving her the entire rental of the Bronte estate. This was how he came to endorse her claim to share in the glory and rewards of the Nile.

He got into trouble with the wording by referring to "any child she may have in or out of wedlock," and Emma told him to burn the memorandum, though she apparently kept her copy. This child was to receive the rents after her death, the income from the sale of Nelson's diamond boxes, and all his money over the sum of £20,000, which was the amount needed to provide a pension for Fanny. He added hopefully, "I shall now begin and save a fortune for the little one." His last will differed in many essentials from this early memorandum, but it is of some importance as containing Nelson's first reference to Emma's services and his public acknowledgment of "a child called ———— in whom I take a very particular interest."

In the accompanying letter he told Emma, "Thank God you want not the society of Princes or Dukes. If you happened to fall down and break your nose or knock out your Eyes you might go to the devil for what they care." There was also the usual little letter to Mrs. T.; it was concerned with christening the child. "Its name will be Horatia, daughter of Johem and Morata Etnorb." He was serious! Fortunately for Horatia Etnorb, the plan was dropped in case the clergyman asked questions, and Johem and Morata reverted to Emma and Horatio.

On his arrival at Torbay Nelson had been to see St. Vincent and learned that he was going to be appointed to a fleet bound for the Baltic. The *St. George,* a ship of shallower draft than the *San Josef* and better suited to northern waters, was coming for his flag. The Earl was pleasant. "You would have thought he would have overwhelmed me with civilities," Nelson told Davison, "nothing *equal* to me, as an Officer *I hope he says true,* but I will not spare him an inch in the point of law."

Davison came down to Torbay on February 6. He arrived at dinner-time and Nelson had already written several pages to Emma. There was a present, a lock of soft fair hair, to be acknowledged; then there had been some trouble with the nurse, and he suggested a small pension if she kept her mouth shut, and now and then an extra guinea; the weather was bad and the boat might not bring his letters and newspaper, "You know I am not a little fond of a newspaper and we have often almost quarrelled for a first reading"; and he was alone except for Hardy and young Lieutenant Parker, because the Rector had returned to town. Edward Parker had belonged to the *Foudroyant.* "Ah those were happy times."

And here was Davison. "He says you are grown thinner, but he thinks you look handsomer than ever. I know he is a very great admirer of yours." Grown thinner, indeed!

William Marsh, of Marsh, Page & Creed, was Nelson's agent; William Haslewood, of Booth & Haslewood, was his solicitor; but it was Alexander Davison, his friend and banker, who had the task of arranging the settlement on Lady Nelson. Davison was a wealthy man with a house in St. James's Square and an estate, Swarland Hall, in Northumberland. He hobnobbed with the great, and could tell Nelson that Lord Spencer spoke of him in raptures; he might have brought Lady Spencer's present of a gold combined knife and fork to the one-armed Admiral. Davison was a financier and dabbled in government contracts. He was normally a discreet man. Above all, he was an admirer of Lady Hamilton's, and the same could not be said for William Marsh and William Haslewood.

The settlement was a generous one. The terms were written in a note by Nelson on March 4, but they were decided on before then, and probably at this meeting. "Lord Nelson's annual income is about £4,000 a year including £200 a year the interest of Lady Nelson's £4,000. My plan is to allow Lady Nelson £2,000 a year subject to the Income Tax, which as I pay the Tax with my own will reduce my nett yearly income to £3,600. Lady Nelson to be paid every Quarter in advance viz. on the 1st January 1801, 1st April, 1st July, 1st October, by Messrs. Marsh, Page, Creed, £400 each quarter, which with the interest of the £4,000 will amount to £1,800 neat money. Lord Nelson has directed Mr. Davison to pay every bill and expence of his and Lady Nelson's to the day of his leaving London. N.B. Lord Nelson gives Lady Nelson the principal of the £4,000 mentioned above to be at her disposal by will."

So he gave Fanny half his income.

Davison returned to town on February 8 and, of course, acted as postman. There was a heroic letter for Emma. "I know you are so true and loyal an Englishwoman, that you would hate those who would not stand forth in defence of our King, laws, religion, and all that is dear to us. It is your sex that makes us go forth, and seems to tell us, 'None but the brave deserve the fair,' and if we fall we still live in the hearts of those females who are dear to us. It is your sex that rewards us; it is your sex who cherish our memories; and you, my dear honoured friend, are believe me, the *first*, the best of your sex."

Inside that, there was a doubting letter. "I do not think I ever was so miserable as this moment. I own I sometimes fear that you will not be so true to me as I am to you, yet I cannot, will not believe you can be false. No, I judge you by myself; I hope to be dead before that should happen, but it will not. Forgive me, Emma, oh forgive your own dear disinterested Nelson."

There was a note on a separate sheet of paper. "I may not be able to write to you tomorrow but thou art present ever to my eyes. I see hear no one else. Parker setts next me to cut my meat when I want it done. May God send us a happy meeting. I am writing in a room full of interruptions therefore give me credit for my thoughts, you can guess them, they are I trust like your own." And there was one for Mrs. T. "Your dear friend, my dear and truly beloved Mrs. T. is almost distracted, he wishes there was peace or that if your uncle would die he would instantly then come and marry you, for he doats on nothing but you and his Child, and as it is my Godchild I desire you will take great care of it. He has implicit faith in your fidelity even in conversation with those he dislikes, and that you will be faithful in greater things he has no doubt. May God bless you both and send you a happy meeting is the wish of your N & B."

In the first week of February Mr. Pitt resigned. Said the *Chronicle*, "Everybody was surprised and everybody was glad." Nelson was not glad. "I am sorry Mr. Pitt is out," he told Emma. "I think him the greatest Minister this country ever had, and the honestest man." How much honesty there was in this resignation is difficult to say. Ostensibly it was over the issue of Catholic emancipation, the King refusing to agree to the repeal of the Test and Corporation Acts. However, the Prime Minister may well have used this issue to leave office before being obliged to face a greater and more challenging one.

The question of peace with France was raised once again by the ratification of the Treaty of Lunéville (February 9), between France and Austria. Great Britain was left, solitary in the lists, against a triumphant enemy who now paraded as the champion of peace. Surely, said the reasonable men, eight years of war is enough and it is time to call quits?

Now it is always easier to lead a country into war than into peace. War does not require the cooperation of the enemy. Then again, it is always easier to negotiate a peace after a victory, or even after a defeat, than during a stalemate. After a victory the terms are dictated; after a defeat the terms are imposed; but after neither one nor the other the terms are subject to lengthy negotiations in which both sides wish to appear to have won, while only one will win and the other will lose. Many a good war has been lost by a bad peace.

The situation in 1801 was not conducive to a good peace for Great Britain. France was stable and triumphant under the First Consul. All her objectives, a frontier from the sea to the Rhine, had been gained at Lunéville. Whereas Britain, while admittedly gaining an empire of colonies, was less secure in 1801 than she had been in 1793. Her objective had not been gained. Peace, then, would cost the sacrifice of that objective, the sacrifice of principle, perhaps of conquests, and ultimately of popularity. It is impossible to say to which of these Mr. Pitt clung the hardest, because he resigned.

The change of an administration might take a week or more, and only the most hardened and cynical empiricist would suggest that a week was a long time in politics. If that was so, we should have a new Prime Minister every week (and perhaps we do). Then, the new one was Addington, a follower of Mr. Pitt, or, as Canning said, a borough of Mr. Pitt.

Pitt is to Addington
As London is to Paddington.

But the week stretched into a month, because King George fell ill, ostensibly catching cold at a service on February 13, the day of the general fast to draw the Almighty's attention to the starvation in the country. So Mr. Pitt and his colleagues lingered in office, anxious to get out, while Mr. Addington and his, including St. Vincent, the First Lord of the Admiralty apparent, lingered out of office, anxious to get in. And apart from them, nobody noticed the difference whether there was a government or not.

This little digression has been allowed by gales that kept Lady Hamilton's letters from Lord Nelson, and Lord Nelson's answers from the page.

No woman of spirit would put up with being told daily that she could not be trusted alone with a man, even if that man was the Prince of Wales. Emma slammed back with a similar accusation, though, from Nelson's protests on February 11, she could not find much to charge him with. He had said that the west country women wore black stockings—how did he know that unless he had been looking? "You cannot help your eyes, and God knows I cannot see much." Aha, then what about the handsome Mrs. Kelly? "I am glad you have found out Mrs. Kelly is so handsome; in that case you will give me credit for never going to make her a visit, but, to say the truth, I think her quite the contrary; red hair, short, very fair I believe, but her face beplaistered with red." And Admiral Kingsmill's friend? "It is now 17 years since I have seen her." He burst out, "I have no secrets, and never had but one only one love in my life, and damn me, if I lose her, if ever I will have another."

One should not laugh at lovers, nor yet pity them, for they hurt each other, and yet have compensations only lovers know.

"I hope my dear Mrs. Gibson that Miss Horatia is well," Emma wrote on the 11th, "if it is a fine day tomorrow bring her in a coach well wrapt up to see me, but let her be well covered getting in and out of the coach. Come at eleven o'clock." So the child was brought to 23 Piccadilly. Would Emma have risked the questions that were bound to follow if Sir William was not in on the secret? And say he left the house at half past ten and went to the British Museum, was there not one person who would have told him of the mysterious visitor that morning? Emma was often unwise, but never downright stupid.

The weather stayed foul down at Torbay and Nelson complained, "I am a miserable fellow shut up in wood." The *St. George* had arrived and he did not like the look of her, but the sea was too high for him to change quarters. He remained, tossed about his cabin in the *San Josef*, thinking of Emma. He wrote on the 14th:

> My confidence is as firm as a rock till you try to irritate me to say hard things that you may have the pleasure of scolding me; but recollect it must remain 4 days before it can be made up, not, as before in happy times, 4 minutes. Consider, my dear friend, what you ought to say if I did not fire at your scolding letters and suppose me, if it is possible for a moment, answering your scolds with a joke. I know I should fire if I thought that of you, that you was indifferent; but firing like the devil with vexation, anger and retorting, can only proceed from conscious innocence. I defy the malice of anyone, and my mind is as pure as my actions.
>
> Only rest quiet, you know that everything is arrainged in my head for all circumstances. You ought to know that I have a head to plan and an heart to execute whenever it is right and the time arrives. That person has her separate maintenance. Let us be happy, that is in our power.

He was alone that evening, reading her letters and crossing out all the scolding words. . . .

"Troubridge is my guest during the absence of the *Ville de Paris*. He always says 'now comes the fourth and old toast, all our friends—the King —success to the fleet, and though last not least, Lady Hamilton.'"

The gales did not abate and Nelson's letters were sent ashore to the peril of the boats carrying them. Emma was upset because a letter had been lost and another had arrived with the seal broken. He did his best to reassure her, fearing she might stop writing altogether. Without her letters he could not have stayed in his voluntary prison. With them he was subjected to the torments of his inflamed imagination, as she told him she had ventured into society again.

"Believe me my dear friend," he cried, "that Lady A. is as damned a W——e as ever lived and Mrs. Walpole is a Bawd. Mrs. V. a foolish pimp eat up with pride that a Prince will condescend to put her to expences."

He sent her some verses he had written during the previous autumn.

> *Though ——'s polish'd verse superior shine,*
> *Though sensibility grace every line,*
> *Though her soft Muse be far above all praise,*
> *And female tenderness inspire her lays,*

Deign to receive though unadorned
By thy poetic Art,
The rude expressions which bespeak
A Sailor's untaught heart.

An Heart susceptible, *sincere and true,*
An Heart by fate, *and nature, torn in Two—*
One half to duty and his Country due,
The other better half *to Love and you.*

Sooner shall Britain's sons resign
The Empire of the Sea,
Than Henry shall renounce his faith
And plighted vows to thee.

And Waves on Waves shall cease to roll,
And Tides forget to flow,
Ere thy true Henry's constant Love
Or Ebb or change shall know.

Horace would not scan, and no one called him Horatio, so he was Henry. Nelson was no poet and the commonplace imagery of his verses fades beside the unique power of his prose; unique, that is, among heroes. Here he is to Mrs. T. on the same day (February 16).

> I set down my Dear Mrs. T. by desire of poor Thompson to write you a line not to assure you of his eternal love and affection for you and his Dear Child, but only to say that he is well and as happy as he can be separated from all which he holds dear in this World. He has no thought separated from your love and your interest, they are wrapped with his own fate, one destiny he assures me awaits you both, what can I say more, only to kiss his Child for him and love him as truly sincerely and faithfully as he does you, which is from the bottom of his soul, he desires that you will more and more attach yourself to dear Lady Hamilton.

Of course, they spoke like that because they learned their language from the Bible and from Shakespeare. Even Emma, who was ignorant until she met Charles Greville and could barely scrawl a letter—"O G. what shall I dow what shall I dow"—could make words leap with a freshness and vitality that was common to country speech.

Nelson was writing two and sometimes three long letters a day. On the 17th he told Emma that he had burned the memorandum of his will, and that anything he left her would have to be in trust, except his diamond star. "Nobody would take that memento of friendship, affection and esteem from you. May curses light on them if they did." He was expecting to be ordered to Portsmouth, from where he would try to get to London for three days. "Ah my dear friend, I did remember well the 12th February and also the two months afterwards. I shall never forget them, and never be sorry for the consequences—I fear saying too much. I admire what you say of my Godchild. If it is like its mother it will be very handsome, for I think her one, aye, the most beautiful woman of the age. Now do not be angry at my praising this dear child's mother for I have heard people say she is very like you. . . . I would steal white bread sooner than my godchild should want."

He was in this sentimental, almost sly, mood when the boat arrived with her letters and everything was changed. The Prince was coming to dinner!

> I am so agitated that I can write nothing. I knew it would be so, and you can't help it. Why did you not tell Sir William. Your character will be gone. Do not have him *en famille,* the more the better. Do not sit long at table. Good God—he will be next you and telling you soft things. If he does, tell it out at table and turn him out of the house. Do not sit long. If you sing a song, I know you cannot help it, do not let him sit next you, but at dinner he will hob glasses with you. I cannot write to Sir William, but he ought to go to the Prince and not suffer your character to be ruined by him. Oh God that I was dead. But I do not, my dearest Emma, blame you, nor do I fear your inconstancy. I tremble and God knows how I write. Can nothing be thought of. I am gone almost mad, but you cannot help it. It will be in all the newspapers with hints. Recollect what the villain said to Mr. Nisbet, *how you hit his fancy,* I am almost dead but ever for ever yours to the last moment your only your . . .

He dropped the pen exhausted, and then snatched it up again. "I could not write another line if I was to be made king." And on he went. He did not blame her, but . . . he would fast that day. Then the thought: "He will put his foot near you. I pity you from my soul, as I feel confident you wish him in hell. . . . He wishes I dare say to have you alone. Don't let him touch, nor yet sitt next you; if he comes get up. God strike him blind if he looks at you—this is high treason, and you may get me hanged by revealing it. Oh God that I were. . . . He will stay and sup and sitt up till 4 in the morning and the fewer that stay the better. Oh God why do I live. But I do not blame you, it is my misfortune." And down he went into the dumps. "I am only fit to be second, or third, or 4 or to black shoes." And there he stayed.

In the little letter, he wrote, "Your most dear friend desires me to say that he sincerely feels for you, and that if your uncle is so hard hearted as to oblige you to quit his house, that he will instantly quit all the world and its greatness to live with you a domestic quiet life."

The fever of jealousy raged over the next day, and four more sheets of paper. He would have bet ten millions that Emma would not receive the Prince. He would have laid his head upon the block for it. "Oh I wish I had been so placed then and there, then my head, my distracted head must have been off. Hush hush my poor heart, keep in my breast, be calm. Emma is true! But no one, not even Emma, could resist the serpent's flattering tongue, and knowing that Emma suits him, that even a stranger would not invite her to meet the fellow, what will they all SAY and think, that Emma is like other women, when I would have killed anybody who said so, must now *hang* down my head and admit it." On, on he went and out of the depths of his misery drew up some fine, half-remembered phrases. "I know my Emma and don't forget that you had once a Nelson, a friend, a dear friend, but alas, he has his misfortunes. He has lost the best, his only friend, his only love. Don't forget him, poor fellow, he is honest. Oh—I could thunder and strike dead with my lightning. I dreamt it last night, my dear Emma. I am calmer; reason, I hope will resume her place, please God."

Reason returned and he wrote again that day to warn her that, when he came to London, he would have to stay at a hotel and not dine out, "unless once it may be necessary at Lord St. Vincent's to hold a candle to the devil." Fanny had written. "I had a letter from that person at Brighton saying she heard from my Brother that I was ill and offering to come and nurse me but I have sent such an answer that will convince her she would not be received. I am almost afraid you will think I have gone too far, for she must see there is some strong reason, but my intentions are in everything to give you satisfaction, therefore do not be angry for the strength of my letter."

Reason stayed the night. Reason was there on the 19th when he took up his pen again. "Forgive my letter wrote and sent last night, perhaps my head was a little affected. No wonder, it was such an unexpected, such a knock-down blow, such a death. But I will not go on for I shall get out of my sences again. Will you sing for the fellow *The Prince unable to Conceal his Pain &c*. No, you will not. I will say no more for fear of my head." But

208

he did say more, about Charles Greville, whom she must have mentioned in connection with the fatal dinner. "Mr. G. must be a scoundrel; he treated you once ill enough and cannot love you, or he would sooner die." And he was going on to say more when alongside came the boat, in came the post, and—"*Forgive every cross word, I now live.*" She had refused to dine with the Prince!

The weather had moderated and Nelson had himself rowed across to the *St. George*. No sooner was he in his new cabin than he was writing again to Emma, promising never to leave it. He could not get over what she had done. "I wish you were my sister that I might instantly give you half my fortune for your glorious conduct. Be firm! Your cause is that of honor against infamy." Mrs. Thomson's friend was at his elbow, "and enjoins me to assure you that his love for you and your child is, if possible, greater than ever, and that he calls God to witness that he will marry you as soon as possible, and that it will be his delight to call you his own." For good measure, he added a letter for Sir William's benefit, warning him about the Prince of Wales: "He is permitted to visit only houses of *notorious ill fame.*"

Sir William was writing to him the same day, Thursday the 19th. Emma's letter to say she would *not* dine with the Prince could not have been written later than Wednesday morning. The old Knight wrote:

> My dear Lord, Whether Emma will be able to write to you today or not is a question, as she has got one of her terrible sick headaches—among other things that vex her is that we have been drawn in to be under the absolute necessity of giving a Dinner to the P of Wales on Sunday next. He asked it himself, having expressed his strong desire of hearing Banti's and Emma's voices together. I am well aware of the danger that would attend the Prince frequenting our House, not that I fear that Emma could ever be induced to act contrary to the prudent conduct she has hitherto pursued, but the World is so ill natured that the worst construction is put upon the most innocent actions. As this dinner must be, or the Prince would be offended, we shall keep it strictly to the musical part invite only Banti, her husband and Taylor, and as I wish to shew a civility to Davison I have sent him an invitation. In short, we will get rid of it as well as we can and guard against its producing more meetings of the same sort. Emma would realy have gone any lengths to have avoided Sunday's dinner, but I thought it would not be prudent to break with the P. who realy has shewn the greatest civility to us when we were last in England and since we returned, and she has

at last acquiesced to my opinion. I have been this explicit as I know well your Lp's way of thinking and your very kind attachment to us and to everything that concerns us.

He went on to refer to the King's cold, his so far unsatisfied claim for compensation and a pension, and the coming sale of his vases and pictures.

What was Emma up to? "I am so ill with a head aich," she wrote the Rector's wife that day, "that I cannot move and I feil I could not take leave of you and Mr. Nelson it would be too much for my heart." If it was a genuine headache, she had good notice of it, and it came on most conveniently. In the balance between the interests of her husband and her lover, she brought her ample weight down on Nelson's side.

She had already bound the Rector and his Sarah to her. He, poor pompous soul, larded her ladyship with praise. "I never knew what it was to part with a friend before, and it is no wonder that my good, my great, my virtuous, my beloved brother should be so much attached to your Ladyship, after so long a friendship, when I feel so much after so short an acquaintance." Well!

Emma took to her bed. "I am so unwell," she told Mrs. Nelson, "that I don't think we can have his Royal Highness to dinner on Sunday which *will not vex me. Addio mia cara amica,* you know as you are learning italian I must say a word or so. How dull *my bedroom looks* without you, I miss our little friendly confidential chat but in this world nothing is compleat." They had hit it off, those two. "You and I liked each other from the moment we met, our souls were congenial, not so with *Tom tit* for their was an antipathy not to be described."

Sir William had the task of writing to Nelson. "You need not be the least alarmed that Emma has commissioned me to send you the News Papers and write you a line to tell you that she is much better having vomited naturally and is now purposing to take a regular one of Tartar Emetic. All her convulsive complaints certainly proceed from a foul stomach and I will answer for it she will and in spirits to write to you herself tomorrow." Was he just provoked by her refusal to see the Prince into that bitter remark about the foul stomach? Convulsive complaints hardly seem to describe a headache.

Nelson's joy was darkened by Sir William's letter of the 19th. Addressing himself to Mrs. Thomson, he advised her that, if her uncle insisted on bringing the Prince to dinner, "You can dine with Lady Hamilton or some other friend, and after all, if the beast turns you out of his house because you will not submit to be thought a w——e, you know then what will happen. . . . If you think that Lady Hamilton or any one else open your letters, tell me where to direct them." One member of the *tria juncta in uno* was flying off the handle.

Troubridge took this note with him when he went to town on February 20. Troubridge was going to be one of the Lords of the Admiralty and Nelson's master. He also took a letter to St. Vincent in which Nelson said he was going to Portsmouth in obedience to orders he had received from his new Commander in Chief, Sir Hyde Parker. The *St. George* was as uncomfortable as he had expected. "I am neither wind or water tight, but she has a Ship's Company which Hardy tells me will do he is sure, and I take the *Ghost's* word. . . . Before we go to the North I shall have to request either public or private leave for 3 days to settle some very important matters for myself." He also asked if he could have a dozen of St. Vincent's musicians for his ship's orchestra.

The *St. George* anchored at Spithead on the morning of February 22 and Nelson went ashore to pay his respects to the Port Admiral and Commissioner. He was back on board at noon with Emma's letters. "In doing what I wish," he wrote to her, "you win my heart for ever. I am all soul and sensibility; a fine thread will lead me, but with my life I would resist a cable from dragging me." He was waiting for his leave. He was contemptuous of the idea that Fanny might come and find him. "After the letter I wrote *her* the other day I do not think she will attempt to either come here or go to London." And, of course, he was keeping his promise.

> I have been pressed to dine ashore by the Admiral, an old man of eighty with an old wife dressed old ewe lamb fashion. Admiral Holloway, an acquaintance of twenty-five years, wanted me to dine with him as today, or Wednesday. He has a wife and four children with not a farthing to give them. Sir Charles Saxton, the Commissioner, an acquaintance of near thirty years, was also very pressing; his wife, I am told, likes a drop, and looks like a cookmaid. But I will dine nowhere without your consent, although, with my present feelings, I might be trusted with 50 virgins naked in a dark room. My thoughts are so fixed that not even the greatest stroke of fortune could change them.

The next day there was a note for Mrs. Thomson. It contained a puzzling reference, perhaps intentionally, which defies explanation. "My dear Mrs. T., poor Thomson seems to have forgot all his ill health, and all his mortifications and sorrows, in the thought that he will soon bury them all in your dear, dear bosom; he seems almost beside himself. I hope you have always minded what Lady Hn. has said to you, for she is a pattern of attachment to her love. I dare say twins will again be the fruit of your and his meeting. The thought is too much to bear. Have the dear thatched cottage ready to receive him, and I will answer that he would not give it up for a queen and a palace. Kiss dear H. for me." Perhaps the twins, like the dear thatched cottage, were for the benefit of the postal clerk, or someone at 23 Piccadilly, that Nelson imagined opening his letters with lascivious glee.

His leave arrived by telegraph that evening and he was off.

He arrived in London at 7 A.M. on Tuesday, Feburary 24, and put up at Lothians Hotel, which was the nearest he could get to the Hamiltons' house. From there he wrote to Fanny. "As I am sent for to town on very particular business for a day or two I would not on any account have you come to London but rest quiet where you are. Nor would I have you come to Portsmouth for I never come on shore." He mentioned the King's illness and Josiah's prospects of getting a ship. He added later, presumably after he had been to the Admiralty, that Josiah was again to have the *Thalia*.

Emma reveled in her triumph. Nelson was there and doing heaven knows what—well, visiting the Admiralty—but heaven knows what else, and Fanny was banished. As he had doubted, so had she; not that he would go off with Mrs. Kelly or the old ewe lamb lady, but that he might ask Fanny back. Triumph, gleeful, spiteful triumph, is in this day's letter to the Rector's wife at Hilborough. "Oh what real pleasure Sir W and I have in seeing this our great good victorious Nelson his eye is better—*tom tit* does not come to town, she offered to go down but was refused. She onely wanted to go to do mischief to all the great *Jove's relations*. 'Tis now shewn all her ill treatment and bad heart—*Jove* has found it out. Apropo Lady Nelson is at Brighton yet. The King God bless him is ill and their are many speculations, some say it is his *old disorder*."

Apart from visiting the Admiralty, Davison's house, and 23 Piccadilly, Nelson made one other call—to 9 Little Titchfield Street. On Wednesday he dined at the Hamiltons' with his brother Maurice and Troubridge, and on Thursday . . . but Emma's letter to Hilborough is as good as a journal.

> We had a pleasant evening I often thought on you, but now the subject of the King's illness gives such a gloom to every thing tis terrible, all turned upside down, Mr. Addington is not minister for his Commission was not signed before the King was taken ill, so Mr. Pitt is yet first Lord of the T——.
>
> What odd circumstances, his Majesty is the same today as *yesterday*, in short —— you know what *I mean*. Their are thou-

sands of coaches every day in the park to enquire—the *Willises* are there. [Dr. Willis and his son had attended King George during his fit of insanity in 1788; they were there when he caught and kissed Fanny Burney in Kew Gardens.] Our good Lord Nelson is *lodged at Lothians; tom tit at the same place* Brighton; the Cub is to have a frigate the *Thalia,* the Earl gives it tis settled, so I supose *he* will be up in a day or so. I onely hope he will not come near me, if he does, *not at home* shall the answer. I am glad he is going, *I hope never to* ———. [The Cub was, of course, Josiah.]

Milord has onely Allen with him; he supped and talked politicks till 2; Mr. East who is a pleasant man was with us. Do you wonder his My's head should be turned with all these things, tis enough to turn ———. Oh my dearest friend our dear Lord has just *come in.* He goes off tonight and sails emediately. My heart is ful to *Burst* quite—oh what pain God onely knows. I can onely say may the Allmighty God bless prosper and protect him. I shall go mad with greif. Oh God onely knows what it is to part with *such a friend—such a one.* We were truly called the *tria juncta in uno* for Sir W. *he* and I have but one heart *in three bodies.* My beloved friend I can onely say God bless you, *he* our great Nelson sends his love to you, give mine to Mr. Nelson. My greif will not let me say more.

Emma's style had deteriorated into a series of explosive dashes, but then she was upset by Nelson's imminent departure. One thing he had done in town, while settling up with Davison, was to pay Josiah's wine bill of £152 10s. 0d. One thing he had not done . . . but he wrote about that himself on March 1.

He traveled back to Portsmouth overnight, arriving on February 27. "Parting from such a friend," he wrote Emma, "is literally tearing one's own flesh; but the remembrance will keep up our spirits till we meet. My affection is, if possible, stronger than ever for you, and I trust it will keep increasing as long as we both live. I have seen Mrs. Thomson's friend, who is delighted at my having seen his dear child. I am sure he will be very fond of it." He was busy taking troops on board the *St. George,* a battalion of the 49th under Lieutenant Colonel Stewart, and in preparing his squadron to sail to join the fleet at Yarmouth.

That night he had leisure to write her a long letter, which, because of a mistake in the date by an early collector, has always been given as having been written at Yarmouth. As a half of it is concerned with instructions as to where his letters should be sent to reach him *on the journey* to Yarmouth, it was obviously written before he left Portsmouth. He wrote intimately as follows:

> You cannot think how my feelings are alive towards you, probably more than ever and they never can be diminished. My hearty endeavours shall not be wanting to improve and to give us *new* ties of regard and affection. I have seen and talked much with Dear Mrs. Thomson's friend. The fellow seems to eat all my words when I talk of her and his child, he says he never can forget your goodness and kind affection to her and his dear dear child. I have had you know the felicity of seeing it and a finer Child never was produced by any two persons, it was in truth a love begotten Child. I am determined to keep him on board for I know if they got together they would soon have another, but after our two months trip I hope they will never be separated and then let them do as they please.

No sooner was he away from London than Nelson began to worry about leaving Emma alone. "If you like to have Mrs. Nelson up," he wrote on March 1, "say that I will pay their lodgings, and then you can have as much of their company as you please; but Reverend Sir you will find a great bore at times, therefore he ought to amuse himself all the mornings, and not always to dine with you as Sir William may not like it." And Nelson would not like it if people said Sir William was supporting his family. "They can twice or thrice a week have a beef steak at home," he said, disposing of them casually. But then they were probably only too willing to be disposed of.

"Tell Mrs. Thomson," he continued, "that her friend is more in love with her than ever, and I believe dreams of her. He was sorry that she was a little unwell when he was in London, as it deprived him of much pleasure but he is determined to have full scope when he next sees her." So that is what he had not done.

Suddenly and unexpectedly Oliver appeared. "So much anxiety for your safety rushed into my mind that a pain immediately seized my heart which kept increasing for half an hour, that turning cold, hot, cold &c I was obliged to send for the surgeon who gave me something to warm me, for it was a deadly chill." But Oliver brought a letter rather like his own, probably full of "if onlys." "Would to God I had dined alone with you," answered Nelson. "*What a desert we would have had.*"

He took the advantage of a safe messenger to write that evening the most important letter of his life. There have been many letters in these pages and, because they are the hearts and minds of these people, there will be more, but none quite like this one. Remember it was written by a man of forty-two, a mutilated, weather-beaten man with a few teeth, a small and often melancholy man, to a woman of thirty-six, a big, coarse, beautiful woman, a used woman, a woman shallow in everything but her capacity to love.

Now, my own dear wife, for such you are in my eyes and in the face of heaven, I can give full scope to my feelings, for I dare say Oliver will faithfully deliver this letter. You know, my dearest Emma, that there is nothing in this world that I would not do for us to live together, and to have our dear little Child with us. I firmly believe that this Campaign will give us peace, and then we will sett off for Bronte. In twelve hours we shall be across the water and freed from all the nonsense of his friends, or rather pretended ones. Nothing but an event happening to him could prevent my going, and I am sure you will think so, for unless all matters accord it would bring 100 of tongues and slanderous reports if I separated from her (which I would do with pleasure the moment we can be united, I want to see her no more) therefore we must manage till we can quit this country or your uncle dies. I love, I never did love anyone else. I never had a dear pledge of love till you gave me one, and you, thank my God, never gave one to any body else. I think before March is out you will either see us back, or so victorious that we shall insure a glorious issue to our toils. Think what my Emma will feel at seeing return safe, perhaps with a little more fame, her own dear loving Nelson. Never, if I can help it, will I dine out of my Ship, or go on shore except duty calls me. Let Sir Hyde have any glory he can catch—I envy him not. You, my beloved Emma, and my country, are the two dearest objects of my fond heart—*a heart susceptible and true.* Only place confidence in me and you never shall be disappointed. I burn all your dear letters, because it is right for your sake, and I wish you would burn all mine—they can do no good, and will do us both harm if any seizure of them, or the dropping even one of them, would fill the mouth of the world sooner than we intend. My longing for you, both person and conversation, you may readily imagine. What must be my sensations at the idea of sleeping with you, it setts me on fire, even the thought, much more would the reality. I am sure my love and desires are all to you, and if any woman naked were to come to me, even as I am this moment from thinking of you, I hope it might rot off if I would touch her even with my hand. No, my heart, person, and mind is in perfect union of love towards my own dear beloved Emma—the *real bosom* friend of her, all hers, all Emma's. . . .

My love, my darling angel, my heaven-given wife, the dearest only true wife of her own till death.

It is interesting to notice that he was not aware of the existence of "little Emma."

The plan to emigrate with Emma to Bronte was firmly fixed in his head. This is what prompted him to write to St. Vincent on March 2, the day he sailed from Portsmouth, "I am so circumstanced that probably this Expedition will be the last Service ever performed by your obliged and affectionate friend." The Earl seized the wrong end of the stick. "Be assured, my dear Lord," he replied, "that every public act of your life has been the subject of my admiration, which I should have sooner declared, but that I was appalled by the last sentence of your letter, for God's sake do not suffer yourself to be carried away by any sudden impulse." Heroes do not commit suicide.

Nelson's last letter to his wife was written on March 4, as the *St. George* sailed into the North Sea in a fog.

Josiah is to have another Ship and to go aboard if the *Thalia* cannot soon be got ready. I have done *all* for him and he may again as he has often done before wish me to break my neck, and be abetted in it by his friends who are likewise my enemies, but I have done my duty as an honest generous man and I neither want or wish for any body to care what become of me, weither I return or am left in the Baltic. Living I have done all in my power for you, and if dead you will find I have done the same, therefore my only wish is to be left to myself, and wishing you every happines Believe that I am Your affectionate Nelson & Bronte.

He put the onus of blame on Josiah, which goes some way to support the contention that it was Josiah's failure to be the son Nelson wanted that was the beginning of the end of the marriage. It gives great credit to Nelson's words to Fanny given by his early biographers, Clarke and M'Arthur, "I call God to witness there is nothing in you or your conduct I wish otherwise." And it gives credibility to the suggestion that Lady Nelson's quarrel with her son was as much over this letter, as over Josiah's visits to Lady Hamilton in London or anything else.

Fanny, probably when she sent the letter to Clarke and M'Arthur during the preparation of their work, wrote underneath her husband's words,

"This is my Lord Nelson's Letter of dismissal which so astonished me that I immediately sent it to Mr. Maurice Nelson who was sincerely attached to me for his advice, he desired me not to take the least notice of it as his Brother seemed to have forgot himself."

Perhaps she was astonished. The word in society, as recorded by Mrs. Fremantle, the wife of one of Nelson's captains, was, "Lady Nelson is sueing for a separate maintenance. I have no patience with her husband at his age and such a cripple to play the fool with Lady Hamilton."

He had not forgot himself, and wrote to Emma the same day to bring Sir William to visit him at Yarmouth.

Emma told Mrs. Nelson she was ill and unable to eat or sleep for "anxiety and heart bleeding." *He* had written to the Lord Chancellor on behalf of his brother. "You will have him at Yarmouth in 2 days oh how I envy you oh God how happy you are to be with that great good virtuous man." The Cub had been to dinner, but she never asked about Tom Tit. "Oh how I long to see you do try and come for God's sake do." Two days later, on March 4, she again begged Mrs. Nelson to come to town. "You will hear all the news of my *Hero* great great glorious Nelson." The Cub had called but she would not see him. "Thank God—they are a vile set tom tit and cub hated by *everybody*." She had taken over the care of their daughter Charlotte from Lady Nelson—well, the girl turned out ungrateful.

On March 6 the *St. George* anchored off Yarmouth in a fog, "thick as mud," said Nelson. He had made his will. Twenty thousand pounds, if and when he had it, was to be put into public funds to provide £1,000 a year for Fanny. "And I having in my lifetime made her a present of £4,000 I think I have done very handsomely towards her." Three thousand pounds was left in trust for Emma, together with three diamond boxes and the picture of the King of Naples. The Grand Signior's diamond star he left her directly. Bronte and the diamond sword were to go to his male heirs. The aigrette, the collar of the Bath, his medals and the jeweled Order of St. Ferdinand, were left to the heirs of his title, "in order that it may be recollected that there was once such a person as myself living." In a codicil, he left Emma his pelisse and two pictures painted by Füger in Vienna, one of her and the other of Maria Carolina. Hardy was to have his furniture, spyingglasses, china and glass. Tom Allen would get £50 and his clothes. "My silver cup marked EH to be returned to Lady Hamilton." There was a second codicil leaving Emma the money owed him by Sir William, which he reckoned to be £2,276.

In the letter to her giving the details, he wrote, "Why should my friends be neglected, and those who I care nothing for have my little fortune, which I have worked so hard and I think so honourably for." But there was no mention of Horatia.

That evening he got into Yarmouth and found her letters. Greville had been at her again about the Prince of Wales.

> What a rascal that fellow must be. It shews, however, he has no real love—not like a person you and I know—and what bitches and pimps those folk must be. I have always been taught that a pimp was the most despicable of all wretches, and that Chap who once treated Emma so infamously ill ought to have, even before Sir William, one of your rebukes in your best and most legible hand. He would never forget it. God forbid that I should deprive you of innocent amusements, but never meet or stay if any damned whore or pimp bring that fellow to you. Let no temptation make you deviate from your oath. I hope Mrs. Nelson will soon be with you; write to her, she will come. I have just received a letter from my brother to say he will be at Yarmouth on Monday, then I will make a point of it.
>
> Lord St. Vincent I see has carried his false suit against his own Secretary, and I suppose I shall be cast, but try it I will. How infamous against poor Nelson. Every body except you tears him to pieces, nor has he but only you as a disinterested friend that he can unbosom to. Aye would to God our fates had been different. I worship—nay adore you, and if you was single and I found you under a hedge I would instantly marry you. Sir. Wm. has a treasure and does he want to throw it away. That other chap did throw away the most precious jewel that God Almighty ever sent on this earth. . . . Just going to bed with much rheumatism.

At Yarmouth Nelson's promise never to meet another woman got him in a ridiculous situation when Davison came to see him bringing his wife and a young lady as her companion. The ladies naturally wanted to see the *St. George* and so Nelson went ashore and walked about with Davison while they were taken over the ship by Hardy. When they returned, back he went on board without exchanging a word. Davison understood and knew very well what was going on.

Others did not understand. Sir Hyde Parker invited Nelson to dine and was put off with a stuffy answer: "My Ship is my home." Sir Hyde had recently married a young lady, a very young lady—"It is nothing surprising," said the *Chronicle,* "that a *twenty* gun sloop should be obliged to *lie to* by a *seventy-four!*"—and was probably very sensitive to the slightest discourtesy. He certainly snubbed Nelson back very decidedly, and Nelson had all sorts of wild ideas as to the reason for it.

Sir William could not accept the invitation to come to Yarmouth. Emma was apparently not quite free from bile, and he was busy opening the crates that had arrived from Palermo. The old gentleman was very happy, as he had found some of his best vases, which he thought had been lost with the *Colossus*.

The Rector did come down and Nelson promptly wrote to Mrs. Nelson, urging her to go to London to be with Lady Hamilton. "I will tell my Brother that you are gone, therefore he shall either meet you in London or go round by Hilborough and arrainge his Church duty."

Sir Hyde was in no hurry to leave. Nelson was in a hurry to go and come back. Emma was writing him upsetting letters again. "It almost appeared that you liked to dwell on the theme that that fellow wished, and what he would give, to enjoy your person," he hazarded, accurately. "My head. My head. No we can never be separated till death divides us."

She talked of parties and entertaining.

> What can Sir William mean by wanting you to launch out into expense and extravagance. He that used to think that a little candle-light and iced water would ruin him, to want to set off at £10,000 a year, for a less sum would not afford concerts and the style of living equal to it. Suppose you had set off in this way, what would he not have said. But you are at auction, or rather to be sold by private contract. Good God my blood boils; to you that everything used *to be refused*. I cannot bear it. Aye, how different I feel. A cottage, a plain joint of meat, and happiness, doing good to the poor, and setting an example of virtue and godliness worthy of imitation even to Kings and princes.

He meant it, he could not do wrong. Is this what makes a hero? The blind conviction that he is always right? Sir William, who whatever he was up to was not up to another man's wife, was a villain; while Nelson, who was up to precisely that, was a hero. The great advantage in not stopping to question is that one gets there before anyone else, but is it the right place? Nelson certainly thought so.

"I suppose I shall lose my cause against Lord S. Vincent, I have only *justice, honour, and the custom of the Service* on my side; he has *partiality, power, money and rascality* on his, but we are good friends and I have the highest opinion of his naval ability." He was writing on March 10. "You know my dear Emma that I would not detract from the merit of my greatest enemies. No, I am above that. You will have Mrs. Nelson with you. She will be company, and the little woman's tongue never lays still—she is a cheerful companion."

Sir Hyde's neglect of Nelson, which was brought about by Nelson's neglect of Sir Hyde, resulted in the strange idea being formed in the hero's head that he was going to be sent into battle all on his own, and while the rest of the fleet looked on. "I declare solemnly," Nelson wrote Davison on March 11, "that I do not know I am going to the Baltic, and much worse than that I could tell you, *entre nous* there is an appearance of a desire to sacrifice, for he has given no support in the *order of Battle*. Burn this letter that it can never appear and you can speak as if your knowledge came from another quarter. Situated as I am will you give Mrs. William Nelson for me one hundred pounds. She is in London by my desire."

The same extraordinary idea inspired his first letter that day to Emma. "You say my dear friend why don't *I* put my Chief forward, he has put me in the front of the battle and *Nelson will be first*. I could say much but I will not make your dear mind uneasy. The *St. George* will stamp an additional ray of Glory to England's fame if your Nelson survives, and that Almighty providence who has hitherto protected me in all dangers and covered my head in the day of Battle will still if it be his pleasure support and assist me." He went on a bit about the Prince—"Never no never suffer that fellow to come within your doors, a Villain"—and mentioned that his brother was there, "and so prying that I have been almost obliged to scold him."

"As to that fool Oliver . . ." Oliver had asked for a recommendation to a writership in the East India Company, and Nelson had written to the chairman. He was infuriated to discover that the usual consideration for a writership was £1,000, and refused to write to the directors.

Then the idea reoccurred to him.

I go God knows with a heavy heart, keep me alive in your remembrance, my last thought shall be fixed on thee, yes *my last sigh* shall go to my own dear incomparable Emma. I see nothing terrible in death but leaving thee, and should you be false to me I only hope I shall be taken off, but I do not believe that is possible, your heart I judge by my own. Say in thy Breast can falsehood e'er be formed—ah no, ah no, ah no. I judge it by my own. May the great God of heaven preserve us for each other.

Tell Mrs. Thomson her friend is miserable at parting with her and his dear Child. He desires me to beg you to be kind to her and to bless his child for him and to comfort his afflicted Wife that is to be, and to make her cheer up against her uncle and his cruelty, for neither he or I can call it by any other name.

The second letter, written at night and they were off at daybreak, was concerned with Romney's portrait of Emma as St. Cecilia, which Nelson wanted to buy before the sale of Sir William's pictures. (He also wanted the picture of Emma in a tiger skin by Madame Le Brun, but that was not in the sale.)

Pray what has Christie done about your picture. I have no letter from him; how can any man sell your resemblance, to buy it many would fly. As for the original, no price is adequate to her merits. Those of her dear mind and heart, if possible, exceed her beauty. All this World's greatness I would give up with pleasure. *So be it. Amen.*

I see clearly, my dearest friend, you are on SALE. I am almost mad to think of the iniquity of wanting you to associate with a set of whores, bawds and unprincipled lyars. Can this be the great Sir William Hamilton. I blush for him. Be comforted, you are sure of my friendship, and Mrs. Thompson's friend desires me to beg of you to tell her that he swears eternal fidelity, and if he does not say true he hopes the first shot from Cronenburgh castle will knock his head off.

The fleet sailed on March 12. Sir Hyde would not have had it, but the Admiralty spoke and the fleet sailed. There was a ball arranged for March 13 and Lady Parker was disconsolate, but Nelson had written to the Admiralty, and the Admiralty spoke, and the fleet sailed.

> *Silent grief, and sad forebodings*
> *(Lest I ne'er should see him more),*
> *Fill my heart, when gallant Nelson*
> *Hoists Blue Peter at the fore.*
>
> *On his Pendant anxious gazing,*
> *Fill with tears (mine eyes run o'er)*
> *At each change of wind I tremble*
> *While Blue Peter's at the fore.*
>
> *All the live-long day I wander,*
> *Sighing on the sea-beat shore;*
> *But my sighs are all unheeded,*
> *When Blue Peter's at the fore.*

For when duty calls my hero
To far seas, where cannons roar,
Nelson (love and Emma leaving),
Hoists Blue Peter at the fore.

Oft he kiss'd my lips at parting,
And at every kiss he swore,
Nought could force him from my bosom,
Save Blue Peter at the fore.

Oh, that I might with my Nelson,
Sail the wide world o'er and o'er,
Never should I then with sorrow,
See Blue Peter at the fore.

But (ah me!) his ship's unmooring;
Nelson's last boat rows from shore,
Every sail is set and swelling,
And Blue Peter's seen no more.

                              Emma Hamilton

CHAPTER NINE

Baltic Visions

HAVING FAILED to get the Prince of Wales to come to dinner, and though the first invitation may have been canceled, the second and third were refused, the Hamiltons decided he was a thoroughly bad influence and gave him up. Fortunately, this failure (or from Nelson's viewpoint, this success) did not affect Sir William's claim to a pension. In the second week in March the King recovered, some said his health others his senses, and took up the reins of government again. The horses were changed, the thoroughbred Mr. Pitt going out to grass, and the hack Mr. Addington going into harness.

The last acts of an administration are usually designed to lay as heavy a burden as possible on their successors, to ensure that they start with no unfair advantages. When the burden takes the form of rewards for themselves, this is statemanship of a high order. Mr. Pitt's last Civil List starred Henry Dundas, with £8,000 a year pension, and Lord Grenville, £7,000 a year and £1,500 a year for Lady Grenville if she survived him. Somewhere near the bottom was Sir William Hamilton, with £1,200 a year on the Irish establishment. It was not the £2,000 he had expected and been promised, but it appears that the claims on government were heavy. The matter of compensation for his losses was left to the new Foreign Secretary, Lord Hawkesbury, who, it might as well be said now, was no more willing to move the Treasury than his predecessor, and indeed together they might just as well have tried to move St. Paul's.

The following advertisement appeared in the *Morning Chronicle* of March 6:

> By Mr. CHRISTIE in his Great Room in Pall Mall on Friday
> the 27th inst. and following day at 12 o'clock. A Select Part of the

capital, valuable, and genuine COLLECTION of PICTURES the property of the Rt. Hon. Sir Wm. Hamilton K.B. purchased by him with great taste, and at a liberal expence, from several distinguished Cabinets in this Country, and during 37 years residence at Minister Plenipotentiary at the Court of Naples, consisting of the Works of the greatest and most admired Masters in the Italian, Spanish, French, Flemish, and Dutch Schools viz.

Leon da Vinci	P Veronese	Cagnacce	V Dyck
Permigiano	Tintoretto	L Giordano	Jordaens
Polidoro	Schiavoni	Velasquez	Teniers
Gerofelo	Caracci	S Rola	Berghen
Titian	Schidoni	Vernot	W de Velde
Giorgione	Guido	Rubens	Wouvermans &c

Particularly a small Portrait, an exquisite Cabinet Picture by Leon da Vinci, formerly in the Collection of the Earl of Arundell and Lady B. Germaine; a Madonna and Child, Permigiano; and St. Sebastian, a noble composition by V Dyck.

Also early in April (together with the remaining part of the above Collection) will be sold his truly valuable Assemblage of Antique Bustos, Marbles, capital and singularly fine Grecian, commonly called Hetruscan Vases, and other rare and curious specimens of Ancient Art, which were saved upon the entry of the French into Naples, and escaped the fatal effects of the storm, by which part of this Unique Collection was lost on board of the Colossus man of war. The former part of the above may be viewed two days preceeding the sale, when Catalogues may be had; and timely notice of the Sale and View of the latter will be given.

The first sale took place as advertised and raised £5,025 13s. 0d. for the old gentleman. Beckford paid 1,300 guineas for the Leonardo, a portrait of Francis I called the "Laughing Boy," and the lot were sold for prices that today would break the hearts of Mr. Christie's successors. However, Sir William was happy and said he got more than he expected.

The second sale did not take place, because the vases were sold as a collection to Mr. Gale Hope for £4,000.

Nelson purchased Romney's portrait of Emma as St. Cecilia for £300 (at those prices he was done) and said, "If it had cost me 300 drops of blood I would have given it with pleasure." Davison was instructed to keep the picture in his house and not to show it to anyone. There were two Emmas already in Nelson's cabin . . . but we will leave him there to contemplate them for the moment.

The Hamiltons stayed in town and Mrs. Nelson came up from Hilborough to keep Emma company. Once or twice a week Mrs. Gibson brought the child Horatia to Piccadilly, and once or twice a week Emma went to Little Titchfield Street. There were problems—"Dear Mrs. Gibson, Pray do send the nurse a way and change the milk for I don't like the nurse much" —but on the whole they were small ones and little Miss Thomson grew up steadily.

The habitual callers at 23 Piccadilly were the Duke of Queensberry, who lived just down the street, and Lord William Gordon, who appointed himself the laureate of Emma's little court. Charles Greville was naturally quite often at his uncle's house, and Mrs. Nelson attended regularly on Emma. From the Rector's letter of March 29 to her ladyship, it appears that his children Charlotte and Horatio were in town for the school holidays. And so was Fanny. "I was rather surprised to hear *Tom Tit* (that bad bird) had taken his flight to Town, but He is a prying little animal and wishes to know everything, and as he is so small and insignificant his movements are not always observed, but for God's sake take care of him and caution our little Jewel [his wife!] to be as much upon her guard as she can. I am terribly afraid this Bird will endeavour to do mischief. He must be watched with a Hawk's Eye—I almost wish some Hawk or *Jove*'s Eagle would either devour him or frighten him away. . . . I am glad my little Horace looks so well, and that you think him so like his great, his Glorious, his immortal uncle; why should he not be like him? is it so very uncommon for such near relatives to have some similitude? they who say otherwise, only say it out of envy, malice and hatred and all uncharitableness, and to make mischief—out upon all such miscreants say I—Love to deary, Charlotte, and the Hereditary Duke of Bronte." It looks as if Emma had been teasing him, but she really seemed to like the great clodhopping clergyman.

Fanny came to London late in March on her way to Bath. She made no effort to speak to the Rector's jewel, though she was still corresponding with the rest of the Nelson family. While at Brighton she had received a friendly letter from Mrs. Bolton dated March 8. Nelson's eldest sister, who knew some but not all the circumstances, asked:

> Will you excuse what I am going to say? I wish you had continued in town a little longer, as *I have heard* my brother regretted he had not a house he could call his own when he returned. Do, whenever you hear he is likely to return, have a house to receive him. If you absent yourself entirely from him, there never can be a reconciliation. Such attention must please him and I am sure will do in the end. Your conduct as he *justly* says is *exemplary* in regard to him and he has not an unfeeling heart.

I most sincerely love my brother and *did quite as much before he was Lord Nelson* and I hope my conduct was ever the same towards you as Mrs. Nelson as ever it was as Lady Nelson. I hope in God one day I shall have the pleasure of seeing you together as happy as ever, he certainly as far as I hear is not a happy man.

The Reverend Edmund also wrote to Fanny this month, to find out how she was and what she intended doing. There is a tone in these letters that is more normal in letters of condolence. "Can I contribute any thing to the farther increase of your comfort," inquired the very old gentleman, "or do your mind feel easy and happy in its present state?"

Nelson was not happy as he sat in his cabin aboard the *St. George* alone with his thoughts. We forget sometimes how often he was alone, and the peculiar nature of his fears and suspicions made them impossible to communicate. He was not in command of the fleet and found himself at a loss for something to do in the mornings.

"His Lordship was rather too apt to interfere in the workings of the ship," wrote Colonel Stewart, "and not always with the best success or judgement. The wind, when off Dungeness, was scanty, and the ship was to be put about; Lord Nelson would give the orders, and caused her to miss stays—he said to the Officer of the Watch—'Well, now see what we have done. Well Sir, what mean you to do now?' 'I don't exactly know, my Lord: I fear she won't do.' Nelson: 'Well, I am sure if you don't know what to do with her, no more do I either.' "

The afternoons were taken up with walks on the quarter-deck to the music of the band and dinner with his officers. But the evenings and the nights were lonely. He would sit in his cabin, gazing at Emma's picture until his brain reeled. He would write her fantastic letters, dwelling on the mystery he was creating around her image, and suddenly becoming clear and decisive when he turned his mind to the conduct and purpose of the expedition on which he was embarked.

In this black Baltic mood Emma and England were opposing poles, tugging at the needle of his heart. He told her on March 13:

Ah my Dearest beloved friend, I see I feel what the call of duty to our Country makes me suffer, but we must recollect, which is the only comfort I can know, the reflection at some future day of what we have both suffered in the cause of our Country. You have sent your dearest friend and I have left mine; the conduct of the Roman matron *return with your shield or upon it;* so it shall be my study so to distinguish myself that your heart shall leap for joy when my name is mentioned.

He still believed that Sir Hyde was intending to disgrace, and even destroy, him by sending him into battle unsupported, "but never mind Nelson will be first if he lives, and you shall partake of all his Glory. Our Breeze is foul, what our Neapolitan Princesses would say fresh gales, but quick quick quick and let Nelson return to his mate for he is disconsolate."

March 14. "For these two nights I have done nothing but dream of you, the first I saw your tears as plain as possible on your left cheek, and waking with anguish I had lost your picture the Hair had broke, last night I thought that poor *Mira* was alive and between us, what can this mean time can discover."

March 16. "All yesterday was such a dreadful nasty day, snow frost sleet strong breezes that I could not put pen to paper, but all my thoughts were fixed on thee all night I dreamed of you. I saw you all in black and that fellow sitting by you—all this must mean something. Before you receive this all will be over with Denmark, either your Nelson will be safe and Sir Hyde Parker a victor, or he your own Nelson will be laid low, in case of the latter I have this day added another codicil to my Will and given you my Pelisse."

Sir Hyde was still not talking to him, but he had heard that the Commander in Chief intended to anchor the fleet off Cronenburg Castle, while the diplomats negotiated in Copenhagen. "To keep us out of sight is to seduce Denmark into a War, which I as an Englishman wish to prevent. . . . I hate your Pen and Ink men, a fleet of British Ships of War are the best negotiators in Europe."

He wrote much the same thing to Davison that day. "A Danish Minister would think twice before he would put his name to war with England, when the next moment he would probably see his Master's fleet in flames and his capital in ruins—*but out of sight out of mind* is an old saying, the fellow should see our flags waving every moment he lifted up his head."

His dreams became wilder. Emma learned from his letter of the 17th, "I dreamt last night that I beat you with a stick on account of that fellow and then attempted to throw over head a tub of Boiling hot water, you may believe I woke in an Agony and that my feelings cannot be very comfortable." He now suspected Lord Spencer and Lord St. Vincent as well as Sir Hyde. "They all hate me and treat me ill, I cannot my Dear friend recall to my mind any one real act of kindness but all of unkindness—but never mind we will be happy in spite of all they can do and if it pleases God."

He was more than ever concerned about the conduct of the campaign. "Why we are not this day off Copenhagen I cannot guess, our Wind is fair, but a frigate is just sent away by the Commander in Chief, perhaps to say we are coming that they may be prepared, or to attempt to frighten at a distance; paltry the last and foolish the first; but mine is all guess. . . ."

Nelson was not the only one concerned. On March 13 the *Morning Chronicle* had asked, "We should be glad to know from whom the instructions for this expedition and its object have come, and who are to be responsible for the measure—the Ministry not yet out, or the Ministry not yet in!" Pitt had planned the expedition and Addington had modified the plans. ("If they are the plans of Ministers," said Nelson, "they are weak in the extreme, and very different to what I understood from Mr. Pitt.")

On the 17th the *Chronicle* reported, "The Commander in Chief is said to be instructed to demand from the Danes, that they shall within 48 hours declare their resolution to separate from the Neutral Confederacy; and in case of their refusal to proceed to hostilities. We can scarcely think it possible that a line of conduct so rash and violent can be resorted to, after all the calamity we have suffered from thoughtless intemperance." The *Post* added, "Ministers boast at once that they will attack the North, and that they have strong hopes of peace with France." And that is what happened. The fleet arrived off Elsinore on March 19 and hung at anchor for a week while Messrs. Drummond and Vansittart went ahead in the frigate to Copenhagen. They gave the ultimatum. It was rejected. They returned to the fleet and then sailed back to England. Then the whole issue of peace or war rested on the table of Sir Hyde Parker. In the meantime, of course, the Danes prepared their defenses. Between two ministries and an undecided admiral, the attack on Denmark was delayed until it was virtually impossible to make it. Nelson made it. The tragedy of it was that had Sir Hyde been allowed to dither a few days longer, it need not have been made at all.

On the 21st Nelson wrote a long exposition to Emma as to why the Danes should not risk going to war. It was superfluous, as by the time she read it the business was done. What is fascinating is the extraordinary hyperbole which it led him into.

> These ideas, my sensible friend, the vicinity of Denmark naturally gave rise to, and I let them out to you as one of the most sensible Women of the age and if I was to add of men too I should be more correct. Your beauty which I own is beyond that of all other women is still below that of your understanding, for I believe

that either Johnson or Burke would be struck with your excellent writings, and both these rare and most extraordinary qualifications are almost eclipsed by your goodness and gentleness of heart. There you shine with unequalled lustre. The first make you the Envy of all the Women in the World (Your wisdom they do not envy you for they know not the worth of it, getting what their want of sence makes them call the honors of this World mistress to a Prince &c &c by their folly.) But your goodness of heart, your amiable qualities, your unbounded Charity, will make you Envied in the World which is to come. There will be your sure reward and where they can never hope to reach. You will not my dear friend at this moment consider these true thoughts of your worth can be with a view of adulation, for it is very possible they may be the last words ever wrote by your old faithful and most attached friend till Death—Nelson & Bronte.

Your heart my friend may feel too much on reading this, pray do not let it, for my mind is tranquil and calm, ready and willing to stand in the breach to defend my Country, and to risk whatever fate may await me in that post of honor, but never mind perhaps I may laughing come back. God's will be done, Amen Amen.

It has always been the story that Lady Hamilton flattered Lord Nelson silly. Well, perhaps she did, for her excellent writings, which would have struck Johnson and Burke, were all in his praise. In default of anything written by her at this time, for he was still burning her letters, here is part of one written on April 2, 1802, the anniversary of the battle that is just about to be fought.

Our dear glorious friend, immortal and great Nelson, what should I say to you on this day? My heart and feelings are so overpowered that I cannot give vent to my full soul, to tell you as an English woman, grateful to her Country's saviour, which I feil towards you; and as a much loved friend that has the happiness of being beloved, esteemed and admired by the good and virtuous Nelson, what must be my pride, my glory, to say this day have I the happiness of being with him, one of his select, and how gratefull to God Almighty do I feil in having preserved you throu such glorious danger, that never man before ever got throu with such Courage, Honner and Success. Nelson I want Eloquence to tell you all I feil, to avow the sentiments of respect and adoration with which you have inspired me. Admiration and delight you must ever raise in all who behold you, looking on you onely as the Guardian of England, but how far short are those sensations to what I, as a much loved friend, feil and I confess to you the pre-

229

dominant sentiment of my heart will ever be, till it ceases to beat, the most unfeigned anxiety for your happiness, and the sincerest and most disinterested determination to promote your felicity, even at the hazard of my life.

This is a real "Britannia" letter and she penned it with some care (though it is deuced hard to find a place to put a full stop). It gives some idea of Emma's high style of letter writing.

With the return of Drummond and Vansittart unsuccessful from Copenhagen, it became apparent to Sir Hyde that he would be obliged to do something, so he sent for Nelson. In the great cabin of the C. in C.'s flagship, the *London*, there were conferences on March 24 and 26. Nelson took over the command of the fleet. "Not a moment should be lost in attacking the Enemy," he said. "They will every day and hour be stronger, we shall never be so good a match for them as at this moment." He outlined the position of the Danish line of defense and explained his plan of attack, which, naturally, gave him the leading part while Sir Hyde and the greater part of the fleet were to be observers. "Here you are," up he stood, "with almost the safety, certainly the honor of England more intrusted to you, than ever yet fell to the lot of any British Officer. On your decision depends whether our Country shall be degraded in the eyes of Europe, or whether she shall rear her head higher than ever: again do I repeat, never did our Country depend so much on the success of any Fleet as on this." Who could say no to that?

On the 26th Nelson shifted his flag to the *Elephant*, a seventy-four-gun ship more suitable for navigating the tricky sandbanks of Copenhagen Bay than the *St. George*. She was commanded by Captain Foley, one of the band of brothers of the Nile. Nelson took Emma's portrait with him; it was the one painted by Schmidt at Dresden. "You know," he wrote her, "I am more bigotted to your picture than ever a Neapolitan was to St. Januarius and look upon you as my guardian angel and God I trust will make you so to me. His will be done. Sir Hyde Parker has by this time found out the worth of your Nelson and that he is a useful sort of man on a pinch, therefore if he ever has thought unkindly of me, I freely forgive him. Nelson must stand among the first, or he must fall."

"I feel very sorry for Sir Hyde," Lord Minto wrote later, "but no wise man would ever have gone with Nelson or over him, as he was sure to be in the background in every case."

Sir Hyde managed to waste a day or two in making up his mind whether to approach Copenhagen through the Belt or the Sound. ("Let it be by the Sound, by the Belt, or anyhow," said Nelson, "only lose not an hour.") Then, having decided on the Sound, he insisted on writing to the Governor of Cronenburg Castle to ask him what he would do if the fleet attempted to pass by. The Governor replied that he would resist the attempt. Sir Hyde construed that as a declaration of war. Nelson was not bothered with such trifles. A battle there was going to be, war or no war. Mind you, it would have to wait a minute. "I must have done," he wrote Emma on the 30th, "for breakfast is waiting and I never give up a meal for a little fighting."

That day the fleet passed through the Sound on the Swedish side and out of range of the cannons of Cronenburg. The day after, Nelson wrote his last note to Emma before the battle. "I have just been reconnoitring the Danish line of defence. It looks formidable to those who are children at war, but to my judgment, with ten sail of the line I think I can annihilate them; at all events, I hope to be allowed to try. . . . May God whom I worship protect and send me victorious. Amen if it be his good pleasure. May the heavens bless you. My best regards to Sir William, I hope his pictures have sold well. Recommend to Lord William not to make *songs* about *us*, for fear *we* should not deserve his good opinion. Once more adieu and may God bless you shall be my last word."

The battle was fought on April 2. Colonel Stewart wrote to his friend Sir William Clinton:

> The nature of the battle of the 2nd is I believe unparalleled in history, and for enterprize, and difficulties, as well as the length of the contest (for we were *five* hours in one incessant roar of cannon) infinitely superior to the famous action of Aboukir. I was during the whole of the action, excepting whilst employed in working my Carronade on the Poop or carrying Capt. Foley's orders to the different Decks, on the quarter deck of the *Elephant* with Lord Nelson, and never passed so interesting a day in the course of my life, or one which so much called for my admiration *of any Officer*.
>
> After the Action had lasted about three hours, and that we had fired about forty broadsides (we fired above 60 in all) he said to me, "Well Stewart, these fellows hold us a better Tug than I expected, however we are keeping up a noble fire, and I'll be answerable that we shall *bole them out* in four if we cannot do it in three hours, at least I'll give it them till they are sick of it." Our grand fleet was under sail all this time, about two leagues on our starboard beam, and as there are a number of Croakers, or what you may call Cautious Men, in it (names I shall not mention)

the signal was made for us to leave off Action—this is a fact, and is a source of much "conversation" in our fleet now. Ld. N. however never answered it, and expressing his astonishment to me at the circumstance, turned and said what I have written above in a most animated manner—the only signal which the hero kept flying was the very reverse, viz. "for Close Action."

(Oddly enough, the Colonel did not mention the incident which he later included in his narrative of the campaign, and which became so famous. "He also observed I believe to Captain Foley, 'You know, Foley, I have only one eye—I have a right to be blind sometimes,' and then with an archness familiar to his character, putting the glass to his blind eye, he exclaimed, 'I really do not see the signal.' ") The letter continued:

His distress at the Pilot's refusing to take the Ship closer to the Enemy was very great, and he called me down at the beginning of the day from the Poop to tell me the indignation he felt at the fellow's refusing to go nearer than $\frac{1}{4}$ less 5—which is *within* a fathom of what the *Elephant* draws. All our fleet engaged at anchor by the *Stern*, in the *Nile* stile. At times the contest was most desperate, for we were opposed to a force infinitely superior to us, from its *composition*, the floating batteries and the Ships of the Enemy being without any rigging, mere hulks, and consequently as difficult to contend with as any batteries on the shore.

The Colonel went on to describe the *Elephant*'s part in the battle and the Danish line, which extended for nearly four miles and consisted of six sail of the line (four more were in the harbor's mouth) and eleven floating batteries of various sizes. Nelson attacked with twelve sail of the line and a squadron of smaller ships which were of little use. The strong points of the Danish defense were two forts built out in the bay called the Crown Islands. There were, said the Colonel, about 500 yards between the two lines. "'Tis this last circumstance which causes us regret now that we have examined the Channel since the Action, for it is proved that we might have gone within pistol shot of their whole line. Whereas we conceived it to be formed on the Southern Shoals, and therefore gave it a *supposed* necessary wide berth—the contest had we been aware of this could not have lasted one fourth of the time."

When seventeen Danish vessels had been sunk, burned, or taken, and the whole line south of the Crown Islands defeated, Nelson sent a flag of truce ashore suggesting a cessation of hostilities—Nelson said in the cause of humanity, to save the Danes in the captured vessels from falling in the crossfire between the squadron and the Crown Islands, and everyone else said to extricate himself from an impossible position.

The Colonel thought it "a masterpiece of policy of the little hero's, for victorious as we were, the narrowness of the Channel in which our Ships were engaged, and the commanding batteries on shore, had left our Ships, six of which were aground, in a most perilous situation. . . . Lord Nelson then *commanded* a cessation of hostilities, and by prolonging it under one pretext or another, in four and twenty hours after got our crippled Ships off the Shoals, and from under the guns of the Enemy's batteries, and he also took possession of all our prizes, which otherwise we should have found some difficulty in doing."

So ended the battle, with a vast number of Danish casualties, seventeen prizes, only one of which could be taken to England, and at a cost to the fleet of no ships, but 254 dead and 689 wounded. "There are many people in this fleet," concluded Colonel Stewart, "about Headquarters too, who think our victory bought infinitely too dearly."

That evening Nelson returned to the *St. George* and wrote a short account of the day's events to Emma, in which he referred to the truce as "not very inconvenient to me." He was tired, "very tired after a hard fought battle," and yet wrote her some lines, or perhaps altered some lines of Lord William Gordon's for her.

Lord Nelson to his Guardian Angel.

From my best cable tho' I'm forced to part,
I leave my anchor in my Angel's heart:
Love, like a pilot, shall the pledge defend,
And for a prong his happiest quiver lend.

Answer of Lord Nelson's Guardian Angel.

Go where you list, each thought of Angel's soul
Shall follow you from Indus to the Pole:
East, west, north, south, our minds shall never part,
Your Angel's loadstone shall be Nelson's heart.
Farewell, and o'er the wide, wide sea,
Bright glory's course pursue,
And adverse winds to love and me,
Prove fair to fame and you.

And when the dreaded hour of battle's nigh,
Your Angel's heart, which trembles at a sigh,

233

> *By your* superior danger *bolder grown*
> *Shall dauntless place itself before your own,*
> *Happy, thrice happy, should her fond heart prove*
> *A shield to* Valour, Constancy, *and* Love.

The negotiations that Nelson undertook following the battle need not be indulged at length. Suffice it to say that he did negotiate with the Danish Regent, the Crown Prince Frederick, son of the mad King Christian VII and nephew of George III. By dint of plain speaking, threats, impatience, and not insisting on the object of the war, the withdrawal of Denmark from the confederacy, he obtained an agreement on April 9, the main provision of which was an armistice for fourteen weeks. Some of his experiences during these days appear in his letters.

On the 4th he told Davison to subscribe £100 for the widows of those killed in the battle and for the wounded, and added, "Sir Hyde having sent me on shore to talk with the Prince, I was received in the most flattering manner by all ranks, and the Crowd was as is usual with me. No wonder I am spoilt, all my astonishment is that my head is not turned."

The next day he wrote Emma that he had told the Prince "such truths as seldom reach the Ears of Princes. . . . You must know you have been in the battle, for your two pictures, one done by Miss Knight crowning the rostral column, the other done at Dresden, I call them my Guardian Angels and I believe there would be more Virtue in the prayers of Santa Emma than any Saint in the whole calendar of Rome, I carried on board the *Elephant* with me and they are safe and so am I, not a scratch." He again mentioned the dead. "It has truly made my heart run out of my eyes. It brought fresh to my recollection that only when I spoke to them all and shook hands with every Captain, wishing them all with laurel, alas, too many are covered with cypress." Twenty officers had been killed, among them Captains Mosse and Riou.

On the 6th he discovered some verses by Miss Knight in Emma's handwriting and sent them back to her saying, "The latter part is a little applicable to my present situation." Here is the latter part.

> *Blest, blest, the compass be*
> *Which steers my love to me!*
> *And blest the happy gale*
> *Which fills his homeward sail.*
> *And blest the boat, and blest each oar*
> *Which rows my True Love back to shore.*

And doubly blest the hour
When love resumes his power,
And when the northern wind,
To long-lorn Emma kind;
Shall change to joy her soul's alarms
And give back Henry to her arms.

So much for Miss Knight's protestations of propriety!

On the 9th he wrote her again. "The Armistice has tied up Denmark and let us loose against her allies, for which I think Russia will go to war with her. If our Ministry do not approve of my humane conduct, I have begged they would allow me to retire and under the shade of a Chestnut tree at *Bronte* where the din of War will not reach my ears do I hope to solace myself. . . ." She must have been at him again, because he wrote further on, "Your Virtue [the paper is damaged here] conduct is admirable and I would not wish to consider you as my friend if you kept such scandalous company as the P—— of W——. How Sir Wm. can bear to associate with such wretches I cannot think."

There was a little letter inside.

You are, my dearest Mrs. Thomson, so good, so right in all that you do, that I will take care your dear friend shall do no wrong. He has cried on account of his child; he begs for heaven's sake, you will take care that the nurse had no *bad* disorder, for he has been told that Captain Howard, before he was six weeks old, had the *bad* disorder which has ruined his constitution to this day. He desires me to say he has never wrote his aunt since he sailed, and all the parade about a house is nonsense. He has wrote to his father, but not a word or message to her. He does not, nor cannot, care about her; he believes she has a most unfeeling heart.

He repeated his determination to go to Bronte "in six weeks after the peace" on the 11th. "*I can assure you that I am fixed to live a Country life and to have many (I hope) years of comfort,* which God knows I have never yet had, only moments of happiness, but the case shall be altered." He was impressed by the humility of this future existence. "Gold silver and jewels may be presents from Royalty. I can only send you a sprig of laurel and the friendship of an humane and generous heart, which I believe you would prize more than all the Riches of this World. What little I have is honestly come by, earned by my Blood, and therefore I may eat my morsel of bread in peace without a sting of Conscience."

He mentioned that he had heard of the death of the Emperor Paul, though he was much more interested in a report that the Swedish fleet was at sea. "All our fellows are longing to be at them, and so do I, as great a Boy as any of them, for I consider this as being at School and going to England as going home for the holidays, therefore I really long to finish my task."

The fleet went off without Nelson, who was stuck in the bay trying to get the *St. George* out over the shallows, with the wind in the wrong direction. On hearing that Sir Hyde was really in pursuit of the Swedes, he ordered out his boat and had himself rowed after them. He spent six hours of a bitter cold night in an open boat without his cloak, caught up, and went aboard the *Elephant* at midnight.

"A celebrated *female attitudinarian*," tittered the *Morning Herald*, "ever since our Northern Squadron has put to sea, has thrown aside all the lighter airs, and positions of gaiety, confining her imitative talents to those of a graver cast. Cleopatra arrayed in *mournful graces* is now the model that she daily copies, and with *singular effect!*"

Strangely enough, Charles Lamb used to contribute jokes to the newspapers at this time, though not this one, because he was employed by the *Post* and the *Chronicle* for 6d. a day—1d. a joke. He used to think them up early in the morning before going to work at the offices of the East India Company. Did he ever take advantage of the easy laugh to be got out of just mentioning Lady Hamilton, the knowing leer? Surely not, though others did.

The newspapers were hard on Copenhagen, the country was hard on it, because everything conspired to turn Nelson's tremendous victory into a disaster.

It began, as we have seen, with doubts cast on the purpose of the expedition. Denmark was a friendly nation; there had been no war with Denmark since . . . King Canute! Then the whole question of the northern confederacy had not been discussed. Parliament had not met since the King's enigmatic speech on December 31. And what was the fleet going to do without any declared policy from the government? "Unquestionably," thundered the *Chronicle* (the *Chronicle* used to thunder then, and the *Times* used to squeak), "Unquestionably this is one of the first examples of a great armament proceeding to the place of its destination, without the power of action, without the authority to make peace or denounce war."

There was nothing but conjecture until April 14, and then the first news to arrive was of the death of Paul and the accession of his son Alexander, who had immediately ordered the release of the English seamen imprisoned in Russia. Paul was reported to have died of apoplexy, though it

was not long before it came out that he had been strangled. When someone asked Mr. Pitt if he thought that Paul had died a natural death, he
answered, "Very natural for such an Emperor."

While the papers were full of Paul and the possibility of peace, the
news came on the 15th that Danish troops had occupied Hamburg and a
Prussian army was marching into Hanover. On the same day it was known
that Captain Otway had arrived from the fleet with dispatches, and there
were rumors of a desperate action off Copenhagen.

On April 16 Sir Hyde's dispatch announcing the victory was published
and the guns were fired in the park and from the Tower. But there were no
illuminations of public buildings and the Lord Mayor advised the people of
London not to decorate their houses and offices, but to give the money to
the widows and orphans instead. Greater prominence than usual was given
in the papers to the lists of killed and wounded, and the *Chronicle* noticed
with gloomy satisfaction that £1,500 had been subscribed at Lloyd's for
the wounded in one hour.

Mr. Addington was said to have announced the victory to the House
of Commons apologetically, and Mr. Grey spoke up, not in opposition to
the vote of thanks, but to protest that the first the House knew of a war
with Denmark was of a victory against Denmark. The motions of thanks
naturally passed in both Houses on the 16th, but when the City came to
consider its vote of thanks on the 27th, not enough members of the Court
of Common Council appeared and it was postponed.

On April 17 there was an absolutely unheard of event, when the
Chronicle and the *Herald* published an account of the battle by the Danish
commander in chief, Commodore Olfert Fischer. Fischer not only claimed
that the contest was unequal but that the English fire was exhausted and
Nelson—"this hero at the very moment and during the very heat of the
battle, sent a flag of truce on shore to require a cessation of hostilities."

Now all this was very bad and very untrue, but that did not stop the
newspapers from printing it, and when the *Post* made a point of praising
Nelson for his "well-timed flag of truce," the *Chronicle* felt bound to reply.
"The proposal of Lord Nelson appears to have been not a measure of humanity, but a *ruse de guerre*, and we are not quite sure if it be a justifiable
one."

Matters were made worse by stories of differences of opinion between
Sir Hyde Parker and Lord Nelson, which sprang from Colonel Stewart's
tale, told with the best of intentions, of the signal to break off the action and
Nelson's refusal to see it. The Colonel arrived at the end of April with the
terms of the convention which Nelson had made with the Danish Court.

When these were known, and it appeared that the only consequence of the battle was a fourteen-week armistice, criticism reached a crescendo.

"The Convention concluded with the Danes does not give very general satisfaction," said the *Chronicle*. "This diminishes the importance, or what is the same thing, the impression, of the late victory." "It is plain," said the *Post*, "that our fleet has been unable to subdue the Court of Denmark." There was a move to shift the blame onto Sir Hyde. The *Chronicle* took up the cudgels. "A Ministerial Paper of yesterday [April 24], without meaning to throw out any insinuation against the conduct of Sir Hyde Parker, expresses considerable regret that Lord Nelson had not the whole command of the expedition to the Baltic. This is a pretty plain proof that the Convention is not entirely to the satisfaction of Ministers. Whether Lord Nelson had the Chief Command or not, it is evident that he had the chief direction both of the war and the negotiation. It was he that first proposed the armistice, it was he, with full powers, that concluded the fourteen weeks Convention."

The victory took on all the effects of a disaster when the price of shares fell in the City. This was unforgivable. Politics are profanities, and we may believe or disbelieve, but shares are sacred. The skies darkened over Whitehall. The *Post* pronounced, "The public censure must fall on the Ministers alone, who planned and have supported this expedition."

The only tangible reward for the hard fought victory of Copenhagen was a viscountcy for Lord Nelson, and a K.B. for Admiral Graves. They could hardly be avoided and were a blatant censure on Sir Hyde Parker, who got nothing. There were no promotions for the lieutenants, and no gold medals for the captains. Difficulties were made about the prize money for the captures, and Alexander Davison became sole agent again, not so much from Nelson's influence as from the reluctance of other agents to deal with the government. Sixteen of the prizes were so battered as to be fit only for burning. The seventeenth, the battleship *Holstein*, was eventually brought to England. Sixty thousand pounds was allowed for the burned ships and £30,000 for the *Holstein*, a poorer reward than was given for the Nile, which had to be divided among a greater number of men.

There was a nice story about one of these prizes. "The Danish officers denied a vessel had struck and insisted on seeing Lord Nelson. 'I am Lord Nelson, see here's my *Fin!*' at the same time throwing aside his green dreadnought and showing the stump of his right arm and exposing also his three stars. The Danes convinced immediately gave up the ship."

However, though the papers moaned and groaned—"It is too well known that the public are displeased with the proceedings at Copenha-

gen," moaned the *Post*—not all the members of the public were so miserable. One April morning the King was out riding in the park when an old
lady called out to him, "God bless your Majesty and Admiral Nelson!" and
George pulled off his hat and said, "Thank ye, good woman, thank ye." At
Sadlers Wells, the public went to see *The Northern Fleet or British Intrepidity Triumphant*. The Royal Circus presented in St. George's Fields,
"For the first time on any stage a Real seventy-four (invented and executed
by Mr. Branscomb) with its full complement of brave officers and seamen,
passes proudly through the Sound, silences the batteries of Cronenburgh,
overcomes every impediment, and destroys the supposed invincible Danish
Navy. This piece will be repeated every evening until further notice." "The
only thing that could be said in favour of the battle of Copenhagen was
that it arrived most opportunely for the playhouse benefits," groaned the
Chronicle.

Mr. Branscomb's 74 did not sail for long. On May 1 the news arrived
that General Abercrombie had defeated the French army at Alexandria. It
was brought by Mr. Lock on his return from Naples in a brief moment of
glory. Soon after, the playhouses were showing the battle of Alexandria and
the death of Abercrombie.

Even the ladies gave up their Copenhagen coats, which after all were
only suitable for winter, and began to dress *à la sauvage*, which meant no
pockets, no handkerchief, no shift, only a muslin dress over flesh-colored
knitwork silk stays, with a purse tucked in the bosom and fan stuck in the
belt. And that was that.

Of course, that was not that in Piccadilly; more particularly in Number
23.

"You would have laughed to have seen what I saw yesterday," Sir William wrote Nelson on April 16; yesterday they had received his letters up to
the 6th.

> *Emma* did not know whether she was on her head or heels—
> in such a hurry to tell your great news that she could utter nothing
> but tears of joy and tenderness. I went to Davison yesterday morn-
> ing, found him still in bed having had a severe fit of the gout and
> with your letter which he had just received, and he cried like a
> child, but what was very extraordinary assured me that from the
> instant he had read your letter all pain had left him and that he
> felt himself able to get up and walk about. Your Brother, Mrs.
> Nelson and Horace dined with us—your Brother was more ex-
> traordinary than ever— He would get up suddenly and cut a caper
> rubbing his hands, every time the thought of your fresh laurels

came into his head. In short, except myself (and your Lordship knows that I have some phlegm), all the Company which was considerable after dinner—The Duke, Lord William, Mr. Este &c were mad with joy—but I am sure that no one realy rejoiced more at heart than I did. I have lived too long to have *Extacies,* but with calm reflexion I felt for my Friend having got to the very summit of Glory—the *ne plus ultra*—that he has had another opportunity of rendering his Country the most important Service and manifesting again his judgement, his intrepidity and humanity. God bless you my very dear Lord and send you soon home to your friends. Enemies you have none but those that are bursting with envy and such animals infest all parts of the world.

Sir Nathaniel Wraxall, Sir William's old correspondent, was at the party after dinner and recorded that in the company were the Dukes of Gordon and Queensberry, Lord William Gordon, Charles Greville, Kemble the actor and his wife, the Rector, and a Neapolitan Duke de Noia. Emma danced the tarantella.

Sir William began it with her and maintained the conflict, for such it might well be esteemed, during some minutes. When unable longer to continue it, the Duke de Noia succeeded to his place; but he too, though near forty years younger than Sir William, soon gave in from Extenuation. Lady Hamilton then sent for her own maid servant; who being likewise presently exhausted, after a short time, another female attendant, a Copt, perfectly black, whom Lord Nelson had presented her on his return from Egypt, relieved her companion. [And a wild dance it was.] It was certainly not of a nature to be performed except before a select Company; as the Screams, Attitudes, Starts and Embraces, with which it was intermingled, gave it a peculiar character.

Emma soon had a new verse of "God Save the King" to sing.

> *He who twice saved our Isle*
> *First in the floods of Nile*
> *Then near the Pole;*
> *Him still oh him defend*
> *Who made his foe his friend*
> *Still on his steps attend*
> *From Pole to Pole.*

There was also a verse which delighted her so much she put it in her letters.

> Two thirds of Caesar's boasted fame
> Thou Nelson must resign.
> To come and see is Parker's claim,
> To conquer only thine.

And there was a splendid song for her songbook, written by Miss Metcalf (at the age of ten) and Mr. C. Metcalf, which she must have rendered at the musical treats and drawing rooms she attended that spring.

> Awake awake my lyre awake
> Attend a Briton's lays,
> A Briton calls, obey and sound
> Brave Nelson's worthy praise.
> Brave Nelson's praise, brave Nelson's praise,
>   brave Nelson's worthy praise.
>
> Him England's foes shall ever fear
> Him Britons shall admire,
> The glorious bay of Aboukir
> Is witness of his fire.
> Is witness of, is witness of,
>   is witness of his fire.
>
> 'Twas there he nobly fought, 'twas there
> He conquered Gallic foes,
> 'Twas there he risked his life, his fame,
> To ease all Europe's woes.
> To ease the woes, to ease the woes,
>   to ease all Europe's woes.
>
> His fame still spreading far and wide
> Extends to northern shores,
> From Danish fleets, from Danish walls,
> His thundering cannon roars.
> His thundering can, his thundering can,
>   his thundering cannon roars.
>
> But while terrific scenes of death
> He newly serves to brave,
> Humanity is proud to learn
> He conquers but to save.
> He conquers but, he conquers but,
>   he conquers but to save.

In high circles it had already been decided to salvage Nelson from the general censure. Mr. Addington wrote on April 20, "You will have heard from Lord St. Vincent how entirely the whole and every part of your Lordship's conduct is approved of by the King, and you must have been informed from various quarters of the impression it has made upon Parliament and the public. It remains for me only to express the sentiments of admiration and of complete satisfaction, with which I contemplate what has passed, under your Lordship's auspices, in the Baltic and at Copenhagen." There was some duplicity in this, as the Convention was only approved officially "under all considerations."

St. Vincent, who knew about battles, was more sincere in his praise. "You have greatly outstripped yourself and all who have gone before you, in the late most glorious conflict." There was a tribute from Lord Spencer, who had retreated to Bath. "You have done what I firmly believe no one but Nelson could have done, and what the whole country felt certain you would do whenever the opportunity again offered itself to you. . . . The Battle of Copenhagen will be as much coupled with the name of Nelson as that of the Nile."

Staying in Bath, though in separate lodgings, were Nelson's venerable father and Lady Nelson. His father wrote:

My Good Great and affectionate Son, He who created all things, He to whom all creatures bow, He by whom the very Hairs of our heads are numbered, Have covered your Head in the day of Battle. He has bestowed upon you great abilities and has granted you His Grace, to use them to His Glory, the Good of your fellow creatures and the salvation of your own Soul. I have sometimes a Hope of receiving you once more, surrounded not with publick Honors alone, but what must add pleasure to every other gratification, a return to Domestick joys, the most durable, and solid of all others. Be it so, O God. Yesterday I recd. your joyous news, but all things have their alloy. Lady was Heavily affected with Her personall feelings at not receiving a Line from your own Hand. In all things may you have a right understanding. Writing is not easy task.

His wife drafted a letter which, though he said he had not heard from her, Nelson may well have received.

My Dear Husband, I cannot be silent in the general joy throughout the Kingdom, I must express my thankfulness and happiness it hath pleased God to spare your life. All greet you with every testimony of gratitude and praise. This victory is said to surpass Aboukir. What my feelings are your own good heart will tell you. Let me beg, nay intreat you, to believe no wife ever felt greater affection for her husband than I do. And to the best of my knowledge I have invariably done everything you desired. If I have omitted any thing I am sorry for it.

On receiving a letter from our father written in a melancholy and distressing manner, I offered to go to him if I could in the least contribute to ease his mind. By return of post he desired to see me immediately but I was to stop a few days in town to see for a house. I will do every thing in my power to alleviate the many infirmities which bear him down. What more can I do to convince you that I am truly your affectionate wife?

What care must have gone into the composition of this letter, what tears! And how wretched Fanny must have felt to receive the congratulations of her friends in the black-bordered tones of condolence. She bore it all and went up to London to show herself at Court. Mrs. Bolton wrote to her on May 14 and addressed her as Viscountess though Nelson's new creation was not announced until the 19th.

I suppose by this time, my dear Lady Nelson, you are returned to Bath after your appearance in the Drawing Room which I hope you found as pleasant as you expected. I find by a letter from Mrs. Nelson that you saw her. She thinks of bringing Charlotte to Hilborow to spend her holidays, I believe she is heartily tired of London and my brother will not be sorry to come into the country unless Lord Nelson wishes for his company there. I thought perhaps you would have stayed in town until my brother arrived, but you and my father are better judges than I am what is proper and you are with *his* father. Keep up your spirits my dear Madam and all will come right again, for tho' he is warm, he has a truly affectionate mind.

You talk of making a visit to Wolterton [the home of the Walpoles]. If it does take place, I hope you will favour us with your company, here. Do not say you will not suffer us to take too much notice of you for fear it should injure us with Lord Nelson. I assure you I have a pride, as well as himself, in doing what is right, and that surely is to be attentive to those who have been *so to us* and I am sure my brother would *despise* us if we acted contrary. Ah Lady Nelson, you and I have lost our best friend in my dear brother Maurice. What a shock to us all. Do you see the poor blind widow when you were in town? Mr. Bolton and the girls join in best wishes to all the party in both houses. [The letter from this friendly soul was addressed to Bath.]

Poor Maurice, who was forty-eight, died on April 24. He was just about to achieve his life's ambition, had got one step toward it, when he suffered an inflammation in the brain and died nine days later. This obituary appeared in the *Gentleman's Magazine*.

> April 24. Of a brain fever, after a very few days illness, Maurice Nelson Esq, one of the secretaries to the Navy Board, a brother to Lord Nelson. He was about to be appointed a Commissioner to the Customs and Excise, till a vacancy should have happened at the Navy Board to which he would have been removed. He was the favourite and elder brother of Lord Nelson. No man ever lived more truly beloved and respected by his friends and acquaintances, and none ever carried to the grave a more sincere and tender regret.

And there, on this unhappy note, we must leave the people in England in the spring of 1801, and return to the little Admiral, freezing cold and wringing wet, climbing up the side of the *Elephant*.

"*Here I neither can or will stay*." Nelson wanted to go home. He felt sure that there would be no more fighting—"The Swedes cannot be such fools as to wait for us"—and he wanted to be in England before May 25, the day fixed for the hearing of his case against Lord St. Vincent. "My Commanders in Chief run away with all the money I fight for," he wrote Davison, "so let them I am content with the honor, there they cannot get a Scrap, but damn me if I suffer any man to swindle me out of my property whilst he is at ease in England."

He was right about the Swedes. On April 19 he saw them snug inside the harbor of Karlskrona. Three days later Sir Hyde learned that the new Emperor Alexander had ordered his ships to abstain from hostilities, and he took the fleet back to anchor in Kioge Bay.

There, on April 23, Nelson sent Davison a letter which suggests that he had heard from Fanny. "You will at proper time and before my arrival in England signify to Lady Nelson that I expect and for which I have made such a very liberal allowance to her, to be left to myself and without any enquiries from her, for sooner than live the unhappy life I did when last I came to England I would stay abroad for ever. My mind is fixed as fate therefore you will send my determination in any way you may judge proper." He sealed the letter with the impression of an intaglio of Emma's head which he had bought in Naples.

To her, he wrote, "My dearest amiable Friend, this day twelve months we sailed from Palermo on our tour to Malta. Ah! those were happy times, days of ease and nights of pleasure. How different, how forlorn. . . . I am truly anxiously looking out for my leave of absence, or that the whole fleet may be ordered home. Stay I will not, if the Admiral would make me Lord High Admiral of the Baltic."

He was busy sending out invitations to a dinner on the 26th, like the one he sent Captain Fremantle. "My dear Fremantle, If you don't come here on Sunday to celebrate the Birthday of Santa Emma, Damn me if I ever forgive you, so much from your affectionate Friend as you behave on this occasion. Nelson & Bronte." He even invited Sir Hyde, who said he would attend on his Saint with peculiar pleasure.

The day before the party he told his Saint that he would not stay in the Baltic if they made him a duke with £50,000 a year.

I wish for *happiness* to be my *reward*, and not title or money. Tomorrow is the birthday of *Santa Emma*. She is *my* Guardian Angel and sure she has more Divinity about her than any other human form now alive. It is not in my power to do much honor to it in this place, but I have invited the Admirals, and all the Captains who had the happiness of knowing you and of course experiencing your kindness when in the Mediterranean. They are invited to assist at the fete of Santa Emma, in the morning I have Divine Service, then as good a dinner and Wines as money can purchase. You may rely my Saint is more adored in this Fleet than all the Saints in the Roman Calendar, but my dear friend you are so good so virtuous, there is certainly more of the angel than the human being about you, I know you prayed for me both at the Nile and here, and if the prayers of the Good, as we are taught to believe, are of avail at the Throne of Grace, why may not yours have saved my life. I own myself a *Believer in God* and if I have any merit in not fearing death, it is because I feel that his power can shatter me when he pleases, and that I must fall whenever it is his good pleasure.

How extraordinary this is! The gross and self-indulgent Emma canonized! It goes far beyond the limits of infatuation, beyond even the boundaries of love, and into some strange Italianate temple raised in the febrile imagination of the English parson's son. This is all right from Beckford, writing to Emma late one evening with the candles almost out: "That light alone, which beams from your image, ever before my fancy like a vision of the Madonna della Gloria, keeps my eyes sufficiently open to subscribe myself with tolerable distinctness. . . ." Life was a joke for Beckford. Nelson was serious, serious about glory, serious about Emma, and now, it seems, serious about Emma with a halo and glory in the background. His friends indulged him. The Reverend Mr. Scott, Sir Hyde's chaplain, wrote in his journal, "April 26th. I have given the people a Sermon on board the *St. George*. St. Emma's day!"

Nelson followed his star. "Yesterday," he told her, "I had twenty-four at dinner and drank at dinner in a bumper of champaine 'Santa Emma.' The fourth toast after dinner came as usual, your mortal part. Without a compliment, for I scorn to say what I do not believe, it is that you are an angel upon earth. I am serious . . ." and he went on to say that Sir Hyde and Scott had sworn they had seen her in the opera house at Hamburg, where they had been—Emma transmogrified! "But you are above mortal, nothing ever did or ever can equal your excellent head, heart, person, and beauty. Bless you for ever. Curse them that treat you unkindly."

When he was not thinking about Emma he was reasonable enough. He had heard from Troubridge that Josiah's commission for the *Thalia* was not going through. "Although I know that Captain Nisbet does not care if I was dead and d——d, yet I cannot but be sorry that he is not to have the *Thalia* or some other good Ship. His failings I know very well, but as I have the testimony of Duckworth and Inglefield of his improved conduct as an Officer, I care not what Lt. Colquit may say." But his lieutenant's charges, as Duckworth had thought, were too much for Josiah, and there ended his naval career.

On the night of the 27th Nelson suffered one of his spasms of the heart; it was a severe attack and made him very ill. He asked Sir Hyde for permission to go home, which was given, and he was busy having his belongings transferred to the *Blanche* frigate for the next few days. He sent Emma six bottles of old hock, very old hock, "200 years of age, if you believe it," he said, "so says the Prince of Denmark's Aide-de-camp." There was also a sketch of the Danish line of defense. "Have a good glass and frame to put to it. I shall repay you the expense when we meet—'tis to add to the Nelson Room." So there was a Nelson Room in Piccadilly. Come and see my Nelson Room and have a glass of 200-year-old hock. Well, other men have made monuments to themselves out of their houses. The Duke of Wellington had a huge naked statue of Napoleon in his, and so did Napoleon until the Duke took it.

Everything was ready aboard the *Blanche* on May 5, when Colonel Stewart returned from England with orders recalling Sir Hyde and appointing Nelson Commander in Chief. The *Blanche* sailed with, as far as Nelson was concerned, the wrong admiral on board; and he was left to complain: to Emma, "To paint or describe my grief is impossible," and in a lovely sentence, "It must soon happen, and I will live to see you once more, and that once will last, I hope, till time as far as relates to us shall be no more"; and to Davison, "A Command never was, I believe, more unwelcomely received by any person than by myself."

After his initial disappointment Nelson began to feel angry, really angry. Not only had the Admiralty ignored his pleas of ill health, but they had made his command worthless by forbidding him to take prizes. Then again Stewart had brought the newspapers with him, and Nelson read the criticisms of the armistice and, worse for him, the accusation that the flag of truce sent ashore during the battle was no more than a trick.

He determined to make the most of his command, and the day after he got it the fleet was at sea. Half the ships were left to cruise off Bornholm to watch the Swedes—Nelson wrote politely to the Swedish admiral to tell him he was not obliged to abstain from hostilities if he met him at sea— and the other half he took to look at the Russians in Revel.

On May 8 he set about answering his accusers. It is as well to mention here that he knew about Commodore Fischer's account and he had an-swered it to the Danish Adjutant General Lindholm on April 22. Lindholm replied, "I do not conceive that Commodore Fischer had the least idea of claiming as a victory what, to every intent and purpose, was a defeat. . . . As to your Lordship's motives for sending a Flag of Truce to our Govern-ment, it can never be misconstrued, and your subsequent conduct has suffi-ciently shown that humanity is always the companion of true valour." It was hard for Nelson to find his own countrymen taking the opposite view.

He wrote to Mr. Addington, "I am sorry that the Armistice is only approved under *all* considerations. Now I own myself of opinion that every part of the *all* was to the advantage of our King and Country," and he sent his arguments justifying the armistice and the flag of truce. He repeated his arguments in a long letter to Emma, with instructions to have them pub-lished. "If after this either pretended friends or open enemies say any thing upon the subject, tell them *they be damned*." They were not published there, nor are they published here, for, by the time they reached England, no one was interested.

Emma got two more angry letters written that day, one all about how the command was going to ruin him financially—"This is the honor, this is my reward—*a prison for debt*"—and the other about how it was going to ruin him physically—"It is downright murder to keep me here."

"Damn our enemies," he concluded, "bless our friends. Amen amen

amen. I am not such a hypocrite as to bless them that hate us, or if a man strike me on the cheek to turn the other— No, *knock him down* by God."

By May 11 he had quietened down. He had written the Admiralty so strongly that they could not avoid sending someone to replace him. He was sitting staring at her picture again. "I have, my dear friend, taken it into my head that within these few days your picture has turned much paler than it used to be, it has made me quite uneasy. I hope to God you have not been unwell, or anything happened which could make you look differently on me. If it has, I care not how soon I leave this world of folly and nonsense, but why should I think so. Innocent myself, I feel I deserve and shall have a just return. Without friendship this life is but misery and it is so difficult to find a true friend that the search is almost needless; but if ever you do, it ought to be cherished as an exotic plant."

The next day the squadron was in the Gulf of Finland, "the air like a fine January day but my heart as warm towards you as the sincerest friendship can make it and as if I was upon the Equator." He was now hoping to live a few years longer. "I did not, my dear friend, come to the Baltic with a design of dying a *Natural* death, who will thank me, *those* who care not one farthing for me. Our *friend* Troubridge has *felt* so little for my health that I have wrote him word I should never mention it again to him." He was thinking of the future and had a new plan. "It is to take a small neat house from 6 to 10 miles from London and there to remain till I can fix for ever or get to *Bronte*." The idea of going to Bronte was now second and was soon shelved. He began to think of a house, a house where he could live and have the happiness, everyday happiness, that he had never known.

On the 13th the squadron sailed into the roads at Revel and found, with some disappointment, that the Russian fleet had gone off toward Kronstadt. Nelson wrote a polite note to Count Pahlen, the Prime Minister at the Court of St. Petersburg, and went ashore to pay his respects to the Governor. "It is a horrid nasty place," he told Emma, "and nothing less than the arrival of the Emperor shall get me ashore again." But his reception . . . "Except to you my own dear friend I should not mention it, 'tis so much like vanity, but hundreds come to look at Nelson, *that is him, that is him*, in short 'tis the same as in Italy and Germany." It was different in a way, because the Russians thought he looked like their hero Suwarrow, a young Suwarrow.

When the Court of St. Petersburg learned that there was a powerful British squadron anchored in the bay of Revel, they were deeply suspicious. A closed curtain, iron or otherwise, is nothing new in Russia. What was the value of Lord Nelson's pacific overtures, thought Count Pahlen, without considering that the hero resembled a young Suwarrow, when he brought his fleet into a Russian harbor? He wrote as much to Lord Nelson. And Lord Nelson sailed with his squadron a few hours after receiving the letter on May 16.

Nelson did not care, now that there was no chance of fighting, whether he stayed in Revel or anywhere else. He only cared that he was not in England and he went on damning those he called his enemies for keeping him away. "I cannot obey the Scriptures and bless them." He was very ill.

As he took the squadron toward Rostock to victual, he exchanged notes with Lord St. Helens, who was going in a frigate to St. Petersburg to negotiate a treaty with the Russian Court. This was ratified on June 17 and ended the northern confederacy.

When Nelson cried out that he had not come to the Baltic to die a natural death, he meant it. The six hours in an open boat had given him something like consumption. "A cold struck me to the heart," he wrote later. On the 27th he had what he called "a heart-stroke" and, as he told Emma when he was better, "from that time to the end of May I brought up what every one thought was my lungs, and I was emaciated more than you can conceive." He said he was cured by seeing Lieutenant Parker back from England with her letters and the St. Cecilia portrait. His doctor would have given the credit to his keeping inside his cabin and drinking warm milk every morning.

Parker was there when the squadron anchored off Rostock on May 23. With the rest, he brought the news of Maurice's death. "As the dead cannot be called back it is of no use dwelling on those who have gone," Nelson wrote Davison. "I am sure you will do everything which is right for his poor blind Wife . . . it is the only true regard I can pay to his memory, he was always good and kind to me." He told that lady, "You are and ever shall be considered by me as the honoured widow of my dear brother," and, as Maurice died in debt, he made her an allowance of £100 a year. He asked Emma to comfort her and to look after an old black servant, James Price, whom he remembered from his uncle Suckling's house in Kentish Town.

Little Parker, who was probably smaller than Nelson, as he called him little, had his treasures from Emma, "*all all* my treasures, your dear kind friendly letters, your picture as 'Santa Emma' for a Saint you are if ever there was one in this World. For what makes a Saint—the being so much better than the rest of the human race, therefore as truly as I believe in God do I believe you are a Saint; and in this age of wickedness you sett an example of real Virtue and goodness, which, if we are not too far sunk in Luxury and Infamy, ought to rouse up almost forgot Virtue, and may God's curse alight upon those who want to draw you, my dearest friend, from a quiet home into the company of men and women of bad character; and I am one of those who believe that in England the higher the class the worse the Company, I speak generally, I will not think so bad of any class but that there may be some good individuals in it."

Nelson's moral blind spot was never more evident than in this letter. Of course, we do not know what she had written to him. We can guess that she had turned down some invitation to dine out and meet the Prince of Wales and that started him off. "The higher the class the worse the company" is a good indictment of society. But none of this takes away from the assumption that his own relationship with Emma was above reproach. Surely no other lover ever praised his mistress's virtue, though he praised everything else about her from her toenail to the top of her head? If she was his wife, Nelson could not have written more devoutly of her. But then, as far as he was concerned, she *was* his wife.

On June 1 Nelson was about to take the fleet back to Kioge Bay to wait for his successor, when he heard that Queen Charlotte's brother, the Duke of Mecklenburg, had come to Rostock to see him. For an hour the Duke and his Court, about a hundred men, women and children, pottered about the *St. George* to the Admiral's annoyance. Then the fleet was away.

They arrived off Denmark on the 4th and Nelson had to fret away another fortnight before his release. He wrote every day to Emma; he was better, "It is odd but after severe illness I feel much better." The Danes, infuriated by the seizure of St. Thomas and Santa Cruz, their West Indian islands, were breaking the terms of the armistice, but they would not fight, said Nelson, not against him.

> June 11th. This day 22 years I was made a Post Captain by Sir Peter Parker, as good a man as ever lived, if you meet him again, say that I shall drink his health in a bumper this day, for I do not forget that I owe my present exalted rank to his partiality, although I feel if I had even been in an humbler sphere that Nelson would have been Nelson still. My Eyes are almost stretched out looking at that Point of Land where Ships come from England, but alas not a thing to be seen.

He wrote the same day to his old captain, Sir Edward Berry, "All those who have been at Rostock *on shore* will remember it, therefore you have had a good escape, for *you* are *mortal* man. I have not been out of the Ship . . ." which suggests, as Nelson was a mortal man like his officers, that Emma's ban on his leaving his ship was not mere caprice and saved him from an irritating, if temporary, affliction.

On the 12th a cutter arrived with letters—"I am overjoyed"—and the news that Admiral Pole was on his way to take over the command. "I wish I had a rope fast to him," Emma was told the next day, "I believe I should pull myself to pieces, but I will have a little more patience; but my nails are so long, not cut since February, that I am afraid of their breaking, but I should have thought it treason to have cut them, as long as there was a possibility of my returning for my old dear friend to do the job for me." Nothing is trivial in love!

Nelson's last official act in the Baltic was to invest Admiral Graves with the Order of the Bath, and an impressive ceremony it was on the quarter-deck of the *St. George*. Emma's green chair represented the throne, and the ribbon, star and commission were borne on her blue satin pillow. Apparently Nelson did not appreciate the irony of it. He placed her chair and her pillow above King George's.

The letters stopped on June 15. "The next," as he once said, "will be myself addressed to you." He had to wait four more days for his release, and then sailed for England in the *Kite* brig, taking young Parker with him. The fleet saw him go with regret. "I can do my duty as well as any of the very strict gentlemen," he told Davison, "and still have the affection of the whole body." There was a new toast in the Baltic: "May he, who is no longer our Commander, ever be our Example."

> June 30th. ½ past 1—running in for Yarmouth. My Dearest Friend, I hope in God to be with you long before this letter. Best regards to Sir William. I have neither seen or heard of any thing like you since we parted. What Consolation to think we tread on the same Island.

CHAPTER TEN

The Amusements of a Dirty Seaport

WHILE LORD NELSON was in the Baltic and Sir William and Lady Hamilton were living comfortably in London, one person, of whom we have heard little but who nevertheless was always there, went on a visit to the north of England. Mrs. Cadogan returned to Hawarden after an absence of sixteen years.

We have seen that Emma was not ashamed of her mother, that she had no reason to be ashamed of her, and that Mrs. Cadogan was treated with respect by Sir William and Nelson, the King and Queen of Naples, and indeed everyone except Lady Elgin and Mrs. St. George. The only trace of snobbery Emma ever revealed was when she applied for a coat of arms so that her name might be enrolled in the Order of Malta with the proper distinction. She gave the name of her father as Henry Lyons of Preston in Lancashire. (Even then, the Heralds may have misread her atrocious handwriting or, having failed to discover Henry Lyon of Nesse in Burke's *Peerage* or *Landed Gentry*—they might have found him in Anvil's *English Blacksmiths* if there had been such a book—they may have picked on the gentleman nearest in name and place of residence as a suitable progenitor for Lady H.) In any event, the arms were granted in November 1806 and were described as, "Per pale Or and Argent, three Lions rampant, Gules on a chief Sable, a Cross of eight points of the second."

Emma did not blush for her humble birthplace. She did not ignore her relations: on the contrary, she helped them all. Mrs. Cadogan, who had been Mrs. Lyon and before that Miss Kidd, had a brother and three sisters. The brother and his family were living at Hawarden in poor circumstances. The sisters had done better for themselves. One of them had married Mr. Moore, a Liverpool merchant. Another was Mrs. Connor, who had five daughters, Ann, Eliza, Sarah, Cecilia and Mary, all of whom were well educated, and a son, Charles, whom Nelson took as a midshipman. The third was Mrs. Reynolds and she had a daughter, Sarah. Some of the Connors were already in London, and perhaps the Reynolds also.

There was another very close relation of Emma's, and Mrs. Cadogan wrote about her on April 16.

My dear Emma, I have to inform you that I arrived in Chester yesterday and am happy to say that I left all friends at Hawarden very well. I mean to stop in Chester two days and then go to Liverpool and to stop there two or three days and then I mean to proceed on my journey to Manchester. I beg you will send me Mrs. Blackburn's directions and send me every particular how I am to proceed about the little girl. The next letter you send must direct for me to Tho. Moore, Moore St. Liverpool. My sister Kidd and all her Family sends their kind love to you and they are all very well. Give my kind love to Sir William and accept the same yourself from your loving and affectionate mother, M. Cadogan.

Sarah sends her love to her Mother and sisters and brother and to you which I am happy to say we are both well.

The little girl with the Blackburns was "little Emma" of the worms and plain features, who was now nineteen. What happened to her next is really unknown, though, called Emma Carew, she was later found in company with the Connors and Mrs. Denis, Lord Bristol's ex-mistress and dear friend of Emma's, a vulgar woman sometimes referred to as Fatima. Mrs. Cadogan was back in London in May.

Nelson landed at Yarmouth on June 30. He was received with flags, cheers and bells, and was not the less popular for going directly to the hospital to visit some of the wounded from the battle who were lying there. At the Wrestlers—but now we must call it Nelson's Hotel, for the name had been changed in his honor—he met again the great people of Yarmouth, and then set out in a post chaise decorated with ribbons and escorted as before by the Volunteer Cavalry. He was in London on July 1.

Nelson was in town for a week, putting up at Lothians Hotel, but spending most of his time at 23 Piccadilly. He paid his respects at the Admiralty and went to see Sir Hyde Parker. Because of the tacit censure of the part he had played at Copenhagen, Sir Hyde had asked for a court-martial to clear his name, and it had been refused. Nelson did his best to dissuade him from pursuing a matter that could never do him credit. By chance, Nelson was exchanging letters at this very time with another admiral he had pushed into the background. Sir John Orde had not recovered his self-esteem after having been sent home by Lord St. Vincent in 1798 for protesting at Nelson's appointment to command the detached squadron in the Mediterranean. He had gone as far as to challenge St. Vincent to a duel on his return to England, and the King had intervened to prevent it. Since then Orde had devoted his time and fortune to the writing and posting of pamphlets, and the formation of a considerable body of opinion hostile to St. Vincent. As there was scarcely an officer who had not a complaint of one kind or another against the Earl, Orde gained a lot of sympathy. But, needless to say, none from Nelson.

During this week Nelson may have heard from Fanny in this letter, only a draft of which exists.

> My dearest Husband, Your generosity and tenderness was never more strongly shewn than your writing to Mr. Marsh yesterday morning for the payment of your very handsome quarterly allowance, which far exceeded my expectation knowing your income, and, had you left it to me, I could not in conscience have said so much.
>
> Accept my warmest, my most affectionate and grateful thanks. I could say more but my heart is too full. Be assured every wish, every desire of mine is to please the man whose affection constitutes my happiness. God bless my dear husband.

Alexander Davison had not obeyed his friend's harsh instructions to forbid Fanny to communicate with him. However, on July 12 he felt it necessary to write something.

> I have long wished to write to you, which nothing but the want of something to say to you prevented. I have nothing to relate particular, yet it is with unspeakable pleasure I can assure you, that Lord Nelson is better in health than I had ever reason to expect. He had been extremely ill indeed, and there yet remained a very troublesome disagreeable Cough. I hope it will go off, and that we shall see him resume his former and natural good state of health.
>
> A few days quiet retreat in the Country I trust may be of use to Him. I hardly need to repeat how happy I should have been to have seen Him and You, the Happiest.
>
> His Heart is so pure and so extremely good that I flatter myself he never can be diverted from his affection. I have the same opinion I ever had of his sincere Respect for You. I have no right to doubt it.

This was unfair on Fanny, because he had every right and every reason to tell her that it was hopeless for her to expect to live with her lord again. She had to discover it herself in the hardest and cruelest way possible.

Nelson went into the country on July 8 with the Hamiltons, the Rector and his family, and young Parker. They made a three-day excursion to Box Hill, staying at the Fox & Hounds in Burford Bridge. He wrote Davison on the 9th that it was a very pretty place and they were all very happy. He mentioned his surprise that the City had not recognized the victory of Copenhagen: "I look forward with confidence to a Sword from the City of London and their thanks, and the Freedom in a gold box to Adl. Graves. . . . I remember a few years back on my noticing to a *Lord Mayor* that if the City continued its generosity that we should ruin them by their gifts, his Lordship put his hand on my shoulder and said—*aye the Lord Mayor of London said,* do you find victorys and we will find rewards."

They were back in town on the 11th, but left again almost at once for Staines. Nelson wrote from there to St. Vincent the next day, "Before I saw you yesterday and afterwards I was so unwell with the pain in my Stomach that I have been forced to get again into the Country." He certainly had less stomach for dining out than he had the previous winter.

Staines is as pleasant a place to spend a summer's day as any in England, and it was even more pleasant in 1801. The party put up at the Bush and went fishing in the *clear* waters of the Thames. Lord William Gordon celebrated the occasion with verses written in the Duke of Queensberry's window seat in Piccadilly. They hardly bear quoting; each member of the party had a verse and the best is on the Reverend William Nelson, and that must do for all.

> But, to return to this same worthy Vicar,
> Who loves, you say, good eating and good liquor,
> Know, Lady, that it is our earnest wish,
> That we, ere long, may greet him—Lord Archbish . . .

These high jinks did not pass unnoticed in the papers. The *Oracle* was scornful: "The gallant Lord Nelson, the terror of the French, the Spaniards, and the Danes, is now amusing himself with Sir William and Lady Hamilton by *catching gudgeons* at Shepperton. Sic *parvis* componere *magna* solebam." The *Herald* was spiteful: "Lord Nelson is now at Staines with Sir William and Lady Hamilton on a fishing party. Sir William who is said to be one of the first *anglers* in the kingdom, devotes much of his time to that species of sport." While the *Post* denied that Nelson had gone fishing at all: "He flew to Chippenham near Bath to wipe away the tear from the widow's a dependant sister's eye." In fact he visited Old Blindy at Laleham, two miles from Staines, to make sure she had everything she needed.

Nelson was back at Lothians on July 25 and there met his father, who had come up from Bath to see him. The old gentleman was going on to Burnham Thorpe. They could have spent only a few hours together, because Nelson was off the next day to take up his new command.

"On Wednesday evening," said the *Post* on Thursday, July 25, "Mr. Vansittart, one of the Secretaries of the Treasury, waited on the Lord Mayor from the Chancellor of the Exchequer to represent that *His Majesty's Ministers* FULLY EXPECTED *the French would attempt an* IMMEDIATE DESCENT *on this island.*"

This was the beginning of the great invasion scare of the summer of 1801, which interrupted the peace negotiations between England and France, and which gave Nelson the most unsatisfactory command of his career.

His commission was to be Commander in Chief of a fleet of small ships stationed from Beachy Head to Orford Ness. He had the double task of defending the coast and of attacking any concentration of enemy boats prepared for the invasion. He did not like it, boat warfare was not the business of a hero, and it appears that the appointment was a sop to public opinion. The *Chronicle* was pleased. "Every person must rejoice to see Lord Nelson, whose courage, enterprize, and vigilance, are so preeminent, employed in such a service."

If the threat had been real, there might have been some point in putting Nelson at the head of the country's coastal defenses. As it was a false threat, and this was soon apparent, it was a mistake, almost a disaster, to risk a life like Nelson's to gain cheap popularity for an indifferent government. The risk was implicit in the man. Given a Union River barge to fight in, and he was, he would take it over to France and fight in it.

He lost no time. On July 27 he was at Sheerness writing to Emma, "Today I dine with Adl. Graeme, who has also lost his right arm, and as the Commander of the Troops has lost his leg, I expect we shall be caricatured as the *lame* defenders of England." And two days later, in response to a letter from her: "Your letter of yesterday naturally called forth all those finer feelings of the Soul which none but those who regard each other as you and I do can conceive. Although I am not able to write so well and so forcibly mark my feelings as you can, yet I am sure I feel all the affection which is possible for man to feel towards *Woman* and such a Woman. Not one moment I have to myself and my business is endless." He was going to Faversham to organize the Sea Fencibles (a sort of naval Home Guard) and then to Deal; the next day he would be off the coast of France. "Be where I may you are always present to my thoughts, not another thing except the duty I owe my Country ever interferes with you, you absorb my whole Soul. Whether I write little or much never mind, I am yours for ever and ever."

He was much calmer, his black Baltic mood had been dispelled and he was certain of her—well, as certain as a fervent exchange of vows in a fishing boat could make him. There was a plan, something to do with a house, because he wanted to know if she had heard from Mr. Christie about one. "I am very anxious to have a home where my friends might be made welcome." So the idea of a house where they would, presumably, all live together, first mooted in the cabin of the *St. George,* was advanced to the stage where Mr. Christie had been approached. This prospect of domestic pleasures with Emma is what calmed the little Admiral, damped down the fires of jealousy, and got him off the boil.

Sir William left for a tour of his Welsh estate with Charles Greville and wrote her complaisantly from Burford on July 27, "Here we are my dear Emma after a pleasant day's journey. No extraordinary occurrence. Our chaise is good and would have held the famous 'Tria Juncta in Uno' very well, but we must submit to the circumstances of the times." He probably did not know what they had in store for him.

Nelson went to Faversham and harangued the Sea Fencibles. They were, doubtless, very worthy men, but they were very reluctant to go aboard a ship in case they found themselves pressed into full-time service. So, where there were no regular seamen to spare, the defense of the country fell to Greenwich Pensioners. Captain Hervey's frigate, defending Margate, was manned by them. He complained that twelve had wooden legs and kept falling over, eight were ruptured, thirty were senile, and one had scurvy.

The Admiral was at Deal on the 31st, grumbling that he could not sleep. It was not his command that kept him awake until he heard the clock strike one, nor, for a change, any fears for Emma. "Give 10,000 kisses to my dear Horatia," he told her. "Yesterday the subject turned on the Cow pox, a Gentleman declared that his Child was Inoculated with the Cow pox and afterwards remained in a house where a Child had the small pox the natural way and did *not* catch it; therefore here was a full trial with the Cow pox; the Child is only feverish for 2 days and only a slight inflammation of the arm takes place instead of being all over *Scabs,* but do what you please." (According to *Lady Hamilton's Memoires*, Horatia was inoculated with the smallpox at the end of the summer and stayed in a house in Sloane Street with a nurse and Oliver until she was well. In spite of Dr. Jenner's discovery, this was the more usual method at the time.)

Nelson was also concerned about the patent of his peerage. "The patent must be a new creation, first to my Father if he outlives me, then to William and his sons, then to Mrs. Bolton and her sons, and Mrs. Matcham and hers, further than that I care not, it is far enough; but it *may* never get to any of them, for the old patent may extend by issue male of my own carcass. I am not so very old and may marry again a Wife more suitable to my genious." There was a new creation and the title was changed to flatter William to Viscount Nelson of the Nile and Hilborough.

"Lord Nelson's Peerage," said the *Post*, "has, perhaps, more cross remainders than any other on the list: by what secret contrivance of nature does it happen that heroes seldom have heirs of their own body?" If they only knew!

Lord St. Vincent thought that the pier at Boulogne would be a good place for a bombardment and the newspapers agreed with him. "In a short time Lord Nelson will make an experiment," said the *Post* on July 30. "Boulogne will be bombarded." Thus giving the enemy good warning of what to expect.

On August 1 Nelson sailed in the frigate *Medusa* for the French coast to have a look at Boulogne. It was the anniversary of the Nile and he was miserable to be away from Emma. Young Parker told him to cheer up. Young Parker knew everything. He had seen Horatia, and Emma joked that he might marry her one day. There were contrary winds and the *Medusa* did not come in sight of the harbor until the 2nd, then Nelson saw batteries being erected along the coast, and about two dozen brigs and flatboats in the harbor. He sent for his bomb ships, and at dawn on the 4th the bombardment began.

Hundreds of people gathered on the cliffs to listen and occasionally to catch a glimpse of the squadron. The firing lasted until dusk and it was generally agreed that Boulogne was in ruins. Nelson himself was optimistic at first. "Boulogne," he wrote Emma, "is evidently not a pleasant place this morning. . . . I hope and believe that some hundreds of French are gone to hell." His mind was not entirely on the work in hand. "Buy the house at Turnham Green, I can pay for it. . . . Damn that Christie, how negligent he has been."

Everyone waited for Lord Nelson's public dispatch announcing the victory. There was no news on the 5th. On the 6th there was none. "It is not the practice of that renowned hero," preached the *Herald*, "to relate any part of his brilliant exploits until he has fully completed the whole of his undertaking." People were entertained on the 7th with a report of Nelson's death in action. And on the 8th they finally read that five flats and a brig had been sunk and that Boulogne had not been touched! Nelson was reported as saying, "Oh this is but a shabby affair, but it is necessary to convince the enemy they shall not threaten invasion with impunity, and to do something to quieten the minds of the women and children in London." What he actually said in his dispatch was, "The whole of this affair is of no farther consequence than to shew the enemy that they cannot, with impunity, come outside their ports."

It was a sad anticlimax. Too much had been expected, too little had been achieved. Bonaparte's mouthpiece, the *Moniteur*, crowed, "Of 800 bombs which Nelson threw, 200 fell on the sands and were carried to the arsenal. The rest were thrown fruitlessly without wounding a single man." "If there be anything to be regretted in this affair," concluded the *Chronicle*, "it seems to be that so great a Commander as Lord Nelson should have been employed in a business of no great importance as now appears."

But where had Nelson been? Well, on August 5 he had sailed with the idea of looking into Flushing. He seemed more worried about the house than anything else, and complained to Emma, "It is, my dear friend, extraordinary but true that the man who is pushed forward to defend his Country has not from that Country a place to lay his head in, but never mind. . . ." Then he had changed his mind and sailed for Margate, anchoring in the roads on the evening of the 6th. The next day he sent his dispatch to the Admiralty, and wrote his dearest friend, "I could not drink Champagne, a sure sign that all is not right, but indeed I am not to call ill, but sometimes the exertion of my mind is beyond the strength of my body."

In spite of reassuring noises from St. Vincent and Troubridge, he was upset at the futility of the Boulogne bombardment and the reaction in the press. "I am vexed such a racket should be made of these trifling things." He did not want to be seen. "I have given directions to Captain Gore (or rather requested) not to let anybody come into the Ship but who had business with me, for the *Medusa* would be full from morning to night. Fifty boats I am told are rowing about her this moment to have a look at the one-armed man."

On the 8th Nelson sailed for Harwich, perhaps with the aim of distracting the enemy's attention away from Boulogne, for he intended to attack that harbor again. Two letters followed him; one from Troubridge to warn him, "All your Lordship's plan has got into the newspapers, there is some Active Agent writing from your Division all that passes"; the other from St. Vincent, "The public mind is so very much tranquillized by your being at your post, it is extremely desirable that you should continue there." Incidentally, Troubridge added a postscript referring to an old acquaintance: "Mrs. Lock report says has taken a *Russian General for her Guardian.*" And another gentleman who dined out on his scandalous stories of Nelson and the Hamiltons was himself served up with the entrée: William Wyndham, home from Florence, failed to get a divorce even though his wife had gone off with the Earl of Wycombe, because of his own affair with a certain Madame Mara. Providence can be very obliging.

Nelson was piqued, though he protested to Emma on the 9th, "I wish my dear Emma that my name was never mentioned by the newspapers, it may create poor Nelson enemies, not that I care, only that I hate to be praised except by you. My conduct at this time of service is not to be altered, by either praise puffs or censure. I do my best and admit that I have only zeal to bear me through it." He was piqued. "You know my quick temper," he told her the next day when she had scolded him for some trifle. "You know my quick temper, and cannot bear false accusations." He was on his way back to the Downs. Much the same thing had happened at Tenerife in 1797 when, after the failure of his first attack on Santa Cruz, he had led a second forlorn attempt which cost him his right arm and his squadron nearly 100 dead. There was little enough justification for a second attack on the same place then, and there was less now.

"The story of invasion," said the *Chronicle* on the 10th, "is nothing but a Ministerial *Humbug.*" Nelson said the same to St. Vincent. "Where, my dear Lord, is our invasion to come from. The *time* is gone . . ." And Troubridge himself wrote privately to say that the peace negotiations had recommenced and that their troubles would soon be over. Yet the second attack on Boulogne was made.

On August 11 Nelson was at Sheerness fending off the Mayor and Corporation of Sandwich who had brought him another freedom. Now he considered all visits as an imposition on his freedom and complained bitterly, "Oh how I hate to be stared at." On the 12th he was off Margate and asking Emma to lay out £50 on a silver teakettle for Captain Gore. "That beast Allen" had left his papers behind, but there they were, "Huzza Huzza." The next day he was in the Downs.

"You may rely it is not my fault I cannot get to London to see you and Mrs. Nelson, but I believe it is all the plan of Troubridge." He was going over to the French coast, "but I assure you, my dear friend, that I am going into no danger." There was no need for the personal exertion of a vice-admiral.

The attack made on the night of August 15 by some seventy small boats on the flats and brigs in Boulogne harbor was a desperate attempt to pull some little victory out of the fire of war before it went out. The difficulties were enormous, *and Nelson recognized them.* In the draft plan of attack he wrote, "Although the risk may be great, from the circumstances of wind, setting of tides, uncertainty of finding the ships in a dark night from their great distance, not much less than twelve miles, and many other incidental circumstances, yet the object is great, and will justify the attempt." Yet what was the object? To carry off a dozen or two dozen flat-boats from under the nose of the enemy. To show Old Boney a thing or two. To work off a bit of Lord Nelson's pique. Or is that unfair? He usually knew when an attack would succeed.

He said in his plan of attack, "The enemy may naturally be supposed to be alarmed." Yet Troubridge had warned him that another attack on Boulogne was openly canvassed in the newspapers, and he could read it for himself. It is strange and defies explanation, unless he was ordered to make an attack, or unless he was determined to reassert his reputation, which he felt was diminished after the fiasco of the bombardment. There were no orders, though plenty of encouragement from St. Vincent, so we are left with the unhappy alternative.

His letter to Lady Hamilton on the 15th began about the house. Was the house in Chiswick furnished? "I am very anxious for a house and I have nobody to do any business for me but you, my dear friend." He wanted to know when she and Sir William would come to see him, and whether at Margate or Deal. He was unwell with a fever in his head, which was swollen, and toothache. He was obviously uncertain about the outcome of the night's business.

As you may believe, my dear Emma, my mind feels at what is going forward this night; it is one thing to order and arrange an attack, and another to execute it; but I assure you I have taken much more precaution for others, than if I was to go myself— then my mind would be perfectly at ease, for after they have fired their guns, if one half the French do not jump overboard and swim on shore, I will venture to be hanged, and our folks have only to go on, never think of retreating. This will not go away till to-morrow. Many poor fellows may exclaim, *Would it were bed-time, and all were well;* but if our people behave as I expect, our loss cannot be much. My fingers itch to be at them.

The attack was made at midnight with four divisions of boats. The first ran alongside a brig which they captured but could not tow away because it was chained to the shore: they came under heavy fire of musketry and grapeshot and were forced to retreat. The second, under Captain Parker, reached the enemy commodore's brig, but were unable to board her because of a heavy netting stretched above the bulwarks: the French were waiting for them too, there were 200 soldiers aboard the brig, and two-thirds of Parker's men were killed or wounded, he being shot in the thigh. The third division met such heavy fire that they never reached the enemy ships. The fourth was swept out of the attack altogether by the tide. Inevitably, the casualties were heavy; 44 officers and men were killed and 128 were wounded.

In his dispatch to the Admiralty Nelson gave as the reasons for the failure the very circumstances he had mentioned in the plan of attack—the darkness and the uncertainty of the tide. He made the most of the vessel chained to the shore, and it became "the vessels being, as I am informed, chained to the shore, but certainly hauled on shore. . . ." Very likely, as the men returned to the *Medusa* and the other warships, all he heard was of the damned French and their damned chains. He could not say too much of the courage and perseverance of his men.

He told Emma the news on the 16th, but he could not write much. "This letter will be opened to a certainty to hear news from Boulogne."

The dispatch arrived at the Admiralty on the 17th. "It is not given to us to command success," wrote St. Vincent, using the same words he had written to Nelson on his return from Tenerife, "your Lordship and the gallant officers and men under your orders certainly deserved it. . . ." "We must lose Men in all sorts of Warfare and in the one you are employed on in particular," wrote Troubridge, who was a little indifferent in the matter of life and death.

The news was published the next day and the papers, except for the *Times,* which was the Minister's puppet, were critical. The *Herald* was quick to spot that only one boat had been chained to the shore. On the 21st the French account of the attack was printed, claiming 500 English casualties and admitting ten Frenchmen killed and thirty wounded: "We did not trifle away our time in making prisoners, nor in saving the shipwrecked, we minded nothing *but to destroy;* accordingly there are only two English in the Hospital of Boulogne, and it is not thought that even they will survive their wounds." Was Lord Nelson, the French asked, now to be created "Baron of Boulogne and Chevalier of the Channel"? Bitter reading for the hero, who learned that the French commander opposed to him was La-touche Tréville, who had taken his ships into Naples in 1793.

"The enemy expected the attack," said the *Post*, "and was well pre-pared for defence both by troops and batteries." But the *Post* backed the government and went no further than that. The *Chronicle* did not back the government. "Our readers will lament to hear that the second attack on the enemy's flotilla has produced only a melancholy carnage." That was on the 18th, and the next day they said, "There seems to have been a fatal want of information, as well as of respect for the skill of the enemy, which however the daily sycophants of office may gloss over, will be a serious and grave subject of regret to every British bosom."

However, these were days when patriotism was neither an eccentricity nor a sign of insanity, and the *Chronicle* could applaud it. "His Lordship," went the story on the 19th, "has visited the wounded in the Royal Naval Hospital at this place [Deal]; he was observed to pay particular attention to every individual, inquiring their cases and consoling them with a promise that he would send them good news shortly. Of a seaman which he recol-lected, his Lordship asked him how he was; the gallant tar replied, He had lost his arm; to which the Admiral said, 'Never mind that, I have lost an arm, and perhaps shall shortly lose a leg—they cannot be lost in a better cause than fighting for our Country.' This had such an effect on the sailors, that several of them exclaimed, They only regretted their wounds, as it prevented them from accompanying him in another attack on their ene-mies the French."

Perhaps this account has been hard on Nelson. To redress the balance, here is Collingwood's opinion of him, given in a letter dated August 24, which is unfortunately damaged at the bottom.

> Lord Nelson is an incomparable man—a blessing to any Country that is engaged in such a war—his successes in most of his undertakings are the best proofs of his genius and his talents—without much previous preparation or plan, he has the faculty of discovering advantages as they arise—and the good judgement to turn them to his use—and it comes to him with an impetuosity that allows him no time to recover . . . he is kind hearted . . . said his attachment in Italy altered him. . . . I could not discover any great change in him. . . .

Nelson was at Deal on August 17. He was furious at the Admiralty, and blamed Troubridge for it, for not allowing him a day's leave to go to

London. He was ashore, he *had* to go ashore, he assured Emma, for the cabin of the *Medusa* to be washed and purified. Parker and young Lieutenant Langford had been lying there and their wounds stank. He had got them lodgings in Deal and visited night and morning. "I would lose a dozen limbs to serve him," poor Parker wrote to Lady Hamilton. She had called him *a Nelsonite* and it was better than being called a Duke.

If the failure of the bombardment piqued Nelson, the failure of the attack pierced him like a sword. "I own I shall never bring myself again to allow any attack to go forward, where I am not personally concerned," he wrote St. Vincent. "My mind suffers much more than if I had a leg shot off in this late business." In this mood he addressed the squadron publicly, praising their efforts and promising, "The Vice Admiral begs to assure them that the enemy will not have long reason to boast of their security; for he trusts, ere long, to assist them in person, in a way which will completely annihilate the whole of them."

"I long to pay them for their tricks t'other day the debt of a drubbing which surely I'll pay," he wrote Emma on the 18th, in a long letter about a house, and a teakettle, and Troubridge, and the funeral of two young mids, "but *where when and how*, it is impossible your own good sence must tell you for me or mortal man to say. I shall act not in a rash or hasty manner, that you may rely and on which I give you my word of honor."

He was back on board the *Medusa* and reconsidering his promise to tackle the enemy in person, but he would not have anyone tell him to do so. "How often have I heard *you* say that you would not quit the deck if you came near a Frenchman," *you* was Emma. "Would you have your attached friend do less than you purpose for yourself, that I am sure you would not. In these bombardments there is no risk for my rank, therefore I pray be quiet." He was looking forward to seeing them in Deal. "The Three Kings I am told is the best house (it stands on the beach) if the noise of the constant surf does not disturb you. . . . Your interest with Sir William is requested to come and see a poor forlorn sailor."

That day, the 19th, he wrote to Mrs. Nelson, who was getting fed up with being kept in town waiting on Lady Hamilton and wanted to go home. "My dear Mrs. Nelson, I beg intreat and pray that you will not leave our dear Excellent Lady Hamilton. She is miserable at the thought of it, so am I, therefore by everything which is dear to me I entreat you will not leave her. Send for my Brother to come up, you can have good lodgings and no Bugs and they shall be no expence to you, only my dear Mrs. Nelson do not leave our dear dear friend. Come down to Deal with her and Sir William, I shall rejoice to see you, do me this favor. . . ." Do not leave our dear virtuous Lady Hamilton, he might have said, in case she opens the door to all the whores and pimps in London.

At last she had got him a house. He had not the slightest idea of what it was like but, "I approve of the house at Merton," he wrote with delight on August 20, "and as the Admiralty are so cruel (no I never asked the Board of Admiralty) as Troubridge and the Earl are so cruel as to object to my coming to London to manage my own matters, I must beg and entreat of you to work hard for me." Booth & Haslewood would manage the law business. He had £3,000 ready to put down. "How often have I, laughing, said I would give you £500 to furnish a house for me—you promised me and now I claim it, and I trust to your own dear good heart for the fulfilment of it." And he told her gleefully how he had escaped from some people who had actually managed to get aboard to see him.

The weather was bad and Nelson was seasick—late August and the equinoctial gales were brewing up in the Channel—and he would not leave his ship. Nelson was almost certainly the only admiral with a coastal command who did not put up on shore in a comfortable house, and all because of his promise never to be in company with a woman other than Emma.

He had heard that the Duke of Queensberry had offered to lend Sir William, back from his Welsh trip, his villa at Richmond. "I entreat you my dear friend to work hard for me and get the house and furniture and I will be happy to lend it to you and Sir William, therefore if you was to take the Duke's house, *a Cake house* open to everybody he pleases, you had better have a booth at once, you never could rest one moment quiet. Why did not the Duke assist Sir Willm. when he wanted his assistance—why not have saved you from the distress which Sir William must every day feel in knowing that his Excellent Wife had sold her Jewels to get a house for him, whilst his own relations, great as they are in the foolish World's Eye would have left a man of his respectability and age to have lodged in the streets. Did the Duke or any of them give him a house *then*. Forgive me, you know if anything sticks in my throat it must out." He went on about the people who had come to see him the day before. "I was stout and will not be shewn about like a *Beast*."

He booked three rooms at the Three Kings, and two sitting rooms facing the sea and joined by a gallery. He was hoping to see them on the 28th or 29th. "I know not why but today I am ready to burst into tears." He was still seasick, "and I am damned sick of the sea."

Then, on the 23rd, with all the arrangements for the visit made, word came from his masters at the Admiralty that he must go and look at Flushing. "The First Consul has declared himself Generalissimo of the Army of Invasion," wrote St. Vincent, "and that we are to look to Flanders for the grand effort." So, at Bonaparte's behest, poor Nelson had to sail, fearing that his friends would arrive in his absence, find Deal unbearable, and cut short their visit. He recommended Emma to meet Admiral and Mrs. Lutwidge. Very many years before, as a boy of fourteen, Nelson had gone on an expedition to the Arctic in a ketch commanded by Captain Skeffington Lutwidge, and now the old admiral commanded the Downs station. "I know very little of her," Emma was told, "she is a very good woman, but her figure is extraordinary. Oh that I could stay. How I hate going to sea."

When Nelson is on the scene it is always difficult to find room for anyone else. Fortunately, the two other members of the *tria juncta in uno* were reasonably quiescent in this hot month of August.

Sir William went off on his leisurely trip to Milford, doubtless enjoying the intelligent company of his nephew, and certainly being persuaded that the management of his estate could not be in better hands. He was pushed for money. The proceeds of the sale of his pictures and vases had gone to pay part of his debt to his bankers. The upkeep of 23 Piccadilly took all his pension and more. He would have liked more money from his estate, he would have liked to exchange it for an annuity, but Charles Greville persuaded him, for once in his life, to think of the future. "Milford," Sir William wrote Nelson hopefully, "will surely be a great Town." After some three weeks' pleasant perambulation, the old Knight returned to London and was ready to accompany his lady to Deal.

She, in the meanwhile, had been quietly living in Piccadilly, with the Rector's jewel for company. There were the usual visits to and from little Miss Thomson and, of course, the outings to Turnham Green, Chiswick and Merton to look at houses for Nelson.

The Rector wrote to her regularly on the subject nearest his heart. Someone had told him the Dean of Exeter was eighty and infirm. "It would be a most desirable thing if Mr. Addington would make me Dean of Exeter . . . now we have secured the Peerage we have only *one* thing to ask, and that is my promotion in the Church, handsomely and honourably, such as becomes Lord Nelson's brother and heir apparent to the title." The Dean of Exeter was only one of several elderly churchmen he would have gladly seen go to their last rest, provided that he could slip into their surplices. He was obsessed with stalls and deaneries, and knew the ages and infirmities of the incumbents better than any Crockford. "I am told there are two or three very old lives, Prebends of Canterbury, in the Minister's gift, near

£600 a year and good houses. The Deans of Hereford, Exeter, Litchfield and Coventry, York and Winchester, are all old men. . . ."

Emma, who could match him in vulgarity, wrote him on August 24.

> My dear good Mr. Nelson, How much oblidged to you I am for your kind letter. Sir William, Mrs. Nelson and I am going down to Deal to see Milord and our Dear glorious friends Parker and Langford *allso*—if Horace comes, my Mother will take care of him and *when we return* I will bring her to Norfolk and Sir William will get *a pike*. Pray could not we come across from Deal, or could you not come to Deal to us, Lord that would be nice as the children say. I long to see you. . . . Tom tit has been in town I heard and Mrs. Nelson a few days ago saw, *met the Cub*, but he looked as if he was going to be hanged, but did not speak to her. The precious couple are fit for each other.

Fanny was in town looking for a house where she hoped she would one day receive her husband again. There was not a move of his or the Hamiltons that escaped her, for they were all reported in the newspapers. Yet she continued to hope, and it was greatly to Alexander Davison's discredit that she did. No one in communication with Fanny knew as well as he that there was no hope, and he did not tell her. She heard from "our father," who wrote firmly from Burnham Thorpe on August 21, "I can only repeat what I have often declared that whenever you have a house likely to be your residence, which is convenient for receiving me, I will be ready." He did not mind London or Bath, though he preferred Bath. He was determined to go and stay with her.

Old Edmund Nelson was saddened and bewildered by his son's behavior, but all he could give to rectify it was saintly and rather vague advice. "May your ways be ways of pleasantness and all your paths be peace," he wrote. "My bodily decay is sometimes uncomfortable and wants that support which a tranquill mind can only give and Humanly speaking I avoid offence towards God and Man. I have just received a most beautiful present of choicest fruit from Lady H. . . ." His dear Hor's adventures troubled him. "It is with the utmost concern I hear of the dangers you are dayly exposed to, patriotism has surely its Boundary," and again, "Nobody will say you are in arrears to the Country. . . . You must today, whilst it is called today, remove those obstacles that impede your personal happiness." Nelson only wished he could!

But the old man played it both ways—and who, at the age of seventy-one and wishing to spend his last years in peace, would not?—and wrote to

Emma on the eve of the trip to Deal, "Tho the amusements of a dirty sea port are not the most refined, good health and domestick cheerfulness will be a happy substitute."

Mrs. William Nelson was fed up with London. Apart from the bugs it was hot and there was nothing to do. Emma, who seemed to spend the greater part of her time in bed, neglected her when she was there, but threw a fit when she suggested going home. The trips to the country to look at houses were a relief, and Merton was a pleasure. "It is in Surry," she told the Rector, "seven miles from Town. I think your Brother will like it, and I hope we shall all spend many happy days there." She was going on the journey to Deal, "and nothing I hope will again prevent my coming home *as soon* as we get back to Town."

Nelson looked at Flushing and was back at Deal on August 28. He shifted his flag from the *Medusa* to the *Amazon* frigate, gave Captain Gore his teakettle, and went on shore to the Three Kings. "You have acted very wisely in giving up the meditated attack upon the Naval Force of the Enemy at Flushing," said Lord St. Vincent. "I hope your Bilious complaint will go off," said Sir Thomas Troubridge. "The French funds rise which looks peaceable."

The Hamiltons and Mrs. Nelson were already there. Emma and the jewel had already been out bathing. Ladies used to bathe from machines not unlike gypsy caravans and drawn by horses; gentlemen went to the opposite extreme and bathed naked. At Margate recently there had been a scandal when two gentlemen had landed inadvertently among the machines. The *Morning Herald* was shocked. "The Ladies could not use their *handkerchiefs* because the mode forbids their use, and they could not lift their gowns as being most fashionably unsupplied with any *under* garments."

Emma was in high feather. "Mrs. Nelson and I are going to bathe this morning," she told the Rector. "Tomorrow we dine at Admiral Lutwidge's, but you know we want not company when we are *tout en semble*, the Hamiltons and Nelsons have resources enough in themselves without the help of company. Well but we should be glad if you was here that would be compleat. Hang the Ministers—*shame to them*—for letting Lord Nelson's brother be a slave to a little Country parsonage house, when at least he ought to be in the palace of Lambeth for to pay Lord Nelson and his family for the great and important services he has rendered his Country. He ought to be a Duke greater than Marlbrough, you an archbishop, his father with a title, fortune, and being old his *otium cum dignitate*, your children booth in the title, and all his sisters and their children's children for ever lasting provided for, and if they did this what would it be but justice. If I was a King or Queen, I would not hesitate a moment but *do it*—they be d—— if they do not amen." Nelson added on the bottom, "As my Lady writes so much and so well it is unnecessary for me to say more than God bless you best regards to all our friends at Swaffham."

So the holiday began and, apart from the visits to Parker and Langford lying in their lodgings, went on pleasantly enough. Poor Parker, whose thigh was broken in three places, was not doing well, but they took some comfort from his brave smiles, and he and young Langford were promised rooms at Merton.

The purchase of Merton was the great business of the moment. It was now in the hands of Mr. Haslewood, who had advised Nelson that the owner, Mrs. Greaves, was asking £9,400 for the house and fifty-two acres of land, and the furniture to go at valuation. Haslewood was not at all keen on the house and had sent a surveyor, Mr. Cockerell, to look it over. Nelson, on the other hand, was falling over himself to buy it. He wrote the solicitor on August 27:

> I wish very much to have the place at Merton and agree that £9,000 with the furniture should be given for it. You will take care that the title is good. £3,000 I can pay tomorrow and if necessary great part of the other very soon, the remainder to be left on the estate and paid off as I please. So that all be paid in 2 or 3 years. The place I wish much to have and Sailor like a few pounds more or less is no object. I never knew much got by hard bargains. I trust to your doing the needful and quickly. I approve of the Gentleman's plan that went to see an estate, bought it as it stood, Dinner on the table, the former owner sat as his guest.

Now Nelson's whole fortune did not come to £10,000, he would not get much for Copenhagen except for £500 of plate voted him by Lloyd's, useful for putting in a house but not for putting down on it. Mr. Haslewood was determined to see that his client would get his money's worth. So when Mr. Cockerell's report arrived, he hurriedly forwarded it to Nelson, with a note to say that the place was not at all desirable and the price was too high. "I should write to Lady Hamilton as she requested me to do so"—he did not like Lady Hamilton—"but that I conceive it to be unnecessary while your Lordship is in England."

Mr. Cockerell's report is a model for all surveyors.

There are so many insurmountable objections as a Residence, that I am astonished anyone can think of it as nearly compleat for any family.

The House itself standing on only an acre and half of Ground is surrounded on three sides within 20 yards of it by the property of others, continually in Tillage, and is liable to be annoyed by the meanest buildings or other nuisances which may be placed close to it;—and within that straightened boundary is circumscribed by a dirty black looking canal, or rather a broad ditch, which keeps the whole place damp.

The House itself consists of an old paltry small dwelling of low stories and very slightly built, at each end of which has been added (very unsubstantially) a very gross room, and nearly the whole of the body has been rendered weak for communication to them. The Offices behind are even worse than the House and the roof and other parts are so much out of repair that before they can be furnished and comfortably inhabited at least £1,000 must be laid out, exclusive of furniture, and the present furniture of the principal apartments is so inferior that it must also be replaced with new, in which £1,000 more may be easily expended;—and when done there will be but one Bed Chamber in the House fit for a Gentleman's accommodation, and that without a Dressing Room or other convenience, and not one Room to the south of the House.

Add to all this the Land is entirely detached by the Turnpike Road and is surrounded by Public Roads possessing not the least privacy as a place for pleasure—on a dead flat and a clay soil and the whole most scantily worn and out of condition—but if all these things were otherwise, it is wanting in the most essential requisites; there is no kitchen garden or a foot of fruit wall nor any proper situation to make one and no Stabling belonging or even a Shed or out-houses for cows or other necessary live or dead stock without which the land cannot be occupied—In short it is altogether the worst place under all its circumstances that I ever saw pretending to suit a Gentleman's family.

And that was Merton, "paradise Merton." Only a hero would have bought it after that!

The day he received the report, August 31, Nelson told Davison, "I am after buying a little farm at Merton, the price £9,000 I hope to be able to get through it, if I cannot after all my labour for the Country get such a place as this, I am resolved to give it all up and retire for life." And to Haslewood the next day he wrote, "I do not understand all the difficulties stated. I would have the place bought, as good a bargain as can be made. Your friend Mr. Cockerell is not a Judge of what may suit my fortune," and he made a point of wanting all the furniture.

Nelson instructed his agents to sell his remaining shares and they raised £6,000 toward the purchase price. The remainder was made available through the generosity of Alexander Davison. "You tell me you are buying a place at Merton and that the price is £9,000," he replied. "You must have more money than I know of, if you have sufficient to pay for this Farm. But that you may have *no* difficulty about it, I request you will not use your usual delicacy with me, but draw on me for whatever you may want for this purpose, and I am sure I shall be more gratified by paying your Bill, than the pleasure you will have in the possession of the Estate. Whilst I have the means, you will command them."

Now there remained the business of persuading Mr. Haslewood to allow his client to throw his money away. "I was in hopes this day to have had your letter to say *Merton Farm* was mine," Nelson wrote him on September 4. "I cannot afford a fine house and grounds, therefore I wish for Merton *as it is* and the sooner you can accomplish the purchase as it stands the more you will oblige—N & B."

But what do sailors know of buying houses? What does anyone know of the mysterious delays, of the unimaginable difficulties that arise in lawyers' offices, except that he is obliged to pay for them? Could you go up to Mrs. Greaves and say, "Madam, here is £9,000, Merton Farm is now mine?" Well, neither could Nelson. The business dragged on and was still unsettled at the end of September.

Before returning to the holiday makers there is a small and unpleasant matter to be dealt with. Nelson received a threatening letter. A certain Mr. Hill sent him an article accusing him of incompetence, even criminal negligence, in the attack on Boulogne; unless Lord Nelson sent a £100 note to a certain post office in London, the article would be forwarded to the papers. Nelson quite naturally defied him. "I have not been brought up in the school of fear and therefore care not what you do." He sent to Mr. Nepean at the Admiralty to have the post office watched. Mr. Hill was not caught and perhaps that was a pity. He gave as his excuse that his relation had been killed in the attack and he knew of no other way of providing for the man's widow.

However, the criticism of Nelson was not confined to this one misguided man. There were no promotions of the officers involved in the attack, and Nelson took this as a personal insult from his friends at the Admiralty. Troubridge answered him on September 20. "I feel much distressed at the part of your letter, *which I construe* that this Board would *envy any success your Lordship might have,* and *feast on your failure,* if I am right I will venture to say that never was a charge so unmerited on your *real Friends,* and I cannot persuade myself but some person has been poisoning your mind against us."

But it was not one person whispering in Nelson's ear that the Lords of the Admiralty were secretly saying he had failed at Boulogne. It was the whole fleet saying it out loud. The evidence is in a letter from the Admiral to Nepean, when, late in September, an expedition was proposed against Flushing and there was a question of who was to command it.

A diabolical spirit is still at work. Every means, even to posting up papers in the streets of Deal, has been used to sett the Seamen against being sent by Lord Nelson to be butchered, and that at Margate it was the same thing; whenever any boats went on shore, "*What,* are you going to be slaughtered again." Even this might be got over, but the subject has been fully discussed in the Wardrooms, midshipmen's berths &c. &c. and it must give me more pain to mention a subject which the Admiralty have decided against, that no promotion should take place for the gallant but unsuccessful attempt at Boulogne; this matter I now find has been discussed in such a manner that its influence has spread through the whole fleet under my orders. It seems to be a matter of some doubt whether, if I was to order a boat expedition, it would be obeyed, certainly not in such a zealous manner as to give me either pleasure or confidence.

If I might be allowed to recommend, *Lord Nelson* should not command the present enterprize; first Adl. Dickson must feel mortified and I suppose would strike his flag; if the thing succeeded the hatred against me would be greater than it is at present, if it failed I should be execrated. My wish, dear Sir, has not been to put myself forward, nor if I know myself to send any Man where I should not wish to be first, and as I must probably be, from all the circumstances I have stated, not much liked by either officers or men, I really think it would be better to take me from this Command.

It is worth knowing that Nelson experienced the hurts of failure and criticism, as well as the balms of success and praise. He was human after all.

Deal, as the Reverend Edmund Nelson had foreseen, was not a place where anything happened. "What can one have to say every day?" Mrs.

Nelson asked her husband. The ladies went swimming before breakfast and then joined Sir William and the Admiral in their sitting room facing the sea. There was usually the company of an officer or two at dinner, and always a knot of curious people near the hotel to gaze at them, and, if the people were great enough, in the hotel to be introduced to them. Each day they visited the invalids and shook their heads over little Parker, whose wounds showed no signs of improvement. "Little true spirit of Nelson," Emma called him.

She was blooming. She could find things to say to the Rector, though he owed her a letter. She wrote him on September 4:

> You will say psha, what a scrap of paper this is, yet 'tis the best I could get and I would not put off writing all tho you Reverend Sir have not addressed a line to me these 5 days now. Can you think Mr. Nelson that I will give all and not receive —no, give and take for my money. Fye uppon you counting the bricks of my aunt mary's house instead of writing to us all about every one thing that has happened. [Nelson's Aunt Mary was dying.] You go jaunting to Swaffam—well their is a marriage going on—tell us how the bride blushes, how the gallant bridegroom with love on his steps and ardour in his eyes speaks the yeilding vow one then t'other—Misses that envy her, the old Ladies that look knowing, the father and mother sighing to lose their darling, who is going to launch in to this world of wickedness, and the poor soul her self wishing, sighing, groaning and dreading —Lord bless the poor Soul!
>
> Well Mr. Nelson, I expect a long long account and how goes on the other 2 old souls your aunts—but aunt Mary for my money. I wish I was with you at the press, and like to be in a press, and put the Bride in one, throw the stocking, drink the posset, put them to bed—up and be doing God will prosper! What an epistle for a parson—I dare say you will be scandalised. I don't care I am a rattle and today am in a foolish mood. Your jewill will come home so fresh and fine from Sea Bathing and Country air that a little Emma soon will call papa. I fancy it will be your fault if it is not. Good by Mr. Nelson, I am angry not having a letter so will not say dear Mr. Nelson.

This was good farmyard stuff and had the Rector skipping coyly in his rectory. He answered that he had been waiting to hear from her,

> and now this morning comes your roguish, waggish Letter on a Sunday morning (amidst all my meditations for the good of my

parishioners) about Love, Courtship, marriage, Throwing the stocking, going to bed &c. &c. &c.—quite shocking to write to a Country Parson who can have no Idea of such *things*, it might do well enough for a King's Chaplain or a Church Dignitary, who is supposed to have more *learning* and more knowledge of *things in general*; I wish you was here, and you should not laugh at me for nothing, I would give you as good as you brought any time;—I'll have no Emmas at present, stay 'till there comes one or two of another sort to keep the line of the Nelsons, in the true name and blood, without being obliged to go to others to assume a Name which scarcely belongs to them, and then as many Emmas, Elfridas, Everildas, and Evelines as you please. But I hope to God, the present young Horatio, will go on as we all wish, and transmit a long race to Posterity.

Emma caught the intended slight on the Boltons and Matchams, whose children would have to assume the name of Nelson if ever they inherited the title. She was quite ready to abuse the Boltons because Lady Nelson was going to visit them. "Is tom tit going their," she asked brother William, "is not a nest for her, or has their been a kick up? Cub will be their, but the Boultons are as close Tounged about *her* as they are *close fisted*—well never mind. Oh Lord how I should like to bring *my Hero* down to Hilborough, stay a month with you, have the Children down, eat drink walk talk—about my aunt Mary God rest her soul."

Cub had been to Deal to see Nelson. Jewel wrote on September 9, "Capt. Nesbit has been to call upon your Brother. I was at Church, so I did not see him. Your Brother *did not* ask him, and I am glad I was out, for I never wish to see him again."

What Josiah wanted does not appear, but he probably told Nelson that his mother was annoyed and had quarreled with him. It might have been about his career, or about the separation. Troubridge's name was mentioned, because Nelson wrote to him and Troubridge answered, "I think your Lordship must have been mistaken about Nisbet, I have never seen him since your Lordship sailed for the Baltic, and then only for a short time. I was written to—enquiring if Capt. Nisbet could find you at Deal, I answered yes by note." Whatever it was, we can be sure Josiah did not get it.

There was a good deal of what can only be called bitching about Tom Tit and Cub between Emma and her friends. The Rector informed her, "I find Lady N. has taken a house in Somerset Street Portman Square, she and my Father are to spend the Winter in London—and I am informed he is to pay half—whether it is ready furnished or not I can't tell." Emma was not to rest until she had driven the lady she called Tom Tit, one way or another, out of every Nelson home.

The holiday was planned to end on the 16th. Emma wanted Mrs. Nelson to return to town with her. "My jewill must stay a week with me for I shall dye if she quits me emediately," she told the Rector, "oh she is the dearest soul living and I never loved any female, the Queen of Naples excepted, better than her." She invited them all to Merton for Christmas. One room in the new house was to be theirs. However, Sir William was persuaded to stay a few more days. Troubridge had written that they might as well stay another month, "they will not find a Christian in London." More likely Nelson wanted them to be there when Parker's father arrived. The doctors were going to amputate the young man's leg, and that meant kill or cure.

The operation was performed on the 18th. Nelson was terribly distressed and wept when he spoke of it with Mr. Parker. Emma bore up well and spared a line in her letter to Hilborough telling of the events to her favorite subject. "The Cub I hear from Mrs. Denis is in town, were ever he is I am sure he can be doing no good, like tom tit boath false and deceitfull. You cannot conceive how unhappy I feil in leaving our dear friend, but I hope soon he will be out of this *paultry work*, all his real friends *wishes it*. . . . Such fine weather and such a glorious harvest, what the devil do they mean by raising the bread."

On Sunday, September 20, the Hamiltons returned to town and Nelson was left to what Captain Gore of the *Medusa* considered, "a Dull, Monotonous, Uninteresting State of Tame Defence than which nothing can be more uncongenial to your Soul." The Admiral went back on board the *Amazon*. Mrs. Thomson's lover took up the pen.

> I came on board, but no Emma. No, no, my heart will break. I am in silent distraction. The four pictures of Lady Hn. are hung up, but alas, I have lost the original. But we part only to meet very soon again, it must be, it shall be. My dearest wife, how can I bear our separation. Good God what a change. I am so low that I cannot hold up my head. When I reflect on the many happy scenes we have passed together, the being separated is terrible, but better times *will* come, *shall* come, if it pleases God. And to make one worse, the fate of poor Parker. But God's will be done. Love my Horatia, and prepare for me the farm. If the furniture will not

suit we must get other, there are sales every day. My head is almost turned. Continue to love me as Lady Hamilton does, she knows my thoughts, and although this letter is incoherent, you will explain it all. May the heavens bless you. Amen amen amen.

They were fiercely in love. They were like young lovers who could only meet fleetingly and in secret. Indeed, they *could* only meet fleetingly and in secret. They had no time to come to know each other as a husband and wife know each other, to become familiar with each other's ugliness. To Nelson, Emma was always beautiful—he probably never saw her wake up in the morning. To Emma, Nelson was always heroic—she probably never saw him shaving. This love affair remained a love affair because of the constant presence of Sir William. Their moments together were always stolen moments. Their smiles were illicit smiles. Their touches were secret and conspiratorial. They could never become bored with each other or surfeited with their emotions. They were always kept wanting, Nelson particularly, because he lived like a monk when she was away. In that way, they were fiercely in love, and they had Sir William to thank for it. He . . . he went fishing.

"Expences at the Inn at Deal paid by Lord Nelson," noted brother William, unhappy that his inheritance was being squandered, "for three weeks—£265 Exclusive of Wine." He copied a joke from the newspapers, but he was not amused. "The Duke of Bronte says that the French will not come to the English Coast if they are wise. They will never be able to support the *charges* of the Inn-keepers."

"Nelson cannot be like others," Nelson wrote Davison, "everybody knows that Lord Nelson is *amazingly rich*." He had spent £1,000 in six weeks. He had to borrow it, of course, for there was no money coming in apart from his pay (£2 10s. 0d. a day) and his pension. We do not think of Nelson being in debt, but he was, and Emma put him there.

The war, the greatness and the glory, was fizzling out. "I fear that the Scoundrel Buonaparte wants to humble us as he has done the rest of Europe," said the hero, "to degrade us in our own eyes, by making us give up all our Conquests as proof of our sincerity for making a peace . . . he be damned and there I leave him." Little Parker was dying.

All Nelson's thoughts, when he could tear them away from the agony of the sickroom, were concentrated on Merton. Emma was to go to Mr. Dod's warehouse where his furniture and civilian clothes were stored and sort out his things from Fanny's and send them to Merton. He hoped that the purchase would be completed before October 10, the date arranged between Haslewood and Mrs. Greaves; he hoped the Admiralty would relieve him of his command.

"My dear Emma," he wrote on September 23, "I received your kind letters last evening and in many parts they pleased and made me sad, so life is chequered and if the good preponderates then we are called happy. I trust the farm will make you more so than a dull London life. Make what use you please of it. It is as much yours as if you bought it, therefore if your Relation cannot stay in your house in Town, surely Sir William can have no objection to your taking her to the farm." He is talking about one of the Connors, a Reynolds, or perhaps even Emma Carew. "The pride of the Hamiltons surely cannot be hurt by sitting down with any of your Relations. You have surely as much right for your Relations to come into the house as his could have. It has vexed as I know it must give you great pain, make use of me for your happiness. . . . I am sure you will not let any of the Royal blood into your house. They have the impudence of the Devil. His mother was a bastard of my relation's Sir Edward Walpole. . . ." What an extraordinary libel on dear Queen Charlotte! She was the daughter of the Duke of Mecklenburg and her brother had visited the *St. George* at Rostock. "But let us turn our thoughts to the dear farm. . . ."

On the 24th Parker rallied and Nelson, who was himself suffering the torments of seasickness aboard the *Amazon*, asked Captain Sutton to sail. The ship was off Folkestone the next day when a boat brought a message from Dr. Baird, the physician at Deal, to say that Parker was worse and that a day or two might see the end of his suffering. They turned back to the Downs. "God's will be done," Nelson wrote the doctor, "I beg that his hair may be cut off and given to me, it shall remain and be buried with me. What must the poor father feel when he is gone." But Nelson felt as if he were the father. "He is my child," he wrote, "for I found him in distress."

Thoughts of Merton were a refuge from sickness and death. It would be the prettiest place in the world and he would buy the Duck Close and the field adjoining it if he could afford it. They would employ the local tradesmen. Little Horatia would be there in the spring. "Have we a nice Church at Merton, we will set an example of goodness to the under Parish." The dream was interrupted. "I had yesterday a letter from my Father, he seems to think that he may do something which I shall not like (I suppose he means going to Somerset St.) and shall I to an old man enter upon the detestable subject it may shorten his days, but I think I shall tell him that I cannot go to Somerset Street to see him, but I shall not write 'till I hear your opinion. If I once begin you know it will *all out*, about her and her ill treatment to her son, but you shall decide."

His father had written, "Surely no act of mine will ever seem to cast an obstacle in the way of your happiness, nor anything but death separate our affections."

On September 27 at nine in the morning Parker died. "I believe we ought to thank God," said Nelson. "He suffered much and can suffer no more." To St. Vincent he wrote, "I fear his loss has made a wound in my heart which time will scarcely heal. But God is good and we must all die."

The young captain was buried the next day with full honors. Flags flew at half mast and minute guns were fired from the *Amazon* and shore batteries as Lord Nelson followed the coffin to the grave. The poetess Harriet Walker wrote in the *Times,*

> *One proud distinction marks thy glorious grave,*
> *That he from whom thy heart its ardor drew,*
> *To thee Affection's latest tribute gave,*
> *And bad his gallant Friend a fond adieu.*

Nelson returned to the *Amazon.* "Thank God the dreadful scene is past," he wrote Emma. "I scarcely know how I got over it. I could not suffer much more and be alive. God forbid I should ever be called upon to say or see as much again." He paid dearly for that damned raid on Boulogne. He paid in more ways than one, for he found himself landed with Parker's debts and the expenses of his lodgings and the funeral. He lent Parker's father, or rather gave him, £72, and all that, together with a silver cup for Dr. Baird, put him £300 out of pocket.

But what was money? "Lady Hamilton has agreed with Mrs. Grieves for all the furniture &c. as it stands for one thousand pounds. I *approve* therefore my agents do pay it. Hay rick included." There was a Turnip Close which Emma was after too, if he could afford it, so Nelson told Mr. Haslewood.

It had been agreed by Nelson and Emma that Merton and everything in it should belong to him (which meant them) and that nothing in it should belong to Sir William. There was some idea of making Sir William feel like a guest, and perhaps behave like one and leave them alone together; and some sense, because when Sir William died, his heirs would claim his belongings and leave them without a saltcellar or whatever. So while Nelson was busy sending down his crockery and cutlery, Emma was out buying sheets. Sir William was away on a visit to Warwick Castle at this time, and did not yet know that at Merton he would have to manage without his books or his French cook.

Nelson decided to leave Deal, where the last month had been so checkered with happiness and sadness, and the *Amazon* sailed for Dungeness on October 1. Emma's letters followed him, and he answered her the next day. "I am sorry the lawyers should have been the cause of keeping you one moment from Merton, and I hope you will forever love Merton—since nothing shall be wanting on my part. . . . You are right, my dear Emma, to pay your debts—to be in debt is to be in misery, and poor trades-people cannot afford to lay out of their money. I beg you will not go too much on the water, for the boat may upset, or you may catch an autumnal cold which cannot be shook off all the winter. Wrap yourself up warm when you go out of the house, and for God's sake wear more clothes when winter approaches, or you will have the rheumatism. I hope you are this moment fixed—damn the lawyers." There was a postscript. "I hope, Emma, you take care of your relative; when you can get her well married and settled we will try and give her something. Chs. is a good boy." Chs. was Charles Connor, and the relative was very likely Emma Carew.

That day, quite unexpectedly, the nation found itself at peace. The negotiations had been proceeding without attracting the slightest notice. The preliminaries were signed by the Foreign Secretary Lord Hawkesbury and the French Envoy M. Otto. When the terms were known, the reason for the hush and whispers in Whitehall was apparent. M. Otto had gained everything, Lord Hawkesbury had gained nothing but peace. The terms were subject to ratification and can be left for the moment; it is enough to mention here that Charles James Fox said that he liked the peace better because it failed to secure a single object of the war; and the *Morning Post* was shocked out of its usual approval of the administration: "It was unnecessary to appoint the Chief Clerks of Mr. Pitt, with large salaries, to do his business. Any porter at Whitehall, receiving the wages of a guinea a week, any link-boy who could make his mark, could have signed a treaty giving back to France all we had taken from her, and leaving her all she has gained."

"You are right," Nelson told Emma, "*no* champagne till we can crack a bottle together." The preliminaries of peace included a date for the cessation of hostilities, to give time for the order to cease fire to be carried to the various fleets and colonies, and Nelson expected to be kept in his command until that time. "If I can I should like to come on Shore good friends with the Administration or my Brother will stand no chance probably he does not much at present." Perhaps Sir William and Emma could come to Deal again? "I would hire a house and have our own things on shore, and not cost one-eighth part of the other cheating fellow's expense. I hear he has been fool enough to say as nobody goes twice to his house he takes care to make them pay enough the first time. What a fool, but he did not know if it had been 50 times as much I should have paid it with pleasure for the happiness of my Emma's company."

On the 5th, and he was writing to her every day, he reverted to an old theme, presumably stirred up by some reference in her letter to the Prince of Wales. "I am vexed but not surprised, my dear Emma, at that fellow's wanting you for his mistress, but I know your virtue too well to be the ——— of any rank stinking king's evil; the manners of the titled pimps does not surprize me in these degenerate days. I suppose he will try to get at Merton, as it lays in the road, I believe, to Brighton; but I am sure you will never let them into the premises."

"Good Admiralty," he added in a little note, "let me get on shore."

He returned to Deal and there he found Lord St. Vincent's request to stay in his command at least until the official end of hostilities in the Channel; then he could go on leave. It meant staying on board the *Amazon* for perhaps another fortnight. He had to stay on board—good heavens, she had told him off for taking a walk ashore! Did she suspect Mrs. Lutwidge of the extraordinary shape? "I shall *not* set my foot on shore again till I go for good," he promised.

Emma was in a state. Mrs. Nelson had served her week and had then flown to the Rector's bosom at Hilborough. Sir William was still at Warwick Castle, but he was punished for deserting her with poor sport and the drone of Lord Warwick's voice. "The Avon is either poached to death or spoilt," he told Greville, and as for his lordly nephew, "he does not give an echo fair play."

Worst of all, Nelson might get his leave before Merton was ready to be occupied. Mrs. Greaves was due to quit the house on the 10th, but why, Emma asked Mr. Haslewood on the 6th, could not the servants go down to start preparing the place today or tomorrow? Things had been ordered, there were cows and green house plants and painters waiting to get in. Why not then conclude? "We are all on honner, no person wishes to out reach the other, 'tis of no consequence to Mrs. Graves to give it up 3 days before the time and it is of consequence to Milord to have the house put in order." It was hopeless. What? To break the sacred rules of property? Not even for a hero!

She was upset, because Nelson's home, their home, was to be her masterpiece. On top of that, Nelson's father was associating with Tom Tit—it was too much. She poured out her heart to the jewel, and a very black heart it was at this moment. A heart loaded with hate.

His poor father is unknowing and taken in by a very wicked bad artful woman, acting *a bad part by so Glorious a son*. The sin be on their *heads*. Would your father have seen with patience if she had lived with Milord, *his own* flesh and blood set a *side* for who—for Nesbit the Docter's son, a villan who many times has called the Glorious Nelson villan, and that he would do for him! Yet this boy, the son, would if this designing woman had her way have put you all aside—and *your* father, Nelson's father, protects this woman and gives a mortal blow to his son. The old man could never bear her till now and now he conspires against *the saviour of his Country* and his darling, who has risen him to such a heighth of Honner and *for whom—a wicked false malicious* wretch who rendered his days wretched and his nights miserable; (*and the father* of Nelson says "I will stab my son to the *heart*," but indeed he says "my poor father is led, now he does not know what he *does*.") But oh how cruel, shocking it is and I am affraid the Boltons are not without their share of *guilt in this affair*, jelous of *you all. They* with the *Mashams* pushed this poor dear old Gentleman to act this bad and horable part, to support a false proud bad *woman*, artfull and with every bad quality to make wretched those she belongs to and yet command over her own cold heart and infamous soul to shew an appearance to the bad part of the world of gentleness and strugleing with oppression, but let her own wickedness be her punishment, her sins be on her head, she abandons *her Son* alltho a villan, 'tis a bad Bird befowls its own nest.

This outburst of vituperation is Emma at her worst. In her eyes, Fanny was already feathered, now she was tarred. There is a depth of hatred, below the obvious attempt to gratify the William Nelsons, that gives us an indication of the depth of her love. It is a letter written in a passion, not the contrived and theatrical sort of letter she wrote to Greville, but an outpouring of deep-felt hatred. It is full of lies and they tumble out, one on top of the other, just as love and flattery tumbled out on other occasions. If she talked like that, at times she must have been unbearable. Yet there is the feeling that, having got it off her capacious chest, she got up (probably out of bed to judge from the scrawl and slope of the lines) and spent the rest of the day in the best of humor.

She wrote again to Mrs. Nelson on Tuesday the 6th, the same day she talked about "honner" to Mr. Haslewood.

Tuesday in bed. I have got such a pain in my head, my jewill my dear friend, that I am a bed with it. Curse the Lawyers, I hate them all. I shall not get to Merton till Saturday, if then, and that false Mother Greaves, who never intended with her cant to let us —she would be a good match for tom tit—what! does she think a Nelson will cheat her, a nasty B—— I was going *to say*, I am in a passion—the Lawyers are a lot of villans or it might have been finished ten days past. Yesterday I sent Dods [Davison's man] to beg her to give it up as Milord was expected and could not sleep in town. She had the impudence to say, "Well let Milord come down with one servant and stay with us till the thing is finished, we will make it comfortable to him." What do you think, my dearest friend, of her *impudence!* What would Nelson say was I to tell him of it—"She be d——" you know the rest. A likely story, *he* would go down with one servant and stay *with her!* My patience is gone and my head not the better for it. May the heavens bless you.

There is more fun in this and it seems that Mrs. Greaves was a match for Emma. However, it was all for Nelson. The house had to be ready for him.

Hanging off the coast at Deal, Nelson was subjected to a similar bombardment. He flared up and was angry with Haslewood. Then he had a thought about the consequences of peace. "The Peace seems to make no impression of joy on our Seamen, rather the contrary, they appear to reflect that they will go from plenty to poverty. We must take care not to be beset by them at Merton, for every beggar will find out your soft heart and get into your house." He would be going ashore the next day for a visit to Walmer Castle to see the Warden of the Cinque Ports, Billy Pitt. He returned to his favorite theme. "You are to be, recollect, Lady Paramount of all the territories and waters of Merton, and we are all to be your guests, and to obey all lawful commands. What have you done about the turnip field, duck field &c. Am I to have them. I wish I could get up for four or five days. I would have roused the lawyers about."

In the second week of October the association between Fanny and Nelson's father came up again in a manner suggesting that Emma was not satisfied with just fulminating about it. It will perhaps be remembered that when Mrs. Bolton wrote to Fanny in May, she mentioned a proposed visit to Wolterton, the Norfolk home of the Walpoles. In September Fanny made the visit and then went on to see the Reverend Edmund at Burnham Thorpe for a day or two. After she left him, she wrote him a letter of which this is the draft.

My dear Sir, My visit to Burnham was one of duty rather than of pleasure, I assure you it called forth all my feelings. [She had lived there with Nelson for nearly five years.] The Impression your situation has left on my mind is so strong that I cannot delay any longer offering my opinion on the subject of your living with me—which from your conversation makes it *impracticable;* the deprivation of your seeing your Children is so cruel, even in thought, that it is impossible you can any longer indulge the desire.

I am not surprised for I know Lord Nelson, even supposing his Lordship resided in Italy the offence would be just the same and in my opinion greater. I told Mrs. M. at Bath that Lord Nelson would not like your living with me, "Oh! My Dear Lady Nelson, My Brother will thank you in his heart—for he knows no one can attend to my father as you do." I had seen the Wonderful Change pass belief. She had not. . . .

Underneath she wrote, "I thank God I have not yet been led into temptation," and then she crossed it out.

This threat, this hidden threat, came out when the old clergyman wrote to his son on October 8. He congratulated him on the return of peace, "You have fought the good fight," and so on. Then he continued, "As a publick character, I could be acquainted only with what was made public respecting you. Now, in a private station possibly you may tell me where it is likely your general place of residence may be, so that sometimes we may have mutual happiness in each other, notwithstanding the severe reproaches I feel from an anonymous letter for my conduct to you, which is such, it seems, as will totally seperate us. This is unexpected indeed. Most likely the winter may be too cold for me to continue here, and I mean to spend it between Bath and London. If Lady Nelson is in a hired house and by herself, gratitude requires that I should sometimes be with her, if it is likely to be of any comfort to *her.* Everywhere age and my many infirmities are very troublesome, and require every mark of respect." He finished with a word about the parsonage where he lived retired, and an invitation to visit him.

Now Nelson drafted a mild reply, saying that the old man would always be welcome at Merton, that nothing in his conduct would ever cause a separation, and that "as to anonymous letters, they made no impression where they did not fit, and that I should ever conduct myself towards him as his dutiful son." He sent it to Emma with a note. "Tell me, my friend, do you approve. If he remains at Burnham he will die and I am sure he will not stay in Somerset Street. Pray let him come to your care at Merton. Your kindness will keep him alive, for you have a kind soul."

Emma's kind soul was less in evidence in this affair than her heavy hand. There had to be time for these letters to go and arrive and the next we hear of it is on October 17, when Emma wrote from Merton to Mrs. Nelson.

> My dearest friend, I had letters yesterday from our dear Lord. He has sent me a letter up for me to read and put in the post which I have done this day, but I send you an extract. "My dear Father, I have received your letter and of which you must be sensable I cannot like for, as you seem by your conduct to put me in the wrong, it is no wonder that they who do not know me and my disposition should, but *Nelson soars* above them all and time will do that justice to my private character which she has to my public one. I that have given her with falsity and lies £2,000 a year and £4,000 in money and which she calls a poor pittance, and with all that to abandon her son bad as he is and going about defaming me—may God's vengeance strike me dead if I would abandon my Children—if he wants reformation who should reclaim him but the mother. I could say much more, but will not out of respect to you my dear Father, but you *know her* theirfore I finish. On the 23rd I shall be at Merton with Sir William and Lady Hamilton and them with myself shall be happy, most happy, to see you my dear beloved Father, that is your home. My dear Brother and sister, the dear Children, will soon be with us and happy shall *we all* be, but more so if you will come. Plenty of room for you and your servant. Abram's Brother will live with us, Allen's wife is the dairy maid. Ever my dear Father's dutiful son, NB." This is an extract what do you think of it. When you and Mr. Nelson *has read it pray burn it.* I would have sent you the letter but am obliged to send it today. God bless you in a hurry, Sir William is gone to fetch Charlotte.

Allowing for some peppering with Emma-isms, this is far from a mild letter in which there was no mention of the quarrel between Fanny and Josiah. It seems likely that Emma prompted Nelson into writing something like this when she found the anonymous letter had had no effect. This had no effect either. On the same day, the old gentleman was telling Fanny that he held fast to his integrity and would join her in London when she was ready. "In respect to this business, the opinion of others must rest with themselves, and not make any alteration with us."

The episode was an unpleasant one and shows both Emma and Nelson in the most unfavorable light. Fanny was to be driven away, no matter how abusive or underhand the methods. She had spent the last thirteen years looking after Nelson's father, and that was her reward.

October 8, and Nelson did not go and see Billy Pitt because the weather was bad. He fretted himself into one of his "heart attacks" instead. He was angry now with another father, poor Parker's father, who, it appeared, had begged, borrowed and stolen from every officer in the squadron. "I am so vexed that he should have belonged to our dear Parker."

The next day he was still stuck in his cabin and rampaging about the peace. "There is no person in the world rejoices more in the peace than I do, but I would burst sooner than let a damned Frenchman know it. . . . We have made peace with the French despotism and we will I hope adhere to it whilst the French continue in due bounds; but whenever they overstep that and usurp a power that would degrade Europe, then I trust we shall join Europe in crushing her ambition; then I would with pleasure go forth and risk my life for to pull down the overgrown detestable power of France."

Thoughts of peace led to thoughts of Merton. "We will eat plain, but will have good wine, good fires, and a hearty welcome for our friends, but none of the great shall enter our peaceful abode. I hate them all."

In most of his letters he referred to Emma's economy. This was a myth, of course, as Sir William knew very well. He told Greville on his return from Warwick Castle, "I see as fast as I get money in my banker's hands, the housekeeping draughts draw it off. I have a bill for wine only, since we came home, of near £400. I know not what I am to receive from the Treasury, nor when, but a few thousands at my command will always be agreeable, and prevent the dread I have of being dunned in my old age."

Sir William had not been consulted in any of the plans for Merton. It was tacitly assumed by the other two that he would not object to living there and it was equally tacitly assumed by Emma that he would keep the house in London. Nelson had to have a house and he could not consider one that did not have Emma in it. Sir William had to have a house and he could not consider being dependent on his friend for a bed, for his wife's bed. Yet no one seemed to consider where the money was to come from for two establishments. Nelson took a house too large for him, and Sir William kept one he hardly used. Debt, of which they both had a very proper horror, was implicit from the beginning. They both had to pay for Emma!

Merton was to be occupied on the 10th. The day before, there was a note for Mrs. Gibson. "My dearest Mrs. Gibson, I have sent a person to you to take your orders for Miss T's things—pray tell her what you want. I am going out of town but come back on Tuesday and shall have the pleasure of seeing you. I recommend Miss T to your care. Write to me at Merton place, near Merton surry, and tell me how you all are. Milord will be in town soon. Kiss my god daughter for your affectionate friend, E. Hamilton."

Milord wanted Horatia at Merton, but that would never do. How could Sir William go there if the child was on display? and how could Emma go there without Sir William? Perhaps that is what Nelson meant by virtue?

He was feeling virtuous. He had had a letter from Mr. Addington about his high character and Mr. A.'s public duty, which depended on Nelson's flag flying until the definitive treaty was signed. "You will then have seen the Ship safe into Port and may close with honor a career of unexampled success and glory." Of course, peace meant the end of Nelson's career. He summed it up rather neatly on a scrap of paper.

Wounds received by Lord Nelson.
His eye in Corsica.
His belly off Cape St. Vincent.
His arm at Teneriffe.
His head in Egypt.
Tolerable for one war.

There were cold gray fogs on the south coast. Then a break in the weather and Nelson went to Walmer early in the morning on the 12th, but found Billy fast asleep. He walked back to Deal, a road he had walked with Emma—"ah how different"—and climbed back aboard his ship. "I am in truth not over well, I have a complaint in my Stomach and Bowells but it will go off. If you was here I should have some Rhubarb but as you are not I shall go without." He had heard that the Rector was going to Cambridge to be made an honorary D.D. "What can Revd. Sir want to be made a Doctor for, he will be laughed at for his pains." Emma had written him about the garden. "I would have everybody like your choice for I am sure you have as fine a taste in laying out land as you have in music. I'll be damned if Mrs. Billington can sing so well as you. She may have stage trick but you have pure nature."

Mrs. Billington, of whom the Prince of Wales said "the only satisfaction he enjoyed in her society was when he shut his eyes and opened his ears," was back in London after a protracted stay in Italy. She was in the news because both the theaters, Drury Lane and Covent Garden, were bidding for her services. That season she performed at both alternately in the same part, Mandane in the opera *Artaxerxes,* for a fee of £4,000. Someone said that it was more than the Prime Minister earned; someone else said that whatever the Prime Minister earned it was too much.

The next day Mr. Pitt returned Nelson's visit, coming aboard the *Amazon.* It seems doubtful that they exchanged much more than civilities, because Nelson had pains in his stomach, head and teeth, and could only think of Merton. He refused to dine at Walmer and the meeting sounds as unsatisfactory as most meetings of great men.

Almost incidentally, Nelson picked up a fourth knighthood and star. "I have this day received a curious letter," he wrote Emma, "from the Order of Joachim in Germany, desiring to elect me Knight Grand Commander thereof. I shall send it to Mr. Addington that he may give me his opinion, and obtain, if proper, the King's approbation—this is very curious." It was even more curious that Nelson was quite happy to be enrolled in an order neither he, nor anyone else outside its members, had ever heard of. The members, who were extraordinary in the length of their names and titles and nothing else, were minor German noblemen, and the order was devoted to maintaining their rank and nothing else. It had been going for about fifty years, and with the knighthood went a dark green ribbon and a star like that of the Thistle, and that was all that was known. That was all Nelson wanted to know.

The weather got worse and the Admiral raged against the Admiralty for keeping him where they knew he did not want to be. Troubridge was the great object of his anger, and he listed everything he had done for him, all the rewards he had obtained for him at Naples—"What rewards!" Troubridge would have said. But Nelson was sick and nothing would do until he got to Merton. Emma was farming. "I rejoice at your occupation. Live pretty and keep a pig. Have you done anything about the turnip field." And his brother was making an ass of himself, now they would all call him the Doctor. "His being a Doctor is nonsense, but I must write tomorrow and congratulate him or else the fat will be in the fire."

He wrote to Sir William at Merton that day, the 14th, "I am quite rejoiced to hear that you have got possession, and I assure you every study of mine shall be to make you happy in it. I shall buy fish out of the Thames to stock the water, but I bar barble. I shall never forget the one you had cooked at Staines. Sutton, Bedford, Peard and Hardy, are all determined to come and see us, and I know that, as strangers, you would rather have well-informed Sea Officers than any Country squires, lords &c. &c. The Admiralty will not let me escape. . . ."

The cold got into his head, his toothache plagued him, but now he had a date, October 22, when the hostilities would end officially and he could get on shore. He would be there on Friday the 23rd. "What a Bitch that Miss Knight is." What had she done? This was the day he sent Emma the letter for his father. "I could not say less, I hope you will approve."

On the 16th he went ashore for an hour. Mrs. Lutwidge pressed him to dine with them. "I told her I would not dine with the Angel Gabriel if he was to ask me to be dragged through a night surf, her answer was that she hoped soon I should dine with an angel for she was sure you was one. In short she adores you, but who does not, you are so kind so good to every body, old, young, rich or poor it is the same thing."

On he went about Merton. Pigs, poultry, sheep—"Do *you* get paid for them and take care that they are kept on the premises all night, for that is the time they do good to the land"—he was going to get a farming book. "I am glad to hear that you get fish, not very good ones I fancy." Poor Sir William. And Troubridge—"I have a letter from Troubridge recommending me to wear flannel shirts. Does he care for me—*No*, but never mind." He had written to the Reverend Doctor and Emma had sent a present. "I hope you ordered something good for him, for those big wigs love eating and drinking."

Sir William's first letter from Merton was written on the 16th, an important letter, because on it depended the future harmony of the *tria juncta in uno*. Mr. Cockerell was consigned to the henhouse!

We have now inhabited your Lordship's premises some days, and I can now speak with some certainty. I have lived with our dear Emma several years. I know her merit, have a great opinion of the head and heart that God Almighty has been pleased to give her; but a seaman alone could have given a fine woman full power to chuse and fit up a residence for him without seeing it himself. You are in luck, for in my conscience I verily believe that a place so suitable to your views could not have been found, and at so cheap a rate, for if you stay away three days longer I do not think you can have any wish but you will find it compleated here, and then the bargain was fortunately struck three days before an idea of peace got abroad. Now every estate in this neighbourhood has increased in value, and you might get a thousand pounds to-morrow for your bargain. The proximity to the capital, and the perfect retirement of this place, are, for your Lordship, two points beyond estimation; but the house is so comfortable, the furniture clean and good, and I never saw so many conveniences united in so small a compass. You have nothing but to come and enjoy immediately; you have a good mile of pleasant dry walk around your own farm. It would make you laugh to see Emma and her mother fitting up pig-sties and hen-coops, and already the Canal is enlivened with ducks, and the cock is strutting with his hens about the walks. Your Lordship's plan as to stocking the Canal with fish is exactly mine. I will answer for it, that in a few months you may command a good dish of fish at a moment's warning.

So it was paradise Merton after all.

Off Deal there were gales and bowels and colds and troubles—"I wish the Admiralty had my complaint," said Nelson, "but they have no bowels, at least for me." The government wanted him to do something (it was to speak in favor of the peace in the Lords) and he would do it for his brother's sake. "I shall talk and be much with Mr. Addington if he wishes it." But his release was in sight. He could talk of going ashore on Thursday and being with her on Friday.

It was Monday the 19th and he told Emma, "I assure you my dear friend that I would rather read and hear all your little story of a White hen getting into a Tree, an anecdote of Fatima, or hear you call *Cupidy Cupidy* than any speech I shall hear in Parliament, because I know although you can adapt your language and manners to a Child, yet that you can also thunder forth such a torrent of eloquence that corruption and infamy would sink before your voice in however *exalted* a situation it might be placed."

She thundered at him for what he had said about Mr. Addington. "How could you think for a moment," he answered, "that I would be a time server to any Minister upon Earth . . . living with Mr. Addington a good deal never in your sence of the word shall I do it. What—leave my dearest friends to dine with a Minister—damn me if I do." It was the Reverend Doctor who liked going about, who wanted to come up with an address of thanks on the peace to the King. "The King will not notice him although he is a Doctor and less for being my Brother for they certainly do not like me."

He had two more days to serve. "I believe I leave this little Squadron with sincere regret and with the good wishes of every creature in it. How I should laugh to see you, my dear friend, rowing in a boat, the Beautiful Emma, rowing a one armed Admiral in a boat, it will certainly be caricatured. Well done farmer's wife, I'll bet your turkey against Mrs. Nelson's, but Sir William and I will decide. Hardy says you may be sure of him, and that he has not lost his appetite, you will make us rich with your oeconomy." People were writing to him for money, a person from Yorkshire asked for £300 to set up a school. "Are these people mad or do they take me for quite a fool. However I have wisdom enough to laugh at their folly and to be myself."

The last letter from Deal, written on Wednesday, October 21, was concerned with the preparation for his appearance in the House of Lords. "Has Mrs. Cadogan got my peer's robe for I must send for Mr. Webb and have it altered to a Visct." Lord Hood wanted him to dine with him on the 24th. "I'll be damned if I dine from Home that day." The farm would prosper. "I expect that all animals will increase where you are, for I never expect that you will suffer any to be killed." The Duke of Queensberry had lent Sir William a pony. "I am literally starving with cold but my heart is warm."

This series of letters covers an end and a beginning. The end is that of the months of uncertainty, of doubts, of feverish dreams, of seclusion. The beginning is that of living in retirement together, Emma and her two husbands. That is what the peace meant for them, day after day together. Nelson could not get to Merton quick enough. As for Emma, she wrote on the cover of one of his letters, sealed in black for young Parker's sake, *"friday friday friday* and Saturday."

CHAPTER ELEVEN

In Retirement at Merton

MERTON LIES eight miles from Westminster bridge on what used to be the old turnpike road to the south coast. It was the site of a famous old priory, the school of Thomas à Becket and Walter de Merton, the founder of the Oxford college. Henry VIII had seized the priory and used its stones for his palace of Nonsuch, and when the palace followed the priory into oblivion, the villagers took the stones for their cottages. Merton already had associations with the sea—what place in England has not?—the land had once belonged to Pepys' cousin Tom, and Captain Cook lived for many years in the village. Izaak Walton praised the Wandle, the river that wandered round Nelson's house, and that alone would have been enough to have drawn Sir William Hamilton there.

Nelson's post chaise clattered through the village under a makeshift triumphal arch, the people smiled and waved, the postboy shouted from his box—did his lordship know the way to the house? His lordship had to admit he did not. It was not far from the road, opposite the old priory wall . . . there it was, that red brick villa, through the leafless branches of the trees, and there was a large lady in a flowing gown, very low around the bosom, and an elderly gentleman, stooping in the silk and brocade of an earlier age, and a little grandmotherly woman in black with an apron, and the butler and the maids, the coachman and the gardeners.

"Is this mine too?" asked Nelson as they showed him around the farm and the dairy, and took him through the tunnel beneath the road to view his estate. There was the canal formed by a branch of the Wandle, "the Nile" as Emma called it, and the terrace, "the poop" as Emma called that. The boundary on one side was certainly close to the house and two days after his arrival, Nelson was writing to the owner of the fields beyond, one Mr. Axe, to see if he could extend his property in that direction. Mr. Axe was willing, but his tenant who farmed the fields was not. Eventually, Nelson was obliged to offer for the whole farm, another property deal that exhausted his money and patience.

The house itself was, according to Mr. Cockerell, paltry. Sir William admitted it was small, small for those days anyway. There was a cellar with a good deal of wine in it. Every ship's captain abroad was liable to find himself acting as a wine merchant for his friends at home. The advantage was that it was cheaper to ship wine oneself and pay the duty than to buy it in England. The disadvantage was that one was liable to be landed with a load of vinegar. Sir William did not think much of Nelson's port.

On the ground floor there were the hall and the kitchen and the dining room, all rather cramped up together in the middle; the drawing room was on one side, and the library, which at once became the Nelson Room, on the other. Upstairs, and here we must guess, there was one decent bedroom, another less decent bedroom, and perhaps six indecent bedrooms. There had to be about eight bedrooms from the number of people who stayed in the house, unless they were very indecent, which was quite possible. There were, of course, no bathrooms or lavatories to be accounted for.

The house needed some improvements, this was agreed from the beginning, but for two of the *tria juncta in uno* it was the happiest place on earth, and the third could always escape for a quiet day at the British Museum, about an hour and a half's trot away.

Emma wrote Mrs. Nelson:

I am sorry to tell you I do not think our dear Lord well. He has frequent sickness and low and he throws himself on the sofa *tired and says I am worn out,* but yet he is better and I hope we shall get him up. He has been *very very* happy since he arrived and Charlotte has been very attentive to him, indeed *we all* make it our constant business to make him *happy.* Sir William is fonder than ever and we manage very well in regards to our establishment, pay share and share alike, so it comes easy to *booth* parties. When will you come, pray do as soon as possible for *we long to see you.* We were all at Church and Charlotte turned over the prayers for her uncle. As to Sir William, they are the greatest friends in the world; and our next door neighbour Mr. Halfhide and his family, they would give us half of all they have, very pleasant people; and Mr. and Mrs. Newton allso, but I like Mrs. Halfhide very much indeed and she sent Charlotte grapes &c. &c. We *could* have plenty of visiting in the *neighbourhood* but we none of us *like it.* Sir William and

Charlotte caught a large pike. She helps him and Milord with their great coats on, so now I have nothing to do.

Nelson took his seat in the House of Lords as a viscount on October 29 and on the next day he made his maiden speech. He seconded the vote of thanks to Sir James Saumarez, his second at the Nile, for his victory over a superior Spanish squadron at Algeciras in the previous July. He spoke for too long and when he finally made the customary apology to their lordships for troubling them there was a general cry of "Hear! Hear!" "You will see my maiden speech," he wrote Captain Sutton, "bad enough but well meant."

He was at Court on the 30th with Sir William, and a week later they were both once again in the Lord Mayor's Procession. Nelson was as popular with the mob as ever. The *Morning Chronicle* of November 9 reported, "Viscount Admiral Lord Nelson, accompanied by Sir William Hamilton, in Sir William's carriage, was drawn to the Guildhall by the populace; they greeted his Lordship with repeated plaudits, and stopped the carriage several times to have the gratification of taking him by the hand. A seaman who had served with the Admiral after giving him the salute exclaimed: 'By God your Lordship has got a delicate soft hand.' "

The 9th was the day of the debate on the peace in Parliament. Though Lord Cornwallis was negotiating the definitive treaty with Talleyrand at Amiens, it was expected that it would not differ greatly from the preliminary treaty. Certainly England had little left to give up. In the war she had won Ceylon and all the French and Dutch colonies in the East except Batavia and Mauritius; the settlement at the Cape of Good Hope; Tobago, Martinique, St. Pierre and Miquelon, St. Lucia in the West Indies; Surinam, Demerara and Curaçao in South America; Minorca, Malta and Egypt in the Mediterranean. In the peace she kept Dutch Ceylon and Spanish Trinidad, the Cape was to be a free port, and all the rest was given up! In the war France had won Belgium and all the territories west of the Rhine; control over Savoy and Piedmont; domination over all Italy; the virtual domination of Spain and the subjugation of Portugal; control of Holland and Switzerland through client republics; the Spanish half of Santo Domingo. In the peace she kept it all; her conquests, republics and puppet kingdoms were recognized. The Revolution was accepted; and the cause of the Bourbons, to the extent that it ever was a cause, was abandoned.

This peace was a triumph for Bonaparte. "It was the only event wanting to complete his destiny," trumpeted the *Gazette de France*. In England the Whigs supported the peace without enthusiasm. As Sheridan said, "It was a peace of which every body was glad and nobody was proud; it was such a peace as such a war deserved." Addington's Tories had made the peace and were stuck with it, but it was bitterly opposed by those Tories who had gone out of office with Pitt and their followers. Pitt himself, who had probably foreseen that peace would be popular but that the terms of peace would not, committed himself neither way.

As the majority of abandoned conquests had been made by the navy, Addington hoped to gain support by producing the navy's hero to speak in favor of the peace. It was a mistake. Nelson had neither the eloquence nor the arguments to support such a shabby affair and he spoke only to curry favor on behalf of his brother. He said that Malta was of little importance to England and that the Cape was no more than a tavern which might as well be kept by anyone provided it could be used on the route to India. He went into some detail about the price of cabbages there. Huskisson wrote to Henry Dundas:

> I was obliged to Lord Nelson for giving me anything that could create a smile on such a grave and awful subject. His Lordship's experience might have convinced him that a Seaman could find a tavern nearer home than the Cape of Good Hope, and if Malta is not to be considered of importance because it does not serve to blockade Toulon, we must be obliged to conclude that no Station in the Mediterranean is a good one. How can Ministers allow such a fool to speak in their defence?

His lordship did better on the 12th when he seconded the Vote of Thanks to Lord Keith and General Hutchison for their services in Egypt. And he was on safe ground when he supported the convention with the northern powers that allowed for the return of the Danish islands in the West Indies in exchange for the evacuation of Hamburg. Hanover was to be given up by Prussia. England maintained the right of search in wartime; and the proposition that free ships made free goods, abominable to the English, was abandoned by the neutrals.

He was in town at least twice more in November. On the 14th he and Sir William dined with the Levant Company, and on the 18th Emma let him go and have his dinner with Mr. Addington.

The London papers maintained a friendly interest in the whereabouts of Nelson and the Hamiltons. The attacks and sneers were replaced by something approaching sympathy. They found a good ally in Mr. Perry, the editor of the *Morning Chronicle*, who was their neighbor at Merton.

One of the sneers in the *Oracle* of September 3 is interesting because it refers to Emma's brother. That such a person ever existed rests on the slender evidence of a remark by her cousin Thomas Kidd in 1809, "I have to inform you that your brother Charles is in Greenwich College and has been here since the 6th inst." Thomas Kidd had been a sailor and had retired to the hospital at Greenwich. Was this brother also a sailor? Certainly not in 1801.

> The *Brother* of a celebrated *Fair One of Quality* who some years since most fortunately persuaded a *virtuoso Baronet* to put on the *matrimonial fetters,* though the attempt was nearly as arduous as digging up the ruins of *Herculanaeum,* keeps, to the disgrace of his Sister, an obscure *Pot-house* in the vicinity of *Swallow-street,* where, doubtless over the enlivening brew of *Sir John Barleycorn,* he very frequently has occasion to remember "The Goddess of Health."

This does not prove that Emma had a brother; all the Kidds had an affinity with pothouses and it might have been cousin Tom or uncle William. As a rule, single references are misleading unless we know all the circumstances surrounding them. But two references are better than one.

Two papers mentioned on November 5 that Lady Nelson had arrived at her house in Somerset Street from Lord Walpole's. On the 2nd Nelson's father wrote that he would accept the invitation to Merton, "after finishing some necessary business in town." The old gentleman certainly stayed with Fanny, bravely under the circumstances, and then went on to Merton, where he arrived on November 18. "My Father came here yesterday," Nelson wrote Davison on the 19th, "and we shall be truly happy to see you here and give you a bed any night except Sunday." The accommodation at Merton was obviously limited.

The contentment that Nelson found in his new home, in the uninterrupted company of Lady Hamilton, and, in spite of his transgression, in the presence of his father, was complete but for one irksome omission. The battle of Copenhagen had not been recognized by the King or the City. He could do nothing about the King. It had taken the King a year to consent to the official announcement of his foreign orders in the *Gazette,* and even then the Crescent was not included. But he thought something might be got out of the City.

On November 20 he drafted a letter to the new Lord Mayor, which he sent to Mr. Addington for his approval. He took the occasion of the City's Thanks to the army and navy in Egypt to state that the only battle the City had not noticed was Copenhagen. "For myself I can assure you that if I was only personally concerned, I should bear the stigma, first placed upon my brow, with humility; but, my Lord, I am the natural guardian of the characters of the officers of the navy, army and marines who fought and so profusely bled under my command on that day."

Nelson waited three days without hearing from the Prime Minister and then sent the letter to the Lord Mayor. Within a week he was obliged to withdraw it. St. Vincent said it was improper, and Addington that it would cause serious embarrassment. Nelson then declared that he would not wear his other medals until a Copenhagen medal was awarded and he would not dine with the Lord Mayor again.

The continued absence of one medal was made up for to some extent with two ribbons. Nelson had declared himself to be the first Knight of the Order of the Crescent. He presumed a trifle because no such order existed. However, word got back to Constantinople that the Crescent was appearing in Lord Nelson's list of his titles, and the Grand Signior decided to establish the order. Early in January 1802 the hero received a peach-colored ribbon, which he sent to Addington to know if he would be allowed to wear it.

He also heard again from the Order of St. Joachim. The Baron d'Eiker and Ekoffen, Knight Grand Commander and Chancellor of the Seals of the Most Illustrious Order Equestrian Secular and Capitular of St. Joachim, Knight of the Royal Order of Stanislaus, Actual Chamberlain to the late King of Poland, and Grand Drossard to His Serene Highness the reigning Duke of Brunswick, as well as actually Councillor Intime to the reigning Prince of Hohenloe, wanted to know if he was going to join. On a second sheet of paper he gave a few details of the order in case his lordship had not heard of it.

"It has above all as its *principal object* to maintain the tranquility of the Publick and to excite the highest degree of fidelity for the Sovereign to whom you are subject or in whose Service you may be engaged." The Grand Master was the reigning Count of Leiningen Westerburg, and there were a Great Prior, twelve Grand Commanders, seventeen Commanders, forty-two Knights, one Lady of the Great Cross, nine Ladies of the Little Cross, "besides many in expectation."

On February 19 Mr. Addington wrote to say that the King had agreed that Nelson could wear both new orders, and on March 20 they were gazetted. He now had four ribbons—red, blue and gold, peach, and green— and four stars—the chelengk for his hat, the pelisse for his shoulders, and a variety of swords, miniatures and boxes.

He did not have the boxes much longer. There is a letter to Davison of

December 18 which tells of their fate. "The valuation of the Diamonds is as far as I have been told shameful, therefore although I am naturally very anxious not to obtrude more on your goodness than necessity obliges me, yet I wish to talk to you on the subject of being *even* a little longer in your debt. . . . I would sooner beg than give those fellows my Diamonds."

That he did sell the diamonds appears in a letter to William Marsh on December 29. He wanted some money to pay his old secretary John Tyson £4,000, which he owed him from the Mediterranean days. Marsh was to sell his East Indian stock, there was some prize money to come, and he was even prepared to mortgage part of Merton. (His case against St. Vincent was still not settled, having been referred to the High Court.) "I have sold diamonds," he wrote, "to pay one person to whom I was indebted by his goodness in trusting me £3,000. *I take no shame to be poor*, never for myself have I spent sixpence, it has all gone to do honour for my country and in a way which, whether the persons have deserved it or no, is for their consideration, not for mine."

Nelson was not alone in financial straits. Sir William was there with him. The Knight was a little grudging in his appreciation of Merton. "I do not see any chance of our being much in town until after Xmas," he wrote Greville on December 5. "I shall go to attend my particular business at the Museum or Royal Society occasionally. This air and early hours seems to agree with me, and to get over the winter tolerably in this climate is a great object to me at my time of life, and accustomed to a much better climate." He had been obliged to sell £1,000 of stock. "Nothing is to be got out of the Treasury. . . . If we had given up the house in Piccadilly, the living here would indeed be a great saving; but, as it is, we spend neither more nor less than we did."

Very likely Sir William had particular business in town on December 15, as on the 14th Emma sent a note to Mrs. Gibson. "If you will take a post chaise tomorrow *Tuesday* and set off at half past ten a clock and bring my God daughter and your little girl with you, I shall be glad to see you. Tell them to drive you to Merton and the best way you can come is over Clapham Common. Hire the chaise for the day, you can go back at 3 o'clock. Do not fail. . . ." For sure Nelson stayed home that day.

The Doctor and Mrs. Nelson with Charlotte and Horace were at Merton by December 15. On that evening they went with the Admiral and his friends to the Barn House Academy at Mitcham, where the young gentlemen performed *The Siege of Damascus* and *No Song No Supper* in their honor. The Reverend Edmund had left for Bath at the beginning of December. He had written to Mrs. Matcham, "Your good brother is truly in better health and happier in himself than in good truth I have in any passed time observed him to be." He admitted to his son on the 5th, "I now rejoice to see so few impediments to as much felicity as falls to the share of mortals." It was an admission of Fanny's defeat.

Fanny's final rejection came that month. It appears that she must have received some notification from Davison that her husband had no wish to hear from her, but it was not in sufficiently strong terms to prevent her from writing this last letter to him. It was addressed from Somerset Street to Viscount Nelson, St. James's Square, where Davison lived. It was dated December 18.

My dear Husband, It is some time since I have written to you. The silence you have imposed is more than my affections will allow me and in this instance I hope you will forgive me in not obeying you. One thing I omitted in my letter of July which I now have to offer for your accommodation, a comfortable warm house. Do, my dear husband, let us live together. I can never be happy till such an event takes place. I assure you again I have but one wish in the world, to please you. Let every thing be buried in oblivion, it will pass away like a dream. I can now only intreat you to believe I am most sincerely and affectionately your wife, Frances H. Nelson.

The letter was returned to her with a note on the cover: "Opened by mistake by Lord Nelson but not read. A. Davison."

Surely the banker could have spared another word even if the Admiral was adamant? It was bitter cold.

"Even the severity of the Season, which makes many a poor creature such as myself to shake, gives much pleasure to the skating parties." The Reverend Edmund was writing to Lady Hamilton on December 21. "So that I hope all in their Turns have their Hours of enjoyment at a Season when all the Xtian world do celebrate with songs of praise the return of Xmas. Long may you all feel the happy influence of such an event Here, and the inestimable benefit of it Hereafter."

So ended a year, a strange long year. There was peace, uneasy and unaccustomed, like a girl at her first ball. It was a goose-pimpled peace that might die of a fright or a chill, or languish from lack of partners. There was our hero in his home, a little man unremarkable in a plain dark suit. The house full of people coming and going, and full of Emma rushing about and pressing food and presents on them, and full of Nelson trophies and portraits and pictures of battles. Unbearable people for an elderly gentleman used to the company of wits and scholars; unbearable pictures, not a patch on his; unbearable songs about the same battles and the same man who was in the pictures; unbearable extravagance, for he paid for half the table and none of the people who sat at it were his. But if Sir William's philosophy taught him anything it was to endure.

The first fashionable event of every year was the Queen's Birthday Drawing Room, which took place on January 17. Fanny was there, "dressed in the most simple but elegant style which consisted of a white satin robe and petticoat, ornamented with gold fringe cord and tassels. Headdress, plain white and gold with a beautiful plume of Paradise and ostrich feathers." She had covered her sorrows with a new hat. Emma was not there, and the reporters spotted that too. The *Post* had a poem on it.

> *To Lady Hamilton.*
>
> *What, tho' thou visitest not COURTS,*
> *Where FOLLY grins, and NONSENCE sports!*
> *EMMA; thou hast no cause to* pine—
> *Know that the loss is* theirs, *not* thine.
>
> *Impartial.*

Nelson caught a bad cold and his face swelled up. His father wrote to Emma on January 7.

> Madam, Your polite congratulation upon the entrance of a new year, I return sevenfold to you, and the whole of the party now under the hospitable roof of Merton Place. Time is a sacred deposit committed to our trust, and hereafter we must account for the use we have made of it. To me, a large portion of this treasure has already been granted, even seventy nine years. The complaint my dear son has felt is, I know, very painful; and can be removed only with much care and caution; not venturing without a thick covering, both head and feet, even to admire your parterres of snow drops, which now appear in all their splendour. The white robe which January wears, bespangled with ice, is handsome to look at; but we must not approach too near.

The old clergyman was at Bath, living in lodgings and visited regularly by the Matchams. Nelson had persuaded his sister Matcham to come to Merton with some of her brood, but one or two fell ill and they could not make the journey.

Even when the Matchams did not come and the William Nelsons had gone the house was full enough. To give an idea what it was like, here is a letter from Emma to Mrs. Nelson written some time after young Horace had returned to Eton at the end of January.

Lord Minto arrived at dinner time and we passed a most pleasant evening. After supper I began on purpose to *tell him* of all the ill usage (*before Nelson*) that he had suffered of the Doctors not being provided for. He was *astonished* and outraged and when Nelson said "I onely wanted a Cannonship or Deanery for my onely Brother," Lord Minto answered, "Fye fye he ought not to accept that, Ministers ought to have thrown a Bishoprick at you saying give it to your Brother, you are our *Saviour*." He then said he wished onely to be Minister to do it—so you see my dear friend this will be of use, for Lord Auckland is his brother, Lord Hobart his nephew, and in short I was determined *he* should know all, for he will raise a clamer. You and the Doctor would like him. Of all things he goes at 12 o'clock to town but he will come soon and stay. He doats and worships Nelson, he is a great friend of ours.

My head is not yet over well. These winds kill me, but we have a deal of Company today and a great dinner. We shall be 19 at dinner. Lord Minto is charmed with Charlotte, he says she will be a beautiful woman and he likes her manner. Miss Furse is not grown a bit, but she holds herself remarkably well, so does Charlotte, much better. Miss Furse eat so much that in the evening she vomited before us all. Charlotte covered her *retraite* and got her out. She came in again and played at Cards. I *tipt* them both. Lord Minto played. Mrs. Tyson was drunk and when she talked nonsence her husband tipt her the wink and she held her Tongue. Charlotte is now practising as we do not go to Church, the day being bad, and Lord Minto not having ordered his Coach till past 12, I am writing and they are talking politicks. Oliver is gone for the turtle. I expect tomorrow Mrs. Denis, Miss Hornby and Mrs. Broadhead. The Cub is in town and he called at Tysons so as Sir E. Berry. *Tom tit* is despised and hated and even those that pretend to protect her *fell off*. She is now *bursting* and abuses him, you and us openly and all our *friends*. I wish she would *burst*, but their is no such good luck. Does she ever write to the Boltons, I dare say. Mother Blindy comes today. Charlotte and Miss Furse sleep in your room in Horrace's bed. I shall send this tomorrow and perhaps have some news to send you.

What a picture! Emma constantly on about the oafish Doctor; Miss Furse, Charlotte's school friend, being sick; Mrs. Tyson drunk; an expensive turtle on its way with some more awful people; and Emma, off the Doctor, on about Tom Tit and the Cub! What else? Lord Minto wrote:

I went to Lord Nelson's on Saturday to dinner and returned today in the forenoon. The whole establishment and way of life is such as to make me angry as well as melancholy. . . .

She looks ultimately to the chance of marriage, as Sir William will not be long in her way, and she probably indulges a hope that she may survive Lady Nelson; in the meanwhile she and Sir William and the whole set of them are living with him at his expence. She is in high looks, but more immense than ever. She goes on cramming Nelson with trowelfuls of flattery, which he goes on taking as quietly as a child does pap. The love she makes to him is not only ridiculous, but disgusting; not only the rooms, but the whole house, staircase and all, are covered with nothing but pictures of her and him, of all sizes and sorts, and representations of his naval actions, coats of arms, pieces of plate in his honour, the flagstaff of *L'Orient* &c.—an excess of vanity, which counteracts its own purpose. If it was Lady Hamilton's house there might be a pretence for it; to make his own a mere looking-glass to view himself all day is bad taste.

Minto did not know that it *was* Lady Hamilton's house, but Nelson certainly conspired with her to fill it up with Nelsoniana.

"The love she makes to him is not only ridiculous, but disgusting." At Merton, Emma behaved like Nelson's wife and Sir William was relegated to a corner by the fire and he resented it. There is a sort of behavior which is tolerable, even charming, in young people, which becomes absurd and embarrassing when the people are older. Young hands may steal into each other, young eyes may gaze into each other, and we may smile. But when the hands and eyes belong to an immense woman of thirty-six and a haggard little man of forty-two, we can only look away. Happily in possession, Nelson damns us and Emma hopes that we might burst. Lovers are always young to each other.

Sir William resented it. In May 1801 he had made a will leaving his estate to Charles Greville, with a charge on it for Emma of £300 down and £800 a year, and for Mrs. Cadogan of £100 down and, if she survived her daughter, £100 a year. This was not generous and, compared to what Nelson had done for Fanny with less means than Sir William, it was niggardly.

Let us not be mistaken. It was possible for a family to live on £800 a year, the William Nelsons lived on less, but they lived in the country and Nelson paid for Horace at Eton, while Emma was always tipping Charlotte.

It was not enough to live on in London in a style in which Sir William had educated Emma, or led her to expect. He might have guessed that his pension would not be extended to her and that the Treasury would be no more beneficent to her than it was to him. We cannot know what was in Sir William's mind when he fixed on that particular sum, but if the probability of Emma living with Nelson after his death was out of it, it would be surprising.

Emma knew of the terms of the will—of course she knew of them, she had been in on them from the beginning when Old Pliny made Young Pliny his heir. Moreover, she had been at Sir William to change them. Who else could be referred to in the first sentence of this letter in which Sir William expresses his intentions toward Greville and his dissatisfaction with his life at Merton? The old gentleman wrote on January 24:

I return you my Dear Charles the inclosed paper with the addition you wished for, my partiality to you and the thorough confidence I have in you, in spite of many attempts that have been made to disturb them, remains and will I am confident to my last moment in full force.

My visit to Milford last year convinced me of the propriety of all your operations there and which may still operate in my favour during the short time I can expect to live, but must be attended with immense profit to my Heirs hereafter. You are perfectly acquainted with the present state of my finances and are giving me your active and friendly aid to get me as soon as possible out of my difficulties. I saw enough when at Milford that was I to take upon me the management of your plans there I should rather do hurt than good, and you know that I gave a publick Testimony at the Dinner there, that I should continue to give you the full power of acting for me after your having given such proofs of your ability. Knowing as you do the whole of the dispositions I have made after my death, I am sure it is quite unnecessary for me to repeat to you that I expect in cases of necessity every assistance from my Estate in Wales that it is capable of affording—but you will see whether such aid will be further necessary or not. It is but reasonable after having fagged all my life that my last days should pass off comfortably and quietly. Nothing at present disturbs me but my debt and the nonsence I am obliged to submit to here, to avoid coming to an explosion, which would be attended with many disagreeable effects, and would totally destroy the comfort of the best man and the best Friend I have in the World. However, I am determined

that my quiet shall not be disturbed, let the nonsensicall World
go as it will.

This is clear enough. He does not like it, but he will put up with it for
Nelson's sake. An explosion, a divorce or separation, would indeed involve
Nelson in an even greater scandal than the one in the winter of 1800. So he
was obliged to suffer the bad taste that so upset Lord Minto, the noise and
the company, and seek his moments of peace in the British Museum. The
expense of these annoyances he could not avoid, and that seemed particularly unfair to him.

Emma wrote their friend Captain Bedford on February 13:

> Nelson the glorious Nelson is the truly great man in his re-
> tirement. He seldom goes to town and for that reason he is much
> desired and sent for—"keeping men off, you keep them on" will do
> for men as well as women. If ever he is employed, which will be if
> their is a new war, you will be one of *his select*, for such he calls
> you, but he will not take such a Command as he had last year—
> *shame* on them for giving it him—but Nelson is a being of a
> superior Class, the most trivial Command he makes of impor-
> tance, and I look on the attack off Boulogne as the bravest thing
> ever done. It was not his fault it did not succeed—alas the poor
> brave little Parker—but we must not dwell on trist Ideas. . . .
> We are very busy planting, and I am as much amused with pigs
> and hens as I was at the Court of Naples Ambasadress.

No compliment to the Court of Naples. But what about this new war?

"We may be wanted in 7 years," Nelson sent to Bedford in the same
packet, "but I do not think there is a probability of its being very soon. The
French wish for peace if possible perhaps more than ourselves, and the
Continent must go to war before us, and I say let them fight for some years
before we begin."

The Queen of Naples gave the peace ten years. She wrote to Emma
every now and then. Nelson's support of the peace had upset her. "One
must be silent even when laughed at and asked if our Anglomania is cured.
I grieve and my tears suffocate me. My attachment may be unfortunate,
but cannot be destroyed, and leads me to hope that England will not before
ten years have to repent of this peace, now concluded with a nation whose
activity, pugnacity, and good fortune, will make such efforts as will surprise
and incommode her."

There were gloomier prophecies than that. There was still no definitive treaty; the two sides could not agree on the future of Malta, and the *Post* found room for "apprehension, anxiety and speculation." There was alarm at the sailing of a French expedition to Santo Domingo to quell the revolution of the slaves led by Toussaint L'Ouverture. (The alarm was not for Toussaint, who was setting a bad example to slaves everywhere, but for the British colonies.) War had broken out in Egypt between the Turks and the Beys and, once the British army had left, it might easily fall again to France.

In Europe even more disturbing events were taking place. Bonaparte was at Lyons and announced early in February that Genoa, Parma and Lucca had been annexed and a new Italian Republic had been created of which he had consented to become President. This casual assumption of a title embracing all Italy, advancing the frontiers of France while the peace negotiations were in progress, gave everyone good reason to be gloomy. "He is giving wars to Europe for generations," said the *Chronicle*.

In England the general expectation that income tax would end was disappointed, and the army and navy were kept on a partial war footing. The merchants were also concerned that there were no signs yet of any commercial exchanges with France—well, there was one sign. The *Post* noticed it. "The commercial intercourse between England and France has hitherto extended to a fair exchange of *Cyprian nymphs*. Several French covies have already alighted in London, whilst English covies have taken a speculative flight to Paris."

Late in February Nelson heard about his father. "I am sorry to say that he is not so well as when he came to Bath," wrote Mrs. Matcham, "his cough was very troublesome and he is weak in the extreme." There was a letter dated the 26th. "My Dear Hor, This is the title that with me will ever supersede all others which the Empire of the World can ever give you." And the good old man could not resist a little sermon: "The post of Honor is the post of Danger, and to be exalted is to be tempted; but God tempteth not man beyond what he is able to bear." He was going slowly that cold winter.

There was one branch of the Nelson family that Emma had not as yet plucked. It was done in March with the present of a pipe of wine for Mr. Bolton and an invitation to Merton for his wife and the girls. Mrs. Bolton answered:

I shall my Dear Lady be happy to visit you and my Brother at Merton, to be sure Mrs. Matcham will be an agreeable addition to the Party. Poor thing, she is not very able to cope with a cough. I should be alarmed but that I know it in some degree belongs to her situation which I am sorry enough to hear as I am afraid she will breed herself to Death, which was the case with our poor Mother. Some time the beginning of April I hope to see you, with your permission I shall bring Kitty with me. I am sorry to hear you have all been ill and hope Sir William is daily getting strength. The weather is not very favorable for Invalids, with us the ground is now covered with snow.

There was always someone dining or staying at Merton, a captain or two, young Langford, Emma's frightful friends. Whoever was there in March was in for a treat. The *Morning Herald* reported on March 8, "The epicures are probably to be gratified by Lady Hamilton as much as antiquaries have been by Sir William's researches in Italy, by her bringing to their knowledge a new dish; for, in the manifest of the *Shelburne*, Captain Hopps, from Sicily and Mahon, entered at the Custom House for the 16th ult, there appears a case of *sows udders* a present for Lady Hamilton." The *Oracle* enlightened its readers, "The *teats of a sow* it is well known were esteemed a delicious treat by the Roman Epicureans. The Lady of a *celebrated Antiquarian* has lately imported a large quantity, flattering herself that their *salubrious* effects will ever continue her the blooming 'Goddess of Health.'"

None of them was very healthy that spring, least of all the Reverend Edmund Nelson, declining at Bath. He wrote what was, in the event, his last letter to his famous son on March 23.

Amongst many others may your lott be cast where there is not only a goodly Heritage but also abundance of internal *peace* such as you have never yet enjoyed much of, but are now of age to enjoy. When the expected stranger is arrived in Kensington Place and I can see your sister in a way of recovering, I shall then begin to think of leaving Bath. . . . My strength returns very slow, yet still have hopes I shall with the assistance of the May sun-shine get able to travel, and smell a Merton rose in June. Lady Hamilton's promised gazette is very tardy in its appearance, pleasant news is always acceptable. God bless you and all who dwell under your roof.

At the end of March 1802 Lord Cornwallis returned with the Treaty of Amiens. In the illuminations to celebrate the event, no house shone brighter than that of M. Otto, the French Envoy. Above the glowing façade, spelled out in lights, was the word "CONCORD." Before long the mob had gathered menacingly around the house, and Monsieur Otto sent to inquire the reason. The answer was that they were not conquered, and in any event some ignorant Frenchman had spelled it wrong! "CONCORD" was taken down and replaced by "AMITY."

The terms of the treaty were, as expected, those already specified, with one exception. Neither side wanted Malta, but neither side wanted to see it in the possession of the other. They fell back on the old compromise: Malta was to be restored to the Order of St. John and its independence was to be guaranteed by France, Britain, Austria, Russia and Prussia. Since the Emperor Alexander had given up all claim to Malta and the remaining Knights belonged to the chapters of countries under French influence, it was apparent that the island would fall to France the moment the British withdrew their forces. The treaty had a built-in breakdown.

On the anniversary of the battle of Copenhagen Lady Hamilton wrote the eulogistic letter to Lord Nelson, who was sitting in the same room, that we have already seen. She addressed it, "Emma the real sincere and true friend sends this greeting To the Victor of the Nile, the Conqueror of Copenhagen, the Terror and Stop of the Northern Confederacy, St. Vincent's Prop and the Hero of the 14th of February, the restorer of the King of Naples, the preserver of Rome, the avenger of Kings, the Guardian Angel of England, and the *man of men* who in this war as been in one hundred and 24 battles and come off covered with Glory, Honner, Virtue and modesty, the pride of his Country and friends."

A few days later, when he was complaining in a letter to Davison about the City's continued refusal to thank the victors of Copenhagen, Nelson said that there was still time to make amends. "The Framing of a Motion can easily be made from the direction of a letter sent to Lord Nelson by a Dear friend on the Anniversary of the 2nd of April—To the Victor of the Nile, the Conqueror at Copenhagen, St. Vincent's Prop . . ." and he went through the list, modestly altering Emma's 124 battles to "127 days in battle." In the same letter he stated his willingness to give up part of his prize money to make up Colonel Stewart's share to that of a junior flag officer.

What a strange compound of self and selflessness he was! Not that £100 to a friend was particularly selfless, but people must have liked him for something. They forgave him a lot.

Nelson was not always welcome, as appears from a note to the Doctor of April 10. "I have seen Mr. Addington now and then, but only for a moment, and there generally seems to be a fear that I am come soliciting, but my spirit is too independent to be a beggar." But he did go soliciting for what he believed was his right. At a time when patronage was the reward of virtue, the withholding of patronage suggested imperfection. It was a burden to Nelson.

On April 19 the new little Matcham was born. The Reverend Edmund sent the news to Fanny, adding that he intended to leave Bath in the next month. His journey was hastened. On the 24th Mr. Matcham wrote Nelson, "Your good old father is very ill, and I have directions from Dr. Perry and Mr. Spry, to say to you that he is certainly in great danger. Whatever orders you send me shall be executed."

Nelson answered, "From your kind letter of yesterday describing my Father's situation I have no hopes that he can recover. God's will be done. Had my Father expressed a wish to see me, unwell as I am, I should have flown to Bath, but I believe it would be too late, however, should it be otherwise and he wishes to see me, no consideration shall detain me for a moment."

One person did not wait to ask whether she was asked for. Lady Nelson flew to Bath and was with her old friend when he died on April 26.

Sir William wrote from Piccadilly:

> Emma says I must write a letter to you of condolence for the heavy loss your Lordship has suffered. When persons in the prime of life are carried off by accidents or sickness—or what is I believe oftener the case, by the ignorance and mistakes of the physicians, then, indeed, there is reason to lament. But as in the case of your good Father the lamp was suffered to burn out fairly, and that his sufferings were not great, and that, by his Son's glorious and unparalleled successes, he saw his family ennobled, and with the probability, in time, of its being amply rewarded, as it ought to have been long ago, his mind could not be troubled in his latter moments, as to his own peace of mind at the moment of his dissolution, there can be no doubt among those who ever had the honour of his acquaintance.

It is a firm and reassuring letter, and Nelson answered it firmly. "I have a consolation in the loss I have sustained that my dear father was a good man and that I feel I never was wanting in kindness to him."

The funeral took place in Burnham Thorpe. Nelson did not attend on account of his health, and the arrangements were left to the Doctor. Nelson need not have stayed away, because Fanny was not there.

Mrs. Bolton wrote to her on May 15.

Your going to Bath my dear Lady Nelson was of a piece with all your conduct to my beloved father. I did not know he was ill till he was no more. To me his loss is great indeed, even as a friend, but more as a parent. He had lived so long that when not with him we always flattered ourselves with a longer time still. He was a truly good Christian and no doubt has met his reward. This must be our comfort and hope to meet again in a better world. . . .

I am going to Merton in about a fortnight, but my dear Lady N. we cannot meet as I wished for every body is known who visits you. Indeed I do not think I shall be permitted even to go to town.

Fanny was now entirely alone. Mrs. Bolton's reward was £100 a year for the education of her children, and a visit to Merton with the Matchams. Nelson wrote Mr. Bolton:

These Rains may give us a little hay. I shall not allow its being cut too soon, nor in too great a hurry to sell, but I mean to sell it in the cock or standing. This weather suits Cranwich, it will give you good turnips and I am farmer enough to know that gives everything. We only regret that we have not the means of doing all the kindness for my Sister which my heart wishes. Mrs. M. goes off Saturday. Mrs. B. on Monday, when we shall be quite alone.

Neither Sir William nor Nelson was doing very well with the subjects nearest his heart, or perhaps next nearest to Emma. The Knight could not get even his proper expenses at Palermo paid by the Treasury and suffered the indignity of being ignored in Lord Hawkesbury's anteroom. The Admiral could not get a word out of the City for Copenhagen, though he went to the extent of declining their thanks for his services in the Channel.

Sir William was worse off of the two, because nothing could detract from Nelson's glory, whereas everything seemed to be detracting from his bank account. Nelson's relations were eating up his half of the household expenses; an apparently endless stream of little boys and girls with ever-open mouths.

The only remedy that seemed to offer was Beckford's old plan, and he took it up again with the Duke of Hamilton and his son the Marquis of Douglas. Sir William's great relations were kind enough to let him down gently.

Then the idea occurred that perhaps something more might be done at Milford if Lord Nelson would propose to the government that the harbor would be ideal for the mail packets to Ireland. From that, a plan developed for them to visit Milford with Charles Greville. But if four were going, why not more? The Doctor and his jewel would be delighted, if they could bring young Horace. Seven. But why not nine, if Mr. and Mrs. Matcham would agree, Bath was on the way? Certainly, if we can bring young George. Ten. With a train of servants—a cavalcade.

There was a general election going on. General elections went on in those days, and on, with rules that were apparently different in each constituency. Some members were elected without a poll, others had several. There was a famous constituency in Lord Clive's day that had one elector, quite a wealthy man, and that was not so long ago. We shall have more than a passing interest in this election, because Mr. Davison was standing for Ilchester against the popular candidate, Sir William Manners.

The election figured in a letter from Cambridge, where the Doctor had gone to cast his vote. "The election for the University took place yesterday," he wrote Emma on July 6, "the whole was over in five minutes. Mr. Pitt and Lord Euston are re-elected. I had a bow this morning from Billy in the Senate House, so I made up to him, and said a word or two to him." Who will bet that the word was about some aged dean or defunct prebendary?

On July 13 Nelson was reported on the hustings at Covent Garden on behalf of Lord Gardner. Perhaps he had some effect, because Lord Gardner got in. Nelson was busy at this time with the purchase of Mr. Axe's estate, which bordered the grounds of Merton Place. He was obliged to take the whole 115 acres and Mr. Axe was asking £8,000. Half this money he was borrowing from George Matcham; it was his sister Catherine's marriage settlement and Matcham was taking it out of the Funds to lend it to him. Nelson was concerned that the Matchams would not lose by the deal, and wrote on July 16, "I will take care if the money is wanted that all shall be done properly for my Sister and family who are of more consequence to me than 50 Axe's Estates. . . . The Star Inn Oxford Wednesday the 21st July. Dinner at 5 o'clock for 8—be so good as to order it, need not say for who." Mrs. Matcham had recommended the Star, or the Bear which was more moderate, so of course it had to be the Star.

The William Nelsons came to Merton, the weather was fine, the party were in anticipation of a pleasant holiday—and Sir William was in his room in Piccadilly on July 16 writing to his wife.

My Dear Emma, It gave me much uneasiness to leave you as I did in a most uncomfortable state but consider you had not had your breakfast and the communication I made you of what passed *amicably* between Oliver and me did not quite coincide with your Ideas—then came *passion humour* and *nonsence*, which it is impossible to combat with reasoning whilst the passion lasts. There is no being on earth that has a better understanding or better heart than yourself, if you would but give them *fair play* and keep down the passions that make you see every thing thro' an improper and false medium. I am an old sinner I confess—but I am not the hard hearted man you do not scruple to make me. Your Ladyship is exactly what your old aunt told you, so *noble*, so *generous*, so *beautifull*, that you would give away your A—— and H thro' your ribs—it is all well and so would I if I could afford it, and our Dear Ld. N. is noble, generous, open and liberal to all and I wish to God he could afford it. In this state you must excuse me if my having lived so long has given me Experience enough that the greatest fortunes will not stand the total want of attention to what are called *trifling* Expences. La Bruyere says *Qu'on se mine plus en faux frais qu'en grandes articles de depence,* that is that any great sum strikes you, but you do not think of Shillings and Sixpences that in time make up a great sum. You charge me with having by my Will left you to poverty and distress, that is by no means my intention. I know your value and mean to do every thing in my power (when I know what I really possess) to prevent that distress, but it is not my fault if by living with a great *Queen* in *intimacy* for so many years that your *ideas* should so far outrun what my means can furnish. Believe me, happiness is in a much *narrower* compass than most people think. But my Dear Emma let us cut this matter short. I am the old Oak and by God I can not give way to nonsence. Do not then strain the bow too tight, as the Duke of Grafton said to Ld. Ossory, least the string should break. I love Ld. Nelson. I know *the purity of your connection with him.* I will do every thing in my power not to disturb the quiet of my best Friend, and his heart God knows is so sensible that a sudden change from his present peace and tranquility might prove fatal to him.

We had yesterday a little tiff about Oliver. Ld. N. and I mean as friendly to him as you do, but do not think I am blind, do not think that I am ignorant that besides *Sabatini Michele* that most *ungrateful* and *impertinent rascall,* not to say *worse* is hidden at Merton. For God's sake as we have cause commune with Ld. Nelson, let us have fair play and do not let your generous and noble way of thinking and acting end in distressing us. I have now done with my Sermon—it comes from my heart which is seldom the case of those that come from the pulpit.

I went at ½ past 11 to the Hustings in Convent Garden yesterday. Luckily for me I was an hour too late for the business was over. The Blackguard Friends of Graham in despair pulled down the support of the Hustings where I should have been and where there were more than 100, and I am told two are killed and many wounded. I went however to Hudsons and, as they told me Ld. Gardner and his friends were to be there at 4 o'clock, I left my billet on his table—"*Sir W.H. at the request of Ld. N. came this morning from Merton to vote for Ld. G.—and was happy to find that there was no need of his vote and wishes his Lp. joy of his success.*"

The Duke of Q. chose to dine alone. Ld. Warwick is gone to the Castle, so I dined at home on *pickled salmon, pidgeon and peas, cold lamb, and Tart*—GOOD PORT which after every delicacy is most necessary. Would to God I could enjoy all that is mine and which I know to be superior to what any other person on Earth possesses, but one can not have eaten one's Cake and have one's cake. Ponder well my Dear Emma these lines, let your good sense come forward—as to me it is perfectly indifferent what may happen! I shall be Patience in Purity. Ever yr. W. Hamilton.

The letter teases as much as it tells. What had passed about Oliver? Who was Sabatini Michele? And above all, what did Sir William intend when he wrote, "I know the purity of your connection with him," and underlined it? One thing is plain, the whole letter is loaded with irony.

Let us take it up again on the road to the Star Inn at Oxford.

CHAPTER TWELVE

Death of a Philosopher

THE LETTER was about money. Sir William was, for a philosopher, very conscious of money, or rather of the lack of it. "He trafficked in the Arts," said Major Gordon, "and his hotel was a broker's shop. No one knew the value of a Greek vase or a gem better than the *Cavaliere Inglese*, or where to place it." He used to think that a little candlelight or iced water would ruin him, remembered Nelson.

The tiff over Oliver was about money. Francis Oliver was a gentleman, Nelson's secretary and interpreter for the journey through Europe. In England, while he lived with the family, he did not seem to have any precise function. He acted as a confidential messenger between Nelson and Emma and was the one person in the household who took an active part in the arrangements concerning Horatia. Nelson had intended to ask the directors of the East India Company to make him a writer, until he realized that a request for such a post was usually accompanied by a guarantee of £1,000. Doubtless Oliver's future was again under discussion and Emma was anxious that he should be amply repaid for his services, and that was too ample for Sir William. However, Emma probably got her way, and Oliver will be found planning to go into partnership with Mr. Matcham to buy an estate in Denmark.

There are two more things to say about Oliver. The first is that he was very attached to Emma. After Sir William's death he began addressing her as "Adorable Lady"; and after Nelson's death, he wrote to her, "I cannot tell you what you already know that I love you and that to hear of your welfare in *every* respect is the *first* and *greatest* satisfaction I can have." The second is that he probably turned against her. Whoever wrote *Lady Hamilton's Memoires* after her death knew what Oliver knew, and what no one

else could have known, about Horatia. If the author of that piously cen-
sorious tract was not Oliver, he at least had Oliver's testimony.

Sabatini Michele was the brother-in-law of Sir William's valet Gaetano
Sabatello. What he had done to be hiding at Merton is a mystery. When
Nelson took him back to Naples, he went off with £70 belonging to
Emma's maid Julia. It would seem that Sir William had dismissed him from
the Piccadilly house, he had taken refuge with Emma, and Sir William had
found him out.

"I love Ld. Nelson. I know *the purity of your connection with him*." If
Sir William meant what he said, he must have been the blind and ignorant
person he denied being a few lines later. However, in a letter in which he
congratulated her on giving her arse and heart away, he presumably did not
mean what he said. And again, if it was a straightforward statement of fact,
why did he underline it? Underlining usually means that the writer wishes
to emphasize what he has written *or to contradict it*. "Then came *passion
humour* and *nonsense*" is an example of plain emphasis. "Your Ladyship
is . . . so *noble*, so *generous*, so *beautifull*" is an example of contradiction,
and he might just as well have said "so stupid, so wasteful, so vain." But he
was determined not to quarrel with her. What he probably meant was, I
know what you and Nelson are up to, but, because I love him and it is
better for him that we live together, I will continue to pretend that you are
just good friends.

The letter ends with a cry from the heart of an old epicure. He de-
scribes his dinner, "good port" is underlined three times, and then says,
"Would to God I could enjoy all that is mine and which I know to be
superior to what any other person on Earth possesses. . . ." We can almost
feel sorry for him!

They dined at the Star on Wednesday, July 21—Nelson, the Hamiltons, Greville, the William Nelsons and the Matchams. The next morning
the Admiral went through the usual crowd to the Town Hall to receive the
freedom of the city in a gold box. In the afternoon there was a tour of
Oxford and his lordship was said to have expressed his admiration of the
jail, where he left a present for the prisoners.

On Friday, in full convocation, Lord Nelson and Sir William Hamilton were installed as Doctors of Civil Law, while Dr. Nelson was made a
Doctor of Divinity for coming along with them. The *Morning Post* suggested that from Nelson's knowledge of *cannon* laws, he should have been
the Doctor of Divinity. The *Morning Herald* was less polite. "When Lord
Nelson had a degree conferred upon him at Oxford, it is said that his friend

Sir William Hamilton had an *honorary* one also voted him at the same time, but whether that of L.L.D. or A.S.S. the Records of the University do not say."

They took the Woodstock Road that afternoon with the intention of visiting Blenheim Palace, the present of a grateful country to that earlier hero the Duke of Marlborough. In Vanbrugh's sprawling barracks they were met by a lackey, though the present Duke was at home, with the offer of a cold collation that was coldly refused. Emma could barely contain herself, and when they were outside she burst out, "The splendid reward of Marlborough's services was because a woman reigned and women had great souls." She told Nelson that if she had been a queen, after the Battle of Aboukir he would have had a principality "so that Blenheim Park should have been only as a kitchen garden to it." It was said for the Duke that he was shy—better that than proud, because his great ancestor's private character does not bear much looking into.

The party stayed the night in Woodstock and traveled to Gloucester on the Saturday. There was no titled nonsense here, but a good honest welcome with bells and crowds, and a visit to the cathedral and the county prison. The Matchams parted company on Sunday and returned to Bath, while the rest drove on to Ross. The welcome of the commonalty was as warm in Herefordshire as in the neighboring county. Nelson was the people's hero and his tour, from the beginning, had something in it of a Roman triumph.

From Ross they went by boat on the river Wye to Monmouth, birthplace of a royal hero, Henry V. Monmouth was busy acquiring a naval tradition. The daughter of Admiral Boscawen had built a pretty pink and blue kiosk on Kymin Hill overlooking the town, which, because it had some famous admirals' names on plaques about it, was called the Naval Temple. Nelson, whose name was quickly enrolled with Rodney, Hawk & Co., was led through the town by the local band to the delight of the people milling in the narrow streets.

The next day, and on to Brecon and the cheers of the Brecknock farmers. And then a dash for Milford, to arrive there a day or two before the anniversary of the Nile.

August 1 was a gala day at Milford. There was a fair, a cattle show and a boat race. At a grand dinner in the New Hotel, Nelson did all that was required of him in pronouncing that the port of Milford would one day be of the greatest importance to Great Britain. He was a true prophet, though he probably did not reckon it would take 150 years to make him one.

A week passed pleasantly, touring Sir William's estate and visiting the local bigwigs; and if Charles Greville was occasionally to be seen gloomily turning over stones on a bright day, he was the only one of the party so affected. He was no part of the *tria juncta in uno*, and the uncouth Doctor and chattering jewel very likely turned his fastidious stomach.

On August 9 they left Milford on the return journey, stopping at Haverfordwest, where the Admiral was drawn through the streets to the house of Mr. Foley, the Captain's brother. He received yet another mayor, corporation and freedom, before continuing the progress toward Swansea. In this seaport the carriage was hauled along by cheering seamen. Here Charles Greville left them, pleading ill health.

"I purpose crossing the Bristol Channel," he wrote Sir Joseph Banks, "to make my journey compensate the inconvenience I experience from indisposition by my observations in the mining country." On his return to London, Sir Joseph answered, "I rejoice exceedingly that you have returned safe from your expedition, which I conclude could not in any part of it be an agreeable one to you, and I think you have done very wisely in prefering a route through Cornwall, where nature would arouse you at every step, to the artificial satisfaction of feasts, Mayors and Aldermen, freedom of Rotten Boroughs &c."

There was a day's visit to Carmarthen on the 14th, and then they were on their way again through Merthyr Tydfil and on to Monmouth. The newspapers had been very interested in the tour and anyone who wished could read that Lord Nelson and his friends were receiving the kind of welcome previously only associated with royalty. At Monmouth, on August 19, the party drove up the Kymin and were met with a salute of cannons and the local militia band playing Emma's theme song, "Rule Britannia." They examined the temple, looked at the scenery, and walked back to the town, "receiving as they passed, the grateful applause of all ranks of people, who seemed to vie with each other in the ardour of their expressions of joy." In the afternoon they dined at the Beaufort Arms, toasts and speeches were exchanged, and Emma sang

> *Come hither all ye youths of Bath*
> *Whose bosoms pant for glory. . . .*

"In short," said the correspondent, "The polite and engaging behaviour of Lord Nelson, as well as of Sir William and Lady Hamilton, impressed on the minds of the visitors the most unqualified respect and admiration of their characters." Emma and Sir William were an integral part of the cavalcade and added a delightful hint of romance to the martial spirit of the triumph.

Wherever Nelson went he left his name behind him. "There is no man so busily employed at present in England as Lord Nelson," said the *Post*. "In one place we meet him as a *gooseberry*, in another as a *carnation*—sometimes we find him a *racehorse* and sometimes a Prize *ram*."

Ross saw them again on August 20, and the Admiral, passing through the Forest of Dean, had some serious thoughts about the preservation of timber for the warships of the future.

From Ross they went to Rudhall, the home of the Westfalings, old friends from Naples. There was a fete in the grounds, supper, fireworks and a ball, quite like old times. They stayed a night or two, and the *Morning Post* tittered, "Sir William Hamilton's party are quite *in love* with each other on the Welch mountains."

The joke makers had more fun when the party reached Hereford. "The branch of an apple tree in full bearing, being presented to Lord Nelson at Hereford, his Lordship, with all the gallantry of Paris, presented the *apple* to Lady Hamilton, thereby acknowledging her Ladyship a perfect VENUS." In fact, after being dragged through the city to the tune of "See the Conquering Hero Comes," and being met by the Duke of Norfolk, Nelson was presented with the freedom in a box cut from an apple tree, but the newspaper story is better.

More important than the jokes, which were for the smart London society, were Nelson's speeches, simple, sincere, patriotic, and exactly what his listeners wished to hear. "From the spirit he had witnessed in the people during his present tour, he was confident the Nation could defy the World," he said at Hereford.

On August 28 the friends were in Ludlow, and two days later in Worcester. Worcester was a great place where they made famous china, and the freedom was presented to his lordship in an elegant vase of local manufacture. The mass of people who crowded around Nelson's carriage and the inn where the party spent the night made him concerned about the vast press he was likely to meet at the next stop, Birmingham. Consequently they set off early on the 31st, arrived two hours before they were expected, and reached Styles Hotel with the horses still in harness.

It was not long before the news spread that Nelson was there, church bells began to ring, a huge crowd gathered before the hotel, and the great men of the city came to welcome him to "the toy-shop of Europe." That evening they went to the theater, the audience stood and cheered and sang "Rule Britannia" while the little Admiral bowed repeatedly. The play was

The Merry Wives of Windsor. In the scene where Falstaff makes up to Ford's wife, he says, "Before the best Lord in the land I swear it." At that point the actor swung his hand up toward Nelson's box, and the applause and cheers started up all over again. After the play the carriage was drawn back to the hotel, with thousands of huzzas and by the light of torches.

"It is a singular fact," the *Post* noted at last, "that more *eclat* attends Lord Nelson in his provincial rambles, than attends the King."

The next morning the whole party went on a round of visits to the various factories in Birmingham: japanners, sword makers, button, buckle and ring makers, the stained-glass factory, and finally to the famous coin and medal makers, Boulton's of Soho. Nelson already had several of Mr. Boulton's products to hang around his neck, and now he got some more, struck in his presence and honor.

There was dinner with the local worthies, where Emma sang, and a second visit to the theater similar to the first. On September 2 there were more visits before the journey was continued once more toward Warwick.

From Warwick, where the scenes were repeated, they went on to Coventry. The last lap was broken at Althorp, the seat of Lord Spencer, and Nelson and the Hamiltons arrived back at Merton finally on September 5.

"Lord Nelson and his party returned on Sunday to Merton from their tour through a part of the west of England," said the *Times*. "If, on the one hand, the Country owes his Lordship a large share of gratitude for the brilliant Services he performed during the war, no man ever had it repaid in a more ample degree." And the country has gone on repaying that debt with affection and gratitude ever since.

In a life as well documented as Nelson's, it is surprising to find a series of incidents which have no fixed date or place. It is even more surprising to find a whole week into which they will fit with only a slight squeeze. The incidents are connected with a visit to the seaside, and the week is September 13–20, 1802.

Nelson and the Hamiltons were back at Merton on September 5. The first letter from there that we have is from Emma to Mrs. Gibson on the 9th, asking her to bring Horatia to Piccadilly the next day. The next is from Nelson to Davison on the 11th. "We have had rather a longer tour than was at first intended, for Merton was not fit to receive us. Dods being so very ill, even at death's door, the work went on so very slowly it is not even yet finished. Our tour has been very fine and interesting, and the way in which I have been everywhere received most flattering to my feelings, and although some of the higher powers may wish to keep me down, yet the reward of the general approbation and gratitude for my Services is an ample reward for all I have done, but it makes a *comparison* fly up to my mind not much to the credit of some in the higher offices of the state." He added that Axe's estate was not yet paid for and that Sir William had gone to Windsor.

The next day Davison replied that he would pay Axe £4,000, thus putting Nelson in his debt once again.

On the 13th Emma wrote to Mrs. Matcham to say that the improvements were still going on at Merton and to exclaim, "Oh how our Hero has been receved. I wish you could come to hear all, *our Story must entertain.*"

Then, for seven valuable days, there were no letters. The incidents require Emma and Sir William to go to the seaside without Nelson. (If he was there he would almost certainly have been spotted and it would have appeared in the papers.) The suggestion is that, as it was uncomfortable at Merton with the builders still in, and as Emma had a passion for bathing, she dragged Sir William off to Ramsgate, where he was soon fed up. At the same time, she arranged for Mrs. Gibson to take Horatia to the less well-known resort of Margate, where Nelson visited her.

The first clues are three undated letters between Emma and Mrs. Gibson.

Mrs. Gibson may go to Margate or Ramsgate with Miss Thompson but not to go with the Hoy as it is dangerous and to let Lord N. know where they are and how Miss Thompson is in her health and spirits and if Batheing is necessary to let her Bathe.

Hond. Lady—This with my Duty to you to inform you of our safe arrival on Wednesday night. Miss Thompson is very well and self—from your Humb. Serv. M. Gibson.

Ramsgate. Dear Mrs. Gibson, I was yesterday at Margate and had lost your direction and sent the servant all over the town to Church square—Church place—but could not hear from you. Write me a note directly and send me your proper direction, My love to H. and believe me. . . . [In another hand there is the address] Mrs. Gibson 115 High Street Margate.

The next clue is a very doubtful one and assumes that Emma dived straight into the sea on her arrival and was spotted by the correspondent of the *Morning Herald*. It is in that paper's issue of September 14. "A Lady *swimmer* at Ramsgate, who is said to be a perfect *attitudinarian* in the water, is now the morning gaze of the place. She *ducks* and *floats* with infinite dexterity, and seems secure against any *marine enemy*; but as she is

young and beautiful she is perhaps in more danger from the *land sharks!*"
An attitudinarian nearly always meant Emma and the rest of the report is
contrived to make the pun at the end, but there is the squeeze.

The last clues are a fascinating exchange of notes between Emma and
Sir William, written on one piece of paper, without a date. Emma began
it.

> As I see it is a pain to you to remain here, let me beg of you
> to fix your time for going. Weather I dye in Piccadilly or any other
> spot in England 'tis the same to me, but I remember the time
> when you wished for tranquility, but now all visiting and bustle is
> your liking. However, I will do what you please, being ever your
> affectionate and obedient E H.

Sir William wrote on the back:

> I neither love bustle nor great company but I like some em-
> ployment and diversion. I have but a very short time to live, and
> every moment is precious to me. I am in no hurry, and am ex-
> ceedingly glad to give every satisfaction to our best friend, our
> dear Lord Nelson. The question, then, is what we can best do
> that all may be perfectly satisfied. Sea bathing is usefull to your
> health; I see it is, and wish you to continue it a little longer; but I
> must confess, that I regret, whilst the season is favourable, that I
> cannot enjoy my favourite amusement of quiet fishing. I care not
> a pin for the great world, and am attached to no one so much
> as to you.

Emma turned the page back and wrote, "I go when you tell me the
coach is ready."

Sir William had the last word, the last written word anyway. "This is
not a fair answer to a fair confession of mine."

Well, there it is, and whether or not the Admiral ever slipped off to
Margate in plain clothes to play with a tot on the sands remains doubtful.
If not, why did Emma ask Mrs. Gibson to let him know where they were?
Let us hope he did, because he would have loved it.

Whatever happened, they were all at Merton on September 20. Nelson had certainly been in town, as he wrote Davison, "London seems absolutely deserted and so hot and stinking that it is truly detestable. . . . We
are fixt here till next year and it is not impossible but we may make a
northern visit . . ." presumably to include Davison's home in Northumberland. Poor Dods was dead and the house still not finished. He had

heard from his friend Abraham Gibbs in Naples that his manager of Bronte, Mr. Graefer, was also dead. "How short sighted we are." However, his affairs at Bronte were looking up, "rather more than £3,000 a year nett, and increasing every year in value. General Acton has taken possession of every thing for me and is behaving very friendly." Acton was behaving less friendly to Troubridge—Rome and Civita Vecchia had been given up in the peace and there was to be no prize money for them.

Emma added a note to the letter. "I am very sorry you are not near us to keep the Hero of Hero's Birthday the 29th but you will drink his health. . . . We have had a most Charming Tour which will Burst *some of them*, so let all the Enimies of the greatest man alive, and bless his friends."

Nelson's birthday party was a great event in Merton, and, because the editor Mr. Perry was invited, it was reported in the *Morning Chronicle*. Sir William gave a dinner to a select party, which included the Doctor and his family, their neighbors the banker Abraham Goldsmid and his family, and the Perrys. Afterward there was a concert: the Miss Goldsmids performed a concerto and several Italian singers from the opera displayed their talents. The apogee of the evening was Emma's singing.

> There is no voice in England which combines such uncommon volume and quality of tone with such richness of cultivation; and which receives from expression, gesture, and articulation such force of truth and feeling. In an Italian cantata composed by Bianchi, Lady Hamilton displayed the wonders of her talent. . . .

> *Then live, ever live, to our gratitude dear,*
> *The hope of our Navy! May Fortune endeavour*
> *His days and his friends to increase ev'ry year,*
> *And Nelson and Glory be coupled for ever.*

It appears that immediately after this event Sir William was allowed to have his way. "PATIENCE IN A PUNT!" headlined the *Times* of September 30. "Undaunted by the ridicule thrown on this inactive species of virtue, the HERO OF THE NILE sits, *die in diem* to witness the gudgeon fishing of Sir William and Lady H——. Sir William who is liberality itself, pays the boatman a Guinea a day for his exertions." The *Post* took up the story the next day: "Sir William and Lady Hamilton are at present daily engaged in a punt on the Thames about Kingston and Hampton, fishing for *gudgeons*; Lord Nelson being constantly at her *Ladyship's elbow*." There was, apparently, something very sexy about elbows. "The arm is naked," said the *Morning Post's* fashion correspondent, "to the shoulder and the more ruddy and athletic it appears, especially about the elbow, the more it excites admiration." Today the same thing could be said about knees.

A little quiet fishing on the cool river fringed with willows under a glorious September sky . . . and over the hill the white puffs of a paper war. The battle of the newspapers in the summer and autumn of 1802 was a unique event which contributed significantly to maintaining the hostility between France and England. The main protagonists were the *Moniteur* and the *Times*, but all the daily columns were employed, supported by the *tiraillerie* of pamphlets and caricatures. It began with the criticisms of Bonaparte that appeared regularly in the English papers after the peace.

"Bonaparte certainly is much offended with the freedom of the English press," stated the *Chronicle* of August 13. "He manages the press in France better; but, thank God, we are beyond the range of Fouche's jurisdiction."

The early answers of the First Consul were mildly contemptuous. "There is no taste in that country and that accounts for their disposition to abuse."

But before long the *Moniteur* took a big stick to its rival the *Times*. "Two of its four dull pages are every day employed in accrediting foul calumnies. Everything that the imagination can depict that is low, vile, and wicked, the miserable journal attributes to the French Government." And added for good measure, "The English Government does not deserve the name of Government, because it cannot repress calumny."

The miserable journal answered, "Let Bonaparte go before an English Jury in Westminster hall and prove the calumny—then will he obtain redress. Is this beneath him? The King of BRITAIN has sought and obtained redress in the same place for personal calumnies—and we trust no Corsican Consul, Egyptian Catholic, Turk or Mahometan will ever be placed above him!" Bonaparte's recognition of Allah in Egypt and God in Europe was always good for a jibe.

At the end of August the battle became one-sided as English papers were banned in France, but English readers could still see the more virulent passages from the French journals, translated and printed for them with suitable high-toned comments below.

The only other channel of communication between the two countries, because as yet there had been no exchange of ambassadors and no commercial intercourse, was the stream of British visitors to Paris. Society went to the palace of St. Cloud to be nodded at by Madame Bonaparte. Josephine was known as "the sovereign nodder." The result of one meeting, between the First Consul and Mr. Fox, the First Consul of England, was eagerly awaited. Fox was apparently quiet enough, but Bonaparte propounded his theory of European unity, the old demon of France that everyone ought to be French, which is still knocking around. The dictator told the demagogue:

> There were in the world but two nations, the one inhabits the East, the other the West. The English, French, Germans, Italians &c. under the same civil code, having the same manners, the same habits, and almost the same religion, are all members of the same family, and the men who wish to light again the flame of war among them, wish for civil war.

Unity is the very devil. In the name of unity Piedmont was formally annexed to France, and in unity with Russia the German principalities on the east banks of the Rhine were shuffled about to compensate the princes of the west bank dispossessed by France. For unity the revolution of Swiss patriots against the puppet government of the Helvetian Republic was crushed by France.

> *Forgive my Freedom! O forgive those dreams!*
> *I hear thy voice, I hear thy loud lament*
> *From black Helvetia's icy caverns sent . . .*

cried Coleridge. Switzerland, the cradle of liberty, became the grave of liberty. Bonaparte claimed to be the agent of Providence come to restore the Swiss to their true independence. All in the name of unity.

October was a quiet month—quiet, that is, except for the silent thunderings of the press. "I am really so very little in the world," Nelson told Davison on the 20th, "that I know little if anything beyond a newspaper." He had seen Mr. Addington and Lord St. Vincent several times. "We felt our importance in the scale of Europe degraded if Buonaparte was allowed to act as he has lately done and that it was necessary for us to speak a Disguised language, but when where and to whom all this was to be done I know no more than your Ploughman."

In spite of the Prime Minister's double-talk, or perhaps because of it, Nelson did not consider the situation between the two countries as serious. "I do not believe we shall have a war," he wrote the Doctor, "Neither France or this Country can wish for it and I think Buonaparte is too politick to risk his downfall which both Countries would then have an equal interest in accomplishing."

Others disagreed. The First Consul was making an ostentatious tour of the Channel ports and being greeted with patriotic speeches, just as Nelson was greeted on his tour. The Treaty of Amiens was already being reversed by Addington's administration, which, having dashed into peace, looked like dashing back into war. The *Morning Post* approved: "With the design of resisting the ambitious strides of France, dispatches have been sent to the Mediterranean to retain everything in our possession, and to put our forces on the best footing." The *Chronicle* accused France of aiming at universal domination: "To give up Malta is to surrender to France." Being a reasonable paper, it added, "Upon the strict letter of the Treaty of Amiens we do not see that France has given any ground for war. Indeed, every stipulation in that Treaty being favourable to her, it is not easy to see that she should have violated them."

Between one day's papers and the next, there was little enough to disturb the autumn at Merton. Sir William went fishing, he hauled sixty pounds of assorted catches home one day. Emma was busy with Charlotte and Horace. Nelson was anxious to complete the purchase of Axe's fields, to start turning them into his park.

Nelson had another worry. He had been to the doctors about his eye. He wrote Dr. Moseley, an old friend, on October 26, "I shall be in Town in a few days, and will endeavour to see you. I agree with you that (if the operation is necessary) the sooner it is done the better. The probable risk is for your suggestion; I cannot spare very well another eye." Nelson's one eye, his one good eye, was, said Captain Bowen to Emma, "the Brightest jewel in the Crown." What was wrong with his eye is difficult to say; one modern expert has said "bilateral pterygia" which might mean something; Nelson just said that his sight was failing.

November began with a blast from the *Moniteur*. The General dismissed European unity as quickly as he had called it up.

> Great Britain has no right and shall have no right to interfere in the concerns of the Continent; her only relations with France shall be the Treaty of Amiens, *the whole Treaty and nothing but the Treaty of Amiens*. Nothing shall be obtained from France by menacing proceedings: France will remain in the attitude in which the Athenians placed Minerva—*her helmet on her head and her lance in her hand*.

This was followed by the unexpected arrival of a French Ambassador, General Andréossi. The English Ambassador elect, Lord Whitworth, went posthaste to Paris. Mr. Addington was baffled by the hostile pronouncement followed by the pacific gesture and doubtless it was intended he should be so. Andréossi's arrival was at once followed by a second blast from the *Moniteur*, concerned with the impossibility of dimming the star of the French people, and reports of a great armament preparing in Toulon. This in turn was followed by the news that, on the occasion of the death of the infant King of Etruria, the Italian provinces of Parma, Piacenza and Guastalla had been annexed to France. Professions of peace and acts of aggression were the two pillars of Bonaparte's policy.

The confusion in the political atmosphere had an unhappy echo in the domestic life at Merton. The quiet of the previous weeks was broken. Lord Nelson was required in town, he was to speak in the next session of Parliament in the address to the Throne and on a bill to inquire into abuses in the navy. Lord Nelson's friends came to Merton for dinner, naval officers, politicians, new faces to the old gentleman at the other end of the table. The costs were running out of control. The carriage was never there. Lady Hamilton was always busy with other people's greatcoats, or the girl Charlotte and her scales and singing lessons, or young Horace and his dog. . . . Sir William sat down to write his wife another letter.

> I have passed the last 40 years of my life in the hurry and bustle that must necessarily be attendant on a publick character. I am arrived at the age when some repose is realy necessary, and I promised myself a quiet home, and although I was sensible, and said so when I married, that I should be superannuated when my wife would be in her full beauty and vigour of youth. That time is arrived, and we must make the best of it for the comfort of both parties. Unfortunately our tastes as to the manner of living are very different. I by no means wish to live in solitary retreat, but to have seldom less than 12 or 14 at table, and those varying continually, is coming back to what was become so irksome to me in Italy during the latter years of my residence in that Country. I have no connections out of my own family. I have no complaint to make, but I feel that the whole attention of my wife is given to Lord Nelson and his interest at Merton. I well know the purity of Lord Nelson's friendship for Emma and me, and I know how very uncomfortable it would make his Lordship, our best friend, if a separation should take place, and am therefore determined to do all in my power to prevent such an extremity, which would be *essentially detrimental* to all parties, but would be more sensibly felt by our dear friend than by us. Provided that our expences in housekeeping do not encrease beyond measure (of which I must own I see some danger) I am willing to go on upon our present

footing; but as I cannot expect to live many years, every moment to me is precious, and I hope I may be allowed sometimes to be my own master, and pass my time according to my own inclination, either by going my fishing parties to the Thames, or by going to London to attend the Museum, R.Society, the Tuesday Club and Auctions of pictures. I mean to have a light Chariot or post Chaise by the month, that I may make use of it in London and run backwards and forwards to Merton or to Shepperton &c. This is my plan, and we might go on very well, but I am fully determined not to have more of the very silly altercations that happen but too often between us and embitter the present moment exceedingly. If realy we cannot live comfortably together, a *wise* and well *concerted separation* is preferable; but I think, considering the probability of my not troubling any party long in this world, the best for us all would be to bear those ills we have rather than flie to those we know not of. I have fairly stated what I have on my mind. There is no time for nonsense or trifling. I know and admire your talents and many excellent qualities, but I am not blind to your defects, and confess having many myself; therefore let us bear and forbear for God's sake.

On November 19 the *Herald* noted, "Sir William Hamilton sported an elegant new chariot on Wednesday last, for the first time." Doubtless he used it a great deal as the activities at Merton intensified.

Parliament reassembled on November 16. King George made a suitably baffled and baffling speech, which ended, "You will, I am persuaded, agree with me in thinking that it is incumbent upon us to adopt those means of security which are best calculated to afford the prospect of preserving to my subjects the blessings of peace." The same day a party of dissident soldiers led by Colonel Despard was discovered and arrested and later charged with high treason. They were accused of plotting to fire the old cannon on the Horse Guards to blow the King to pieces on his way to Parliament.

On Thursday the 18th Lady Hamilton breezed into town. From her letter to Mrs. Nelson we can see that Sir William had something to complain about.

Here we are come up to breakfast this morning. Horace is come with me and we have been out to buy a pair of Boots. He has got a pair big enough I was quite *determined on that*. Charlotte is not come as today she has 2 principal lessons. We went the other day to Mr. Young's in St. James Street to see Andreossi go to Court. Charlotte was admired and thought improved. Mr. and Mrs. Young come to Merton Saturday week and stay till Monday. My Cold is so bad I can *hardly speak*. Horace goes to school Sunday, he is got very well and in high spirits. Charlotte and I come to town Monday and Tuesday for my Lord and Sir William are obliged to be in town on business and we shall continue to have Viganoni and Mr. Ottwood. Monday my Lord dines with Lord Pelham *at my desire*. I think it right. *Tuesday* the *House* and between *you and I*, but do not mention it for you life, my Lord I believe is to second the address. Wednesday we return to Merton, dine at Mr. Lancaster's Thursday were there is to be a play performed. Mrs. Bianchi comes Friday after to stay a *fortnight* with us. Mr. Blake I shall have Monday and Tuesday in Town, he is today at Merton, so is Oliver, so Charlotte is kept pretty well to it, so she *must* be. Direct your letters to us in Piccadilly Monday and Tuesday. It is by express intreaty of A. and P. that *he* seconds the address. Say nothing about it as it may not yet take place. If he does, it is my earnest wish that he goes up with it to the King. Let them see that he does what is right when it is *necessary*—a set of ungratefull wretches. But how dreadfull is this villan Despard business. I hope the plot will be fully discovered and all of them brought to punishment. Horace is gone to buy tooth brushes &c. &c. Ever yours, love to the Doctor. . . .

When Horace came in he added a note. "I came to London this morning and my uncle has given me a new pair of boots they are very large."

In the middle of all this to do, there was a minor crisis about little Horatia Thompson. Nelson himself wrote to Mrs. Gibson on the 19th, "Mrs. Gibson is desired on no consideration to answer any questions about Miss Thompson nor who placed her with Mrs. G. as ill tempered people have talked Lies about the Child." On the 22nd Emma summoned Mrs. G. to come to Piccadilly alone the next day. It is to be assumed that some gossip about Horatia had got back to Merton, but nothing was made public and the Grub Street gentlemen were not usually reticent about these affairs.

Nelson's speech in the Lords on November 23 was important enough to be covered in the newspapers outside the normal Parliamentary report. "No man was more for peace than he was," paraphrased the *Chronicle*, "it was to obtain it he fought, and the enjoyment of it constituted the chief part of his happiness. But he deprecated having it on dishonourable terms; and it was purchased at too high a price with a particle of our honour." He continued in general terms that, as the nation was sincere in wishing for peace, "so, now that a restless and unjust ambition in those with whom we desired sincere amity has given a new alarm, the country will rather prompt the Government to assert its honour, than need to be roused to such measures of vigorous defence as the exigency of the times may require."

Here is Sheridan, a few days later in the Commons, on the same subject.

> I think an important lesson is to be learnt from the conduct of Bonaparte. He tells us that he is an instrument in the hands of Providence, an Envoy of God. He says that he is an instrument in the hands of Providence to restore Switzerland to happiness and to elevate Italy to splendour and importance. I think he is an instrument in the hands of Providence to make the English love their Constitution better; to cling to it with more fondness; to hang round it with true affection. Every man feels, when he returns from France, that he is coming from a dungeon to enjoy the light and life of British independence! Sir, whatever abuses exist, we shall still look with pride and pleasure upon the substantial blessings we still enjoy. I believe too, that this man is an instrument also to make us more liberal in our political differences, and to render us determined with one hand and heart to oppose any aggression that may be made upon us. If that aggression be made, we ought to meet it with a spirit worthy of these Islands; we ought to meet it with a conviction that Britain, which has achieved such greatness, has no retreat in littleness; that if we could be content to abandon everything, we should find nothing but contempt in poverty; no security in abject submission. Finally, Sir, that we ought to meet it with fixed determination, to perish in the same grave with the honour and independence of our Country.

While Nelson was engaged in Parliament and at Court, a judgment was reached in his case against Lord St. Vincent. It was indecisive, as the judges were divided, two for and two against him. To save the expense of a new trial, and to allow for an appeal, his counsel prayed for a *pro forma* judgment against him, and this was given. The appeal was duly lodged.

On December 21 Thos. Coutts & Co. wrote to Lady Hamilton, "Madam—Agreeable to your Ladyship's desire we have the Honor to acquaint you that the present balance of your money in our hands is twelve shillings and elevenpence."

Sir William sent the note to Charles Greville with his comments.

> My Lady having left this letter on her Toilet, I supposed necessities were pressing and I have given her an additional credit

on Coutts for £130—so that of the £700 wanting to clear all, having had £120 before, I am to pay £450, if I am not soon paid by the Treasury I am determined to apply to Mr. Addington myself, it is most shameful.

I am returning today to dinner at Merton. I attended the Council yesterday at R.S. Sir Joseph came but was too ill to come upstairs. I went down to him and was glad that I had it in my power to assist him, so I took the Chair at Council and in the Evening. I think of going on Sunday to stay a day or two at Windsor to have an opportunity of wishing their Majesties a merry Xmas. PS. Do see what you can do with Vansittart but surely I will not tamely submit to be robbed by the Treasury much longer.

So Emma already had debts of £700 on her own account over and above the expenses of Piccadilly and Merton. That was a portent of the future. Sir William was hardly generous, but perhaps he reckoned that the more he gave her the more she would spend.

Nelson appeared that day in the House of Lords and made a long speech on the abuses practiced by prize agents to deprive sailors, "from the highest admiral in the service to the poorest cabin-boy that walks the street," of their rewards. The Bill for a Commission of Enquiry, instituted by St. Vincent, was passed. It was to have a very surprising effect on the next First Lord, though cabin boys continued to walk the streets.

Christmas was coming and there was a house party at Merton hardly conducive to Sir William's desire for peace and quiet. Nelson was still arguing with Matcham over the terms of the loan, which he considered too generous. In order to raise £4,000, Matcham had sold stock worth nearly £6,000, and Nelson insisted on making the larger sum the amount on which interest was to be paid. He wrote about this on the 23rd, and Emma added her bit.

Here we are as happy as kings and much more so. We have 3 Boltons, 2 Nelsons, and only want 2 or 3 little Matchams to be quite *en famille*, happy and comfortable, for the greatest of all *joys* to our excellent Nelson is when he has his sisters or their children with him, for sure no brother was ever so much attached as he is. . . . Our Hero was most *graciously* and particularly secured by her Majesty when he went with Sir William to the Drawing Room. Sir Wm. who is often in private with the Royal Family as had opertunity of letting them know many truths concerning our incomparable Nelson—don't you think he speaks like an angel in the House of Lords. As he must and *shall* go to Court the Birth Day to pay his *devoirs* to her Majesty, we shall go for a month to Piccadilly *near that time.* Lady Mansfield as promised me to take charge of him and Sir Wm. that day and get them near the K and Q with out Crowd—on this condition he goes he says, but don't you think it right. I love him, adore him, his Virtues, his Heart, mind, soul, courage, all merit to be adored and every thing that concerns his Honner, Glory and happiness will ever be dear to his and yours, my dear Mrs. Matcham, ever affectionate friend, Emma Hamilton.

The Tysons joined the party for Christmas and if she drank and talked too much, let us hope that, for Sir William's sake, *he* tipped her the wink.

The year ended with the adjournment of Parliament, to the delight of the *Moniteur.* The opponents of the peace—Grenville, Windham, Minto, and Henry Dundas, now Lord Melville—were the targets of Bonaparte's anger. Their voices had spoken in criticism of the General.

"Our voice," shouted the *Moniteur,* "shall still be *peace, peace,* nothing but *peace* can make Europe, and especially England, happy. It would be a wise and beneficent law to ordain that no Ministers should be capable of sitting in the British Parliament for the first seven years after their dismissal out of office. Another highly wise law would be that which should condemn to Paltry silence for the space of two years, any Member whose voice should insult a people, or power, with whom the nation was in amity." With growing hysteria, the paper accused the English of spreading their agents throughout Europe, and of sending parties of assassins in fishing boats from Jersey to the French coast to murder helpless women and unarmed husbandmen. War was coming closer.

Early in the new year there came news of Fanny. In a letter from George Matcham on January 9 there was this: "Lady Nelson, we understand, has taken a house at Clifton. She called upon us, Mrs. Matcham was at home. She did not come in nor make the least inquiry about us, but left a card and rolled off as she came in Lord Hood's carriage and four. We should have told her, as we have always declared, it is our maxim if possible to be at peace with all the world."

Nelson replied, *"What upstart Pride may do is not worth consideration except return the Card from whence it came."* Emma added, *"As to that fool's impudence I would do as milord says, send her card back,* a nasty vulgar bad hearted wretch. God bless you."

The whole party at Merton were well, there had been a little ball for Charlotte, and the children had all behaved themselves, and Sir William was getting his appetite back. The Knight attended the Queen's Birthday Drawing Room on his own. Nelson stayed away and perhaps it was to avoid the possibility of finding himself in his wife's company.

The Hamiltons were in town again at the end of the month and Emma was noticed by the *Post*, watching the skaters in the park. "Among the fashionable, Lady Hamilton was much noticed at the Serpentine for the elegance of her dress and appearance. Her Ladyship was in plain white, with a rich white satin cloak, trimmed with ermine, and lined with amber."

The great event that month was the publication in the *Moniteur* of the 30th of Colonel Sebastiani's report of his tour through Egypt. Fears for the future had been somewhat allayed by the absence of news from the Continent in the bad weather, and the good news from Santo Domingo that the French troops were dying in their hundreds from fever, and among the dead was Bonaparte's brother-in-law, General Leclerc. Then came Sebastiani's report.

"It now appears evident," fluttered the *Post*, "that Sebastiani's mission is connected with the ultimate design of the French Government on the conquest and possession of Egypt." Very sinister.

"Not a fort escapes notice," the *Chronicle*'s man had read it, "a regular statement of the forces, means, resources, temper and disposition of the Country is given, and all this is followed up with the reflexion that *six thousand French troops would be sufficient to conquer the country*. It would scarce be possible not to infer from such a *secret* paper that a hostile attack was in contemplation. Does its publicity then alter the case and change the conclusion we ought to draw?" Yes. Bonaparte had a system. "The grand principle of that system is to alarm us, to keep us in perpetual uncertainty, to vex our spirits, to injure our manufactures, and depress our funds." Still sinister, but not if we keep our heads.

"The report of Colonel Sebastiani respecting Egypt is universally laughed at, even in the French capital," said the *Herald*, keeping its head. So this famous report, which is preserved in textbooks like a squashed fly, was dropped in the wastepaper basket a week after its publication, and was only brought out again when the English government wanted a reason for hanging on to Malta.

Sir William fell ill at the beginning of February. "Poor Sir William is rather delirious," Nelson wrote Davison on February 8. He was not physically confined, because on the 16th he was at a levee and in the evening Emma gave a grand concert, but on the 8th poor Sir William was rather delirious. He was 72, admitted to be a bit tottery, and there is not a note to be found from him that year. Would it be strange if his mind was wandering? But delirious is a hard word for the old philosopher, and no one else said another one about it.

In Davison's letter Nelson wrote about the prize money for Copenhagen, which was still not settled, his bad eyesight, and Despard's trial the day before where he had been called as a witness to the Colonel's character.

Nelson had not seen Despard since 1780, when they had both served in a disastrous expedition against the Spanish settlement in Nicaragua. However, his testimony had its effect and, though Despard was found guilty, the jury recommended him to mercy. That, however, was hardly to be expected where the source of mercy was the very head at which the plotters intended to point their cannon, and Despard and six others suffered the dreadful penalty for high treason at the New Prison, Horsemonger Lane, on February 21.

"Lady Hamilton had a grand concert a few evenings since in Piccadilly," wrote the *Post* on February 19. "About one hundred fashionable were present, many of whom were *amateurs*. Her Ladyship sang several bravura songs, and played very difficult concertos on the piano-forte, with such rapidity of execution, as not only astonished but electrified her auditors."

It was the swan song of the *tria juncta in uno*.

War was the word for March. It was in the bustle and disturbance of an approaching war that Sir William Hamilton declined and died. It would be too much to say that with him died an age; an age of elegance, of immorality, in which it was no sin to please oneself; an age of complacency called reason, when whatever was, was best; when the poor deserved to be poor and the rich to be richer; an age of amateurs, when one man might hold the sum of human knowledge in his head. It would be too much to say that, because some of the good things had already gone, and some of the bad flourished to become worse. However, manners were giving way to urgency, dinners were getting later and shorter, port was replacing claret on a gentleman's table, and, on the whole, life was becoming a more serious matter. It was not a bad time to go out, just before a war. War is a great changer.

What the devil the King was about nobody knew, least of all George III, but on Tuesday, March 8, he sent a message to Parliament. "His Majesty thinks it necessary to acquaint the House, that as very considerable Military Preparations are now carrying on in the Ports of France and Holland, His Majesty thinks it expedient to adopt measures of precaution for the safety of his Dominions."

This thoroughly belligerent message, a shot across the bows of France, was followed by a burst of activity in the dockyards and the calling out of the militia. Nelson, sitting in on the debate on the message, sent a note to Mr. Addington: "Whenever it is necessary I am *your* Admiral." And he was at the Admiralty with increasing frequency. The country, as unexpectedly as it had found itself at peace, found itself preparing for war.

Some clue as to the secret exchanges with France that presumably inspired the message appeared in the reports on March 14 of a conversation the British Ambassador, Lord Whitworth, had held with the First Consul a few days before in the salon at the Tuileries. Bonaparte had at first denied that there were any preparations going on and had asked, reasonably enough, why there should be. Then he had returned to the Ambassador and said loudly, "Inform your Court that if, on the receipt of your dispatches, orders are not issued for the immediate surrender of Malta, *then War is declared.*" He had come back again a few moments later and added, "My Lord, your Lady is indisposed. She may probably breathe her native air rather sooner than you or I expected."

So Malta was to be the *casus belli.* Addington's cabinet had already issued orders for the retention of Malta, Egypt and the Cape. They arrived too late for Egypt, which was evacuated, and for the Cape, which was reoccupied, but soon enough for the garrison on Malta to stay where it was. Yet in its blundering indecision, stumbling between the rotten wall of the treaty of Amiens and the rising buttresses of French aggrandizement, the Cabinet approved the election of a new Grand Master of the Order of St. John, who was by virtue of his office the legal ruler of Malta. The treaty obliged the Cabinet to order the evacuation of Malta. The unwillingness of the Cabinet to execute the unpopular terms of the treaty caused the retention of Malta. The steps of 10 Downing Street were too high for Mr. Addington, he tripped, and the country fell into war.

The demand for a change of administration came too late, and when it did come, it was for the old firm of Pitt & Co.

The King's message did not pass unnoticed in France. The answer came in an unusual way, printed in the *Hamburg Correspondenten* on March 30. Bonaparte, posing as the champion of Europe and of peace, chose the journal of a free and neutral state to publish his counterblast. He denied that there were any preparations. "From the sudden appearance of this message, people doubted whether it was the effect of treachery, of lunacy, or of weakness. In short, no rational motives remain to which it can be ascribed, except bad faith, except a sworn enmity to the French nation, except perfidy and the desire of openly breaking a solemn Treaty. . . . France will fight for the liberty of the nations of Europe, and for the sanctity of their treaties: and if the English Government wishes to render it a national war, it may easily happen that their naval power, now so formidable, might be unable to decide single-handed the fate of England and to insure her victory." The gauntlet had been dropped and was taken up.

"Thanks my dear Lady for your letter," Mrs. Bolton wrote Emma on March 22. "I am afraid all hopes of keeping our dear Brother with us is now over (Bonaparte must be severely punished for his *Insolence*). God preserve and restore him again to *us* in safety, then what a happy Party we shall all meet at Merton, may it be *soon* is my Prayer. I find by a letter from Captain Bolton Sir Wm. has taken a medicine which has made him better. This mild weather must be greatly in his favour. I sincerely hope he will be restored to you." Captain Bolton was the lady's nephew and was engaged to her daughter Catherine.

Sir William's recovery was short-lived. In a letter dated March 26 Nelson told Sir Edward Berry, "You will be truly sorry to hear that good Sir William is I fear very near his last breath, he is all but gone. You may readily conceive Lady Hamilton's and my feelings on such an occasion, indeed all London is interested." Berry had asked to join him in the event of war, but his captains, Hardy and Sutton, were already chosen. His flagship was to be the *Victory*, which was then lying in the Medway without ballast, beds or guns.

The news was the same on the 30th. "Dear Sir William is very very bad," Nelson wrote Mrs. Bolton. "He can't in my opinion get over it and I think it will happen very soon." Emma added, "I have only to say, dearest Mrs. Bolton, Sir W. was so ill yesterday he could not live we thought. Today he is better. I am worn out but ever your affectionate E.H."

They took the old gentleman to Piccadilly. In an affidavit made to support his claim to £7,000 of stock left by Sir William, Charles Greville stated that he had called to see his uncle on April 1. Mrs. Cadogan was asked to leave the room and they were alone. Greville took a chair close to the bed and heard Sir William say quite distinctly that he was to have the £7,000 in the three per cents. There were some other small bequests—a collection of stones which fitted into a ring was to go to the Princess Elizabeth; the Queen was to have a canister of old Havana snuff which had been a present from the King of Spain to the King of Naples; and the annuities to his four old servants were to be continued.

The Knight paused for a moment, "I am sure that you will do all that I have forgot or omitted for we always have thought alike. . . . I am so weak I am sure I cannot last many days, I hope it will not be protracted with encreased sufferings. Do you think it will?" Greville recalled, "I told him that the progress of the weakness and the little sustenance he took must satisfy him that his dissolution would be easy, and his mind be supported as it then was by the calm recollection of a Virtuous Life." "I hope so, I know the weakness of Humanity. In health I meditated without finding limits to the Sublimity of Power, or to the Infinity of Goodness of the Almighty. In my weakness I dwell on it with encreased humility and resignation. I do not wish to see any Friend who is wiser or better than I am, and may be desirous to prepare me for death. You will not, I know, let them intrude, to disturb my Tranquillity."

"He desired me to seal up his keys, which he directed to me and I replaced them in his pocket. This was the last conversation with me alone. He lingered a few days and died without a groan."

It is difficult to say how much credit should be given to this testimony. It covers the £7,000 and the fact that no clergyman was brought to the deathbed. Was this the language of a dying man who was said to be delirious a month before? Or a carefully fabricated conversation to conceal the feebleness of the old man's mind? Heaven only knows. At least there was no hypocrisy in it and Sir William died as he had lived, without the help of the church.

"Our poor dear Sir William is no better today," Oliver wrote Mr. Matcham on April 2, "there is not the smallest hopes of his recovery. Dr. Moseley attends, my Lady and Mrs. Cadogan nurse him. He sees all his Relations. He feels no pain. There has been a Consultation of Phisicians all advice, human aid is now too late. He is going off as an Inch of Candle."

He lingered for four more days. Then there is a little sad note. "April 6th. Unhappy day for the forlorn Emma. Ten minutes past ten dear blessed Sir William left me."

Nelson also wrote a note, to Davison. "Wednesday, 11 o'clock, 6th April, 1803. Our Dear Sir William died at 10 minutes past Ten this morning in Lady Hamilton's and my arms, without a Sigh or a Struggle. Poor Lady Hamilton is as you may expect desolate. I hope she will be left properly but I doubt."

Tyson called that day and found the house in mourning. "I could not go upstairs nor indeed did I think it prudent, as your Lordship was out and her Ladyship in such deep distress." Nelson obviously could not continue living in the house and he moved to a nearby hotel. Mrs. Nelson was called to town to stay with Emma. No matter what we may call death, providential, glorious, peaceful, it is still an unutterable sadness. "I shall almost hate April," said Nelson.

Sir William's obituary was published in all the papers on the 7th. It was a remarkable compliment to a man who had spent all his life in pleasing himself.

> Sir William was a man of most extraordinary endowments, and his memory will be dear to the literary world by the indefatigable exertions which he made through life to add to our stock of knowledge, and of models in the fine arts. His whole life, indeed, was devoted to studies connected with the arts and he made every interest contribute to the passion of his soul. He was the foster brother of his present Majesty, which laid the foundation of that gracious attachment and friendship with which he was honoured by the King through the whole of his public service. By that immediate protection he procured the favourite appointment of Minister at the Court of Naples, which he enjoyed with the uninterrupted approbation of the two Courts for thirty-six years, and which he would not change for more lucrative situations: during all this time, we need not enumerate the zealous and successful efforts that he made in bringing to light the buried treasures of antiquity, and in promoting a just and correct taste in the arts, by making known in his works the specimens of the pure and chaste stile of the classic aera, that he had discovered. He was equally active and successful in the duties of his appointment. He maintained the most perfect harmony between the two Courts, at a period when it required all his influence and address to counteract the designs of those who had an interest in the breach of the amity that so happily subsisted. And the English Nobility and Gentry who travelled into Italy, speak with the warmest acknowledgements of the splendid hospitality with which he represented his Sovereign. About twelve years ago, he married Lady Hamilton, and never was union productive of more perfect felicity. The anxious solicitude, the unwearied attentions, the domestic duties, joined to the uncommon talents and accomplishments of Lady Hamilton, were the sources of the purest happiness to them both, as well as of delight to the circle in which they lived. Sir William derived from his lady, in his last illness, all the consolation of which life was susceptible, and he at length, without a struggle or sigh, breathed his last breath in her arms.

And the irony of it is that, had it not been for Nelson, few people would ever have heard of Sir William Hamilton.

On April 11 the funeral cortege left Piccadilly for Pembrokeshire, where Sir William was to lie by his first wife in Slebeck Church. Emma did not go, but kept the proprieties as she recognized them. She instructed Mrs. Gibson, "Horatia nor anybody can go out till after the funeral as we are very close and sincere mourners." Nelson wore black and canceled all but his official appointments.

The terms of the will were soon known; by April 18 they were public property and the subject of much discussion. Emma's immediate legacy had been increased to £800 by a codicil, and she was to have £800 a year from the estate that was known to produce £5,000 a year. Mrs. Cadogan's legacy was unchanged. Emma's outstanding debts of £450 were to be paid, hopefully, from the money owed Sir William by the Treasury. The rest went to Greville, apart from two guns at Merton which were for Nelson, and this: "The copy of Madame Le Brun's Picture of Emma in enamel by Bone I give to my dearest Friend Lord Nelson, Duke of Bronte, a very small token of the great regard I have for for his Lordship, the most virtuous, Loyal and truly Brave character I ever met with. God bless him and shame fall on those who do not say Amen."

The *Morning Herald* could not resist the opportunity. On April 29, "Lord Nelson has received his celebrated picture of *Emma* by Madame Le Brun, conformably to the Will of Sir William Hamilton: another beautiful piece is also said to have devolved on his Lordship, in consequence of the demise of that friendly Connoisseur!"

The *Herald* took great interest in the concerns of the late Sir William. Noting on April 19 that his pension ceased with his life, it reported, "Lady Hamilton, not having been left in independent circumstances, the Minister, it is said, means to recommend to His Majesty to grant a pension to her Ladyship," and added the next day, "It is said that a Naval Officer is soliciting a pension for Lady H——, but on what grounds has not been declared."

The claim for the continuation of part of Sir William's pension for his widow was pressed by both Nelson and Charles Greville. Emma herself wrote to Mr. Addington on April 13.

> Sir, May I trouble you for, and but for a moment, in consequence of my irreperable loss of my ever-honored Husband. Sir William Hamilton, being no more, I cannot avoid it. I am forced to petition for a portion of his pension, such a portion as in your wisdom and noble nature may be approved, and to be presented to our most Gracious Sovereign as being right. For, Sir, I am most sadly bereaved and I am now placed in circumstances far below those in which the goodness of my dear Sir William allowed me to move for so many years, and below those becoming the relict of

such a public minister, who was tried so very long (no less than 36 years) and all his life honored so very much by the constant friendly kindness of the King and Queen themselves. And may I mention what is well known to the then Administration at Home how I too strove to do all I could towards the Service of our King and Country. The Fleet itself, I can truly say, could not have got into Sicily but for which I was happily able to do with the Queen of Naples, and thro' her secret instructions so obtained, on which depended the refitting of the Fleet in Sicily and with that all which followed so gloriously at the Nile. These few words, tho' seemingly wrote at large, may not be extravagant at all, they are indeed True. I wish them to be heard only as they can be proved, and being proved may I hope for what I have now desired. Your &c. &c.

Mr. Addington was reported to be favorably disposed. Indeed, society thought she was hard done by. Lord Minto wrote on the 18th, "I have seen Lady Hamilton, who is worse off than I imagined, her jointure being £700 a year, and £100 to Mrs. Cadogan for her life. She told me that she had applied to Mr. Addington for a pension, and desired me to promote it in any way I could, and Lord Nelson coming in, made the same request. I promised to do so. She talked very freely of her situation with Nelson and of the construction the world may have put upon it; but protested that their attachment had been perfectly pure, which I declare I can believe, though I am sure it is of no consequence whether it is so or not. The shocking injury done to Lady Nelson is not made less or greater by anything that may or not have occurred between him and Lady Hamilton."

That was the problem and there was Fanny, in town at 54 Welbeck Street and often in the drawing room calling herself Duchess of Bronte, as a perpetual reminder of it.

Emma was in mourning.

"How her Ladyship will manage to live with the Hero of the Nile now, I am at a loss to know, at least in an honorable way," said Captain Hardy.

The problem hardly had time to arise. A month after Sir William's death, General Andréossi was asking for his passports and Lord Whitworth was packing in Paris. Early in May Mr. Addington's government, with all the belligerence of which a group of stupid men are capable when they know they are in the wrong, sent an ultimatum to the First Consul and demanded his submission to its terms within a week. French troops were to evacuate Holland, the Swiss were to be allowed to choose their own government, and Great Britain was to keep Malta until its independence was properly secured. Bonaparte agreed at once to the first two conditions. He had no wish for a war when he was gaining everything from peace. The third condition he could not accept, because it contravened the treaty of Amiens, which gave his rule legality throughout Europe.

This was enough for Mr. Addington, who had accepted the treaty, and been encumbered with the treaty, and longed to be rid of the treaty. On May 16 it was reported that the Channel fleet was at sea. Lord Nelson was appointed Commander in Chief of the Mediterranean fleet and would be leaving town at once. Letters of marque were issued allowing for the seizure of enemy shipping. The *Morning Post* of May 18 buried the peace. "Any hopes of peace that remain must vanish before the London *Gazette* of last night, which contains the Order of Council for issuing Letters of Marque and Reprisal, the only declaration of war this Country ever makes."

The last few weeks of Nelson's stay in England were crammed with events which hid the death of his friend, though he certainly took his opportunities of consoling his friend's widow. Apart from this *affaire*, which was as intimate as ever, he was bedeviled with the affairs of other people.

There was the affair of Captain Macnamara, an old acquaintance, who had killed a gentleman in a duel over whose Newfoundland dog had attacked the other. Nelson was called as a witness to the Captain's character in his trial on April 22. In England, a gentleman could kill another over a dog, as was shown when the jury ignored the judge's directions to bring in a verdict of manslaughter and pronounced the Captain not guilty.

There was the affair of Alexander Davison, which was more serious as far as Nelson was concerned. In the general election of July 1802 Davison had stood for the borough of Ilchester against Sir William Manners. Stood is really the wrong word: to use the contemporary expression, he had been mugged into an attempt to bribe his way into the seat. The villain, whose name was Mr. White Parsons, had offered to arrange Davison's election for the sum of £500 for himself and £30 for each of the 150 or so voters. "No man," said Mr. White Parsons, "had ever been known to go against the money." Davison had agreed, paid up, and promised Mr. W.P. a dinner with Lord Nelson to celebrate the victory.

It was not long before Mr. W.P. was back again. Sir William Manners was the local landlord and might, if defeated, evict the voters responsible. Now, if Mr. Davison was to build thirty or forty houses at Ilchester . . . quite by chance Mr. W.P. had half an acre of land which he would give away for £400, and there was another half an acre for another £400, and luckily the local builder was his wife's cousin and would do the job quickly and cheaply . . . why, Mr. Davison could look on it as a good investment.

Mr. Davison did. The houses were built and were promptly christened "Davison's Folly." By this time Sir William Manners and his friends were taking a keen interest in what was going on. So keen that Davison became worried and tried to give up Ilchester and White Parsons altogether. It was too late. He was charged with bribery and brought to trial at the bar of the House of Commons on May 18, 1803.

Now Davison had friends too, and at the head of them was Lord Moira, an ambitious politician and profligate companion of the Prince of Wales. Part of the price of Lord Moira's support was Lord Nelson's proxy in the House of Lords. As the Prince's party was in opposition, Nelson's vote was used against those who placed him in his command and he later regretted it. Worst of all, the trial was delayed, Lord Moira and his friends got tired of waiting and left the House, there was a quick division and Davison was done for.

Moira's letter to Nelson on May 19, when the Admiral was about to cast off from England, is a nice comment on the politics of the day. "The decision of the question last night against our Friend Davison frets me more than I can express. Not so much from apprehension of any inconvenient consequence to him, as from the knowledge that it will wound him, do not, however, let him be cast down at it, because there is nothing discreditable in the imputation of that which every Member of the House of Commons is known to have done."

There was an inconvenient consequence, most inconvenient, and Davison was eventually committed to the confines of the King's Bench for a year.

Apart from these distractions, Nelson's time was filled with his own affairs, public and private.

On May 6 he heard from St. Vincent. "As far as I am able to judge, your Lordship will be called upon in a very short space of time, and I think you may, without much risk of disappointment or loss, commence your preparations." "I have had my Tradesmen and ordered my things," he replied. "I am going to Merton in the morning to settle my matters there. Government cannot be more anxious for my departure than I am if a War to go and I trust to return in Peace."

Servants, wine, sheep, poultry, hay, groceries, furniture, crockery, everything for a gentleman's drawing room and kitchen, had to be carried down to Portsmouth where the *Victory* now lay. Then a doubt arose whether or not he was to have the *Victory*; and he had to come up to give evidence at the Committee of Naval Enquiry; and then there was the impending ceremony of Installation of Knights of the Bath that was to take place on May 19, and if Nelson could not be there he must have a proxy, and the proxy would have the honor of being knighted, and Nelson chose Davison, and nobody was going to knight him!

And as if this was not enough, there was some very important private business to be settled. On May 10 Nelson made a new will. On May 13 he and Emma took little Horatia to Marylebone Church, the old church and the one where she had married Sir William, to be baptized. "To give the Clergyman a double Fee and the same to the Clerk," Emma wrote to the Clerk, "the Register of the Baptism to be taken out." But it was not taken out and it is still there. "May 13, Horatia Nelson Thompson, B. 29 October 1800." The new birthday was invented to support the proposition that Nelson had acquired his godchild before his arrival in England. Emma passed the new information on to the nurse. "Horatia Nelson Tompson. Born October 29th 1800. Father and mother being dead are unknown to Mrs. Gibson." So the little girl got a name and her parents became her godparents.

The last of this private business was contained in a note to Davison on May 17. "I beg that you will have the goodness to Pay on my account to Emma Lady Hamilton the Sum of One Hundred Pounds on the first day of every month till further orders, the first payment to be made on the first day of June next 1803."

Nelson obtained his commission as Commander in Chief of the Mediterranean on the 16th. Early in the morning of the . . . the Installation! "A very unpleasant thing has happened that you cannot be my Proxy," he wrote Davison, "the King insists on my naming a Naval Officer." Which naval officer? They are all at sea. Oh no, here is Captain William Bolton, in town for his wedding to his cousin. Nelson had no great opinion of him, but he had to do. Early in the morning . . . Mr. Addington had at last agreed and the Doctor was to be a Prebendary of Canterbury—thank heavens! Early in . . . the Prince of Wales had called, but never mind. At 4 A.M. on Wednesday, May 18, Lord Nelson left town and, with his friend Davison for company, went on his way to Portsmouth.

"You will believe," he wrote Emma on the 20th, "that although I am glad to leave that horrid place Portsmouth, yet the being afloat makes me now feel that we do not tread the same element. I feel from my soul that God is good, and in His due wisdom will unite us, only when you look upon our dear Child call to your remembrance all you think that I would say was I present, and be assured that I am thinking of you every moment. My heart is full to bursting. May God Almighty bless and protect you."

CHAPTER THIRTEEN

Emma and the French Fleet

THE *tria juncta in uno* was dissolved. Sir William was in his grave. Nelson was in the *Victory*. Emma was in London. Nelson and Emma were to meet once more, for twenty-five days in the summer of 1805. From the day of their first meeting they were actually together for only three years and nine months, and Sir William was with them for all but two months of that time.

Nelson left England in hopes of a short and profitable campaign. He was going as Commander in Chief on a station where he might expect to make his fortune. He went to war with a fine touch of gallantry. "Believe me, my dear Emma, although the call of honour separates us, yet my heart is so entirely yours and with you, that I cannot be faint hearted, carrying none with me."

Emma stayed, more matronly than ever, the hero's accepted consort, once again pregnant, in debt, in short, just like Britannia.

Debt was the most pressing circumstance. Charles Greville was his uncle's executor and her friendship with him was broken by their new relationship. Sir William had left a fine estate and Emma was to have her £800 down and £800 a year; and the furniture in Piccadilly was hers by the deed of gift executed after she had bought it with her diamonds. However, he had also left debts to a total, said Greville, of £5,500: and he left Emma's debts to the Treasury: and wine merchants and linen drapers, butchers, bakers and candlestick makers, were as clamorous to be paid then as their descendants are today: and they all knew that nobody ever got anything out of the Treasury unless they or their friends were in it. Greville was forced to sell out the stocks he had taken such pains to acquire in order to satisfy the creditors. This made him unhappy.

At the same time, he was demanding those of his uncle's possessions which were not part of the furnishings at Piccadilly; his pictures, which Greville took from the walls, his books, his fishing rods, and telescope from Merton. He was also agitating for the lease of the house in Piccadilly to be given up to be sold by Mr. Christie as soon as possible. This made Emma unhappy and led to her putting her affairs into the hands of Mr. Booth of Booth & Haslewood. Then there was the question of income tax, which made everyone unhappy.

In the first week of June Emma went off to stay with Mrs. Nelson at Hilborough. She left her mother at Merton, Oliver in London to look for another house for her, and nothing settled as it ought to have been. Her insistence on keeping up two establishments was guaranteed to ensure that nothing ever would be settled, for no sooner was one bill met than another was presented.

Nelson was never out of debt from the moment he bought Merton. While he was on shore, his income, which was made up of his pensions for the Nile and the loss of his arm and eye, and his half-pay, was £3,418 a year. His outgoings, the allowances to Lady Nelson, Old Blindy, and Horace at Eton, and the interest on his borrowings, were £2,650 a year. He was left with £768 a year to live on. At sea he was on full pay, about another £450. As he had already arranged for Emma to be given £100 a month, it is apparent that he had budgeted to the last penny. The mortgages on Merton and the Axe estate totaled £10,000.

Emma went into Norfolk, wearing black for Sir William. She was, very likely, accompanied by the Doctor and his wife, who were returning after the installation ceremony at Canterbury Cathedral. The Doctor was at last in his prebendal stall. He would browse the lush Canterbury pastures and munch his winter fodder, ruminating on his brother's next victory, which might reward him with a miter. Emma went into Norfolk, in her double widowhood, to quiet warm days in a country parsonage. She was indifferent, "but *Dispatches* and Sea Breezes will surely restore you," said sister Bolton. They were brothers and sisters now, and Nelson passed as surely into her possession as if the Reverend Doctor had married them himself.

The dispatches came with the postboy's shout and in the unmistakable backward scrawl of the hero, as if a line of ships was beating against the wind across the page.

He had taken a rich Dutch prize. He would return soon with honor and riches and they would live together to a good old age. She must tell Mrs. T. that his love was unbounded to her and her dear sweet child, "and if she should have more it will extend to all of them." He was close in to

342

Brest, looking for Admiral Cornwallis to offer him the *Victory*, but the Admiral was away and he was losing the wind to the Mediterranean. He was leaving the *Victory* and going into the frigate *Amphion* to catch the wind, but now the wind was foul and he did not reach Gibraltar until June 3. "I am much hurried for they know nothing of the war."

He was at Malta on the 15th, calling on the Governor Sir Alexander Ball. Then he was off Capri and exchanging letters with Acton and King Ferdinand: "The King is very low, lives mostly at Belvedere." He had written to the Queen, "Your Majesty never had a more sincere attatched and real friend than your dear Emma. You will be sorry to hear that good Sir William did not leave her in such comfortable circumstances as his fortune would have allowed." Maria Carolina had returned "a Political letter" without a mention of her friend. "If she can forget Emma I hope God will forget her."

Hugh Elliot was now British Minister at Naples and, to redress the balance, there were 13,000 French soldiers in the Adriatic provinces. Gaetano, who had been home, returned. The Palazzo Sessa was a hotel. The Admiral left a ship in the bay for an emergency and sailed to join the fleet off Toulon.

July 8 and he was there. "I hope they will come out and let us settle the matter, you know I hate being kept in suspence." The business of his command was immense and manifold, from the ever-present problem of obtaining beef and onions for 5,000 men to occasional charades; like the affair of the Consul at Algiers who was expelled when two Moorish women were discovered in his house, and that of the Naval Hospital at Gibraltar where the surgeon was accused of having criminal intercourse with the nurses, and the patients said the matron was more like a boatswain's mate than a matron.

And every day he thought of Emma.

> I sincerely hope that Mr. Booth has settled all your accounts. Never mind, my Dear Emma, a few hundred pounds, which is all the rigid gripe of the Law not Justice can wrest from you, I thank God that you cannot want, (although that is no good reason for its being taken from you). Whilst I have 6 pence you shall not want for five pence of it, but you have brought your experience that there is no friendship in money concerns and your good sence will make you profit of it. I hope the Minister has done something for you, but never mind, we can live upon Bread and Cheese.

On August 1 the *Victory* arrived and he transferred to her and was "well mounted" with his steward Chevalier, and his two Scotts; his secretary John Scott, a treasure, and his chaplain the Reverend Alexander Scott, who was called the Doctor to distinguish him from the other and not because the poor man suffered mental aberrations, having been struck by lightning in the West Indies. Hardy was hanging up the pictures of Emma and Horatia in the Admiral's cabin. Nelson had Emma's first letter, "although you said little I understood a great deal and most heartily approve of your plan and Society for next Winter, and next Spring I hope to be rich enough to begin the alterations at Dear Merton; it will serve to amuse you and I am sure that I shall admire all your alterations, even to planting a gooseberry bush." Society meant Nelson's relations. From Hilborough the party went to find the sea breezes at Southend. Emma in the company of a clergyman was a great joke. Giggled the *Morning Herald* of August 18, "The Rev. Dr. Nelson expects a *dispensation* daily, to enable him to hold his domestic Chaplainship to Lady Hamilton, with his prebend stall, which gives rise to some extraordinary *Canterbury Tales!*"

Southend was a newly fashionable resort where the bathing was famous. It was a favorite place of the Cockneys and their "slapbangs," the fine strapping London girls who filled the streets of the city with their brats, but culture, in the form of a tea garden and Mr. Trotter's theater, was creeping in. The Cockneys have stayed true to Southend, though culture, unnoticed, crept out.

"I hear the Sea Air and amusements of the Watering Machines have contributed very much to restore my Lady Hamilton's health and spirits," Davison wrote Nelson, "the Doctor and Mrs. Nelson have benefited wonderfully."

Davison, in spite of the doom hanging over him, was now a partner in a respectable banking firm, "so much for sheer integrity," and was busy raising his own volunteer corps. There were to be 2,000 men in his regiment, the uniforms were to cost three guineas each, and they had the brave title of "The Loyal Britons." "Soldiering and the lottery," said the *Morning Chronicle*, "engross almost the whole of the public mind."

At the beginning of the war, which, as we have seen, was announced by the capture of every Dutch and French vessel unlucky enough to fall in the way of a sea captain out to make his fortune, the French had retaliated by arresting every Englishman between the ages of eighteen and sixty then traveling in France. This outrage was followed by the French invasion of Hanover and the buildup of their forces in the Channel ports for the proposed invasion of England. Ladies in their bathing machines on the Kent and Essex coasts shuddered delicately in anticipation of the sort of atrocities that were being perpetrated just across the sea.

"The French soldiers have the most unbounded indulgence of their ruling passions, of rapacity, cruelty, and lust," reported the *Gentleman's Magazine*. "In the city of Hanover, and even in the public streets, women of the highest rank have been violated by the lowest of that brutal soldiery, in the presence of their husbands and fathers, and subjected at the same time, to such additional and indescribable outrages, as the savage fury of their violators inflamed by drunkenness could contrive."

The response in England was immediate and impressive. Kemble appeared in *Henry* V at the Haymarket Theatre; gentlemen joined volunteer regiments and formed squares as eagerly as they had previously formed quadrilles; honest workmen volunteered to put on a uniform and drink a pot of porter once a week, though it was uncharitably said that most volunteered to avoid being drafted into the militia; pikes were issued from the Tower and innkeepers and coachmakers promised to provide horses for the cavalry when the invasion came; uniforms were the rage, and the assemblies were glorious with the gentlemen all in red and the ladies all in white; the final flush of patriotism came when the ladies adopted a new fashion and gave their appearances the military flash of red stockings.

That summer Bonaparte toured the Channel coast. "A Providential Christ is come," said the Archbishop of Rouen. "God created Bonaparte and rested from his labours," said the Prefect of Calais. "Let England tremble!" said Bonaparte. England went to the seaside. Bond Street and St. James's Street were deserted but for the Duke of Queensberry and Colonel Hanger on their solitary perambulations in search of a pretty ankle.

There was very little of the serious business of war. The West Indian islands given up the year before were soon retaken. There was a premature uprising in Dublin, sparked off by the assassination of Lord Kilwarden and squashed out by the execution of a few dozen rebels. There were new taxes on nearly everything that moved—servants, carriages, carts, horses and hair powder—and on nearly everything that stood still—houses, windows, hats, armorial bearings, malt, sugar, coffee and tea. There was plenty of pluming, strutting and crowing, but no fighting.

September was lively with routs, balls and parties. "I suppose you have been engaged lately with your Fete on Miss Moseley's Birthday," Mrs. Bolton wrote to Emma, who was still at Southend. "I hope you was well enough to enjoy it as you always do when you are promoting other People's amusements." The children were going back to school and Mrs. Matcham had assured her that she was not expecting. The Matchams were going to

Denmark, and Oliver and Mr. Matcham were to set up as partners doing heavens knows what in Husum.

Emma was in town in October, rotating in fashionable circles around the node of her new house in Clarges Street. Propriety forbade in London what was permitted at the seaside, but passersby heard singing in Clarges Street and saw the shadows of attitudes upon the blinds.

News of the world came from Mrs. Denis.

> A curious circumstance happened yesterday. I want a cook for my little Inn on the Windsor Road, one comes and drops a curtesy with "Ma'am I was informed you wanted a cook." "Yes, where was your last place?" "I was on a job with Lady Nelson." I kept my countenance and ask questions about her health. She certainly has bad health and is obliged to live on mutton—mutton &c. &c. mutton. She said she was Emable and no more pride for she used to come into the kitchen and talk to her, and used to say she must be saving as her income was so small—at that I lost my mask and I flew into a rage—and she said that indeed Samuel the servant who lived with her and my Lord said he allowed her 2000 a year and that it was a shame for her to make such a poor mouth.

Mrs. Denis moved among the demimonde, where all worshiped, cheated, obliged, and pimped for that tarnished demigod the Prince of Wales. Madame Beaufrere had got a girl for him, "that unfortunate tripe Sally Brooks," but he had declared himself disgusted with her, "a broad flat face, narrow shoulders out of proportion, and no breasts." And who should be flirting with the Princess of Wales but Sir Sidney Smith! And Lord L. had thought that S.S.S. was in love with Emma! Whereas Mrs. D. had told Lord B. . . . and so on through the alphabet of light-headed peers and fashionable demireps.

Emma, to whom all this was quite delightful, put it in her letters to Nelson.

"I have not a thought except on you and the French fleet," the sailor wrote his love in August, "all my thoughts, plans and toils tend to those two objects, and I will embrace them both so close when I can lay hold of either one or the other, that the devil himself should not separate us. Don't laugh at my putting you and the French fleet together, but you cannot be separated." Rule Britannia.

He was sending home an order for £2,100 to pay off Mrs. Greaves's mortgage. "It is the first fruits of prize money, not much you will say, but I am not over fortunate in that respect." He was writing to an old acquaintance, Mr. Gibbs, about Bronte. It had cost him a fortune, favor and jealousy, "I did my duty to the sicilifying my own conscience." Graefer had been a bad manager, using three years' rents to build a farmhouse, no, a palace. Perhaps the King would buy the estate back? Or he might rent it for £2,000 a year, "that will be a pretty addition to our housekeeping."

Lord Bristol was dead. Lord and Bishop, he perished after a severe attack of gout at Albano near Rome. The greatest of English travelers, well, he was never at *home*, died at his post surrounded by artists. He cheated his tribe of sycophants with a last grand gesture, tearing up the will they had wheedled out of him. Nelson had the great corpse shipped to England with its treasures. To fool the seamen, Lord Bristol was crated up and labeled "Antique Statue." How he would have loved the compliment!

Nelson wrote again on August 26. He had received her letters written in May, "the next best thing to being with you. I only desire, my dearest Emma, that you will always believe that your own Nelson's *alpha* to *omega* is *Emma*." He was longing to meet her again at Merton and find "the new room built, the grounds laid out neatly but not expensively, new Piccadilly gates, kitchen garden &c. . . . and H. shall plant a tree."

She had given Mrs. Bolton £100. "Your purse, my dear Emma, will always be empty, your heart is generous beyond your means." He would help young Tom Bolton through college, but if only a vacancy would occur in his list of pensioners! and the one he meant was that filled by Fanny. He had written to the Duke, Emma had hopes of Old Q., "but I would not let him touch you for all his money, no that would never do."

Under cover of this letter there was one for Mrs. T., who was now so much part of their correspondence that Nelson wrote in the first and third person indiscriminately.

My Dearest beloved Mrs. T., to say that I think of you by day night and all day and all night, but too faintly expresses my feelings of love and affection towards you and our dear little girl, the first fruit of unbounded affection. Our dear excellent good Lady Hamilton is the only one who knows anything of the matter, and she has promised me, when you are in the straw again, to take every possible care of you as a proof of her never failing regard for your own dear Nelson. Believe me that I am incapable of wronging you in thought word or deed. No, not all the wealth of Peru could buy me for one moment. It is all yours and reserved wholly for you, and you will certainly be with child again from the first moment of our happy dear enchanting blessed meeting.

The thoughts of such happiness, my dearest only beloved,

makes the blood fly into my head. The call of our Country is a duty which you would deservedly in the cool moments of reflection reprobate was I to abandon, and I should feel so disgraced by seeing you ashamed of me, no longer saying, "This is the Man who has saved his Country, this is He who is the first to go forth to fight our battles and the last to return;" and then all these honours reflects on you, ah, they will think, what a Man—what sacrifices has he not made to secure our houses and propertys, even the society and happy union with the finest and most accomplished Woman in the World. As you love how must you feel, my heart is with you, cherish it. I shall, my best beloved, return if it pleases God a Victor, and it shall be my study to transmit an unsullied name. There is no desire of wealth, no ambition that could keep me from all my soul holds dear, no, it is to save my Country, My Wife in the Eye of God, and my children. Talk with dear good Lady Hamilton. She will tell you that it is all right, and then only think of our happy meeting. Ever for ever I am yours only yours even beyond this World, Nelson & Bronte. For ever for ever your own Nelson.

September—"buffeting the stormy Gulph of Lyons." By a codicil to his will on September 6, he left £4,000 to Horatia, the interest to be paid to Lady Hamilton until she was eighteen. "It would add comforts to my last moments to think that she would be educated in the paths of religion and virtue, and receive as far as she is capable, some of those brilliant accomplishments which so much adorn you."

He had not heard from the Admiralty for weeks and got his news from the French papers obtained from Spain and sometimes from France when the boats came out with provisions. He sent her £100 for presents for herself and her mother, Charlotte and the eldest Miss Connor, who was under Emma's wing. He had sent to Naples for some shawls and Venetian chains. John Scott had two chains from Venice for her, but only *he* must give her presents and he had bought them and sent them to her.

"I am sorry to say Lady Hamilton is very unwell with a stiff neck and headache. She has now a blister on her neck." Charlotte Nelson was writing to her mother on November 11 from Lady Hamilton's new house, 11 Clarges Street. The house was smaller than 23 Piccadilly, but it was not a *small* house and it was quite fashionable. Charlotte was being very well brought up. Davison, writing four days later, said Emma had blisters on her back and stomach.

Davison's news was dramatic. "Your great cause is decided in *your* favour and that too Unanimously—what a *Glorious day!!!*" This was the final judgment in the case against Lord St. Vincent. The lawyers left Nelson about £10,000. "This happy event will My Dear Friend relieve you of all your anxieties regarding pecuniary matters," wrote Davison later. It would have done, had not Mr. Matcham wanted his £4,000 back for his Denmark business, and there had been no new room at Merton and none of those improvements that cost more than building a new house! But it was good news and the Merton mortgages were paid off and the deeds were lodged with Emma.

Mrs. Nelson said that the Doctor had come jumping in with a letter in his hand to tell her of it. But how sorry she was that Emma was in bed and she was not there with her. "You should really take more care of yourself *for the sake of somebody.*"

The London house was full of visitors. The Bianchis were always in and out, Eliza and Ann Bolton came to stay for two or three days, fat Fatima Denis had called, Mr. Rose had dined with them, and General Dumouriez had come in the evening and read a French play out loud.

There was one regular visitor, whose arising from what everyone thought was his deathbed was greeted with wonder and wicked glee. Here is a handful of notices from the *Morning Herald* which, like a hand of good cards, are better together than apart.

November 19. "Yesterday the Duke of Queensberry paid a morning visit to Lady Hamilton in Clarges-street. His Grace's *convalescence* is no longer questionable."

December 17. "Mrs. Billington and Lady Hamilton are become a *duo of musical inseparables* and his Grace of Queensberry is admitted about three times a day at Clarges Street to make up a *terzatto con amore!*"

December 19. "The harmonies in a street in Piccadilly are classed in due variation to the taste of the several visitors. The approach of the amorous old Duke is generally welcomed with '*The wanton God who pierces hearts,*' but when a Reverend Dignitary of the Church appears the stop is divinely shifted to '*Pious orgies, devout prayers.*'"

December 27. "A certain venerable and sporting Peer has had a slight *relapse*, and no wonder when the nature of his disorder is understood. . . . His Grace on returning out of Clarges Street the other morning was heard to exclaim, 'an oyster may be crossed in love.'"

So numerous were the visits that winter that Emma felt obliged to issue a disclaimer. It appeared in the *Morning Post* of December 21. "We are desired to contradict a paragraph in one of the morning papers relative to Lady Hamilton giving concerts and parties. Her ladyship lives very retired, and she has been and still continues very unwell, and does not see any company, but a very few near relations." That was just before she went to Merton for a great party over Christmas.

What had happened to the invasion? The threat was ever present, reinforced by reports of preparations on both sides of the Channel. Bonaparte declared himself head of the Army of England, 100,000 men and an appropriate number of flat-bottomed boats. Mr. Pitt inspected the Broadstairs volunteers. Bonaparte put in an indent to heaven for three days' fog. All England offered a general fast for gales. The Bourbon princes appeared on parade when King George reviewed the volunteers in Hyde Park. Lieutenant Colonel Davison marched past with his Loyal Britons, all 127 of them. Bonaparte practiced climbing into a boat on the Seine. Bonaparte came to Boulogne in his portable house. Bonaparte made a special visit to Bayeux to look at the tapestry.

The Royal Theatre presented " 'The Army without Reserve, or the British Amazons.' In the course of which will be performed a Grand Military Dance by Female Volunteers in full uniform." The Prince of Wales protested that he was the oldest colonel in the army, and why could he not be a general? On December 24 there was a great storm and Admiral Cornwallis was blown off his station before Brest. The Prince's regiment was moved from Brighton to Guildford. The King's standard would be raised at Chelmsford. Now, surely, the invasion was coming? No? In a performance of *Cinderella* at Drury Lane they were singing,

> *O! what a farce is Invasion,*
> *And O! what a wonderful Farce.*

Emma had expressed a wish to come out to the Mediterranean. Nelson's letters were full of reasons why she should not. "You must let your own good sence have fair play," said he, echoing Sir William. If she came to Malta he would never see her, he would see her in Merton before he saw her in Malta. Sicily and Italy were in danger. As for joining the colors, "We have a hard gale every week, and two days heavy swell, it would kill you and myself to see you, much less impossible to have Charlotte, Horatia &c. on board Ship, and I that have given orders to carry no women to Sea in the *Victory* to be the first to break them."

He diverted her with plans for Merton, the new entrance, the drive through the plantation, the covered passage. This was in October. "You have sent me in that lock of beautiful hair a far richer present than any monarch in Europe could if he were so inclined. Your description of the dear angel makes me happy. . . ." Horatia wanted a watch, she was nearly three, he would send to Naples for one, "if it does but tick, and the chain *full* of trinkets, that is all which is wanted."

He was short with her friends.

> Mrs. D. is a damned pimping bitch what has she to do with your love. She would have pimpt for Ld. B. or Lord L. or Capt. Macnamara, Prince of Wales or anyone else, she is all vanity, fancies herself beautiful, witty, in short like you. She be damned. [So much for Mrs. Denis.] As for old Q. he may put you into his Will or scratch you out as he pleases, I care not, if Mr. Addington gives you the pension it is well, but do not let it fret you. Have you not Merton . . . and my dear Horatia is provided for, and I hope one of these days that you will be my own Duchess of Bronte and then a fig for them all.

> I am glad to find my Dear Emma that you mean to take Horatia home, *aye* she is like her mother, will have her own way or kick up a devil of a dust, but you will cure her. I am afraid I should spoil her for I am sure I would shoot any one that would hurt her. She was always fond of my watch and very probably I might have promised her one, indeed I gave her one that cost 6 pence.

> December 13th. Although I have not been ill, yet the constant anxiety I have experienced have shook my weak frame, and my rings will hardly keep upon my finger, and what grieves me more than all is that I can every month perceive a visible (if I may be allowed the expression) loss of sight. A few years must, as I have always predicted, render me blind. I have often heard that blind people are cheerful, but I think I shall take it to heart. However, if I am so fortunate as to gain a great Victory over the Enemy, the only favor I shall ask will be for permission to retire, and if the contrary, I sincerely pray that I may never live to see it. We must all have an end—but my Dearest Emma let us hope the best, my last thought will be for you and those we hold most dear, but I will have done this triste subject.

The fleet was anchored off the Maddalena Islands, waiting for the victualers to come up from Malta, and resting after six months of patrolling the stormy seas. Little Charles Connor had something wrong with his head and was seeing ghosts. "Was any of his family in that way?" Poor Dr. Scott, learned, religious and sickly, was at that moment abed not scarcely knowing anyone. "The watch spring came in the right time for the other was very rotten, and as it came from H. it is of more value to me than if it was covered with diamonds. She must be grown very much, how I long to hear her prattle."

He had written to H. on October 21, his first letter, and a very serious one. "I have left Dear Lady Hamilton your Guardian. I therefore charge you my Child on the value of a Father's blessing to be obedient and attentive to all her kind admonitions and instructions." Well, it would do for later if she kept it, and of course she kept it.

Christmas Day. "Off Toulon. Here we are and there (in Toulon) are the french."

While Nelson was locked in his wooden prison, tossed into seasickness, periodically stretched on the rack of expectation by reports of activity in Toulon, occupied each morning with paperwork, each afternoon with protracted dinners, each evening with Emma's pictures, and the only changes those in his barometer and the direction of the wind, Emma was spending the last weeks of her pregnancy in bed, in Merton and in town, surrounded by servants, Nelson's nieces, and visitors, fashionable ladies and demimondaines.

Emma's second child by Nelson was probably born in London in February, though it may have been earlier. Very little is known about the poor infant for, no sooner was she about to be born in a Nelson letter in January than she was no more in one in April. Of course, there was no word about it from the household in Clarges Street, and there was little difficulty in disposing of a tiny corpse at a time when there was an abundance of them.

The infant died, Emma was very ill and Horatia was ill, all at the same time.

On March 2 Emma received a great packet of letters from Nelson, the last one dated January 21. He had sent her, she told Mrs. Nelson, a beautiful watch, a comb, and other presents. "I have not been out these three weeks, so very ill I have been," she added.

Among the letters was one for Horatia written on January 13, 1804.

My Dear Horatia, I feel very much pleased by your kind letter and for your present of a lock of your beautiful hair. I am very glad to hear that you are so good and mind everything which your Governess and dear Lady Hamilton tell you. I send you a lock of my hair and a one pound note to buy a locket to put it in and I give you leave to wear it when you are dressed and behave well, and I send you another to buy some little thing for Mary and your Governess.

As I am sure that for the World you would not tell a Story, it must have slipt my memory that I promised you a Watch, therefore I have sent to Naples to get one and I will send it home as soon as it arrives. The Dog I never could have promised as we have no Dogs on board Ship. Only I beg my dear Horatia be obedient and you will ever be sure of the affection of, Nelson & Bronte.

Mary was little Mary Gibbs, who had lived with them at Palermo and who had been sent to England to be educated under Lady Hamilton's guardianship. Horatia's governess was the eldest Miss Connor.

Emma's watch was sent on January 20, and the comb the next day. In the accompanying letter Nelson wrote, "Kiss dear Horatia for me, and the other. Call him what you please, if a girl, Emma."

Very much later Horatia, with her watch before her, recorded, "It is a small French watch set around with pearls, a chain and seals attached. . . . He could not bear that I should have a dog as I should perhaps love it better than Lord Nelson, but that he sent me a gold chain with the medallion of a greyhound in the centre."

Hugh Elliot called Nelson's service "a Campaign of Protection," and it was a good description. While the fleet patrolled Toulon, with regular calls at the Maddalena Islands to take on water and provisions, ships policed the Adriatic, the North African coast, and the Straits of Gibraltar, guarding the trade from Algerian corsairs and French privateers. It was a wearing business. "What is man," the Admiral asked Lord Minto, "a child of the day." His physicians wanted to send him to Bristol to recoup his health. "Whatever happens I have run a glorious race." It was an unprofitable business. He welcomed the news that his case against St. Vincent was won, but, as he told Davison, his only prospect of fame and riches was in the sight of the French fleet at sea. Davison had gout: "You will never be able to run after Buonaparte."

Early in February it seemed as if his wish was to be granted. "We are on the eve of a battle," he wrote Emma from the Maddalenas, and, with concern for her situation, added, "I only hope our dearest friends are well and happily past *all* dangers." Brother William was told grimly, "You will have £2,000 a year with the Title and that will be very handsome and if you vote with the Minister you may be a Bishop." It was a false alarm.

In February Nelson finally reached an agreement over Bronte which promised to put him in better financial circumstances than he had ever known before. Gibbs and a Sicilian banker called Forcelli rented the estate for ten years for £3,200 a year, which, after taxes, would provide an income of £2,000 a year. Nelson's first thought was for Emma and by another codicil dated the 19th he left her £500 a year from Bronte. By Nelson's will of May 10, 1803, Emma was to receive only his diamond star and a silver cup which she had given him: the three codicils we have seen added the house and grounds at Merton, but not the Axe estate, the interest on Horatia's £4,000, and this £500 a year. The main provision of the original will was of a pension of £1,000 a year for Lady Nelson, which was to cease, however, if she was granted a government pension equal to that sum. His titles, pension, and awards, were to descend in the male line of his family.

In London people were behaving much in the way we have come to expect them to behave. King George was getting better. He had been getting better since he was reported ill with a dropsical fever in the middle of February. Every day the bulletins said he was getting better until they destroyed the very hopes they were supposed to raise up. "The distraction of a country without a King and left in the hands of Mr. Addington was a subject well calculated to inspire exultation in every French heart," said the *Chronicle*.

Emma was petitioning for her pension with the advice of Mr. Rose. "In your situation the attempt (however hopeless) is worth making," he told her, "if it does not succeed now it never will." It did not. Her interest in herself was soon lost in anxiety for her love. "*Secret* and private to everybody. His letter is the 10th February," she wrote to Canterbury. This was his "eve of battle" letter. "Now my friend judge of my feelings, of my anxiety—our children are well, the Ball with Miss Scott is tomorrow . . ." and she went on to tell of the entertainments planned for the week, "but my Heart is bursting with anxiety about my Nelson."

Emma had only recently recovered from her illness and the emotional disorder following the death of her child. Horatia had just got over some childish ailment. Yet her activity is remarkable, her energy, and she was pushing forty, unabated. She was coming out of her period of mourning for Sir William and into the season of balls, routs and assemblies in which society exhausted itself before disappearing into the country for the summer. Here she is to Dr. Nelson on March 28.

> My dear Doctor, Thank you for your letter. We shall soon be with you and I long I do assure you to give you a kiss. We are to be at Goldsmid's great fete the 10th given on purpose, the 11th we shall rest and the 12th be with you. As to the great routs I hate them, but I thought it right to shew myself in some respectable Houses as *Tom Tit* said she would shut me out. I have been invited to every party about Town, so has Charlotte. We went to the Ladies Concert and to two most chosen places to shew *we could do so*, and your good sense will aprove I am sure. Charlotte

is so much admired and *justly so I think*. The Duchess of Devonshire was so civil to Charlotte and told Her she would invite Her to all Her Balls. The Walpoles were there, every body came and spoke to me and made so much of us. The most fashionable Ball next week is Mrs. Orby Hunter, all the girls of fashion are to be there, allso one on Friday at Mrs. Broadhead's, and one at Mrs. Wolf's on Wednesday were we are invited, allso to Lady Louisa Manners. Tom Tit is in Town bursting with rage and envy.

One thing about the *tria juncta in uno*, none of them ever did things by halves.

Emma was waiting for news of a great battle. What she got was a long letter mainly about money. "A £1,000 will not go far and we need be great oeconomists to make both ends meet and to carry on the little improvements," Nelson wrote her on March 14. He went on to talk about the new room and entrance and drew a little sketch of the drive curving through the garden between plantations. He asked, as Horatia was to be at Merton, "that a strong netting about three feet high may be placed round the Nile that the little thing may not tumble in then you may have ducks again in it." He would pay for the improvements which he longed to see completed, "but I fear this miscarriage of Pichegru's in France will prolong the war, it has kept the French fleet in port which we are all sorry for."

He was referring to an abortive attempt by the exiled French General, in conjunction with Royalists and a faction hostile to Bonaparte led by the hero General Moreau, to topple the First Consul. The plot failed, the ringleaders were arrested and Pichegru was reported to have committed suicide. Bonaparte took a swift revenge on the Royalists. The Duke d'Enghien, son of the Duke de Bourbon and nephew of the exiled King Louis XVIII, was kidnapped, taken to the castle of Vincennes, tried and shot. The plot was used as a political expediency for Bonaparte's assumption of the title of Emperor. It sent a chill through the civilized world.

Later that month Nelson heard of Emma's misfortunes in February. "Horatia's being so ill and you so much indisposed gave me a raging fever all night." He did not as yet know of the sad fate of the second "little Emma."

It is disheartening how many of his letters were concerned with money matters. "There is not a farthing of prize money stirring here," he told Davison, "I have not got enough to pay my expences." Emma had lent the Boltons £200 and he wanted it placed to his account. "She is generous beyond her means and therefore she should not be asked for what is not in her power to spare." Poor old blind Mrs. Nelson was in debt and he would help her out. And there was an amusing sidelight on a hero often accused of peacock vanities. He asked Davison to order two or three pairs of shoes from Rymers the shoemakers, "but they must be at least one size if not two larger than the last for I cannot wear them they are so small, *no square toes or new fashion.*"

On April 2 a ship arrived with letters from England.

> I opened, opened, found none but Decr. and early in January. I was in such an agitation. At last I found one without a date which, thank God, told my poor heart that you was recovering, but that dear little Emma was no more, and that Horatia had been so very ill. It altogether upset me, but it was just abed time and I had time to reflect and be thankful to God for sparing you and our dear Horatia. I am sure the loss of one, much more both, would have drove me mad. I was so agitated as it was that I was glad it was night and that I could be by myself.

He was severe once again on her friends. The Marquis of Abercorn, "the Great Bashaw at the Priory, he be damned." Lady Harrington was as great a pimp as any of them—what a set! "I care not what they do, even less envy them their *Chere Amies.*" He preferred the poor people who loved them, "if we assist our friends, and I am sure, we should feel more comfort in it than in loaded tables and entertaining a sett of people who care not for us." When he returned, he would settle £4,000 on Horatia so that she would not have to depend on the provisions of a will which might be challenged. "I would not have H. think of a dog. I shall not bring her one and I am sure she is better without a pet of that sort, but she is like her Mother, would get all the old dogs in the place about her."

Nelson was expecting the *Swift* cutter with Admiralty dispatches, letters, and two prints of Emma. He was preparing his own letters. He wrote to Horatia and sent her twelve books of Spanish dresses and told her to be good. He wrote to Charlotte and thanked her for looking after "the dear little orphan"—"*curse* them who *curse* her and Heaven *bless* them who *bless* her"—a strange letter for a refined young lady to receive.

Then he heard that the cutter had been taken by a French privateer and carried into Barcelona. Nelson was disgusted. "The *Swift* of the force of 23 men and boys is taken by a thing of 53 men and boys." All the dispatches were gone and the foreign correspondence of the government— it was worse than the loss of the *Hindostan* storeship that had caught fire and gone up with the provisions and good things coming out to the fleet.

He remembered her birthday, of course, and wrote Emma on April 28.

> I did not, my dearest Emma, pass over the 26th without thinking of you in the most affectionate manner, with the truest love and affectionate regard of man to a dear beloved woman, which could enter into my mind. I have been for some days and am still very unwell, without being seriously ill, but I fret absolutely like a fool for the faults of others. It was no fault of mine that the dispatches were taken, but of those who sent them in a vessel not fit to trust my old shoes in. . . ."

The birthday did not pass unremembered at Merton either. "We sat down about eighty to supper and we danced till six in the morning," said Charlotte.

England had now been at war for nearly a year, had garnered her West Indian islands, and was wondering what was going to happen next. King George had got better and Mr. Addington was languishing. "It is thought," said the *Chronicle,* "that if Dr. Slop had been still alive, there would have been a hard run between him and Dr. Addington for the *premiership.*" The Whigs and die-hard Tories were united against what Mr. Pitt called "the imbecile administration." There was talk of a general election, and the *Chronicle* remarked, "He would be a bold man, indeed, who would advise a dissolution of Parliament in the mere hope of prolonging the existence of a feeble and inefficient administration." That was a time when members of Parliament *could* bring down the government, and did, when it was obvious that it had lost the capacity to govern.

So, at the end of April, the ministry which had taken the country into peace and into war with an equal lack of success collapsed. The King sent for Mr. Pitt. There is a glimpse into the political caldron among the papers sent to Nelson at this time.

> The most singular junto took place betwixt the Grenvilles, Foxes, Windhams, Canning and all Mr. Pitt's old friends to drive out Mr. Addington, unite Pitt and Fox, and form a new and popular Ministry. All this was defeated by the King who gave Pitt the seals and utterly rejected Fox—the consequence is that Pitt is Minister, with all the others likely to be his opponents. . . . I am truly sorry to add, that His Majesty is still highly deranged at times, and though as yet they have endeavoured to keep the matter from discussion, the case is too notorious to be long unobserved. If a Re-

gency takes place, Mr. Fox will inevitably be the Minister, the Prince has redoubled his efforts and has all the party to dinner every fourth day.

On May 11 Mr. Pitt was once again Prime Minister. Lord Melville, who as Henry Dundas had been Secretary to the Navy in Pitt's old ministry, became First Lord. For the rest, as the *Post* had it, "The offices are filled, either with subordinate members of the late 'imbecile Administration,' as Mr. Pitt was pleased to term it, or with persons, whose chief if not only recommendation is their servile and slavish attachment to a man, who has been justly described as, 'having added more to the burdens and taken more from the liberties of the people, than any Minister the Country ever knew.'" "The whole administration is a job," said the *Chronicle*, "a contrivance for the personal aggrandisement of Mr. Pitt and Lord Melville."

This is hard on Pitt, who, looking back from our viewpoint, towered above his contemporaries as the architect of great coalitions against France, and great exactions from England. But they did not think he towered, only that he had got in again, and we must think the same. Very few politicians are statesmen in their own lifetime.

The political struggles in England and in France ensured that there was no break in the absence of hostilities in the war. Nelson, who on April 23 was promoted to Vice-Admiral of the White, would continue to fret. The French were not coming out that year.

"I find, my dearest Emma, that your picture is very much admired by the french Consul at Barcelona . . ." He made light of the loss of her letters, "from us what can they find out—that I love you most dearly and hate the french most damnably." Everybody knew that anyway. "I do not say all I wish and which my Dearest *beloved* Emma (Read that whoever opens this letter and for what I care publish it to the World) your fertile imagination can readily fancy I would say, but this I can say with great truth, that I am for ever yours." He underlined the last three words several times.

"People who don't love don't quarrel," said Emma. She loved dearly. Poor Nelson, though perhaps we should say lucky Nelson, was on the receiving end of her letters in which gossip, endearments, praise and reproaches, flowed indiscriminately, climbing the hill of her stomach as she lay in bed, and chasing down the other side. A ship had arrived from the Mediterranean without bringing a word from him. He had not seen the ship. Davison, now in the King's Bench serving his year's sentence, would not give her money for the improvements. He had instructed Davison to pay all the bills, though he did not know where he would find the money.

Mr. Marsh had put £6,000 in the three per cents. He could not tell Mr. Marsh *everything*, he would settle all this in time. What was her dear Maria Carolina doing about getting her a pension? Well now, that was a story. . . .

"The Queen," Hugh Elliot told Nelson on May 6, "has for a considerable time past been entirely absorbed by an unrequited passion for a French Officer in this Service of the name of St. Clair, who has unfortunately a pair of Irish shoulders, and who was long the Parish Bull of this Capital." St. Clair and his relations were in close touch with the French Ambassador, M. Alquier, and had joined in a plot to drive old General Acton out of the government. A threat of war by Bonaparte forced Acton to retreat to Palermo. King Ferdinand was sulking at Caserta. Maria Carolina, at the age of fifty-two and the mother of seventeen children, alternately stormed and swooned as St. Clair blew hot and cold.

A lover would not have mattered, said Elliot, "for I do not believe that there ever existed a more indolent, dissipated, frivolous or dissolute Court, than that in which their Sicilian Majesties have long given a loose to every passion." But a French lover was too much.

Nelson pressed the matter of Emma's pension. All he asked was that the Queen should write to Addington, or Pitt, to acknowledge the famous services that Lady Hamilton had performed. Elliot finally answered him on July 27.

> I enclose a letter from the Queen to Prince Castelcicala. I believe she makes use of that channel to solicit the pension for Lady Hamilton. This is not what you askd for, nor what I think at all adequate to the purpose. Castelcicala is to my knowledge no friend to that Lady. And now, my dear Lord, allow me to speak plainly to you upon this subject, though with real confidence that you will never allude to what I now write. The Queen may have been *once* the friend of Lady Hamilton, but she is certainly not so *now*. On the contrary, I always avoid the subject with Her, as she speaks in terms which do Herself no credit, and which without doubt proceed from her new French connection.

Perhaps Hugh Elliot's own dislike of Emma crept into the proceedings too, but certainly times had changed since the two large and passionate women had sworn eternal friendship to each other.

Charles Connor, Emma's cousin, was causing concern. He had a kind of silly laugh when spoken to and always complained of a pain in the back of his head. Now, a fellow midshipman had flicked an olive stone at him which had gone into his eye and half blinded him. Nelson paid his bills and took him into the *Victory*.

Nelson wrote to Emma twice on May 30. She had sent him a present. "Your dear Phiz, but not the least like you, on the cup is safe, but I would not use it for the World for if it was broke it would distress me very much." The Frenchman at Barcelona was bragging about her pictures. "What if he had a hundred—your resemblance is so deeply engraved in my heart that there it can never be effaced, and who knows some day I may have the happiness of having a living picture of you."

He had heard of the political upheaval in England. "I wish Mr. A. had given you the pension. Pitt and hard hearted Grenville never will." His thoughts, however, had, always had, one refuge of peace. "Everything you tell me about my dear H. charms me: I think I see her, hear her, and admire her, but she is like her dear dear Mother. I wish I could be at dear Merton to assist in making the alterations. I think I should have persuaded you to have kept the Pike and a clear stream and to have put all the Carp, tench and fish who muddy the water into the Pond, but as you like I am content. Only take care that my darling does not fall in and get drowned. I begged you to get the little netting along the edge and particularly at the Bridges. I admire the seal and God bless you also *amen*." (She was using a seal about an inch across with "LORD NELSON GOD BLESS HIM AMEN AMEN AMEN" written on it. She had another, showing a ship in a stormy sea, with the motto "Nelson Victory Si je la perd je suis perdu." Nelson used several seals, the big one of his arms for formal letters, and a lovely head of Emma from an intaglio carved at Naples.)

The second letter was about himself. "We have nothing in the least new here. We cruize, cruize, and one day so like another that they are hardly distinguishable, but *Hopes* blessed *hopes* keeps us up, that some happy day the french may come out, then I shall consider my duty to my Country fullfilled." He complained of "a slow nasty fever" and was short with her for conning over every word in his letters. "My saying we are on the eve of a battle could only be intended to convey my belief that the French intended to put to sea . . . therefore do not fancy this that or the other as how where or when I can get at them. I cannot do impossibilities or go into Toulon, but all that man can do shall be done, and the sooner it is done the sooner I shall certainly be at dear Merton."

Dear Merton was in a mess. The trouble was that Emma's plans exceeded Nelson's pocket. Davison, who kept the flap of Nelson's pocket, was tethered within the confines of the King's Bench, stuck across the river by St. George's Fields in the Terrace, in sight of Melancholy Walk and spitting distance of Dirty Lane. Emma badgered him for money, visited him, flattered him, and assaulted him with a broadside of letters in her best fighting style.

She began with a bracer that he, deprived of his family, his Swarland Hall, and his house in St. James's Square, might have found too stiff. "How do you do my dear Sir, I sincerely wish you joy. The vagabonds can't not do more or they would. I am glad you have no money to pay and as to one *year* what does it signify, the air will agree with you. . . ." Then she sent him Mr. Cribb the gardener for a little money to pay his men. She and Cribb were laying out the grounds, while Mr. Chawner the architect was planning the new extension.

"I am myself the surveyor of *the alterations* of the grounds as my Lord wished it should be by my taste," she wrote on June 13, "therefore the *Builder* can have nothing to do with my department and I shall have nothing to do with his. . . . We do not want a Capability Brown for we refused one that Mr. Greville recommended—we have spent little money considering what has been done and this I can assure you, not to be all ways asking." Of course, she did ask that time and he refused.

She wrote the next day, "I only beg again if the rooms are to be built let them, if they can't why we will wait Lord Nelson, my dear Nelson's return. As to the garden Cribb and myself are the planners and gardners and if you can allow him eight men for 3 months he will be content." And off she went to Canterbury for a fortnight.

Davison answered her on the 18th. "I ever have most studiously avoided meddling with your exclusive prerogative in your schemes and plans." But they would cost Nelson £4,000 at least. "Now, my dear Madam, let me ask you if you really seriously believe it to be our Dearest Lord's intention to expend this sum upon the Premises? If my recollection is correct, I think He once said to me, that all the alterations and improvements He was desirous of making would not cost more than three or four hundred pounds."

Emma tried another tack. Nelson had told her everything he wanted, and by her reckoning it would only cost £1,500. She could not even have that! "I thought on Nelson and wept myself to sleep." Davison apparently felt that this required no answer and the correspondence lapsed for a while.

She was at Canterbury. What she made of the clerical colony, clinging to the cathedral like fat garden slugs to the underside of a rockery, we do not know, because Nelson, as usual, burned her letters. What they made of her appears from a cruel reminiscence in the *Memoires*. Invitations to Dr. Nelson and his family used to have "But not Lady Hamilton" written on them. She would not tolerate much of this and swept on to Ramsgate, where she took a house, 10 Albion Place. In her train were her three maids, Julie, Marianne and Fatima, Charlotte Nelson, and Eliza and Ann Bolton, and Miss Connor was with them to tutor the girls. Horatia stayed with Mrs. Gibson until Merton should be ready and safe for her.

From Ramsgate on June 27 Emma reopened her campaign. She sent Davison Mr. Chawner's plan once again.

> I had a letter from Crib this morning *which I wish I had not receved,* but I cannot help it. I have no money for him. I have written to a person to see what we can do. *My* dear Nelson did not think of the difficultys I should have, to accomplish what *he* desired, and now, dear Sir, as our Correspondence will for ever close *about Merton* improvements, I can onely say I have not acted for myself in any way. What I have done as been to make comfortable the man that my *soul doats* on, that I would think it little to *sacrifice* my life to make him happy. Nelson and Emma can have but one mind, one heart, one soul, one *enterest,* and I can assure you that if the nation was to give my beloved Nelson a Blenham, Merton would be the place he would live in. Therefore as *I know* all *his* thoughts on this point, I need not say how anxious I was to go on with what he so ardently desired. I daresay your prudence is right, that I can not say anything about.

This was the right approach to Davison, who replied at once, "My Prudence, as you call it, can only be connected with that Duty, Regard, and affection I owe to our Dearest Nelson. . . . I feel, and must ever feel, the most lively solicitude in *Every thing* in which our dearest Nelson's interest, wish, gratification, Happiness, or by whatever term it may be called, is concerned—I trust we shall see him in England before the year is out, and in that good state of Health and Spirits as to afford Joy, transporting bliss to His Emma—and not a little pleasure to myself." They were both great bidders in the auction of Nelson's esteem. Davison added a postscript: "I am told you do not like Canterbury."

"Nothing new has happened," wrote Nelson on June 6, "except our hearing the *feu de joie* at Toulon for the declaration of Emperor. What a capricious nation those french must be. . . . I rather believe my antagonist at Toulon begins to be angry with me, at least I am trying to make him so and then he may come out and beat me as he says he did off Boulogne. He is the Admiral who went to Naples in Decr. 1792, La Touche Treville, who landed the Grenadier. I owe him something for that." He remarked on the same subject on the 17th. "My friend Monsieur La Touche has got his fleet fully manned—he sometimes plays bo-peep in and out of Toulon, like a mouse at the edge of her hole; but as these playful tricks, which mean nothing serious, may be magnified by nonsensical letters, of which too many are wrote, I desire and beg that you will never give any credit to them."

There was a letter, however, which he took very much to heart. On June 14 La Touche was bolder than usual and actually came out of Toulon, though on Nelson's approach he soon went back in again. The Frenchman wrote an account of the affair which ended with the assertion that he had pursued the British fleet and that it had fled from him. This letter was published in the English papers, appearing in the *Chronicle* on July 11. Nelson was furious, protested to the Admiralty, sent home the log of the *Victory* as evidence of his movements that day, and, for some weeks, persisted in telling his friends that when he caught La Touche he would make him eat his letter. This was all the result of months of waiting and worrying. He was eventually consoled by the news of La Touche's death on August 18. The French papers said he died from his exertions in walking regularly up to the signal post above Toulon to look at the English fleet. "I always pronounced that that would be his death," said Nelson.

In the meantime, Emma was living retired at Ramsgate. There were a few ladies for company, and some old acquaintances, Lord Keith and his sister, and the Wraxalls, but for the rest it was "bathe walk and sing" and early to bed. Heaven knows what those two old gossips Keith and Wraxall made of Lady H. and her troop of girls. She was in high looks and high spirits. She resumed the attack on Davison with force enough to make the poor man glad he was in prison.

On July 11 she had received a bundle of Nelson's letters. "He seems to hope the rooms are done and has written a deal about improvements." And on the 15th she exclaimed,

I adore Nelson and my only pleasure is thinking on him and his dear return—may God only send him home safe to his Emma. What a sad thing it is to think such a man as him should be entrapped with such an infamous woman as that apoticary's widow, no more like him, without youth, beauty, riches, talents, or any one thing to recommend her. A woman that has done all she can to ruin, vex and blast his fair and upright Character. Whilst I am free—with talents that he likes, adoring him, that never a woman ever adored a man as I do my Nelson, loving him beyond all this world, and yet we are both miserable . . . *patience*. God bless you. I shall be most obliged to you to send me a Hundred pounds as I have left all I had with my mother for Merton.

Here she is back on the stage of her imagination, denouncing Fanny—like Tamora the Queen of the Goths denounced Lavinia—with all the venom and as little justification. Fanny's crime was that she prevented Nelson from marrying Emma, that was the ground of all Emma's bitterness. As in all her moments of passion, she flew into drama. Davison was her audience, her captive audience. Here she is on July 24. She has received Nelson's letter about hopes; there is talk in England of a war with Spain, which would make the Mediterranean rich with prizes.

He says that hope keeps them on and I know if it was not for hope I should die—the blessed hope of his returning safe. I love him too much and his enterest to wish him to come home in case of a Spanish War, for as he has had the sours, let him have the sweets poor fellow. That I adore him above all this world is true, and that I would sacrifice my life for his happiness, but I have the vanity and pride to be sure that the happiness of His depends on mine. Ours is not a common dull love. My mind was taken with Glory, my Heart beat high with His great deeds, and I never can nor ever will try to get the better of my true and virtuous passion that I feel for Him. My soul owns Him for its Lord and I Hope yet our Love will be crowned with success, and that we shall lawfully belong to each other.

The apoticary's widdow, the Creole with Her Heart Black as Her feind-like looking face, was never destined for a Nelson, for so noble-minded a Creature. She never loved Him for Himself. She loved Her poor dirty Escalopes [Aesculapius] if she had love, and the 2 dirty negatives made that dirty affirmative that is a disgrace to the Human Species. She then starving took in an evil hour our Hero. She made him unhappy. She disunited Him from His family. She wanted to *raise up* Her own vile spue at the expence and total abolation of the family which shall be immortalized for having given birth to the Saviour of His Country. When He came home, *maimed, lame,* and covered with Glory, She put in derision His Honnerable wounds. She raised a clamour against Him, because He had seen a more lovely, a more virtuous woman, who had served with him in a foreign country and who had her heart and senses open to His Glory, to His greatness, and His virtues. If He had lived with this daemon, the blaster of His fame and reputation, He must have fallen under it, and His Country would have lost their greatest ornament. . . . No, let him live yet to gain more victory and to be blessed with his idolizing Emma.

This is not far from Shakespeare and, given a jog, it would fall into blank verse. It gives us some idea of what her letters to Nelson were like. His passion was great, hers was greater. Now, perhaps, we can begin to understand what Sir William meant when he said women had great souls "at least his had," and the extent of Nelson's and Emma's love. This is heady stuff to distill from one letter, and words are difficult to find—but there is nothing like this in literature or in life. There *was* an Admiral, small and sick, mutilated, half-blind, with few teeth, who regularly damned the French, loved England, and wrote heart-thumping letters to a fat woman of forty. There *was* this woman, gross, vulgar and extravagant, her beauty blown like a September rose all open to the bees, who loved, adored him, "that never a woman ever adored a man as I do my Nelson." What more can be said that they did not say themselves?

Emma to Davison again, late in July 1804:

> Nelson has ordered me to go in to Norfolk to stand for Lady Bolton's Child which I do the 17th and then to town and I shall emediately come and see you and carry you off to see dear Merton, which will be ten thousand times dearer when I get *our* Glorious Nelson there. You say I must not be jelous of you—I am not jelous of man or woman. Nelson loves you and theirfore I do the same, but I am so confident of His love, His adoration of His idolizing Emma, that nothing can shake him, nor nothing can change me. I would prefer Him in rags with His wounded glorious carcasse to bring Empress of the world tomorrow. We are going to Canterbury to pass the Glorious first, so write me a good dear comforting letter directed there. *Hip hip hip* to Him on the Glorious first, I wish you could be with us.

[The Lady Bolton referred to was Mrs. Bolton's daughter Catherine, who had married her cousin William; the young officer was knighted when he stood proxy for Nelson at his Installation.]

Nelson again told Davison to pay the bills for Merton and also, if he could afford it, Old Blindy's debts. He hoped Lord Melville, who had promised much when he was out of office, might do a little for Emma now he was in, but "all their promises are pie-crusts, made to be broken." As for Davison's imprisonment, "Have not I been shut up in a Ship without any one comfort. He is ashore with his friends round him, and even you go to see him. I would change with him with much pleasure." He sent her money, knowing she would need it, £100 for her and £100 for poor Mrs. Bolton. "I shall, if it pleases God, eat my Christmas dinner at dear Merton." There was no change, nothing new. "Well this is an odd war," he wrote on July 9, "not a battle."

He managed to fire a verbal broadside on August 1 against an unexpected foe, the City of London. Late in March the City had voted its thanks to the Channel and Mediterranean fleets for the respective blockades of Brest and Toulon. As the names of Nelson's junior flag officers were not known, they did not appear in the official notice of the thanks. When he received this, Nelson politely told them that Rear-Admiral Sir Richard Bickerton and Rear-Admiral Campbell were entitled to their thanks as much as anyone. He did not miss the opportunity of reminding them of Copenhagen, "a great victory passed over without notice." And he neatly turned the tables on the Lord Mayor.

> I beg to inform your lordship, that the port of Toulon has never been blockaded by me, quite the reverse. Every opportunity has been offered the Enemy to put to sea, for it is there that we hope to realize the hopes and expectations of our Country, and I trust that they will not be disappointed.

On the 9th he wrote to the Admiralty for leave to return home for a few months in the winter for the benefit of his health. He told Emma, "I hope a little of your good nursing, with asses milk, will set me up for another Campaign," and went on to suggest that, while the dining room at Merton was to be extended, a room over it would block up the window on the stairs, and perhaps it ought to be reconsidered.

Horatia caught smallpox (so much for the anti-Jennerians). Nelson sent an anguished little note on the 13th.

> My beloved how I feel for your situation and for that of our dear Horatia, unexampled love, never I trust to be diminished much less broken, death with all his terrors would be pleasant compared even to the thought. I wish I had all the small pox for *her*, but I know the fever is the natural consequence. I dreamt last night I heard her call papa and point to her arm just as you described, give Mrs. Gibson a guinea for me and I will repay you. Dear Wife good adorable friend how I love you and what would I not give to be with you this moment, for I am forever all yours.

366

The same day he wrote a formal letter, presumably for Emma to show inquisitive visitors, asking her to take the little girl to Merton. He said that the child had been left to his care and protection in Italy, that he had presented it to her on their arrival in England, and that he was pleased she had become attached to it, "so did Sir William, thinking her the finest child he had ever seen." The time had now come to take her from the nurse and think of her education. Miss Connor would be her tutor and at Merton, "she will imbibe nothing but virtue, goodness, and elegance of manners, with a good education to fit her to move in the sphere of life she is destined to move in." Perhaps Sir William did see Horatia? This is the only mention of it and, of course, it cannot be trusted.

The weather had changed in the Mediterranean. Though it was the middle of August, there were gales, and Nelson had a fire in his cabin to keep out the damp. There was not much news: Charles Connor had recovered and had gone into the *Niger* under Captain Hillyar; the Neapolitan Court was in a panic at Nelson's impending departure; Messrs. Haslewood, Marsh and Davison were squabbling over his few thousands; Lord Moira had used his proxy against the government.

He did not like that, and told Emma, "I wish my proxy never had been given . . . if Lord Moira was to be First Minister and I First Lord of the Admiralty it would be my duty to support, but I am to expect nothing from them." Moira was of the Prince's party and a Foxite. "And to make enemies of those who are in—I'll be damned if I do—I will stand upon my own bottom and be none of their tools. When I come home I shall make myself understood. I like both Pitt and Lord Melville, and why should I oppose them. I am free and independent."

When he got home he would settle his affairs. "I shall put it out of your power to spend dear Horatia's money, I shall settle it in trustee's hands and leave nothing to chance. If Horace behaves well, he shall marry her."

Money bedevils everything. "Mr. Greville is a shabby fellow," wrote Nelson on August 31. Mr. Greville was deducting income tax from Emma's allowance. "As to Davison I know the full extent of the obligation I owe him and he may be useful to me again but I can never forget his unkindness to you." Davison had apparently been bragging of his wealth and Nelson's poverty, according to Emma anyway. "What I have is my own, it never cost the widow a tear or the nation a farthing, I got what I have with my pure blood from the Enemies of my Country." She and Horatia were on the coast, he was uneasy, for there were rumors of invasion, and he wished they were at Merton.

They were at Ramsgate. Emma had postponed her trip to Norfolk, very likely because of Horatia's smallpox. "I have letters up to the first of July from my dear lord, all well," she wrote Davison on August 16. "I was to have left this day, but Lady Essex would make me stay to meet Lady Cholmondly and a small party at her house, so I set off tomorrow for Canterbury. On Friday I shall be at Merton and on Saturday I shall come and see you and talk about my bravest Lord, for I am more in love than ever with Him. Oh God, the joy of meeting, but I will not think on it as my Head will turn with pleasure." She was at Merton on Saturday the 18th, and on the 22nd she set off for a three weeks' stay with the Boltons at Cranwich.

Mrs. Cadogan was at Merton all this time, coping with Mr. Chawner and his builders and Mr. Cribb and his gardeners. She was not alone, as the place was being used as a holiday home for Emma's relations. Sarah Reynolds was there that summer with one of the Connor girls and "little Emma." Mrs. Cadogan makes several references to an Emma and she must presumably be the "little Emma" of the plain face and sickly disposition. Uncle Thomas Kidd also used Merton as a home from home, drinking with the laborers at the Plough, trying to oust Mr. Cribb, and making Mrs. Cadogan unhappy. There were other visitors: the Tysons used to come over from Woolwich; Oliver was often there; and the Abbé Campbell, an old friend from Naples and the priest who was suspected of officiating at the marriage of the Prince of Wales and Mrs. Fitzherbert, appeared once or twice. Everyone who stayed there did so at Emma's expense, of course.

"My jaunt to Norfolk has cost me more than I intended," she wrote Davison on September 17. It was also lasting longer than she intended. For once, Davison did not object to parting with some of Nelson's money. The rumors of a Spanish war were hardening. The country was short of precious metals for coins and the surest source was the Spanish treasure ships from the Americas. "What a world of matter is now in agitation," Davison answered her. "Everything is big with events, and soon, very soon, I hope to see—what I have long desired, and anxiously waited for—an event to contribute to the glory, the independency, of our Nelson."

He heard from her again a few days later. There was going to be a family party at Cranwich on the 29th, Nelson's birthday. "Now will you do me the favour to send *us* two bottles of Champagne by the coach to Cranwich, you will make us very happy. We will have plenty of geese, but now is He not protecting every goose and gosling in England. God bless you, in haste, going to Church to pray for *my* Glorious Nelson. D—— all his enemies and yours allso amen. You will say that is a good prayer for a Sunday."

Since he had written for his leave, the Admiral himself had not heard a word from the Admiralty. He celebrated his birthday with a letter.

> This day my dearest Emma which gave me birth I consider as more fortunate than common days, as by my coming into this World it has brought me so intimately acquainted with you who my soul holds most dear. I well know that you will keep it and have my dear H. to drink my health. Forty six years of toil and trouble, how few more the common lot of mankind leads us to expect, and therefore it is almost time to think of spending the few last years in Peace and quietness. By this time I should think either my successor is named or permission is granted me to come home, and if so, you will not long receive this letter before I make my appearance, which will make us I am sure both truly happy.

If you turn over the pages of a book of English history too quickly, you will miss the year 1804 entirely. It was a year when virtually nothing happened. When, on August 1, King George III came down to Parliament to make his speech to end the session, the day was hot and clammy. Now George was short-sighted, and, though his speech was short, it was written out large on seven or eight sheets of paper. As he turned them over, two got stuck together by the heat and damp, and he missed out two paragraphs. He did not notice it, nor did it matter. It was that sort of a year.

When the newspapers had nothing else to write about, they resorted to the old bogey of invasion, which no longer scared anybody. Mr. Pitt's Aliens Act provided the Cockneys with a new summer pastime, denouncing genteel-looking people who mispronounced the English language as French spies; Southend was a dangerous place for anyone who used his h's.

There was an Anglo-Russian treaty purchased for a vast subsidy, and a Franco-Prussian agreement obtained by the promise of Hanover. The Continental powers were slowly taking up sides. However, the title of the Emperor Napoleon was generally recognized and there appeared to be no chance of involving Europe in the war that year. That is why Pitt, desperate for some gain to justify his reappearance at the head of government, turned to rob the almost lifeless corpse of Spain. The Earl of Chatham had done much the same in 1761, though that time he had seized the Spanish treasure in anticipation of peace. His son became a pirate in anticipation of many years of war.

On September 18 the Admiralty sent orders to Admiral Cornwallis to detain some Spanish frigates coming from Rio de la Plata with £1,000,000 of gold and silver coin, and on the 25th similar orders were sent to Lord

Nelson to detain all Spanish ships carrying treasure or military stores. Cornwallis, who naturally received his orders first, sent two frigates, the *Indefatigable* and the *Lively,* to Cadiz. He believed there were only two Spanish ships coming. Fortunately, Captain Moore, the General's brother, found two of Nelson's frigates, the *Medusa* and the *Amphion,* already on the station and took them under his command. Captain Gore of the *Medusa,* who knew Nelson well from his days in the Channel, wrote to him of the government's extraordinary orders on October 1.

On the 5th four Spanish frigates hove in sight, were pursued and stopped. For an hour Moore tried to persuade the Spanish Rear-Admiral in command to surrender. Quite naturally he refused. Moore opened fire and, after a short engagement, one Spanish frigate blew up and the others struck and were sent to England. There were several women and children on the one that blew up. None were rescued.

On October 19 the news broke in England. The papers had had little to entertain their readers for several weeks. There had been a farcical attempt to blow up the enemy flotilla in Boulogne, using barges, mined and loaded with stones, which were towed into position by catamarans and exploded. There had been Nelson's letter to the Lord Mayor, which was a laugh on the City. But this news was red hot.

The *Times* and *Morning Herald* took the ministerial line. It was, said the latter, "a measure of mere precaution, and that, though hostile when abstractly considered, it breathes nothing of the spirit of hostility towards Spain. Ministers did not act in the spirit of actual warfare" The *Morning Post* regretted the presence of women and children aboard the frigates, as if the Spaniards might have expected to be attacked without warning. It was left to the *Morning Chronicle* to express the disapproval the act merited. "It may be useful to obtain a *million sterling* (for such is said to be the amount of the prizes), but it is obtained at the expence of the Law of Nations. What turn Ministers will give to their measure of capturing a Spanish convoy pending a negotiation we cannot conceive, except the common excuse of a crime, that it is profitable."

When he received Gore's letter of October 1, Nelson was amazed. More than that, he believed the order originated from Cornwallis, who had no right to send ships onto his station, and he wrote to Gore ordering him positively not to interfere with any Spanish shipping. The letter was not sent, because he received the Admiralty's order the day it was written. Even then he instructed Gore to leave merchant shipping alone until war with Spain, which was now inevitable, should be declared. Once that should happen, he was free to make his, and Nelson's, fortune.

This event was to have considerable repercussions. Let us go first to Cranwich, where, on October 7, Emma was still queening it among the country Boltons, the source of patronage for the girls and much-needed £100 notes for Mr. B. She wrote to ask Davison whether he knew if Nelson's request for leave had been granted. She had received letters, about a month's supply.

> Think of my happiness in having got 54 sides of paper. I read and kiss and cry and laugh all in a breath. The *thought* of seeing him again agitates me and makes me mad with joy, then fear comes across me that he may not come—in short, I am, what with the different feelings that elate and opress me, not well. . . . Your Champagne was most excellent and we drank our Hero's Health and yours. I nurse Little Emma all day [This is Lady Bolton's baby.] and sing to Her, so that I have learnt the *trade of nursing* well against I marry. Oh that I was fairly married to the Man my soul doats on. Distance and time has only I think encreased my love and affection, my passion for Him, and I am miserable and ever shall be till He is mine and I am his.

By October 19 she was back at Merton, where she heard the news. Captain Sutton had written to her the moment he landed. The house rang with joy. "We were all made very happy this morning by hearing that my dear Uncle has got a great prize," Charlotte told her mother. "My Lady thinks his share will be about a hundred and twenty five Thousand Pounds. My Lady expects my Uncle home *very* soon. We have been very busy since we arrived from Norfolk. On Wednesday we went to Town to see the house that my Lady was thinking of taking, but she has not decided on it at present, for it is very dirty and will want a great deal of papering and painting before my Lady could live in it." Emma was thinking of moving from Clarges Street because of the expense, but now Nelson was going to have a fortune the idea flew out of her head. She added a P.S. to Charlotte's letter: "This secret and confidential. Our Nelson comes on leave, the Command kept open for him. Mr. Pitt and Lord Melville has behaved like angels, in haste ever yours and the Doctor's most affectionately, Emma."

It seemed certain that Nelson would share in the prize and that he would come home. Mrs. Bolton rejoiced on the 26th.

> I hope with Captain Sutton that the Prizes will be condemned. Eighty thousand to my Lord's share will be a *pretty* thing . . . do not be surprised if he does not arrive so soon as you

371

expect. I think it is very likely, if he falls in with the *Medusa,* he may cruize a little off Cadiz just to skim a little of the cream and *bring you home a Bushell of Dollars*—I hope the Golden Ships will not slip through his fingers. Kate has had a letter from her husband dated 27th August. Quite in the fidgets at my Lord's leaving the Fleet. He says it is reported that Sir John Orde is to have the command (but we know better).

Unfortunately, they did not know better, and Sir William Bolton, who was with the Mediterranean fleet in the *Childers* sloop, had caught a rumor of an event which was to snatch the golden ships out of Nelson's hand.

Sir John Orde was a pompous and ill-tempered man. He was also a bitter enemy of Lord St. Vincent, and his brother was Lord Bolton, an influential politician. This was enough to make Lord Melville wish to serve him. In October Orde was appointed Commander in Chief of the Cadiz station, which was removed from Nelson's command. In view of the situation with Spain, this was as good as a license to coin his own money. At the end of the month Orde sailed to take over his command, while Mr. Marsden, then Secretary to the Admiralty, wrote to Nelson to tell him that the *Medusa* and *Amphion* were no longer under his orders. The Admiralty's only excuse for this outrageous piece of favoritism was that Nelson was expected home on leave.

As for the Spanish frigates, they were eventually condemned, though only half the value was allowed to the captains who captured them. Nelson's share was to be half of the flag eighth, about £10,000. It was given to Sir John Orde. Orde got ten times that amount in the brief period of his command.

But all this would not have mattered so much had Nelson come home. Emma told Davison on the 30th:

He is *very very* anxious to come and I am anxious and agitated to see Him. I never shall be well till I do see Him. The disappointment would kill me. I love him, I adore him, my mind and soul is now transported with the thoughts of that Blessed Extatic moment when I shall see Him, embrace Him. My love is no common love. It may be a sin to love— I say it might have been a sin when I was *another's,* but I had then more merit in trying to suppress it. I am *now Free* and I must sin on and love Him more than ever, it is a Crime worth going to Hell for. For should I not be an ungrateful unfeeling wretch not to pay two fold with love the man that so idolises me, that adores me. My God only spare Him and send Him safe back.

I shall be at Merton till I see Him as He *particularly* wishes our first meeting should be there. . . . My heart beats every ring of the bell but yet I do not think he will be here this fortnight. . . . We are busy planting today as the rain is favourable for us and He seems very anxious in all his letters to have things finished. God bless you my dear Sir, this weather is not very good for the spirits, but I am ever your affectionate Emma. I would say N. but I am afraid such happiness and honour is not in store for me for She will never burst.

We last heard from Nelson on his birthday. He had just learned of the death of La Touche Tréville and, incidentally, of Charles Lock. Lock had gone out to the Mediterranean again as Consul to Egypt, but he got no further than Malta, where he died in the lazaretto at La Valetta of a fever. "The World," said Nelson, "will go on very well without either of them."

Early in October he wrote home about his proxy, his fears for Naples, and his affairs at Bronte. He had been obliged to give Mrs. Graefer a pension of £100 a year, thus increasing his list of dependents. On the 7th, in a short note, he used a phrase in code which has remained a puzzle to this day. "I shall only say Guzelle Gannam Justem and that I love you beyond all the World. This may be read by French, Dutch, Spanish, or Englishmen." He was quite right because no one has been able to make it out. If it is any help, the e in Justem might be an o. Then at least one can have "Emma" and "Nelson," whom it was presumably all about. He liked anagrams, Horatia's parents were once nearly called Johem and Morata Etnorb, and he mentioned an anagram on his own name, Honor est a Nilo. One can spend hours on this one.

He was waiting every hour for his leave to arrive. His baggage had already been transferred to the *Superb*, which was going home. On the 13th a cutter brought the Admiralty orders regarding Spanish shipping. He thought at first they came too late for him to profit by them and that his successor was bound to be on his way. "I should have, for your sake and for many of our friends, have liked an odd hundred thousand Pounds, but never mind. If they give me the choice of staying a few months longer it will be very handsome, and for the sake of others we would give up, my dear Emma, very much of our own felicity. If they do not, we shall be happy with each other and with dear H."

In fact, the Admiralty had very little idea what they were doing. After the orders of September 25, nothing reached Nelson in November apart from one letter from Lord Melville that began, "I don't know if this will find you in the Mediterranean or on your way home." The letter mentioned Orde's command outside the Straits, but said nothing more about Nelson's return. "Well my dear Lord," answered the Admiral, "be assured that I had rather have the French Admiral alongside of me than the mines of Peru, for if it be a sin to covet glory I am the most offending soul alive, so said Shakespeare and so says from his heart your Lordship's most faithful servant."

While he was waiting, he set his ships to work looking for Spanish prizes. "I am now for the first time in my life likely to pick up some money," he told Emma. But Orde netted the mackerel and Nelson got the sprats. The communications with Spain were now closed. Gibraltar was isolated by a terrible outbreak of fever that had spread throughout southern Spain, everyone on the Rock was virtually under a sentence of death. The only route for letters was by sea and Sir John Orde tried to hang on to every ship that passed from England or the Mediterranean. Nelson was still hopeful, but not now of being home for Christmas. He wrote Emma on November 23:

> I have set the whole Mediterranean to work and I think the fleet cannot fail of being successful. . . . Where is my successor. I am not a little surprized at his not arriving, a Spanish War I thought would have hastened him. Ministers could not have thought that I wanted to fly the Service, my whole life has proved the contrary, and if they refuse me now, I shall most certainly leave this Country in March or April, for a few months rest I must have very soon. If I am in my grave what are the mines of Peru to me, but to say the truth I have no idea of killing myself. I may with care live yet to do good Service to the State. My cough is very bad and my side, where I was struck on the 14th Febry. is very much swelled, at times a lump as large as my fist, brought on occasionally by violent coughing, but I hope and believe my lungs are yet safe. . . . Thompson desires to be most kindly remembered to his dear wife and children. He is most sincerely attatched to them and wishes to save what he can for their benefit.

What did he mean by children? Had he forgotten that little Emma was dead? Or was he thinking, as he certainly did on occasions, of a hot knife slipped under the seal and prying eyes? Lord knows!

Miss Thompson was well and sent a kiss to her ladyship and her Godpapa. So said Mrs. Gibson on November 7 when she presented Emma with her receipt for £30 and bill for a further £24 2s. od. This was probably her final account, as Horatia was going to Merton. The two eldest Bolton girls were there prior to going to school, and the Doctor and Mrs. Nelson were expected.

Mrs. Bolton was upset because Emma had sent her a tippet, so many presents made her feel uncomfortable. "I shall be afraid you think me a mercenary wretch—*who has a Price,* but surely you have a better opinion of yourself and me." The rebuke reveals a flaw in the friendship. The Matchams had finally given up Husum, doubtless for the best, and were still at Bath, where Mrs. Matcham reported "a *certain* Lady . . . so *condescendingly Humble* to those she formerly would not notice, all to be *thought amiable.*" Poor Fanny could not do right.

The Matchams had satisfied their desire for a change of scene by moving from Kensington Place to Portland Place. Mrs. Matcham had not actually seen Lady Nelson. "My only desire is that we shall not be in the same room," she wrote Emma, "and circumstances are *now* so well understood by our friends that I don't think it likely we shall ever meet her."

The year ended in disappointment for Emma. When she knew that Nelson was not on his way home, she left Merton and went to town, consoling herself by lavishing entertainments on the Doctor and his wife and presents and clothes on young Horace. "I have not been well my dear Sir," she told Davison on December 18, "and anxious about my dear Nelson— God knows what will be. My Heart is broke about His not coming, yet I think He will be so indignant of Ord's going to trespas on His ground that He will come home, at least I hope so."

The great excitement in town was not about Orde or Nelson, Spain or France. Even the coronation of Bonaparte took second place to the one topic on everybody's lips. "We are *almost* as anxious to hear how this farce goes off tomorrow at Paris," said the *Morning Chronicle* of December 1, "as to see how Young Roscius is received this evening at Covent Garden Theatre." Young Roscius, Master Betty, twelve years old, was making his first appearance in the capital as Norval in *Douglas* and Frederick in *Lovers' Vows,* two favorites of the public. There were riots outside the theater and inside ladies swooned and gentlemen wept. Young Roscius was the rave of the day. "He alone occupied the public attention," said the *Post,* "and the war and Bonaparte were forgotten." He was introduced to the King. "Young gentleman," said George, "I thought you were not so tall as I perceive you are." That was to be Master Betty's downfall. He grew up. We, who suffer from infant phenomena, can take consolation from that, and the comment on this boy applies to them all; "He rose like a rocket, and fell like the stick."

When he first heard that Sir John Orde was outside the Straits, Nelson thought that he had come to replace him. "If Sir John does not make haste, I shall get hold of the French fleet and then he may hang himself in a golden cord," he told Marsden. He really did not have much hope of seeing the French at sea, however, and said to Captain Capel, who had carried the dispatches home from the Nile, "It is our *old* friend Villeneuve that commands at Toulon, we know he can run away."

The last prospect of an early return to England was shattered when, early in December, his second in command Admiral Campbell fell seriously ill of a mental disorder. The poor fellow's condition can be imagined from his handwriting, which was suddenly that of a very old man. Nelson sent him home without delay. Nelson had to stay, and even offered to serve under Orde should he come to take command. "What greater sacrifice could I make," he wrote Emma on December 4, "than serving for a moment under Sir John Orde and giving up for that moment the society of all I hold dear in this world. Many here think that he is sent out off Cadiz to take a fortune out of my mouth, that would be very curious . . . surely I never served faithfully, I have only dreamt I have done my duty to the advantage of my country, but I am above them, *I feel it,* although not one farthing richer than when I left England."

On the 19th he at last heard from Orde that he was not coming and that everything that appeared too unjust to happen had indeed happened. "But never mind"—how often Emma had read those two words!—"he will get all the money and your poor Nelson all the hard blows. Am I to take this act as a proof of Lord Melville's regard for me, but I submit patiently, but I feel. I have not had a scrap of a pen from England 90 days this day, it is rather long in these critical times."

He made yet another codicil to his will on that day, leaving her £2,000, £100 to John Scott, and £200 to Alexander Scott.

On Christmas Day the day he had longed to spend at Merton for the last eighteen months, he finally received the Admiralty's official permission to return to England. He would be back, he said, at the end of February or the first week in March. There was one consolation for all these heart-rending disappointments. Captain Hardy wrote his brother-in-law on December 30, "I think since the thought of a Spanish War the Commander in Chief looks better, and I conclude as troubles increase he will mend."

CHAPTER FOURTEEN

Glory and Grief

THERE IS a great temptation to say something portentous about the year 1805; to herald it with a fanfare, or a funeral march. It would be very misleading to do so, as the year came in the same old way as all the other years; with a peal of bells across the English countryside, a flurry of snow, the clump of boots on the stone floor of a farmhouse kitchen, the creak of stairs in an elegant town house, the drum in the barracks, the hungry yawn of the poor man, the contented snore of the rich, the splash of water going up and slops coming down—and at sea, bare feet on wooden decks as nine hundred men raced for the eight seats in the heads, and Lord Nelson calling for his breakfast. He was up from his cot, with its white embroidered silk hangings, hours ago.

Emma was in bed at Merton. She was not well. She had a cold. Davison sent her some news to make her better. He had seen Lord Melville. "He tells me he has spoken to Mr. Pitt of the propriety of your having a pension settled upon you of £500 per annum, and that he will speak to him again very shortly about it. I asked Lord Melville if I might say as much to you. He immediately said, 'Yes, certainly.' He spoke very handsomely of you, and of your services in favour of this country when in Naples." Privately Melville assured Davison, "But for the *nice* scruples of a *Great* man it would have been settled long ago."

Mrs. Bolton wrote from Cranwich, "When the year gets up I hope to have the pleasure of visiting you." Mrs. Matcham wrote from Bath, "We were in the same room with *Lady N.* a few nights since for the first time since she came to Bath. She had then an opportunity of showing her insolence *as far as looks could express*; so I was told by some friends of mine, she looked as I passed her in that *scornful way* which could not but be noticed by all that saw her, but be assured there is a strong party against my

Dear Brother, whom *we know* to be all goodness and liberality, different tales are told in different pantrys, but I think a time must come when every thing will appear in a true light."

But proof of Fanny's wickedness, and the prospect of seeing Boltons could not console Emma. She had been saving up her little debts for Nelson's return, they amounted to £530, what was she to do? Davison paid them for her. She could at least get up to town, and she wrote him from Clarges Street on January 26.

I have been very ill, my dear Sir, and am in bed with a cold, very bad cold indeed, but the moment I am better I will call on you. I am invited to dine with Mr. Haslewood tomorrow, but fear I shall not be able to go. I am very anxious about letters, but Admiral Campbell has told me he thinks my dear Lord will soon be at home. God grant, for I think he might remove that stumbling block Sir John *O!* Devil take him. That *Poliphemus* should have been Nelson's, but he is thick in great and *noble Deeds* which t'other poor Devil is not, so let dirty wretches get pelf to comfort them Victory belongs to Nelson. Not but what I think money necessary for comfort and I hope *our yours* and *my* Nelson will get a little for all Master *O!* I write from bed and you will see I do by my scrawl. I send you some of my bad verses on my soul's idol. . . .

> Emma to Nelson
> *I think I have not lost my Heart*
> *Since I, with Truth, can swear*
> *At every moment of my Life,*
> *I feel, my Nelson, there!*
>
> *If, from Thine Emma's Breast, her Hert*
> *Were stol'n, or flown away,*
> *Where! Where! Should she my Nelson's Love*
> *Record—each happy day.*
>
> *If, from thine Emma's Breast, her Heart*
> *Were stol'n, or flown away,*
> *Where, where, should she engrave my Love*
> *Each tender word you say.*
>
> *Where, where, should Emma Treasure up*
> *Her Nelson's smiles and sighs,*
> *Where mark, with joy, each secret look*
> *Of Love from Nelson's Eyes?*

Then, do not rob me of my Heart,
Unless you first forsake it.
And then! So Wretched! it would be
Despair alone will take it!

But there was a storm gathering, and lightning storing up to strike that poor heart.

Nobody in England, and very few people anywhere else, thought the Emperor Napoleon was a gentleman. When, at the beginning of the year, he addressed King George as "Sir, my Brother," old George sidestepped the fraternal embrace and his minister's reply went off to "The Head of the French Government." Bonaparte offered peace. Pitt replied politely that his Sovereign would welcome peace when the French nation behaved peacefully and he was engaging with the other sovereigns of Europe to obtain peace. In the meantime, Sweden and Russia were preparing for war and British envoys in Berlin and Vienna were quietly talking about subsidies and grants of territories. A contract was offered in the papers for the building of 87 Martello towers between Hythe and Beachy Head. When Bonaparte offered peace, everyone wondered where the French were going to attack.

The French Emperor was equally unsuccessful in his correspondence with the King and Queen of Naples. His aim was to force them by threats to dismiss their loyal officers, expel the British minister, and close their ports to the British fleet. "Reject the perfidious counsels with which England enthrals you," he told Ferdinand. Ferdinand went hunting. "Is your Majesty's mind," he asked Maria Carolina, "so distinguished amongst women, unable to divest itself of the prejudices of sex, treating of affairs of state as if they were affairs of the heart? You have already lost your kingdom once, and have twice been the cause of a war, which has shaken and ruined your father's house to its foundation—do you wish to be the cause of a third?" Maria Carolina had hysterics. Hugh Elliot, to do him credit, said he felt like hitting Bonaparte. "Her Majesty remarked to me," he wrote Nelson, "with Her usual spirit, that She would willingly consent to have the french balls flying about Her, if She could witness a second Battle of Aboukir in the Bay of Naples."

Such an event seemed highly improbable until suddenly at 3 P.M. on January 19, when the fleet was at anchor off the Maddalena Islands, the lookout cried—a frigate was in sight flying the signal that the French fleet was at sea. "You will be a peer," Nelson scrawled to Bickerton, "as sure as my name is Nelson."

379

Within three hours the eleven ships of the line were at sea. The wind forced them to sail east of Sardinia and hard gales made their progress slow. Ironically, the same gales drove Villeneuve back to Toulon and Nelson was off on a wild goose chase. He expected to find the enemy in the Gulf of Cagliari. He expected to find them at Naples or Sicily. "You will believe my anxiety," he wrote Sir John Acton, "I have neither ate, drank, or slept with any comfort since last Sunday. . . . I am in a fever. God send I may find them."

Off Palermo there was no word, they had either gone back or gone east. If the first, he could not catch them; if the second, he could. On January 29 the fleet beat through the Straits of Messina. On February 8 they were off Alexandria. On the 11th they were off Crete. "I have consulted no man," he wrote Lord Melville, "therefore the whole blame of ignorance in forming my judgement must rest with me. I would allow no man to take from me an atom of my glory had I fallen in with the French Fleet, nor do I desire any man to partake of the responsibility—all is mine, right or wrong."

On February 19 they were back at Malta and learned at last that they had been chasing shadows. But had the shadows been real, the chase could not have been more glorious.

"I have now traversed 1,000 leagues of sea after them," Nelson was writing to Emma on the 18th. "French fleet, French fleet, is all I want to have answered me. I shall never rest till I find them, and they shall neither, if I can get at them." Two days later he was off Maritimo, beating to get off Toulon. He had heard that a Malta convoy had been attacked during his absence and he was grieved and angered by it. It was the result of the ridiculous division of his command to satisfy Sir John Orde.

"I do assure you, my dearest Emma," he wrote next on March 9, "that nothing can be more miserable or unhappy than your poor Nelson." The fleet was anchored in the Bay of Palma. One favorite officer, Captain Layman, had run his ship aground; another, Sir William Bolton, was jeopardizing his promotion by his tardy arrival. We have seen little of Nelson's concern for his officers, but they did not love him for nothing. He was, in every good sense of the word, their patron, and very many of his official letters to them have a short friendly note, or an invitation to dinner, on the bottom. By March 13 he was back off Toulon. The French had come out once and would probably come out again. "We have had a long run to Egypt and back, but as the French Fleet are now ready for Sea again, I fully expect we shall meet them, and then I would change with no man living."

Everything at Merton was going on swimmingly, Davison assured his friend. All the accounts were paid—but if only there had not been the infernal appointment of Sir John Orde! Nelson had lost £250,000! "It puts me stark staring mad when I think of it." Lord Melville had thought, like everyone else, that Nelson was rich, perfectly independent. Even the King sympathized with Nelson. Captain Gore had talked to him about the Spanish frigates. "The King told me at Windsor that we should have the whole and was angry it was not double the sum—that my orders had prevented me taking merchant vessels—but that 'Nelson had done it and I Glory in Him for it—He never loses twice in Parley—it is always a Word and a Blow with Him—I Glory in Him, I Glory in Him:' these were the Exact Words of His Majesty at the Queen's House spoke to me—before thirty Great People and looking round at them while he spoke."

There was a growing feeling in the country that events were ripening suddenly and the harvest might be a bitter one. Shortly before the Toulon fleet had sailed, the enemy squadron in Rochefort had made its escape and there was some anxiety as to its destination. The attack on the Malta convoy caused alarm, though it was not as serious as first thought. Villeneuve's return to Toulon was reported within a fortnight of his sailing, but the fact that he had been able to evade Nelson's fleet was widely discussed with gloomy looks.

There were diversions. On February 7 Master Betty played Romeo to Mrs. Siddons' Juliet. She was fifty, old enough to be his grandmother. It was a sensational performance and thirty people were pulled from the pit in fainting fits. Then on the 20th there was Lady Abercorn's concert. Lady Hamilton performed. "The Company were in raptures," said the Post, "and particularly several noble amateurs, all of whom declared that her ladyship's voice was equal to that of any professional lady of the present day."

Emma was not much in society in February and we must believe that her complaints were genuine. She heard that poor Charles Connor had been brought home behaving oddly and had finally become so deranged that he was committed to the Naval Hospital at Plymouth. She heard, too, of her old enemy. "I have seen Tom Tit once," Lady Bolton wrote from Bath where she was staying, "she called in her carriage at Lady Charlotte Drummond's who lives next door. The lady was not at home, but she got out of her carriage, walked as stiff as a poker about half-a-dozen steps, turned round, got in again. What this manoeuvre was for I cannot tell, unless to shew herself. She need not have taken so much pains if nobody wanted to see her more than I do." Well, they were all getting on.

On the 20th Emma told Mrs. Nelson she had been ill for a fortnight, but she was cured by letters. She had his letters to February 18. *"Depend on this, we shall see our dear Nelson soon, and with Glory, fresh Glory."* She was revitalized. "Charlotte was at Lady Abercorn's assembly on Monday night after our return from Merton where we had been since Saturday. Tomorrow we go to a great dinner at Lord and Lady Carlton's to meet the Essex's. Friday a small party at Miss Paynes, Lord Levington's sister. Saturday and Sunday, Merton, for we have refused all engagements for those days. . . . Lady Bolton is still at Bath and better. Mrs. Matcham is on the point of being confined—how she laughs out her Children. Merton is *more beautiful,* so improved you would not know it again. My Mother has been very ill with an inflammation on her lungs, but she is better. . . ." She met the Young Roscius at Lady Abercorn's assembly, where she performed her "attitudes" for the last recorded time. She could have made twelve of Master Betty!

The news in March was fairly sparse. Bonaparte declared himself King of Italy. He was like the demon king in pantomime and about to enter on the distasteful farce of making all his brothers and sisters kings, queens and princesses. Our old friend Troubridge was going in the *Blenheim* to the East Indies. There was an expedition preparing to sail for the Mediterranean and the defense of Sicily. The main news was the Tenth Report of the Committee of Naval Enquiry. This had been sitting quietly since it had been established in 1803, and had produced nine reports without exciting a murmur. The tenth, however, was concerned with certain defalcations which had taken place when Lord Melville was Treasurer of the Navy. He was involved, the amounts of money were enormous—the First Lord of the Admiralty had embezzled government funds—what a tremendous scandal!

In the meantime, his lordship's most faithful servant was locked up in the great cabin of the *Victory,* in another world. Nelson wrote on March 16:

> The Ship is just parting and I take the last moment to renew my assurances to my Dearest Beloved Emma of my eternal love, affection and adoration. You are ever with me in my Soul, your resemblance is never absent from my mind, and my own dearest Emma I hope very soon that I shall embrace the substantial part of you instead of the Ideal, that will I am sure give us both *real pleasure* and *exquisite happiness.* Longing as I do to be with you, yet I am sure under the circumstances in which I am placed you would be the first to say—may Nelson try and get at those french fellows and come home with Glory to your own Emma, or if they will not come out then come home for a short time and arrange your *affairs,* which have long been neglected. Don't I say

my own love what you would say. Only continue to love me as affectionately as I do you, and we must then be the happiest couple in the world. May God bless you ever prays yours and only your faithful Nelson & Bronte.

The fleet sailed to find their victualers in the Pula roads south of Sardinia on March 30. Rear-Admiral Louis had brought letters from England. There was a scrawled message from a little girl. "I admire dear H's writing," said Nelson. "I think her hand will soon be like her dear Mother's . . ." Well, it was then, because Emma wrote like a four-year-old on skates, but Horatia improved as she grew older. The Boltons were hard up again, he would do what he could. But Sir William Bolton was lazy and had lost the chance of making himself rich. "I shall not talk of Sir John Orde who must be the richest Admiral that ever England saw. He will torment the Admiralty enough. *How should he know how to behave, he never was at Sea.*"

The fleet was standing out to sea from the Pula roads on April 4. Nelson was writing his letters for England.

> My Emma and God forbid you should belong to anyone else, that goose Sir William Bolton has lost his frigate. . . . The time draws near my Emma, my love, my everything that's dear. . . . I hope a return of post, or at least two, will liberate me (I must not say that) for my liberation makes me *all all yours.* I dare not send a little letter, for what with smoking and cutting all would be read. But let them read this, that I love you beyond any Woman in this World and next our dear Ha. How I long to settle what I intend upon Her and not leave her to the mercy of any one or even to any foolish thing I may do in my old age. Adieu for a very short time.

Within a few hours he was writing again. "You will ever glory in your Nelson whether living or dead. I could not exist long in this dreadful suspense, but I am doing what man can do to find them out." The French fleet was at sea again.

Nelson took his ships south to cover the approach to Sicily and the east. He spread his small ships to search the sea lanes from the African coast to the east of Sardinia. He was in a fever of anxiety, but clear enough in his judgment. He did not believe the enemy would sail to the west and, until he had ensured the safety of Sardinia, Naples, Sicily and Egypt, he could not afford to believe it. On April 18 he learned that his first task was over, the enemy had passed the Straits of Gibraltar ten days before. "I may be abused by some blockheads," he wrote Emma, "but I do assure you that upon a revision of my own conduct, that *I approve* and that is a great thing, for if a man does not approve of his own conduct it is certain nobody else can."

The fleet sailed for Gibraltar into a foul wind, and it was not until May 4 that they anchored in Tetuan Bay to take on water and provisions.

> Your poor dear Nelson is, my dearest beloved Emma, very very unwell, after a two years hard fag it has been mortifying the not being able to get at the Enemy. As yet I can get no information about them, at Lisbon this day week they knew nothing about them, but it is now generally believed that they are gone to the West. My movements must be guided by the best judgement I am able to form. John Bull may be angry, but he never had any Officer who has served Him more faithfully, but Providence I rely will yet crown my never failing exertions with success, and that it has only been a hard trial of my fortitude in bearing up against untoward events. You, my own Emma, are my first and last thoughts, and to the last moment of my breath they will be occupied in leaving you independent of the World, and all I beg in this World is that you will be a kind and affectionate *Father* to my *dear Daughter Horatia.*

On May 7 they were through the Straits. Nelson had expected to find word from Sir John Orde waiting for him, to tell him of the enemy's destination. Orde had five ships of the line and two frigates. Surely the latter had been sent to discover the direction taken by the enemy? No. Orde had been at dinner on April 9 when the French fleet of twelve ships of the line and eight frigates had appeared in company with eight Spanish ships of the line from Cadiz. He had borne away, thinking himself lucky to escape, and had sailed to join Lord Gardner's fleet off Ireland. His letters to the Admiralty had been long and involved and mainly concerned with his indignation at Lord Nelson's appointing a prize agent at Gibraltar to determine whether *his* Spanish galleons had been caught on his station.

Poor Nelson, who was telling Davison, "Salt beef and the french fleet is far preferable to roast beef and champagne without them. May God prosper my exertions I pray most fervently and I think He will in the End."

May 9, off Cape St. Vincent. "My dearest Emma, I think myself a little better, but I can neither drink porter nor eat cheese and that is enough to satisfy me that I am far from well. . . . My Emma you are everything to me and I love you if possible more than ever. I send you a Bill for £300, £200 of which is for yourself and the other £100 make in little presents from me to those about you." There was no certain news, but he was going to the West Indies. The ships were victualing for five months. He was only waiting for the Mediterranean expedition to arrive. He sent Mrs. Bolton £100. "I would do more if in my power. I should have been a very rich instead of a poor man if Lord Melville had not given the galleons to Sir John Orde."

Two days later, having seen the convoy carrying the expedition pass, the *Victory* in company with nine ships of the line and three frigates sailed to the west.

The escape of the Rochefort squadron caused enough trouble in London, especially when it turned up in the West Indies and cruised around the British colonies exacting indemnities. "If anything were wanting to open the eyes of the Nation to the real talents of the present Ministers," lectured the *Chronicle* on April 3, "it would be occurrences like this, which there is but too much reason to fear is but the commencement of a system of attack upon us in every quarter, which will distract the attention of a weak and incapable Government, divide our forces, and finally prepare for that great attack upon the British Islands which has never for an instant been abandoned by the enemy."

When, a fortnight later, it was known that the Toulon fleet was out, the *Chronicle* added, "Should it prove true that the Toulon fleet is on its way to the West Indies, we see no chance of safety to our Colonies, particularly the Windward Islands, without a miracle."

The Admiralty was without a head. Faced with a vote against him in Parliament (the majority was one), Lord Melville resigned. With him went all hopes of Emma's pension. In a way, Melville was hard done by, for of all the jobs he had managed in his time, the one he was accused of was the one in which he had the least culpability. Few wept for him, and Emma was one of them. It was rumored that Nelson was to be the next First Lord, only no one knew where Nelson was. Eventually an elderly and blameless old officer, Sir Charles Middleton, was disinterred, created Lord Barham, and propped up at the head of the Admiralty table.

No one knew where Nelson was, not even Emma. "Of course," Mr. Marsden wrote the Admiral on April 17, "we kept the news of the absence of the Squadron as much a secret as possible, and even to Lady Hamilton's repeated enquiries I thought myself obliged to give obscure answers—such as that 'Your Lordship was perfectly well when the latest accounts came away,' which, I am sorry to say, were not satisfactory, and I have unfortunately incurred her Ladyship's displeasure, as she will probably have told you."

On April 26 it was known that the French fleet had left the Mediterranean and a few days later everyone was asking why Sir John Orde had not left a frigate to watch them. Marsden remembered that in one of Orde's letters complaining about Nelson he had threatened to resign. Permission was hastily granted, and he was ordered to strike his flag and come on shore. Lord Bolton wrote his brother on May 7, "I am astonished at Lord Nelson's strange reserve in correspondence. Nobody seems to know where he is and people are a good deal out of humour." They were a good deal more out of humor with Orde, though he had his thousands to console him.

Some said Nelson had gone to Egypt, others that he was on his way to join the Channel fleet. The *Moniteur* of May 16 enjoyed the joke. "As for Lord Nelson, we do not well know where he is at the present moment; but certain we are, that twenty days after the departure of the Tonlon squadron, he was still at Sicily. Perhaps he may have fallen in with another ——— in that quarter." All the genteel, superior, prurient society of Europe filled in the blank space and sniggered.

By the end of May it was known that Nelson had sailed for the West Indies. Admiral Collingwood and a squadron of twelve ships of the line, who had been ordered there, were sent to Cadiz. There was a great deal of speculation—was Nelson right to have sailed 3,500 miles away from Europe, the immediate scene of immense activity? There was a French army of 100,000 men at Boulogne. Bonaparte, after his coronation as King of Italy at Milan, had come to lead them. The Rochefort squadron was back. Now the Toulon squadron would return. Nelson was wrong. "Admiral Lord Nelson has certainly steered on a fruitless pursuit of the enemy," said the *Herald*. "His lordship has not obtained accurate information," said the *Post*. "The state of anxiety and suspense respecting the enemy cannot long be protracted," said the *Chronicle*, and that was the kindest thing that was said! By the end of June, without a word from Nelson, it was generally determined that he had been hoodwinked. The public anger was wreaked on Orde, Melville, and the government, and there was enough over for Nelson when, as was expected, he would limp home confessing failure.

"Mr. Matcham tells us Merton looked very beautiful," Lady Bolton wrote Emma. "He thought you had made wonderful improvements. I cannot help thinking how delighted Lord Nelson will be with it." Emma was at Merton in May. She had nettle rash, so Charlotte said, one of the trying manifestations of anxiety. On June 4 she and Charlotte went to Windsor for a few days to attend the annual celebrations at Eton. On returning to town, she was once more caught in the social round—Lady Mansfield's small party, Lady Bush's ball, and Lady Barrymore's masquerade, where she sang duets with La Billington dressed as a Neapolitan peasant.

Nelson's squadron took twenty-three days to reach Barbados. He had one opportuniy to send letters on the way and told Emma not to be angry with Mr. Marsden and that he gave her all the information he could. He was concerned about his account with Davison's bank (that gentleman was out, by the way). He was deeply in debt to Davison, but Marsh & Creed had invested his prize money as soon as they received it and he would settle everything on his return to dear Merton. He sent an order to Haslewood to pay Mrs. Gibson an annuity of £20 provided she had nothing more to do with Horatia. "Mrs. G. must not presume to chatter . . ." he told Emma.

From Carlisle Bay, Barbados, he wrote on June 4.

> My own Dearest Beloved Emma, Your own Nelson's pride and delight, I find myself within six days of the Enemy, and I have every reason to hope that the 6th of June will immortalize your own Nelson, your fond Nelson. May God send me Victory and us a happy and speedy meeting. Adl. Cochrane is sending home a vessel this day, therefore only pray for my success and my laurels I shall with pleasure lay at your feet, and a sweet kiss will be ample reward for all your faithful Nelson's hard fag, for ever and ever I am your faithful ever faithful, Nelson & Bronte. The Enemy's fleet and army are supposed to have attacked Tobago and Trinidada and are now about landing.

This last sentence contained false information. Villeneuve and the combined fleet of the enemy were at Martinique.

On June 5 the squadron took on 2,000 troops at Barbados and sailed southward. The next day they were off Tobago, and the next off Trinidad. Their high hopes of a second battle of the Nile in the Gulf of Paria were shattered. They turned north and, on the 10th when they were off St. Lucia, Nelson wrote again.

"Your own dear Nelson, my Emma, is very sad—the French fleet have again escaped me. It appears hard to have had the cup at my lip and to have it dashed from me." Had he sailed north instead of south it would have been all over and he would have added a sprig of laurel to his brow, or his memory. His reports of the enemy were that they were now on the run. "I am carrying every rag, but my hopes are very faint, although I must not despair. If they should attempt Antigua I shall be up with them, and if they run I may by good fortune overtake them before they get to Europe. However mortified I may individually feel at not fighting them, yet my happy arrival has saved all our West India islands and commerce."

On the 12th the squadron was at Antigua, the troops disembarked, and they sailed in pursuit of the combined fleet.

What was the result of this chase? An enemy fleet had fled from a British fleet of half its numbers. The islands, that had been an easy prey to the Rochefort squadron and would certainly have fallen to greater numbers, were saved. More than 200 merchant ships carrying sugar were saved. Nelson was chasing the enemy back to Europe and, if he could get information to England of their course, a fleet could be posted to meet them. It was as good as a battle. It was better than a battle. But Captain Hardy thought, "Patience and Perseverance should be poor Lord Nelson's motto."

None of the circumstances of the chase was known in England until July 10, when the brig *Le Curieux* that Nelson had sent home a month before arrived with his dispatches. Before then the newspapers were laden with gloom and West Indian merchants were in despair. Jamaica would be lost! That was what they feared most of all. The Windward and Leeward Islands were nice little honey pots, but Jamaica was the great queen bee herself. It was the government's fault. "If there be a public crime," thundered the *Chronicle*, "more atrocious than another, it is that of filling eminent stations with persons of no talent at so perilous a moment as the present."

The arrival of *Le Curieux* had a more important consequence than that of lifting the gloom and restoring smiles to the faces of City gentlemen. The brig had sighted the combined fleet north of the Azores and the captain reported that it was sailing in the direction of Ferrol. Admiral Cornwallis was warned and Sir Robert Calder's squadron cruising off Cape Finisterre was reinforced.

Then there was a pause, a time of idle rumors and incidental news. There had been a great sea battle and Lord Nelson had been killed. The Austrian army was marching to the Italian front. General Mack had been given the command of the army in Central Germany. Lady Hamilton had gone to Southend with Mrs. Billington. And on July 30 there was a rumor of an action in fog in the Atlantic.

Emma had been dividing her time between Merton and Clarges Street waiting for news. "We are all anxiety as you may readily conceive for news," one of the Bolton girls wrote her from Bath. "You are we know even more anxious than we are. . . . We hear that *Tom Tit* has been very ill and been attended by two Physicians. She is now however got quite well. She looks shockingly really and very old. Mrs. Matcham often wishes she was in heaven, we join and make no doubt we have your good wishes on the occasion." But the time was over when Emma would rise to the bait of Tom Tit. She only wanted news of Nelson.

It came with *Le Curieux*. "Myself and the whole party at Brancaster participate in your joy at my Dear Brother's *Victory*," wrote Mrs. Bolton on July 16. "I must call it since he has done as much or more than any action could have done. Has he not saved the West Indies? His name is so terrible to the French Navy that they dare not face him—that I have the happiness of calling such a man my brother. Where is the man who would have been so active or done so much? I hope now we shall soon see him home, God grant it."

Emma, doubtless with the idea that a little sea bathing would set her up, and certainly with the intention of escaping the incessant dunning of butchers and bakers, Chawners and Cribbs, gathered up her brood of girls and swept off to Southend. "I am not over rich to go into the Country," she wrote Davison on the 19th, "alltho' I have reduced my Establishment, perhaps you will assist me a little. The time will now soon come when I shall no longer be a plague to you." Glad to say he sent her £100.

On August 1 the true extent of the action in the fog was known. It was immediately classified as a glorious victory. By standards other than those set by Nelson it was a glorious victory. Sir Robert Calder with fifteen ships of the line had met the combined fleet with twenty and had taken two prizes before a thick fog had enabled the enemy to bear away. They were said to be heading for Ferrol, but Calder had given it as his opinion that he would engage them again. Lieutenant Nicholson, who brought home the first dispatches, repeated the opinion in the Jamaica Coffee House. "We are assured," said the *Herald* on August 3, "that Sir Robert Calder has placed himself between the enemy and the shore, so that in no state of the weather could they enter Ferrol or Corunna without coming to action." This was foolish of Calder and even more so of Nicholson. As the days passed without news of a second action, the glorious victory became a doubtful encounter. When, on August 17, it was learned that the enemy had gone into Vigo and then run for Ferrol, so escaping Calder completely, it was as bad as a defeat. Calder, so went the general and utterly superfluous cry, was not Nelson.

Nelson himself had, in the meantime, been making slow progress back across the Atlantic toward the Straits of Gibraltar. He called it slow and, had the winds been twice as favorable and yet not brought them within shot of the enemy, he would still have called it slow. He was haunted by the false information which had deprived him of his battle on June 6. "I have ever found," he told Emma, "if I was left and acted as my poor noddle told me was right I should seldom err." If, on his return, he discovered the enemy to be in harbor, he would relinquish the command and come home. If they were out and he found them . . . "Kiss my angel Horatia, farewell, farewell, I love till Death, and afterwards will be your Guardian. May God bless you my own dearest beloved Emma. If I live I shall soon be with you."

The squadron was in sight of Cape Spartel on July 18. They passed Collingwood, watching off Cadiz, and sailed for Gibraltar to take on water. On July 20 Nelson noted in his journal, "I went on Shore for the first time since the 16th of June 1803; and from having my foot out of the *Victory*, two years wanting ten days." Two days later they were at Tetuan to complete their watering and victualing. They were under way again on the 24th and sailed back through the Straits that night. Without pausing to speak to Collingwood's squadron, they sailed by, "steering for Ireland or England as I may hear my services may be most wanted," wrote Nelson.

They had a tedious voyage north into the wind. There was no news of the enemy, except from the newspapers which were a month old. "We have received accounts that the *Curieux* brig passed the Enemy's fleet on the 19th June," wrote Hardy, "therefore no doubt remains but they are gone to the Northward." Nelson sailed to join the Channel fleet and Admiral Cornwallis. On August 15 the fleets exchanged signals and the Admirals salutes. Nelson learned at last of Calder's battle and the subsequent flight of the combined fleet to Ferrol. Cornwallis dispensed with the formalities of a meeting and sent him home to Portsmouth in company with the *Superb*. On August 18, the two ships anchored at Spithead.

The *Morning Chronicle*, August 10. "There is really something epic in this concentration of incidents and feelings. The occasion is *dignus vindice* and Lord Nelson comes before us again as the hero for whom the grand event of the piece seems reserved."

The *Morning Post*, August 9. "We are not in general very superstitiously inclined, but when a hero and a cause, like Lord Nelson and that in which he is embarked, come home to our bosoms and our business, there is a kind of patriotic superstition."

The Emperor was at Boulogne with the Imperial Guard and 120,000 soldiers of the army of England, the army of invasion. If the French fleets combined, there would be an armada of sixty-two ships of the line. Now, thousands of men stood between Bonaparte and his design, but to them and to England one man stood for them all. The little Admiral on the *Victory*.

And what was he thinking about? "I hope we are not to be put in quarantine." But he was, and he believed it would take an Order in Council to get him out of it.

In the meantime, an express was sent to Mr. Marsden. "A note was immediately sent to Clarges Street," wrote that gentleman on August 18, "and the maitre d'hotel informs me he has forwarded it by express to South End in Essex where her Ladyship is at present." The *Post*'s Southend correspondent reported on the 19th, "Lady Hamilton suddenly quitted this place, in a chaise and four, at five o'clock this morning. She took her departure, I understand, in consequence of an express that arrived here yesterday evening. Miss Nelson set off in company with her Ladyship, but Mrs. Billington still continues here and the young ladies who composed the family party still remain behind." He, or perhaps she, added, without the slightest chance of being believed by anyone, "Lady Hamilton's sudden departure from South End was in consequence of her mother's indisposition."

Nelson fumed away a day. He would have been fumed like his letters if it would have meant his release a minute earlier. He wrote on the 19th to Emma to say he would rejoice to see them all at Merton, "dear Horatia, Charlotte, and Ann and Eliza, and I would not have my Emma's relative go without my seeing her." But "little Emma," the first "little Emma," had gone. He wrote to his brother William, "I am so so but what is very odd the better for going to the West Indies, and even with the anxiety. We must not talk of Sir Robert Calder's battle. I might not have done so much with my small force. If I had fell in with them, you would probably have been a Lord before I wished, for I know they meant to make a dead set at the *Victory*."

On the evening of the 19th, after he had affirmed that the *Victory* had not been in contact with any fever-ridden place or ship, he was allowed to land. As he came ashore, a vast crowd that had assembled on the ramparts cheered him to the skies. They pressed around him as he made his way to pay his respects to the Commissioner and Commander in Chief, Portsmouth. They gathered around his coach and cheered him on his way into the night.

The *Victory* lay dark at her anchorage at Motherbank. Hardy was ill ashore, but the seamen had no leave. Nelson's furniture stayed in his cabin. "The Ship," wrote Hardy, "is to be considered as Lord Nelson's Flag Ship and kept in readiness for him."

It was a fine summer. At Merton, though the new building was by no means finished, the extension to the dining room already promised greater comfort to the diners, and that to the kitchen, greater dinners. It was outside, however, that the real improvement to the beauty of the place had been achieved. The canal had been filled in on two sides and no longer constricted the walks around the house. Grassy slopes led down to shrubberies; gravel paths wound beneath spreading trees for those shaded perambulations so convenient for lovers and so necessary for overburdened digestions; the Nile sparkled, and the pond was clean-swept by those ferocious snappers-up of trifles, the pikes. On every side the prospect was green and pleasing, not in the formal seventeenth-century manner, but in the casual charm of its successor, which always suggested that Nature would have organized her affairs in exactly that way had she been capable of it. It was precisely the place that a sailor returning from the sea would be delighted to come home to.

Mrs. Bolton wrote:

> Thanks my Dear Lady for your *scrap*, it was indeed short and *sweet*, for *sweet* was the intelligence that my Dearest Brother was arrived in England. What a Paradise he must think Merton, to say nothing of the *Eve* it contains. I need not *give* you joy for I am *sure* you have it. The Dr. is at Mrs. Berney's, but depend upon it they will soon be with you and fill your House. When you give me a Hint I will come. God bless you—no time I know to read my thrash.

"We have room for you all my dear Belle soeur," Emma wrote Mrs. Matcham on August 22, "so come as soon as you can. We shall be happy, most happy. Here are Sir Peter Parker and God knows who, so Nelson has not time to say more than that he loves you and will rejoice to see you."

The Matchams could not come at once—one of the little ones was ill—but the Doctor and his wife, Horace and Charlotte, the Boltons with young Tom and the girls, were very soon gathered under the roof at Merton with Nelson, Emma, Horatia and Mrs. Cadogan.

Nelson had arrived home early in the morning of Tuesday, August 20. The next day he went up to town and called in at the Admiralty, before going on to the office of Marsh & Creed, and then to Somerset House. From there he went to Downing Street and spent an hour with Mr. Pitt. Everywhere he was followed by a multitude of people. He was in half-dress and wore a green shade above his left eye. He was looking very well. Fortunately, the King was on holiday at Weymouth, and he was spared a levee. He returned to Merton for dinner.

Thursday was spent at home, doubtless with some of the many letters he received from friends and well-wishers, welcoming him and urging him to go to sea again. On Friday he was in town again and called on Lord

Castlereagh and Lord Sidmouth, the erstwhile Mr. Addington. The news was considerable: Russian troops were marching through Poland, and Austrian troops had crossed the frontier into Bavaria. War on the Continent was imminent. At the same time it was reported that the combined fleet had sailed from Ferrol ten days earlier and had been seen steering WNW. Was Bonaparte about to strike his blow against England before war broke out on the eastern frontiers of France? This was the great question of the day. The Emperor was still at Boulogne, but the weight of informed opinion was on the side of *no* invasion.

One of the most dramatic circumstances of Nelson's return to England was that nearly everyone who had had anything to do with him in his life reappeared, either in correspondence or in person. Here is Lord Minto, writing on Monday the 26th.

> I went to Merton on Saturday and found Nelson just sitting down to dinner, surrounded by a family party, of his brother the Dean, Mrs. Nelson, their children, and the children of a sister. Lady Hamilton at the head of the table and Mother Cadogan at the bottom. I had a hearty welcome. He looks remarkably well and full of spirits. His conversation is a cordial in these low times. . . . Lady Hamilton has improved and added to the house and the place extremely well without his knowing she was about it. He found it all ready done. She is a clever being after all; the passion is as hot as ever.
>
> I met Nelson today in a mob in Piccadilly and got hold of his arm, so that I was mobbed too. It is really quite affecting to see the wonder and admiration and love and respect, of the whole world; and the genuine expression of all these sentiments at once, from the gentle and simple, the moment he is seen. It is beyond anything represented in a play or a poem of fame.

When he was in town, Nelson took rooms at Gordon's Hotel in Albemarle Street for his headquarters. Lord Hood called on him there; Prince Castelcicala called five times without seeing him; and many others, including a deputation of West India merchants who brought him their thanks for saving their bacon, or rather their sugar.

On the 28th the news was that, a week before, the enemy fleet in Brest had made an attempt to come out of the harbor. Cornwallis had drawn up his fleet for a battle, there had been an exchange of broadsides, and the enemy had retreated. The Rochefort squadron was already out roaming the Atlantic. Here was the suggestion of some French plan, perhaps the union of the Brest, Toulon and Rochefort squadrons for a sweep up the Channel or a trip to Ireland, foiled by British promptitude and their own incompetence. "What is to be done," Bonaparte said once, "with Admirals who allow their spirits to sink, and determine to hasten home at the first danger they receive?"

The next morning's *Chronicle* reported, "We are happy to state that the gallant Lord Nelson will very speedily hoist his Flag on board the *Victory*. His Lordship is again to have the Command in the Mediterranean, but we understand that the Cadiz Station is to be included within the limits of that Command."

This was a scoop and, from the detail about the Cadiz station, something more than an inspired guess. Mr. Perry, the editor of the *Chronicle*, was intimate at Merton, Nelson looked forward to meeting him there, and surely he must have got this information from the Admiral himself? If so, Nelson had made up his mind to go back to sea before he knew the combined fleet was in Cadiz. That decided when he would sail, not whether he would sail.

The disappearance of the separate command outside the Straits caused a lot of comment. "That matter deserves and may one day obtain examination," said the *Chronicle*. "The reasons why neither Admiral Cornwallis nor Lord Nelson were admitted to share the profits of that station, we venture to assert, had no reference to public utility or naval glory. We believe George Rose, who hates a job as well as any man in England, could give a very good account of the matter."

Nelson was writing to Mr. Rose on the 29th. "I wish Mr. Pitt would give me for my Brother in Law Mr. Thomas Bolton, Father of one of the heirs of my Title, a Commissionership in either the Customs, or Excise, or Navy Office, the first would be most preferable." They were always asking him for something, and he—well, as he told Rose, "I could not bring my mouth to ask a favour." In fact his letter to Pitt that day was all about Sardinia. Minto dined at Merton in the afternoon and found some more people there, "brothers and sisters with their husbands, and Mr. Greville."

The Matchams had not yet come—the little one had died. "We all feel for your situation," wrote Mrs. Bolton from Merton on the 30th, "but I write now in the name of both my Lord and Lady to say they think the sooner you leave such a melancholy scene the better, therefore let me beg of you to come immediately, lest you should not be in time to see our Dear Brother, it is very uncertain. He looks remarkably well and you will find him such a kind and affectionate Relation and Friend as seldom is to be met with, seeing and hearing him will soothe your grief."

Beckford wrote, Sir Edward Berry wrote, Dumouriez, Tom Allen, Mrs.

Faddy, the mother of the mid Emma mothered in Naples. Baron d'Eiker and Ekoffen did not write, but he was about the only one. Nelson read his letters and waited. "My time and movement must depend upon Bonaparte," he told Davison. "We are at present ignorant of his intentions and whether the squadron from Ferrol are coming to join the Brest fleet, going to the Mediterranean, or cruizing for our homeward bound fleet. . . . I may remain in England for seven years, if the Enemy's fleet are met with." Had he said seven months he might have meant the last remark.

September 1 was a Sunday. At 5 A.M. on Monday Captain Blackwood of the *Euryalus*, lately from Cadiz, stopped at Merton on his way to the Admiralty. Nelson was up and dressed. The Captain's news was decisive: the combined fleet was in Cadiz. Nelson knew it. He would beat them. He would give Monsieur Villeneuve a drubbing!

Britannia found the hero walking up and down on the terrace, on the part he called the quarter-deck. It was her finest moment. He would go, but she could try to stop him. She did not. "Brave Emma," he said, "good Emma, if there were more Emmas there would be more Nelsons." He left for town.

"He looks very well," Emma was writing to Mrs. Lutwidge on Tuesday, "but he is not strong and again he is obliged to go forth for they cannot go on without his powerful arm—he will not be many days longer with us I believe. He has all his Brothers and *Sisters* at Merton and I go there to see them, but for fear of having all the *Cats* on my back I am over cautious so as to be *completely miserable*." There were twelve guests at Merton and obviously some problem getting to bed, Nelson's bed. "He is adored, as he walks the streets thousands follow him, blessing him and wishing him Good Luck. He sits down to dinner, every day his own family, seventeen to dinner. He lives at Gordon's Hotel when in London, but *often often* do we wish you was with us. As the Combined fleets are in Cadiz, he will go off there with a large force, near 40 Sail of the Line, and he says that if he can but lick them well he shall be happy. (*What do you think of Sir R. Calder*—I could have done more than him.) I did not get your letter till yesterday in town and today I am here at Merton. Captains Keats, Culverhouse, Bowen &c. &c. are come to dinner. Charlotte, Mrs. Matcham, Mrs. Bolton, Mrs. Nelson, beg their kind compliments. May God bless you my ever dear Mrs. Lutwidge, you do not know how much I love you. Kiss the Admiral for your ever affectionate and grateful Emma—I should like to say Emma Nelson. How pretty it sounds."

Nelson was also at Merton and wrote to Mr. Rose again to tell him Mr. Bolton was a gentleman in spite of having been a merchant and a large farmer. He added, "I hold myself ready to go forth whenever I am desired, although God knows I want rest, but self is entirely out of the question. I shall rejoice to see you on board the *Victory if only for a moment*, but I shall certainly not be an advocate for being at Portsmouth till one of the *Victory's* anchors are at the Bows." The papers were saying that he would leave immediately.

The next day the reality of the situation struck Emma and she was miserable. She told Lady Bolton, "I am again broken hearted as our dear Nelson is immediately going. It seems as though I have had a fortnight's dream and am awoke to all the misery of this cruel separation. But what can I do, His powerful arm is of so much consequence to his Country. But I do nor cannot say more. My heart is broken."

Reality was the loading of a wagon with the Admiral's things for Portsmouth. It was Charles Greville writing about a party he intended giving at Paddington which would never be given. It was going to town to order double brown stout from the wine merchants, twenty fine hams and six kegs of tripe, pickles, sauces, mustard and pepper, from Burgess's, a new set of stars from the embroiderers, a pair of spectacles from Mr. Dolland, and to dispose of the few remaining presents of value to Rundell, Bridge & Rundell, to pay for it all.

Reality was paying bills and settling affairs: £327 to plumbing, painting and glazing at Merton; £133 to Mr. Peddieson the upholsterer—"To a large Feather Bed & Bolster filled with best goose feathers: £18." And it was hardly used! At Peddieson's Nelson saw his coffin, the one made from the mainmast of *L'Orient*. Afterward, Peddieson used to say that the Admiral had told him to get it properly engraved as he would probably need it on his return. £133 2s. 6d., brother Maurice's outstanding bill for medicines—"I have much to lose, but little to gain," Nelson wrote Davison, sending him the bill, "and I go because it is right and I will serve the Country faithfully."

Reality was, above all, the striking of the clock every hour and the hours racing by until poor Emma felt the clock was mad, or she was mad; but, as usual, it was the world that was mad.

September 6, and the newspapers were full of reports that the French army was quitting Boulogne, the Emperor had gone, and the camp was breaking up. Nelson's sea orders were ready at the Admiralty. Someone had invented a submarine bomb, someone else a waterproof jacket; others wrote for money or appointments; the Duke of Clarence invited Nelson to dinner and, when he could not come, arrived himself at Merton, taking up precious moments of Nelson's time with those dearest to him. Showing consideration, and the house was upside down with preparations, the Boltons and William Nelsons took their leave. Only the Matchams stayed, and they had come late and could not be dismissed to a house of mourning.

Nelson was in town on Saturday the 8th and again on Tuesday. He called to see Lord Sidmouth on the way and drew his plan of attack on a little table with his finger. "Rodney broke the line in one point," he said. "I will break it in two." He went to the Admiralty with Sir Sidney Smith, and afterward to Downing Street. He dined away from Merton for the first time that afternoon, going with Emma and the party to Mr. Goldsmid's.

On Wednesday he was again at the Admiralty. What did he see of Merton? He escaped from one annoyance by withdrawing his proxy from Lord Moira, but had to endure another when he received a summons to call on the Prince of Wales at Carlton House before his departure. He went up the next morning and took his leave of the Prince and the Admiralty. He was using the Duke of Queensberry's carriage and got across to Downing Street without the usual mob. He looked in to say goodbye to Castlereagh at the Colonial Office and found Sir Sidney Smith there and General Wellesley, who had just returned from his famous campaign in India. The newspapers thought some vast Eastern conquest was being planned. Wellesley, dragging his memory for a detail or two years later, said he first thought Nelson a charlatan, but after the Admiral had apparently found out who *he* was and began to talk sense, he was agreeably surprised to find him an officer and a statesman. Perhaps he was talking to S.S.S. all the time? Nelson had his dinner with Old Q., Lord William Gordon and a Mr. Douglas, and returned to spend his last night at Merton.

He found Lord Minto there. "I went yesterday to Merton in a great hurry," his lordship wrote on the 13th, "as he, Lord Nelson, said he was to be at home all day, and he dines at half-past three. But I found he had been sent for to Carlton House and he and Lady Hamilton did not return till half-past five. I stayed till ten at night and took a final leave of him. . . . Lady Hamilton was in tears all yesterday; could not eat, and hardly drink, and near swooning, and all at table. It is a strange picture. She tells me nothing can be more pure and ardent than this flame. He is in many points a really great man, in others a baby." It is a pity we have to rely on this comfortable cynic for a word of Nelson's last full evening at home.

He had a day, a whole day to see what he was leaving, to play with Horatia, to comfort Emma, to talk about the future. He wrote two notes, one very famous, the other inconsiderable except as symbolic of much of what we have read. It was to Marsh & Creed, to pay fifteen guineas to Mr. Burlesworth "when he delivers 100 prints to Lady Hamilton of my Ships and Head." The first . . .

It was dark outside, the chaise was at the door. Before leaving, Nelson went upstairs to Horatia's bedroom and knelt and prayed by the little girl asleep. He came down. Emma would not go outside with him and he left her weeping. George Matcham walked with him to the chaise. Nelson said he would bring back a fortune and share it with all his family. Come back yourself, said Matcham.

In the darkness, carried away along the new gravel drive, Nelson wrote in his pocket book.

Friday September 13th 1805. Friday night at half past ten drove from dear dear Merton where I left all which I hold dear in this World to go to serve my King and Country. May the Great God whom I adore enable me to fulfill the expectations of my Country and if it is his good pleasure that I should return my thanks will never cease being offered up to the Throne of his Mercy. If it is his good providence to cut short my days upon earth, I bow with the greatest submission relying that he will pro-tect those so dear to me that I may leave behind. His will be done. Amen Amen Amen.

The next morning he was at Portsmouth. It appears that Mr. Lancas-ter, the Vicar of Merton and a friend and admirer, was either at Ports-mouth, or followed Nelson there. "6 o'clock, George Inn," the Admiral scrawled hurriedly. "My dearest and most beloved of Women Nelson's Emma, I arrived here this moment and Mr. Lancaster takes it. His coach is at the door and only waits for my Line. *Victory* is at St. Helens and if possible shall be at Sea this day. God protect you and my Dear Horatia prays ever your most faithful Nelson & Bronte."

After breakfast he went to pay his respects to the Commissioner of the Dockyard, Sir Charles Saxton. The crowds were thick on the ramparts and at the usual place of embarkation, and he went down on the South Sea beach where the bathing machines were drawn up. George Rose had come from Cuffnells with Mr. Canning, and they followed Nelson through the crowd of—oh, every sort of person, some cheering, some weeping, and some praying. As the Admiral's barge pushed off, Nelson raised his hat. Then he was gone.

Rose and Canning dined aboard the *Victory* and Nelson, as he told Emma the next day, spoke seriously. "I did not dislike letting out a little

knowledge before Canning, who seems a very clever deep-headed man."
This is interesting in view of General Wellesley's remarks, as it appears that
Nelson adapted his conversation to the intelligence of his companion. He
again pressed Bolton's claims and informed Rose of his own circumstances.
"Rose was astonished at my not being rich and he said he would tell the
whole." The politicians went ashore and the *Victory* prepared to sail.

The wind was fair on the 15th, both anchors were at the bows, the
sails were filled, and the hero left England. The next morning, off Dun-
nose, he wrote to Davison regretting he had been unable to see him. "I
wish I could have been rich enough with ease to myself to have settled my
account with you. . . ." They must settle up the amount owing and he
would give a bond for it. "If you and I live, no harm can happen, but
should either of us drop much confusion may arise to those we may leave
behind." Chawner was to be paid for the work done and new work ordered
in the kitchen, anteroom, and dining room. "The alteration will cost about
three times as much as if it had been done at first." He had given blind
Mrs. Nelson £150 and promised to pay her rent, £40 over the £200 a year
he already allowed her.

There was another letter for Emma that day, written off Portland. He
had read hers:

> and I can only assure you that every tear is a proof to me of your
> most warm attachment, which were it possible would make me
> more yours than I am at present, but that is impossible for I love
> and adore you to the very excess of the passion. But with God's
> blessing we shall soon meet again. Kiss dear dear Horatia a thou-
> sand times for me. I write this letter and I fear I shall too soon
> have an opportunity of sending it, for we are standing near Wey-
> mouth, the place of all others I should wish to avoid, but if it
> continues moderate I hope to escape without anchoring. But
> should I be forced, I shall act as a Man and your Nelson, neither
> Courting or ashamed to hold up my head before the Greatest
> Monarch in the *World*. I have thank God nothing to be ashamed
> of.

They passed Weymouth safely and he did not have to go and see King
George.

On the 17th the *Victory* was off Plymouth, signaling the warships
there to come out. "I entreat my Dear Emma that you will cheer up and we
will look forward to many many happy years and be surrounded by our
Children's Children. God Almighty can when he pleases remove the im-

pediment. My heart and soul is with you and Horatia." The impediment was, presumably, Fanny. Rose got a note that day with a famous phrase in it. "I will try to have a motto," said Nelson, "at least it shall be my watchword *Touch and Take*."

On the voyage to Cadiz the frigate *Decade* was hailed and took home a note for Emma and some advice for the Duke of Clarence. "If your Royal Highness has any weight with our fellow government, let not General Mack be employed, for I knew him at Naples to be a rascal, a scoundrel, and a coward." It was too late. The Austrian army was already in Bavaria and the French army was massing on the Rhine.

September 25 and the Rock of Lisbon was in sight. "We had only one day's real fair wind," he told her, "but by perseverance we have done much. I am anxious to join the fleet for it would add to my grief if any other man was to give them the Nelson touch which *we* say is warranted never to fail."

On the 28th he joined the fleet that was made up of the combined forces of Admirals Collingwood and Calder. The next day was his birthday. He was forty-seven years old.

At once his correspondence swelled to an enormous flood of some twenty letters a day. We are here concerned only with a few old friends. To Sir John Acton he said that here he was again after only twenty-five days in England, and only three visits to London: that was piling it on a bit and he made it up to four later. Mr. Gibbs learned that "good Mrs. Cadogan seems very much broke but Dear Lady Hamilton is as beautiful and good as ever," and Sir Alexander Ball that "Merton is become a perfect Paradise, the House is entirely different, the water changed, and the grounds laid out in the most beautiful manner, and all by her taste, no Capability Brown. Coming forth was really being drove out of Paradise, but I allowed nothing to stand against the call of my Country."

Letters came from Naples. "I predict the greatest successes and glory for you always in our vicinity," spelled out King Ferdinand. "The mere knowledge of our hero Nelson's being in the Mediterranean animates individual courage and contributes to the success of all the operations in progress," effused Queen Maria Carolina.

On October 1 Nelson made time to write home.

> I have had about 4 o'clock this morning one of my dreadful spasms which has almost enervated me. . . . My opinion of its effect some one day has never altered. However, it is entirely gone off and I am only quite weak, but I do assure you, my Emma, that

the uncertainty of human life makes the situation of you dearer to my affectionate heart. . . .

I believe my arrival was most welcome, not only to the Commander of the Fleet but also to every individual in it, and when I came to explain to them the Nelson touch it was like an Electric Shock, some shed tears, all approved, it was new, it was singular, it was simple, and from Admiral downwards it was repeated—it must succeed if ever they will allow us to get at them. You are my Lord surrounded by friends who you inspire with confidence—some my dear Emma may be Judas's, but the majority are certainly much pleased with my commanding them.

He had reports that the enemy's fleet numbered thirty-five or thirty-six sail of the line, he would have twenty-three. (In the event, the combined fleet numbered thirty-three, and the British fleet twenty-seven sail of the line.)

He added another page the next day, mostly about Sir Robert Calder, who had been ordered home to face an inquiry into his actions on July 22. Calder felt the disgrace of being turned out of his ship and Nelson allowed him to sail in her to England. "He is in adversity, and if he ever has been my Enemy he now feels the *pang* of it, and finds me one of his best friends."

It was about this time that Emma went to stay with the Doctor and his family at Canterbury. Miss Connor wrote her from Merton on October 4 and Horatia added a rather splotchy postscript—mind you, there was not much room left on the paper and she was only four and three-quarters. "My dear my lady I thank you for the books. I drink out of my lord's cup every day. Give my love to him every day when you write and a kiss. Miss Connor gave me some kisses, when I read my book well I have kisses. My love to Miss Nelson my dear my lady I love you very much Horatia."

Emma sent Nelson Miss Connor's letter and wrote herself on the 8th. It is one of the very few of her letters to survive and it did so because it never reached him. "My dearest life, we are just come from church for I am so fond of the Church Service and the cannons are so civil, we have every day a fine anthem for me." The Doctor had given a dinner, but it had been all right because Marianna had dressed the macaroni and curry. Marianna was there because Julia was seven months pregnant and had to get married. Horatia had been at the wedding and the other day she said at table, "Mrs. Cadogging, I wonder Julia did not run out of the Church when she went to be married, for I should seeing my squinting husband come in, for my God, how ugly he is and how he looks cross-eyed, why, as my lady says, he looks two ways for Sunday." Emma continued, "Now Julia's husband is the ugliest man you ever saw, but how that little thing could observe him, but she is clever is she not Nelson."

> Charlotte hates Canterbury it is so *dull*, so it is. My dear girl writes every day in Miss Conner's letter and I am so pleased with her. My heart is broke away from her, but I have now had her so long at Merton that my heart cannot bear to be without her. You will be even fonder of her when you return. She says, "I love my dear dear godpapa, but Mrs. Gibson told me he killed all the people and I was afraid." Dearest angel she is. Oh Nelson how I love her, but how do I idolize you—the dearest husband of my heart, you are all in this world to your Emma. May God send you victory and home to your *Emma, Horatia, and paradise Merton,* for when you are there it will be paradise. My own Nelson, may God prosper you and preserve you for the sake of your affectionate Emma.

She was concerned for him. "Write often, tell me how you are and how the sea agrees with you, weather it is a bad port to blockade, in short the smallest trifle that concerns you is so very interesting to your *own* faithful Emma. . . . God bless you my own own Nelson."

She was not well. The papers of the 10th reported that the convoy from the East Indies had brought her a present of muslins and shawls worth £600. Who could have sent her that? Not poor Troubridge, for he was dead, drowned in the wreck of the *Blenheim*. She was not well. How could she be well? The whole country was gloomily awaiting the clash of arms in Europe. General Mack was at Ulm. "General Mack," said the *Chronicle*, "allowed to be a great tactitian, is nevertheless an officer to whom fortune has never been kind."

Mrs. Bolton was summoned from Bath. She answered on the 17th:

> I shall obey your commands or rather I may say wishes, and be at Merton next Tuesday night. . . . I saw Tom Tit yesterday in her Carriage at the next door come to take Lady Charlotte Drummond out with her. She looked then much as usual, had I seen only her hands *spreading* about I should have known her. I hope by the last Lisbon mails you have got Letters from my Dear Brother and that I am sure will drive away all the Blue Devils in spite of Screetch owls, rooks &c.—you must keep up your spirits —what in the world will my Lord think if he comes back and finds you grown thin and looking ill.

Her lord was thinking at that moment of the impending battle. "The Enemy are, I have not the smallest doubt, determined to put to Sea," he wrote Emma on the 6th, "and our battle must soon be fought, although they will be so very superior in numbers to my present force, yet I must do my best and have no fears but that I shall spoil their voyage, but my wish is to do much more and therefore hope the Admiralty have been active in sending me ships, for it is only numbers which can annihilate. A decisive stroke on their fleet would make half a peace, and my Emma if I can do that I shall, as soon as possible, ask to come home and get my rest, at least for the winter, and if other inducement was wanting for my exertion this would be sufficient. To come to you a victor would be a victory twice gained." The next day he added a note and said, "Happy will they be who are present and disappointed will those be who are absent. May God instruct us and Heavens bless."

In those October days the British fleet was slowly augmented by ships from England, and the combined fleet of the enemy—"the Combined Devils" Emma called them—prepared for their run from Cadiz. The Admiral was occupied with his incessant business and his orders, "No Captain can do very wrong if he places his Ship alongside that of an Enemy," "When in presence of an Enemy, all Ships under my command are to bear white Colours, and a Union Jack is to be suspended from the fore topgallant stay." The captains were painting their ships à la Nelson, with broad yellow bands along the sides and yellow hoops on the masts to be immediately recognizable.

There was all the business before a battle, and then the battle came.

Victory, October 19th, 1805. My Dearest Angel, I was made happy by the pleasure of receiving your letter of September 19th and I rejoice to hear that you are so very good a girl and love my Dear Lady Hamilton who most dearly loves you, give her a kiss for me. The Combined fleets of the Enemy are now reported to be coming out of Cadiz and therefore I answer your letter, my dearest Horatia, to mark to you that you are ever upper-most in my thoughts. I shall be sure of your prayers for my safety, conquest and speedy return to Dear Merton and our Dearest good Lady Hamilton. Be a good girl, mind what Miss Connor says to you. Receive my Dearest Horatia the affectionate Paternal blessings of your Father, Nelson & Bronte.

And on the same day:

My dearest beloved Emma the dear friend of my bosom, The signal has been made that the enemy's combined fleet are coming out of port. We have very little wind, so that I have no hopes of seeing them before tomorrow. May the God of Battles crown my endeavours with success; at all events, I will take care that my name shall ever be most dear to you and Horatia, both of whom I love as much as my own life; and as my last writing before the battle will be to you, so I hope in God that I shall live to finish my letter after the Battle. May Heaven bless you prays your Nelson & Bronte.

October 20th. In the morning we were close to the mouth of the Straits, but the wind had not come far enough to the westward to allow the combined fleets to weather the Shoals of Trafalgar, but they were counted as far as forty sail of ships of war, which I suppose to be thirty-four of the Line and six Frigates. A group of them was seen off the lighthouse off Cadiz this morning, but it blows so very fresh and thick weather that I rather believe they will go into the Bay before night. May God Almighty give us success over these fellows and enable us to get a peace.

This was his last letter. His last written words were penned in his journal.

In the great cabin of the *Victory* nearly all the furniture had been taken away and stored. "Take care of my guardian angel," said Nelson as they removed Emma's picture. He had to kneel at his desk to write with his one hand in his journal.

October 21st. At daylight saw the Enemy's Combined Fleet from East to E.S.E.; bore away; made the signal for Order of Sailing, and to Prepare for Battle; the Enemy with their heads to the Southward; at Seven the Enemy wearing in succession. May the Great God whom I worship grant to my Country, and for the benefit of Europe in general, a great and glorious Victory; and may no misconduct in any one tarnish it; and may humanity after Victory be the predominant feature in the British Fleet. For myself individually, I commit my life to Him who made me, and may his blessing light upon my endeavours for serving my Country faithfully. To Him I resign myself and the just cause which is entrusted to me to defend. Amen Amen Amen.

Then he added his last codicil. "Whereas the eminent services of Emma Hamilton, widow of the Right Honourable Sir William Hamilton, have been of the very greatest service to our King and Country, to my knowledge, without her receiving any reward from either our King or Country . . ." He mentioned the two services that we have seen and judged.

> Could I have rewarded these services, I would not now call upon my Country; but as that has not been in my power, I leave Emma Lady Hamilton, therefore, a Legacy to my King and Country, that they will give her an ample provision to maintain her rank in life. I also leave to the beneficence of my Country my adopted daughter, Horatia Nelson Thompson; and I desire She will use in future the name of Nelson only. These are the only favours I ask of my King and Country at this moment when I am going to fight their Battle. May God bless my King and Country, and all those who I hold dear. My relations it is needless to mention; they will of course be amply provided for. Nelson & Bronte.

He sent for Hardy and Blackwood to witness his signature.

The two lines of British ships were bearing down slowly on the long irregular line of the enemy. The sky and the sea were inseparable in grayness. The ships were crowded with men: scarlet-coated marines, bluejackets, midshipmen in white and blue, officers in blue and gold . . .

On the *Victory* the Admiral was walking about with a group of officers, speaking encouragement to the crew, in good spirits. "This is the happiest day of my life," he said, "and it is a happy day too at Burnham Thorpe, this is the day of the fair." The four stars, dull gold on his coat, no sword . . .

He asked Blackwood what he would consider a victory? The Captain answered that if fourteen ships were captured it would be a glorious result. "I shall not, Blackwood, be satisfied with anything short of twenty."

Bands were playing on some of the ships and a group of sailors were dancing a jig.

"Mr. Pasco," the Admiral summoned the Flag Lieutenant, "I wish to say to the Fleet, 'England confides that every man will do his duty,' you must be quick for I have one more to make, which is for Close Action." "If your Lordship will permit me to substitute *expects* for *confides* the signal will soon be completed, because the word *expects* is in the vocabulary, and *confides* must be spelt." "That will do, Pasco, make it directly."

The enemy were firing. Shots passed over the *Victory*. Nelson was on the poop to get a better view. He desired Blackwood to return to his frigate. The Captain shook his hand. "I trust, my Lord, that on my return to the *Victory*, which will be as soon as possible, I shall find your Lordship well, and in possession of twenty Prizes." "God bless you, Blackwood, I shall never speak to you again."

Hardy mentioned to him that his coat with its decorations would make him a target. He replied that it was too late to be changing a coat.

Seven or eight ships were firing at the *Victory*. John Scott was struck down as he stood talking to Hardy on the quarter-deck. As the body was thrown overboard, Nelson asked, "Is that poor Scott who is gone?"

There was a rain of shot on the decks, the wheel was shattered, men lay dead and dying. A flying splinter tore the buckle off Hardy's shoe. Nelson stopped and smiled. "This is too warm work, Hardy, to last long." He added that he had never seen men behave with such cool courage.

They were up to the enemy. Two ships lay ahead. Hardy called that they would have to run aboard one of them. "Go on board which you please," said Nelson. "Take your choice."

The first broadside from the *Victory* was fired point-blank into the stern of the *Bucentaure*, Villeneuve's flagship. Then she ran foul of the *Redoutable* and lay alongside locked together. There was a continual fire of cannon, carronade, and musketry. The air was thick with smoke and dust. . . .

Hardy was walking with the Admiral up and down amidships. He turned—Nelson had fallen to his knees with his hand touching the deck, he sank down on his side. Hardy knelt by him; he hoped it was not a bad wound. "They have done for me at last, Hardy." "I hope not. . . ." "Yes, my backbone is shot through."

He was carried down to the orlop deck below the waterline. Other wounded men were also being carried down. His face was covered with a handkerchief. The deck was painted red to disguise the blood. It was dark and close. Mr. Beatty, the surgeon, and his assistants, examined the wounded as they were handed down. Blood, lifeless corpses, a grotesque pile of amputated limbs . . .

He was carried to the comparative privacy of the cockpit, a niche between the arching timbers of the ship's wall where the midshipmen slung their hammocks. "Ah, Mr. Beatty, you can do nothing for me. I have but a short time to live: my back is shot through." Dr. Scott came to him, and the purser, Mr. Burke. He was stripped and covered with a sheet.

He thought he would soon die and spoke rapidly to Scott in broken sentences. "Remember me to Lady Hamilton . . . remember me to Horatia . . . remember me to all my friends. . . . Doctor, remember me to Mr. Rose, tell him I have made my will and left Lady Hamilton and Horatia to my Country."

406

Beatty examined him. There was no external wound apart from the hole in his left shoulder where the ball had entered. He felt a gush of blood every minute in his breast. He had no feeling in his legs. His breathing was difficult. There was a severe pain where the ball had lodged in his spine. "I felt it break my back."

He was hot and thirsty, and they fanned him and gave him lemonade and wine and water. He was worried about the event of the battle. Burke said that he himself would take home the news of victory. "It is nonsense, Mr. Burke, to suppose I can live: my sufferings are great, but they will all be soon over. Ah, Doctor, it is all over, it is all over."

He kept asking for Hardy. "Will no one bring Hardy to me?" If he did not come he must be dead. Young Mr. Bulkeley, the son of a friend of twenty years, came down and blurted out his official message through his tears: "Circumstances respecting the Fleet required Captain Hardy's presence on deck, but that he would avail himself of the first favourable moment to visit his Lordship." "Who is that?" "It is Mr. Bulkeley, my Lord." "It is his voice. Remember me to your father."

Hardy came down and took his hand. "Well, Hardy, how goes the battle? How goes the day with us?" "Very well, my Lord, we have got twelve or fourteen of the Enemy's Ships in our possession. . . ." "I hope none of our Ships have struck, Hardy." "No, my Lord, there is no fear of that."

"I am a dead man, Hardy. I am going fast: it will be all over with me soon. Come nearer to me. Pray let my dear Lady Hamilton have my hair, and all other things belonging to me." Hardy hoped . . . "Oh no, it is impossible. My back is shot through. Beatty will tell you so." Hardy went back on deck.

"Ah, Mr. Beatty! I have sent for you to say, what I forgot to tell you before, that all power of motion and feeling below my breast are gone; and you very well know I can live but a short time." "My Lord, you told me so before." "Ah, Beatty! I am too certain of it . . . *you know* I am gone." "My Lord, unhappily for our Country, nothing can be done for you." "I know it. I feel something rising in my breast which tells me I am gone." Beatty turned away to hide his tears. "God be praised, I have done my duty."

Beatty asked him if the pain was severe. He said, so much so he wished he were dead, "yet one would like to live a little longer too. . . . What would become of poor Lady Hamilton if she knew my situation!"

Hardy came down again, and took his hand, and congratulated him on a great victory, perhaps fourteen or fifteen ships had surrendered. "That is well, but I bargained for twenty." He gave his last command, "*Anchor, Hardy, anchor.*" "I suppose, my Lord, Admiral Collingwood will now take upon himself the direction of affairs." "Not whilst I live, I hope, Hardy! No—do *you* anchor, Hardy." "Shall we make the signal, sir?" "Yes. For if I live, I'll anchor."

"Don't throw me overboard, Hardy." "Oh no. . . ." "Then you know what to do. . . . Take care of my dear Lady Hamilton, Hardy: take care of poor Lady Hamilton. Kiss me, Hardy."

"Now I am satisfied. Thank God, I have done my duty." Hardy kissed him again. "Who is that?" "It is Hardy." "God bless you, Hardy." The Captain left.

He desired to be turned on his right side and Chevalier, his steward, lifted him. "I wish I had not left the deck, for I shall soon be gone." Scott was kneeling over him rubbing his breast, which gave him some relief. "Doctor, I have *not* been a *great* sinner. . . . *Remember* that I leave Lady Hamilton and my daughter Horatia as a Legacy to my Country . . . and never forget Horatia."

They gave him drinks, and fanned him, and rubbed his body, as the pain slowly consumed him. He spoke quickly, in bursts, and with increasing difficulty. "Thank God, I have done my duty," until the words died on his lips.

They called Beatty. Nelson opened his eyes and closed them forever. A few minutes later Beatty came again. He stopped the Doctor's hand from rubbing a cold, dead breast. The great heart beneath it beat no more.

CHAPTER FIFTEEN

Britannia's Sad End

Henry (off Cadiz) to Emma.

The storm is o'er,
The troubled main
Now heaves no more,
But all is silent—hushed—and calm again,
Save in this bosom—where a ceaseless storm
Is raised—by love and Emma's beauteous form.

No calm, at sea,
This heart shall know,
While far from thee,
Midst lengthening hours of absence, and of woe,
I gaze—in sorrow, o'er the boundless deep,
With eyes—which were they not ashamed would weep.

But hark, I hear
The signal gun.
Farewell, my dear.
The Victory leads on. The fight's begun.
Thy Picture, round this cannon's neck shall prove,
A pledge—to valour, sent by thee and love.

Should conquest smile,
On Britain's Fleet,
(As at the Nile,)
With joyful hearts, upon the beach we'll meet.
No more I'll tempt the dangers of the sea,
But live, in Merton's groves, with love and thee.

Horatio Nelson

EMMA WAS at Merton. On November 2, in the midst of all the gloomy news of the surrender of General Mack and the Austrian army at Ulm, the *Morning Post* reported a rumor of an engagement off Cadiz. Four anxious days dragged by. On the 6th Admiral Collingwood's public dispatch was brought to the Admiralty, rushed into print in a London *Gazette Extraordinary*, and carried to the country on the mail coaches. Carried to Merton . . .

Collingwood's words were heavy with the awe of the occasion. "It pleased the Almighty Disposer of all events to grant His Majesty's arms a complete and glorious Victory. . . ." Yes, yes. "I have not only to lament, in common with the British Navy and the British Nation, in the fall of the Commander in Chief . . ." Oh God! ". . . the loss of a hero whose name will be immortal, and his memory ever dear to his Country; but my heart is rent with the most poignant grief for the death of a friend. . . ." Emma collapsed.

Nelson had been great in his life, but in his death he was sublime. Every man found honor in *his* honor, glory in *his* glory, immortality in *his* immortality.

They knew what they had lost and what they had gained. "While we mourn at the fate of Britain's Darling Son," said the *Morning Post* of November 7, "we have the consolation to reflect, that he has closed his career of glory by a work which will place his name so high in the tablets of Immortality, that succeeding patriots can only gaze with enthusiasm, scarcely hoping to reach the envied elevation, which a Nation's tears, to the latest period of time, will drop like so many bright gems upon the page of history, that records the fall of the Illustrious Hero."

Said the *Morning Chronicle* of the same day, "Not a man who would not have given up his life to achieve such a victory. Not a man who would not have surrendered every part of the victory (except the honour of Britain) to save the life of Lord Nelson." It was a life that from the age of twelve had been devoted to the public service. But Perry knew Nelson. "Never was a man so formed by gentleness of temper and by an affectionate heart for domestic felicity as the Noble Viscount. He was only truly blest in the bosom of his family. It was in this social family circle at Merton that he truly enjoyed the short interval of ease which was permitted to him; and it was here that the genuine, unaffected philanthropy of his heart displayed itself. It is impossible to conceive a human being of more pure benevolence, and of more active virtue than Lord Nelson."

All mourned. The City was illuminated and the blaze of light reflected the sad faces of the people.

At the theaters the players and audiences were one in their mournful tributes—*The Victory and Death of Lord Nelson* at Drury Lane, and *Nelson's Glory* at Covent Garden.

On November 9 a grateful King and County rewarded the hero's brother with an earldom and a pension of £5,000 a year which was to descend with the title; six months later Parliament voted a great grant of money to Nelson's immediate family. The Earl eventually received £99,000 to purchase an estate, and his sisters £15,000 each. Lady Nelson was voted a pension of £2,000 a year for her life.

On the 9th the Earl—and he was called that by the family just as they had previously called him the Doctor—opened his brother's will. The last codicil was, of course, still aboard the *Victory*. He wrote to Fanny, sending her a copy of that part of the will that concerned her, and adding, "If I could find pleasure amidst so many mournful reflections as press upon my mind it would be in the opportunity afforded me of renewing with your Ladyship that intercourse of kind offices which I once hoped would have always marked our lives—which untoward circumstances have occasioned some interruption of, but which I trust will never again be suspended." Fanny was not impressed, but it was significant that, as far as the Earl was concerned, Emma was now an "untoward circumstance."

Two of the provisions of the will were published in the *Chronicle* on the 11th. "The greatest part of his fortune to be sold to constitute a fund to provide £1,000 a year for Lady Nelson. The house and part of the land left to the person of all others he most perfectly esteemed." Perry also obtained (and who could he have obtained them from but Emma?) four of Nelson's last letters to Lady Hamilton, and published them on the 22nd. There was also this disclaimer. "It has been falsely and wantonly asserted that Lady Hamilton has taken a house in Upper Grosvenor Street and that she may soon be expected to revive her festive parties. They little know of this lady, who insult her by such reports. Lady Hamilton has a small house in Clarges Street, and this is certainly not a time for her to think of another. She is more likely to sink into the grave."

The publication of the letters gave concern to Nelson's friends. The prospect of a terrible scandal, a monumental breach of propriety, startled them. George Rose wrote hurriedly to Emma. She answered him from Clarges Street on November 29.

I write from my bed were I have been ever since the fatal sixth of this month, and only to be removed from Merton here. I could not write to you, my dear Sir, before, but your note requires that I should justify myself. Believe then, when I assure you I do not see any one but the family of my dear Nelson, his letters are in the bed with me, and only the *present Earl* did I ever read one and then only a part. 'Tis *True* he is lacking, but I believe would not willfully tell anything. But I have been told something like some of my letters have been printed in some paper. I never *now* read a paper, and my health and spirits are so bad, I cannot enter into a war with vile Editors.

This be assured, no one shall ever see a letter of my glorious and dear departed Nelson. 'Tis True I have a journal from him ever since he came up to Naples to get permission for our Troops in Toulon, when he was in the *Agamemnon*—but his letters are sacred and shall be so. My dear Sir my heart is broken. Life to me now is not worth having. I lived but for him, his Glory I gloried in, it was my pride that he should go forth, and this fatal and last time he went, I persuaded him to it—but I cannot go on my heart and head are gone. . . .

My mind is not a common one and, having lived as a *confidant* and friend with such men as Sir Wm. Hamilton and dearest glorious Nelson, I find myself superior to vain tattling women. Excuse me but I am ill and nervous and *hurt* that those I value should think meanly of me.

It is hard, perhaps, to expect discretion from a woman who had seldom shown it and at a time when even the wisest would find it difficult to exert the smallest degree of judgment.

On December 4 the *Victory* came into Portsmouth with Nelson's flag and colors flying and his corpse in a cask of spirits. Hardy sent Chevalier with Nelson's last letters to Emma. On the one dated October 19/20, she wrote, "This letter was found open upon His desk and brought to Lady Hamilton by Captain Hardy. Oh miserable wretched Emma Oh glorious and happy Nelson."

She wrote Hardy that she wanted to look at her hero for the last time. "As his dear body is in spirits, I think it would be wrong for you to think of seeing him . . ." he replied. He had his hair, lockets, rings, Emma's pictures, all of which he would deliver himself.

Her misery was fed by thoughtful friends who wrote to commiserate with her. She was caught in the rays of Nelson's glory, but as that sun set, so the light faded. Those who offered their services so ardently that winter were cold and distant by the next.

On December 23 the *Victory*, anchored near Greenwich, bid farewell to her greatest captain. Nelson's body, in the *L'Orient* coffin, in a lead coffin, in an elaborate silver-chased coffin, was carried ashore. It lay in state in the Painted Chamber in the Hospital from January 5th to the 8th, attended constantly by Dr. Scott. On the last day it was taken on the river to the Admiralty. On the 9th it was placed on a triumphal car, shaped like a ship with a canopy instead of sails, and drawn in procession to St. Paul's Cathedral. Prominent among the mourners was the Prince of Wales, whom Nelson had damned so heartily and so often. Absent were Lady Nelson and Lady Hamilton. He was buried directly beneath the dome of St. Paul's . . . and there he lies with some of his captains around him.

Emma was left with her grief. Her grief was Emma's pride. What had she left besides her grief?

She had Merton, and with it she had the improvements that Nelson had ordered and which she had to pay for. She had the £2,000 he had left her, and the interest on Horatia's £4,000 all of which, and more, went on her education. She did *not* have the £500 a year from Bronte, because the Earl claimed that the estate could not afford to pay it. Only when she threatened him with legal action in 1814 did he pay the first installment.

Therefore, it was on the income left her by Sir William that she tried to maintain her part, her role, as the mistress of Merton, the guardian of Horatia, the patroness of her poor relations, and the inheritrix of Nelson's glory. The pocketbook codicil was both her glory and her burden. She was Nelson's legacy.

Emma had no chance, nothing, to save her from the slow degradation to which she was doomed. One by one the visible effects of Nelson's glory were stripped from her—his property, his possessions, and at last his letters. But she kept the spirit of it to her death. She kept her dignity, and her generosity, and her love. Emma was never greater than when she was playing Britannia in a garret.

In May 1806 the Earl was busy collecting his brother's treasures. He had already taken the aigrette, the Nile sword, the diamond sword, and the collar of the Bath from Emma, and he was dunning Fanny for a gold box that he had in his possession all the time. Fanny, who knew who she had to deal with, was at law with him over the interpretation of the will. She wanted her pension to be continued and her due, as Nelson's wife, to a third of his personal fortune at the time of his death. In the event, she got the first, which Nelson had not intended, but not the second. Let us take our leave of Fanny now. She lived on, in comparative affluence, in London, Bath and Exmouth. She saw Josiah married and more successful in business than he had been at sea. She survived him by almost a year and died at the age of seventy-three in Littleham, near Exmouth, on May 4, 1831. No doubt she was a proud woman, an injured proud woman. Cold, wicked, malicious she was not. Her granddaughter remembered that she prized a miniature of Nelson, which she would kiss and say, "When you are older, little Fan, you too may know what it is to have a broken heart."

Apart from the Earl, who upset everyone, Nelson's family stayed loyal to Emma, and hostile to Fanny. "I find the Viscountess is going to law," Mrs. Bolton wrote Emma in May 1806. "What for, to enrich that son of hers? For depend on it she will not gain a sixpence, if so much *Income*. What a Vindictive Woman she is. Dispute even the last words of the *Man* she once *pretended to Love*. She has changed her mourning and is off for Cheltenham. I hope it will *purge* away all her sins."

They were all concerned for Horatia. Mrs. Bolton, again in May, said "Every one ought to adore that Child. Give our kind love to her, tell her Emma trys to imitate her attitudes every day." The attitudes that Goethe had praised had found their way into the nursery.

The first "little Emma" left England that summer. Emma had resumed her correspondence with Sir Harry Featherstonhaugh by asking him to lend her £500. He sent a present of some game. On July 2, 1806, in a postscript to her letter, she wrote, "E. goes tonight but she is taken care of in case of any accident." This E. is "little Emma" and that Sir Harry should be told of her departure strongly suggests that he was her father.

"Little Emma" appears once more, when she returned to England in the spring of 1810, and wrote Emma this letter.

Mrs. Denis's mention of your name and the conversation she had with you, have revived ideas in my mind which an absence of four years has not been able to efface. It might have been happy for me to have forgotten the past, and to have begun a new life with new ideas; but for my misfortune, my memory traces back circumstances which have taught me too much, yet not quite all I could have wished to have known—with you that resides, and ample reasons, no doubt, you have for not imparting them to me. Had you felt yourself at liberty so to have done, I might have become reconciled to my former situation and have been relieved from the painful employment I now pursue. It was necessary as I then stood, for I had nothing to support me but the affection I bore you; on the other hand, doubts and fears by turn oppressed me, and I determined to rely on my own efforts rather than submit to abject dependence, without a permanent name or acknowledged parents. That I should have taken such a step shows, at least, that I have a mind misfortune has not subdued. That I should persevere in it is what I owe to myself and to you, for it shall never be

414

said that I avail myself of your partiality or my own inclination, unless I learn my claim on you is greater than you have hitherto acknowledged. But the time may come when the same reasons may cease to operate, and then, with a heart filled with tenderness and affection, will I shew you both my duty and attachment. In the meantime, should Mrs. Denis's zeal and kindness not have over-rated your expressions respecting me, and that you should really wish to see me, I may be believed in saying that such a meeting would be one of the happiest moments of my life, but for the reflection that it may also be the last, as I leave England in a few days, and may, perhaps, never return to it again.

Apparently Emma resisted this sad and dignified appeal. But can there be any doubt that "little Emma" knew she was addressing her mother? She disappeared, and we can only hope that the subsequent years of her life were happier than those that had gone before. That Emma should never have acknowledged this relationship, helps us to understand how it was she never admitted Horatia was her daughter, and only called herself her mother when she was angry with her, perhaps in one of her periods of drunkenness.

To return to the summer of 1806. Emma wrote Davison on July 4:

> I am very unwell. Broken Hearted and going into Norfolk with Lady Bolton. I shall beg of my mother to send you the gun and cantine that our departed angel left you. I have now a wide world before me, nor any friends, although when I was in power many basked in my sunshine. I have done the state *no little service*, in Nelson's dying moments he gave testimony of my very important services, he recommended me to the King and Country when he was bleeding and dying for that King and Country. All is now over, all forgotten, and the poor unhappy forlorn Emma's services allso forgotten—but never mind. May you be happy my dear Sir and I hope you will. . . . I am giving up my home and establishment in Clarges Street and I fear I must give up Merton if Government do not do anything for me.

The last codicil was being bandied about between the Earl and Lord Grenville, who had succeeded as Prime Minister on Pitt's death in January, and in and out of Doctor's Commons. Emma suspected plots and deliberate delays to keep the codicil hidden. She was wrong. She expected ingratitude and she was not wrong.

"Psha," she wrote Alexander Scott on September 7 from Cranwich, "I

415

am above them, I despise them, for thank God I feel that having lived with honour and glory glory they cannot take from me. I despise them—my soul is above them, and I can yet make some of them tremble by showing them how he despised them, for in his letters to me he thought aloud." A dangerous idea! "Look at Alexander Davison courting the man he despised and neglecting now those whose feet he used to lick. Dirty vile groveler."

Davison, who had got himself appointed Treasurer to the Ordnance, could, or would, not help her. He had himself suffered a considerable disappointment at not being made the agent for the prizes taken at Trafalgar. Only four of the twenty captured ships survived the storm that followed the battle, but Parliament voted £320,000 prize money.

In the autumn Emma was at Merton. Harrison was there writing his biography, and there was the usual houseful of girls, most of them Connors. Emma was already having trouble with Ann Connor, who, calling herself Ann Carew, was claiming to be her daughter. It created a small scandal and gave rise to the story that she had had three children by Charles Greville— Eliza, Ann, and Charles—but they were all Connors, and two of them at least were mentally unstable.

She wrote to the Earl in November to ask him, as his brother's executor, to help her to have the terms of the last codicil carried out. The Earl replied that he would do all he could if she would tell him what it was she wanted him to do. She was a legacy to the Country, not to him. One thing he did do, and that was to obtain the King's permission for Horatia to change her name. By royal license she became Horatia Nelson Nelson.

While there was a hope of Emma's claims on the government being met, her creditors extended their terms and totted up the interest. It only seemed justice to Emma, who kept open house at Merton and took another town residence, 136 Bond Street. She was maintaining Nelson's position, and why should not they contribute to it? Old Blindy and Mrs. Graefer were fixed at Merton; the Bolton girls visited; Reynoldses, Connors and Kidds found dinners and beds and presents.

The summer of 1807 meant, like all her previous summers in England, a trip to the seaside, though she did choose the less fashionable resort of Worthing. She wrote Countess Nelson, the jewel of bygone days:

All come to look at Nelson's angel, she improves in Languages, musick and accomplishments. But my heart bleeds to think how proud would her glorious Father have been. *He that lived only for her*, whose last words and thoughts were to her. *She* that would have been *every thing*—'tis dreadful to me. However, she is my comfort and solace and I act as allthough He could look down and aprove, and bless Emma for following up his every wish. We have been at Mrs. Matcham's, a week with Lady Bolton. . . . Every day my affliction increases for the loss of my dearest Nelson. . . . Oh this time Two years, how happy we were—every day we think of what we were doing with that angel, who appeared amongst us for those happy twenty-five days. Time only adds to my grief, and now, as the time approaches towards the fatal 13th of Sept., I am wretched, for I was the cause of his going out unfortunately.

Winter, and the Duke of Sussex was staying at Merton, and, of all people, the Prince of Wales called on Emma. What expenses she must have incurred to entertain these royal profligates! How much *more* credit she must have been offered!

In April 1808 came the first creak of the tumbling edifice of Emma's Nelsonian attitudes. Quite suddenly, Merton was put up for sale, improvements and all. The house was valued at £10,430, and the contents £2,500. The contents were to go with Emma, and most of them did go that summer to Richmond, where she stayed first in Queensberry's house, and later in a small house nearby. This sudden development had the creditors scrambling as they felt the ground slipping away beneath their feet.

The family seemed to be ignorant of the impending collapse. Mrs. Bolton was hopeful at Old Q.'s hospitality. "Poor old man, he must have outlived all his pleasures except looking at your Ladyship, which I hope he will remember with *gratitude*." Mrs. Matcham was upset by the Earl. Apparently Mr. Matcham wanted to change his name to Nelson and the Earl objected. "He is as great an enemy to us, as our dear lost friend was our Patron: the extinction of the whole family would be a matter of the greatest exaltation to him, with the exception of his own dear self and Lady Charlotte. . . . God mend him and preserve his Wife, a wish comprising his punishment and his restoration." She thought, quite rightly as it happened, that "he was much more respected as a *country parson*, and a *happier* man than he is at present."

Emma would gladly have seen the Earl extinguished, and the Countess and Lady Charlotte with him. She had had Nelson's last prayer and the codicil printed and sent two copies to Canterbury. On one is written, "Is it possible that Countess Nelson should have forsaken the person who was the means of her being so much exalted?" and on the other, "Is it true that Lady Charlotte Nelson can be ungrateful to her benefactress Lady Hamilton?" We must assume that the answers were yes.

The Earl was unhappy. He confided to a clerical friend that he feared he was unequal to the great station he occupied. "Pray look among the Peerage," advised his friend. He had hung tight to his prebendary, in spite of his vast fortune and great estate. Now he had heard that the Dean of Canterbury was dead, and he applied at once for the deanery. He was obliged to withdraw his application when it transpired that it was the Dean's brother who had died. He was, as he had always been, a clown. The great tragedy in his life came in 1808, when his son, young Horace, Viscount Trafalgar, died. If William Nelson had one ambition in life apart from self-advancement, it was to see the Nelson line continued. He himself outlived the jewel, who died in 1828, and remarried. He died in 1835 at the age of 78. The title went to Thomas Bolton, little Tom who was not too bright but had a good heart. The Earl had managed to separate the Duchy of Bronte from the title and that went to Charlotte, who had married Lord Bridport.

Emma was in trouble. Mr. Rose, who had been trying very hard to obtain a pension for her, at last wrote to say that he could try no more. She appealed to Lord St. Vincent. He had been Nelson's friend, Sir William's friend and her friend. He knew her services. Surely they deserved something? "Even the widow of Mr. Lock, only about two years Consul at Palermo, a man not remarkable either for great loyalty or the most correct attention to his official duties, had a pension assigned her, almost immediately on his death, of £800 a year; while I, who have been seven years the widow of such a man as Sir William Hamilton, the foster brother of our Sovereign, and have constantly done all in my power to benefit my country, continue to be totally neglected. The widow of Mr. Fox, whose *services* to his country are, at best, very *problematical*, had instantly a grant of £1,200 per annum; and even his natural daughter, Miss Willoughby, obtained a pension of £300 a year. . . . Surely the daughter of Lord Nelson, now Miss Nelson, is not less an object worthy of the attention of her King and Country, than Miss Willoughby, the daughter of Mr. Fox." She should have known, Mr. Fox was a *politician*, and they look after themselves.

On September 4, 1808, she tried Old Q. She begged him to buy Merton, she thought £15,000 would leave her free.

My mind is made up to live on what I have. If I could but be free from Merton—all paid, and only one hundred pounds in my pocket, you will live to see me blessing you, my mother blessing you, Horatia blessing you. If you would not wish to keep Merton, perhaps it will sell in the spring better—only let me pass my winter without the idea of a prison. 'Tis true my imprudence has brought it on me, and villany and ingratitude has helped to involve me, but the sin be on them. Do not let my enemies trample on me; for

God's sake then, dear Duke, good friend, think 'tis Nelson who asks you to befriend, Emma Hamilton.

Nelson asked in vain. Old Q. died in 1810 and left Emma £500 a year in his will, but his affairs were so trammeled up that she never received a penny of it.

In October 1808 Emma made her will. It is a sad, rambling document, containing a pathetic plea that she might be buried near her beloved Nelson. She rebuked the Connors for telling lies and ruining her by their extravagance. There was truth in this, because on December 29 Mrs. Connor was forced to take an oath that Lady Hamilton had spent over £2,000 on her and her children and that the stories she had spread about her were totally untrue. But what had poor Emma to leave? Only the treasured relics of her love, which would be Horatia's.

On November 25 there was a meeting of the friends of Lady Hamilton, who included Davison, Goldsmid, and several other respectable and wealthy gentlemen. They met at the house of Sir John Perring, one of the lord mayors Nelson had been angry with over Copenhagen. Her debts were reckoned to be £8,000, exclusive of £10,000 required to pay off annuitants (apparently a polite term for moneylenders). Merton and her more valuable possessions were now valued at £17,500. She assigned these to the trustees, who raised £3,700 to pay off her most pressing debts. Then, with a vague promise of promoting her claim to a pension, they parted. The immediate danger was over.

Emma wrote Charles Greville to tell him the good news. "Goldsmid and my City friends came forward and they have rescued me from Destruction. Destruction brought on by *Earl Nelson's* having thrown on me the Bills for finishing Merton, by his having secreted the Codicil of Dying Nelson, who attested in his Dying moments, that I had well served my country." She was concerned for Mrs. Graefer. The Earl would not pay the annuity Nelson had given her and she was going back to Sicily. Emma had given her a letter for the Queen, "and begged of Her Majesty by the love she bears or *once* bore to Emma, by all I have done for her, by the sacred memory of Nelson, by the Charge she has placed in me, that she will be good to Mrs. Greffer, whom she has always marked with her Royal notice."

What was "the Charge she has placed in me"? On one occasion Emma deliberately fostered the idea that Horatia was the daughter of Maria Carolina, following an affair with Lord Nelson. "She is the daugher," she wrote, "the true and beloved daughter of Viscount Nelson, and if he had lived, she would have been all that his love and fortune could have made her; for nature has made her perfect, beautiful, good and amiable. *Her mother was TOO GREAT to be mentioned*, but her father, mother, and Horatia had a true and virtuous friend in Emma Hamilton." If this was Emma's, and there is some doubt, it does not appear too extraordinary. One of the government's regular excuses for not noticing her services was that they involved a person too great to be mentioned. It might well have occurred to her that the same person would do very well for Horatia's mother, to enhance her claim to a pension. Horatia was not impressed. "Poor Lady Hamilton was not a strict adherer to truth," she wrote to an inquirer, "and her statement implying that the Q. of N. was my mother was most incredible—had it been so, of course I should have passed as her husband's child." She had seventeen and presumably King Ferdinand would not have objected to another.

Horatia, however, was quite convinced that Lady Hamilton was *not* her mother.

Throughout the year 1809 Emma lived quietly at Richmond. In April, Goldsmid bought Merton. He did not live long to enjoy his purchase. Money killed him, when he committed suicide in the next year on the threatened collapse of his banking house. Charles Greville died in the autumn of 1809, and his collection of stones was sold by his executors to the British Museum for £13,727. Was it worth it? Not the stones, but a life devoted to them? Who was left? Davison—well, he was in prison again for embezzlement. He survived it, and lived until 1829. He was no great friend to Emma and his last good deed was to buy the famous enamel by Bone from her for £200.

On January 14, 1810, Emma lost her mother from whom throughout her life she had never been separated. "Dear blessed Saint," wrote Mrs. Bolton, "was she not a mother to us all." Let us remember Mrs. Cadogan, the silent sharer of her daughter's fortune and misfortune.

Misfortune on misfortune . . . Emma now embarked on a series of brief sojourns in lodgings all within a spit of Piccadilly. Bond Street, Albemarle Street, Dover Street, Bond Street again—everywhere she was cheated, dunned, driven from pillar to post, buying her short respites with loans from Mr. Matcham and the singer Rovedino. Even the Connors quitted her at last.

She had Horatia, an old servant Dame Francis, a female companion, and sometimes the company of a writer, Mr. Russell, who was apparently employed to write her petitions. In each new apartment she set up her treasures: a great fourposter bed, several bidets, a piano, a draughtboard, the remnants of Sir William's library, four or five pictures, portraits of Sir

William and Lord Nelson, a bust of Nelson, a gold box with the freedom of Oxford, a prized dinner service, and the Order of St. Ferdinand and Merit in gold and the Grand Signior's diamond star. Each new room was a miniature shrine to the past. She still entertained . . . and she drank. She was ill . . . and she drank. She quarreled with Horatia . . . and she drank.

Why protract her misery and ours in reading of it? By the summer of 1812 she had placed herself within the rules of the King's Bench, lodging at 12 Temple Place, to avoid imprisonment for debt. She was free again, probably through the efforts of Mr. Perry of the *Morning Chronicle* and a new friend, Alderman Smith. She was busy with memorials to the Prince of Wales, now Prince Regent, and even to the old insane King. Early in 1813 the Prince actually dined with her—she was back in Bond Street—but her flickering hopes were finally snuffed out early the next year by the publication of some of Nelson's letters to her. The Prince, proclaimed by Nelson as the frequenter of pimps and bawds, would not now help Nelson's mistress, even if he had ever intended to.

Who published the letters? St. Vincent said that Emma provided them and edited them, Beckford said she got £1,000 for doing so. But what happened to the money? And would she, who had all along striven to conceal her real relationship with the hero, have declared it all? The letters could have been published with a few more asterisks and *all* the incriminating parts omitted. No, they were stolen. Probably not by Harrison, who has often been accused of it, but who was with her at Merton and showed great restraint and tact in his biography. More likely by Clarke, who acted in her migratory days as her secretary. But possibly by any one of the spongers who infested her lodgings. The publication was a terrible blow, as much to Nelson's memory as Emma's hopes, and she took it terribly to heart.

Before this though, and while she was still living precariously in Bond Street, she taxed Horatia, who was twelve years old, with her behavior. "I grieve and lament to see the increasing strength of your turbulent passions, I weep and pray you may not be totally lost, my fervent prayers are offered up to God for you, I hope you may become yet sensible of your eternal welfare. I shall go join your father and my blessed mother and may you on your death bed have as little to reproach yourself as your once affectionate mother has, for I can glorify and say I was a good child." Could she though? "*Can Horatia Nelson say so—I am unhappy to say you cannot.* No answer to this. I shall tomorrow look out for a school for your sake to *save you,* that you may bless the memory of an injured mother. P.S. Look on me as gone from this world."

"You have helped me nearer to God," she wrote later, "and may God forgive you."

Drink and religion, the two refuges of a hurt soul. Poor Emma could never keep her temper, and neither, it seems, could poor Horatia.

In June 1813 affairs were desperate again. Alderman Smith bought goods and chattels from Lady Hamilton for £490. In July there was an auction of Lady Hamilton's effects—away went the books and the pictures, the box, the order and the star, the dinner service, the piano, the bidets, the fourposter, and the goose-feather bed Nelson had bought from Mr. Peddie-son. Away went everything they could not carry, and it was not enough. Emma and Horatia were back in Temple Place at the end of July. The next month another friend was gone when Mrs. Bolton died.

On April 29, 1814, Emma wrote the Earl.

My Lord, It cannot be more disagreeable to you to receive a letter from me than it is for me to write to you, but as I will not have anything to say or do with Lawyers, without I am compelled to it, I shall be glad to know from your Lordship weather the *first half year* of the Bronte pension, which my ever dear lamented friend the glorious and virtuous Nelson left in his Will I was to receive and which I never have received. I shall be glad to know how it is to be settled, as now from my present situation, which has been brought on not by *any Crime* but by having been too generous to the ungrateful, and I rather Glory in being the injured and not the injurer—and as every sixpence is of the utmost conse-quence to me, on account of Horatia Nelson's education, the be-loved Child of dear Nelson. I do not, in the midst of poverty, neg-lect her Education, which is such as will suit the rank in life which She will yet hold in society and which her great Father wished her to move in. I ask not alms, I ask not anything but right, and to know weather I am to receive my due or not. Believe me, my lord, yours &c. Emma Hamilton.

At last the Earl was forced into parting with some money and on May 6 Emma received her first installment of £225.

Even the allowance from Sir William's estate, now in the possession of Charles Greville's brother Fulke Greville, was stopped, had been stopped for some time, because of the claims of the "annuitants." It was by the £225 and with the help of Alderman Smith, that Emma obtained her discharge in June.

But the creditors were still baying. Emma begged Smith to withdraw his bail so that he would not suffer, and, with Horatia, took her flight to

France. They caught the *Little Tom* packet from the Tower to Calais, one night late in June.

France was at peace, Napoleon was at Elba, and King Louis XVIII was on the throne. There were many travelers to France and the large haggard lady with her little girl passed unnoticed among them.

From the Hotel Dessein in Calais Emma wrote to Davison on July 6. They were well and Horatia was at her lessons. "Education goes on, for I would sooner starve than her fine and beautiful mind should not be cultivated and made rich with Honer, Virtue and Rectitude and accomplishments, such as her Glorious Father wished her to have . . ." She looked back on the past year. "Vile Banco Regio—truly a fit place for Lady Hamilton, the Representative of the Queen of England for many years, with Honer and Respect, and the assistant and co-operator for the good of their Country with glorious Nelson, and allso for Nelson's only Child, his flesh and Blood—fye on them." This was something of the old Emma.

Dessein's was too expensive for them to stay long, and they moved to a village, the Commune de St. Pierre, outside Calais and took lodgings in a farmhouse. From there Emma wrote to the editor of the *Morning Herald* denying a report that she had fled from her bail, protesting her innocence in the publication of the letters, and begging him to contradict malicious reports about her birth. She also wrote to Sir William Scott, an old friend and a prominent lawyer who had done his best to help her. She gave a fascinating picture of her last days.

> From the Common of St. Peter Two miles from Calais Septr. 12th 1814. But pray direct for me if you do me so much Honer and happiness as to write Chez Desin Calais.
>
> Many thanks my dear Sir William for your kind letter. If my dear Horatia was provided for, I should dye happy, and if I could only now be enabled to make her more comfortable and finish her education, oh God how I would bless them that enabled me to do it. She all ready reads, writes and speaks Italian, french and English and I am teaching her German and Spanish. Musick she knows, but all must yet be cultivated to perfection, and then our own language, geography, arithmetic &c. &c. she knows. We read the English, Roman and Grecian History, but it is a great fatigue to me as I have been ill eight months and am now in a state of convalescence. I must be very quick.
>
> I have been at this farm house six weeks; a fine garden, common large rooms. The Ladies of the House lost four and twenty thousand franks a year because their sons would not serve the Emperor. I have an ass for Horatia as she wants, now she is four-

teen, exercise. I go in a cart for my Health—the jaundice is leaving me, but my Broken Heart does not leave me. I have seen enough of grandeur not to regret it, but comfort and what would make Horatia and myself live like gentlewomen would be all I wish and to live to see her well settled in the World. We have excellent Beef, mutton and veal, at five pence a pound, chickens a shilling for two, partridges fivepence for two, a turbot for half a crown; Bread very cheap, milk from the Cows on the Common like cream, 2 quarts for four sous; good Bordeaux wine tenpence a bottle.

All our mornings are given up to studys. We walk and dine at Two, go in my cart, she on her donkey, everybody very kind to us. Every Wednesday there is a Dance, were all the persons of Rank and their Daughters Dance, a mile from this place, we pay 3 pence for going in. Horatia is adored. She dances all there Dances and speaks french like a french girl. She is good, virtuous and religious. We go to the Church of St. Peters and read our prayers in french for they are exactly like our own.

But my dear Sir William, without a pound in my pocket what can I do. The 21st of October, fatal day, I shall have some. I wrote to Davison to ask the Earl to let me have my Bronte pension quarterly instead of half yearly and the Earl refused, saying he was too poor—altho I got the good and great Nelson that Estate by means of the Queen. I set out from town ten weeks or more ago with not quite fifty pounds, paying our passage allso out of it. Think then of the situation of Nelson's Child and Lady Hamilton, who so much contributed to the Battle of the Nile, paid often and often out of my own pocket at Naples for to send to Sir John Jervis provisions, and allso at Palermo for corn to save Malta. Indeed I have been ill used. Lord Sidmouth is a good man and Lord Liverpool is allso an upright minister, pray do, if ever Sir William Hamilton's and Nelson's Services were deserving, ask them to aid us. Think what I must feil, who was used to give God only knows too much —and now to ask. Earl and Countess Nelson lived with me, seven years I educated Lady Charlotte and paid Eaton for Trafalgar's Education. I made Lord Nelson write the letter to Lord Sidmouth for the prebendary at Canterbury which his Lordship kindly gave, and they have never given the dear Horatia a Frock nor a sixpence. But no more for you will be tired, but my heart is full. May God bless you and yours prays, my dear Sir William, your ever grateful, Emma Hamilton.

P.S. I again before God declare I knew not of the publication of those stolen letters and I have taken the sacrament on it. Horatia begs her love.

What more is there to say? The little money they had ran out and Horatia wrote to beg the Earl to advance a part of the interest of the £4,000 Nelson had left for her education. Emma made a last plea to Lord Sidmouth and found a fine phrase even in extremity: "If there is humanity still left in British hearts they will not suffer us to die with famine in a foreign country."

Horatia was very cool when she recollected those final days.

I was but fourteen, true, but circumstances form an almost child's character into that of a woman, and that was unfortunately my case. For a very long time before her death she took little interest in anything but the indulgence of her unfortunate habit, and after the first week of her removal to the lodgings she hired in Calais at Mrs. Dames, but once she left her bed, not absolutely from illness; at that time I never went out. . . . For some time before she died she was not kind to me, but she had much to try her, alas, to excite her. . . . Lady Hamilton for a long time had openly expressed herself as being a Catholic, that must be between her God and herself, but having lived so long with such a decided freethinker as Sir William Hamilton professed to be, it is not surprising that she should not have any very fixed principles.

Emma died on January 15, 1815. It might have been the dropsy, or the drink, or a cold, or she was just worn out—but she would have said that she died of a broken heart.

She was buried in Calais, her grave is lost. . . .

Horatia was collected by the Earl, though it was Alderman Smith who collected the bill for Emma's funeral, and she found a home with the kind Matchams until her marriage in 1822 to the Reverend Philip Ward. So the Nelsons returned to the Church. She lived a good long life and saw more honor done her father by Queen Victoria than had been eked out by the Queen's royal uncles. But then, as Emma used to say, women have great hearts.

A NOTE ON THE MATERIAL USED
IN THE PREPARATION OF THE BOOK

I have used three types of material: original letters, journals and other manuscripts; contemporary newspapers and magazines; published works mainly consisting of letters of which the originals have disappeared, contemporary memoirs and journals, and two or three modern and scholarly works on subjects of specific interest.

I have not tried to write a history of the times, or indeed anything other than the story of Nelson's relationship with Sir William and Lady Hamilton. Wherever possible I have used their words and the words of their contemporaries, as opposed to my own or anyone else's.

Original letters. There are two great collections of Nelson's letters, one in the National Maritime Museum and the other in the British Museum. I would like to express my gratitude to the Trustees of the National Maritime Museum and the Trustees of the British Museum for their permission to quote from the letters in these collections, and to the staffs of both museums for their kind assistance. There is a third collection in the Nelson Museum in Monmouth which has been edited by G. P. B. Naish and published by the Navy Records Society.

The letters are not to be found under a single reference in either collection, but are in many different boxes and bindings under a variety of titles. I give them all in the List that follows. Nelson cared little for punctuation, Lady Hamilton cared nothing at all. I have taken the liberty of punctuating the letters in order to save the reader the trouble of doing it himself. I have, however, kept the original spelling and capital letters, in order to leave some freshness in the correspondence.

Newspapers. These are in the Burney Collection in the British Museum and the Newspaper Library at Colindale. Though the historical value of newspaper articles is questionable, I found them very useful as a daily commentary altogether free from hindsight. The gossip columnists were as busy then as they are now, and their comments were invaluable in building up a picture of Nelson and the Hamiltons as their contemporaries saw them.

Published works. It has been impossible to omit quotations from books, but I have tried to confine these to letters and journals of the day. Some of the original letters have disappeared and are only known from publications. Some memoirs are only available in published form. I suppose there are hundreds of books about Nelson, dozens about Emma, and one or two about Sir William. I have tried to be impartial and to make up my own mind and write my own book.

LIST OF SOURCES

MANUSCRIPT COLLECTIONS IN THE NATIONAL MARITIME MUSEUM

Where the letters are part of a larger collection, the reference numbers are given in brackets.

Phillipps-Croker Collection. This is a very large and important collection, containing a great variety of letters from Nelson's correspondents. Box 19 contains the originals of Nelson's letters to Lady Hamilton, some of which were privately published in 1893. There are also many private letters written by members of the Nelson family to Lady Hamilton.

Phillipps Collection. A small collection of Nelson's letters mostly on official business. It also contains his notes on Miss Williams' book on the revolution in Naples, headed "Pages in which are *lies.*"

Nelson-Ward Collection. The correspondence of Horatia Nelson-Ward and her inquiries about her birth; Mrs. Gibson's notes to Lady Hamilton; many Nelson family letters; some of Lady Hamilton's letters up to the year of her death. It is invaluable for a picture of Horatia's relationship with her mother.

Bridport Collection. Family letters separated from the Bridport Collection in the British Museum. Nelson's niece Charlotte became Lady Bridport and she inherited Lady Hamilton's and Nelson's correspondence with her father and mother, the Rector and his jewel.

Girdlestone Collection. Family papers once in the possession of Nelson's eldest sister, Susanna Bolton. It contains some of Lady Hamilton's notes for the Queen of Naples written aboard the *Foudroyant* in Naples Bay in the summer of 1799.

Matcham Collection. Family papers once in the possession of Nelson's youngest sister, Catherine Matcham. It also contains some of Nelson's letters to Emma.

Trafalgar House Collection. A small miscellaneous collection in which there is one of Lady Hamilton's letters from Nelson and the list of her effects sold by auction in 1813.

Walter Collection. A small important collection containing two "Thomson" letters, Sir William's long complaint to his wife, and her last letter from "the Common of St. Peters Two miles from Calais." Also Nelson's last letter to Horatia.

De Coppet Collection. A small collection of Nelson's letters to Sir John Acton, Collingwood, Sir William Hamilton and others.

Stewart Collection. Another small collection containing Nelson's auto-biography to the year 1793 and copies of the many codicils to his will.

Monserrat Collection. A collection of odd Nelson letters and a sheet of accounts from Merton.

Correspondence of Lady Nelson and James Western. An interesting series between Fanny and her solicitor about Nelson's will. She hoped that "excess of Worldly prosperity had given Earl Nelson the feelings and conduct of a Gentleman."

Transcript of the Nelson Collection in Monmouth. Apart from the series of Nelson's letters to his wife, this collection contains a whole lot of letters to everyone else! Its principal interest (apart from Fanny's letters which have been published) is several new (to me) letters from Nelson to Emma of 1804–1805.

Nelson Papers (reference BGY/5D). Some miscellaneous letters. The most interesting are one from Lady Hamilton to Mrs. Nelson about assemblies and another from Sir William to Charles Greville complaining of same.

Nelson Papers General. A small collection of gems. Nelson to Emma: "I will stand upon my own bottom." Duckworth's report on Josiah. Fanny to Nelson in January 1800: "My dear Husband, Good for nothing Mrs. Franks yesterday was too late with Lady Hamilton's box which was to have been put in your box." This was going to Palermo. "I wish my dear Josiah was with you. He never writes, so much the better for he can never be accused of making mischief."

Correspondence of Lady Hamilton and Alexander Davison (reference LBK/7). This is a continuation of the collection in the British Museum and covers the years 1806–1814. It is important for Emma's last years. In April 1814 she was writing from prison: "I can lay my Head on my pillow with a firm Conscience that I never injured man woman or Child . . ." Poor Emma.

Correspondence of Lady Hamilton and Charles Greville (reference LBK/6). Here are all the early letters when she was in love with Greville, and some from Palermo up to 1799, when she apparently stopped writing to him. These were all published by Morrison in 1893.

Correspondence of Lady Hamilton and George Rose (reference LBK/50). These are mostly concerned with Emma's claim for a pension after Nelson's death. "Nelson Good Glorious Nelson *never never* could have gone the second time to Egypt if it had not been for me." Among the letters is the lock of Nelson's hair that she sent Rose. It is light brown and streaked with gray.

Correspondence of Sir William Hamilton and Sir John Acton (reference HML/21). Neapolitan backstairs politics.

Minto-Nelson-Hamilton Papers (reference ELL/139/163). Lord Minto was a friend of both Nelson and Sir William Hamilton. This correspondence is mainly concerned with the political situation in the Mediterranean.

Hugh Elliot Papers (reference ELL/306). In spite of his dislike of Lady Hamilton, Hugh Elliot apparently pressed her claim for a pension on Queen Maria Carolina when he was Ambassador at Naples in 1803–1805. Nelson thought little of him.

Correspondence of Lady Nelson and Lord Hood (reference HOO/28). An interesting series which shows how Fanny kept the friendship of many influential people after her dismissal by Nelson.

Journal of HMS Thalia (reference JOD/11). Josiah Nisbet was a poor letter writer. Any information about him and his troubled naval career is interesting, particularly as, in my view, Nelson's dissatisfaction with him spread over onto his mother. This is not Josiah's own journal, but probably that of one of his officers.

Miscellaneous Letters in Autograph Collections (reference AGC/3/5/9/ 13/14/17/18/24/32). This is a series of small collections of letters from various people. Nelson's letters are in boxes 17 and 18.

Personal Papers of Sir Edward Berry, Lord Collingwood, Sir John Duckworth, Alexander Scott. Small collections of official papers. There are some fascinating notes for a sermon by Scott: "We are ashamed at being so unfashionable as to appear Xtians, or rather religious! for we allow ourselves to be Xtians!"

The Jervis Papers. Sir John Jervis, later Lord St. Vincent, was the Commander in Chief most closely associated with Nelson. His opinions on his officers are particularly interesting. Sir Robert Calder was "violent, impracticable, ignorant, and illiterate, beyond description," and Sir John Orde, "a vain, ignorant, supercilious creature." St. Vincent himself was called every name under the sun, from "the Grand Presbyter" by Cobbett, to "the Jesuit" by Emma and Nelson.

The Keith Papers. A very large, and so far uncatalogued, collection of official and personal letters. Keith demands a biographer, if only because late in life he married Hester Maria, the daughter of Dr. Johnson's Mrs. Thrale.

The Papers of Sir John Orde. A fascinating collection, mostly concerned with Orde's attempt to revenge himself on St. Vincent for being superseded by Nelson. He bore Nelson a grudge for the "disinclination to temperate resolutions" which he showed in 1787, when he was Captain of the *Boreas* and Orde was Governor of Dominica. As we have seen, he was eventually amply rewarded at Nelson's expense.

Lady Hamilton's Songbook. Emma's repertoire was extensive and included Hindu songs—"Ooody Oody Purbum"—as well as love songs and martial songs in Nelson's honor.

Finally, the National Maritime Museum has photostats and facsimiles of some few letters in private collections. Those of special interest have the following references: PST/10/39 and FAC/1/2.

MANUSCRIPT COLLECTIONS IN THE BRITISH MUSEUM

The references to the various collections fall into two parts. There are the Additional Manuscripts (ADD MSS), and the Egerton Manuscripts (EG). Few of the collections have a title and can only be found under the correspondents' names in the catalogue or by quoting the reference number given in brackets.

Letters of Sir John Jervis (reference ADD MSS 29914–5). A useful collection, complementary to the Jervis Papers.

Letters of Lady Nelson (reference ADD MSS 28333). A small collection, including her marriage certificate and the bottom half of Nelson's letter of dismissal with Fanny's comments on it.

Contracts for the purchase and sale of Round Wood (reference ADD MSS 30170). The sale was dated January 18, 1801, five days after Nelson left London for Plymouth.

Letters of Captain Bedford (reference ADD MSS 30182). Bedford was Captain of the *Leyden* during Nelson's command in the Channel.

Order Book of HMS Vanguard (reference ADD MSS 30260). This is important in judging Lady Hamilton's claim to have been instrumental in getting permission for the fleet to victual at Syracuse. Nelson's order for "The Ships of the Squadron to complete their Water and Fuel with all possible expedition" was issued on July 19, 1798, before the fleet entered the harbor. He did not visit the Governor until the next day.

Letters of Sir William Hamilton to Sir Joseph Banks (reference ADD MSS 34048). Banks was a distinguished naturalist who accompanied Captain Cook on his first expedition. He later became President of the Royal Society. Sir William's long and amusing letters to him are an excellent commentary on the diverse interests of a gentleman in the eighteenth century. His comments on Emma's improvement while at Naples deserve more space than I have been able to give them here: "It is a bad job to come from the nephew to the uncle but one must make the best of it, and I long to get poor Charles out of his difficulties."

A Letter from Nelson to Lady Hamilton (reference ADD MSS 34274–G f61). This is the "Santa Emma" letter: "In this age of wickedness you sett an example of real Virtue and goodness . . ."

Hamilton Papers (reference ADD MSS 34710). There are several lots of Hamilton papers. I could not find much for my purpose in this one.

The Bridport Collection (reference ADD MSS 34902–88). The principal collection of Nelson's letters and documents, inherited by the Earl and left to his daughter, Lady Bridport. There are eighty-six volumes and boxes. This collection formed the basis of Sir Nicholas Harris Nicolas's edition of Nelson's dispatches and letters, but there are many that have not been published. The last volume (ADD MSS 34988) contains family letters.

The Correspondence of Sir William Hamilton (reference ADD MSS 37077). An important collection of official letters from Sir William to Lord Grenville.

Lady Hamilton's Letters to the British Ambassador at Florence (reference ADD MSS 37877 f257, 37878 f159). Wyndham was on the receiving end of much advice and comment. "Her Heart is truly english," said Emma of the Queen of Naples.

A Letter from W. Huskisson, November 10, 1805 (reference ADD MSS 38737 f97). "Conversing one day with Ld. Nelson upon the business of Egypt and Copenhagen, he told me neither He nor the battle of Aboukir would have been ever heard of had it not been for the extraordinary exertion of influence of Ly. Hamilton, by whose means he was enabled most expeditiously to obtain naval provision from the Government of Naples."

Hamilton and Greville Papers (reference ADD MSS 40714–6). A good collection, of interest here for the details of Sir William's finances.

Letters of Lady Hamilton to Alexander Davison (reference ADD MSS 40739). A most important collection which, as far as I know, has not previously been quoted. There are many letters which help fill the gap left by Nelson's habit of destroying his letters from Emma. Few of them are dated, but they cover the period 1803–1805.

Correspondence of Sir William Hamilton (reference ADD MSS 41200). Official and semi-official letters concerning the Court of Naples during Sir William's long residence. It also contains a catalogue of his pictures.

Hamilton and Greville Papers (reference ADD MSS 42071). Sir William's letters to Charles Greville over a long period of years. Greville's account of his uncle's death-bed conversation is here.

A Little Book of Fables and Stories in French, the Gift of Lady E. Hamilton (reference ADD MSS 42241). Dated June 1812 and autographed by Horatia N. Nelson.

Rose Papers (reference 42773–4). Lady Hamilton's correspondence with George Rose concerning her pension.

Paget Papers (reference ADD MSS 48398–400). Paget's correspondence when he was Ambassador at Palermo.

Sir William Hamilton's Correspondence from the Holland House Collection (reference ADD MSS 51315). Some letters of small importance.

Horatia Nelson's Commonplace Book (ADD MSS 52360). The first poem was copied out on September 25, 1819. Unremarkable except for the gloominess of Horatia's choice of poetry. For example, "The Lullaby of a Female Convict to Her Child, the Night Previous to Execution" is no sooner over than we get "Lines Supposed to Have Been Addressed by a Female Lunatic."

Collingwood Papers (reference ADD MSS 52780). Collingwood's considered opinion of Nelson, written on March 6, 1806, is perhaps worth quoting here. "I have indeed had a severe loss in the death of my excellent friend Lord Nelson. Since the year 73 we have been on terms of the greatest intimacy. Chance has thrown us very much together in Service, and on many occasions we have acted in concert. There is scarce a Naval subject that has not been the subject of our discussion, so that his opinions were familiar to me, and so firmly founded on principles of honour, of justice, of attachment to his country, at the same time so entirely divested of every thing interested to himself, that it was impossible to consider him but with admiration. He liked fame, and was open to flattery, so that people sometimes got about him who were unworthy of him. He is a loss to his country that cannot easily be replaced."

Letters of Nelson to Lady Hamilton (reference EG 1614). A very important collection of letters covering the whole period of their relationship.

Letters of the Queen of Naples to Lady Hamilton (reference EG 1617–20). The letters are in French and signed "Charlotte." Very few of them are dated. This collection includes a volume of translations of some of the letters made for T. J. Pettigrew.

Letters to Nelson (reference EG 1623). An assortment of letters from various people, including the instructions for the royal family's flight from Naples, and Emma's formal letter on the anniversary of the Battle of Copenhagen.

Letters of Nelson to Alexander Davison (reference EG 2240). An important collection of personal and business letters. Davison was in Nelson's confidence, lent him money, and looked after his affairs.

Correspondence of Sir William Hamilton and Sir John Acton (reference EG 2639). An interesting series between the two old gentlemen which culminates in the row that ended their friendship. Acton's instructions to Nelson when he went to the Bay of Naples in the summer of 1799 are quite clear: "Whatever intimation Lord Nelson shall think proper to make, the Cardinal is to abide by it, and every precedent is to be void and without effect."

Letters of Sir Horace Mann and Sir Joseph Banks to Sir William Hamilton (reference EG 2641). Mann's letters are outside the scope of this work but make entertaining reading. Banks answered Sir William in the latter's cool style, on one occasion recommending him to leave hunting the wild boar for "a quieter and more certain employment, and in this Emma may have a share."

This completes the list of manuscripts that I studied. It is by no means a list of all the Nelson manuscripts in existence and students with more time and patience than I had would be well advised to visit the Public Records Office. The correspondence of the various consuls and ambassadors in the Mediterranean area for the years 1798–1800 will almost certainly repay investigation. However, there is a limit to the amount of research one can afford to indulge in, and I reached mine.

NEWSPAPERS

Newspapers up to the year 1800 are in the Burney Collection in the British Museum, Bloomsbury. After that year they are in the Burney Collection in the British Museum's Newspaper Library, Colindale.

The Times.	*The Morning Herald.*
The Morning Post & Gazetteer.	*The Morning Chronicle.*
The Oracle & Daily Advertiser.	*The St. James's Chronicle.*
The Sun.	*The Porcupine.*
Courier & Evening Gazetteer.	*The London Gazette.*
The Observer.	*The Evening Mail.*
The British Neptune.	*Say's Weekly Journal.*
General Evening Post.	*Bell's Weekly Messenger.*

FOREIGN NEWSPAPERS: *Le Moniteur, La Gazette de France.*

MAGAZINES, JOURNALS: *The Annual Register, The Naval Chronicle, The Gentleman's Magazine, The Mariner's Mirror.*

PUBLISHED WORKS

It would be a burden, both to the reader and myself, to list every book I have read about Nelson and the Hamiltons and the period in which they lived. Therefore I have confined this list to the publications of contemporary writings, and a very few books of special interest. As every one is out of print almost the moment after they are in it, I cannot imagine that anyone will take offense at not reading their names here.

LETTERS

Letters of Lord Nelson to Lady Hamilton, 2 volumes. London, 1814.
The Dispatches and Letters of Vice-Admiral Lord Viscount Nelson, with Notes, by Sir Nicholas Harris Nicolas, GCMG, 7 volumes. London, 1845.
The Hamilton and Nelson Papers, collected by A. Morrison. Privately published, 1893.
Nelson's Letters to His Wife, and Other Documents 1785–1831, edited by G. P. B. Naish. Navy Records Society, 1958.

JOURNALS, MEMOIRS, LETTERS

Memoirs of Lady Hamilton, Anonymous. London, 1815.
Autobiography of Miss E. C. Knight. London, 1861.
Historical Memoirs of His Own Time, Sir Nathaniel Wraxall. London, 1836.
The Paget Papers, edited by Sir Augustus Paget, GCB. London, 1896.
Journal of Elizabeth Lady Holland, edited by the Earl of Ilchester. London, 1909.
Memoirs of the Margravine of Anspach (Lady Craven). London, 1826.
Fifty Years Recollections, Cyrus Redding. London, 1858.
Life and Letters of Sir Gilbert Eliott (Lord Minto). London, 1874.
The Remains of the Late Mrs. Trench (Mrs. St. George). London, 1862.
Recollections of the Life of the Rev. A. J. Scott. London, 1842.
Memoirs of Mrs. Billington. London, 1792.
Letters of Lady Elgin, edited by Lt. Col. N. H. Grant. London, 1926.
Personal Memoirs, Pryse Lockhart Gordon. London, 1830.
Memoirs of Jacques Casanova de Seingalt. Various editions.
My Confidences, F. Locker Lampson. London, 1896.

BIOGRAPHIES CONTAINING ORIGINAL LETTERS

Life of Lord Nelson, J. Harrison. London, 1806.
Memoirs of the Life of Nelson, 2 volumes, T. J. Pettigrew. London, 1849.

SKETCHES

Lady Hamilton's Attitudes, F. Rehberg. 1794.
A New Edition Considerably Enlarged of Attitudes, Humphrey. 1807.

TOURS AND JOURNALS

A Tour through Sicily and Malta, P. Brydone. London, 1790.
Travels through Italy in the years 1804–1805, Augustus von Kotzebue. London, 1806.
Italy with Sketches of Spain and Portugal, W. Beckford. London, 1834.
Journal of a Tour in Italy, J. P. Cobbett. London, 1830.

POETRY

The Works of Peter Pindar. London, 1794.

WORKS OF SPECIAL INTEREST

The Bourbons of Naples, Harold Acton. Methuen, 1956.

The Locks of Norbury, Duchess of Sermonetta. London, 1940.

Naples in 1799, Constance Giglioli. London, 1903.

Narration of the Events Which Have Taken Place in France, etc., Helen Maria Williams. London, 1800.

Nelson and the Neapolitan Jacobins, H. C. Gutteridge. Navy Records Society, 1903.

INDEX